Explanation and Cognition

Explanation and Cognition

edited by Frank C. Keil and Robert A. Wilson

A Bradford Book
The MIT Press
Cambridge, Massachusetts
London, England

This book was set in Bembo by Best-set Typesetter Ltd., Hong Kong and was printed and bound in the United States of America.

Library of Congress Cataloging-in-Publication Data

Explanation and cognition / edited by Frank C. Keil and Robert A. Wilson.
  p. cm.
"A Bradford book."
Includes bibliographical references and index.
ISBN 0-262-11249-3 (alk. paper)
  1. Cognition. 2. Explanation. I. Keil, Frank C., 1952– II. Wilson, Robert A. (Robert Andrew)
BF311 .E886   2000
153—dc21

                                                                    99-087946

Contents

Preface

From very different vantage points both of us have had longstanding interests in the relations between cognition and explanation. When the opportunity arose through the kind invitation of Jim Fetzer, editor of *Minds and Machines*, to put together a special issue on the topic, we eagerly agreed and assembled a series of seven papers that formed an exciting and provocative collection. But even before that issue appeared, it was obvious that we needed a more extensive and broader treatment of the topic. We therefore approached The MIT Press and suggested the current volume, containing revised versions of the seven original papers plus seven new papers. All of these chapters have been extensively reviewed by both of us as well as by other authors in this volume. There have been many revisions resulting from discussions among the authors and editors such that this collection now forms a broad and integrated treatment of explanation and cognition across much of cognitive science. We hope that it will help foster a new set of discussions of how the ways we come to understand the world and convey those understandings to others is linked to foundational issues in cognitive science.

We acknowledge thanks to the staff at The MIT Press for help in shepherding this collection of papers through the various stages of production. Many thanks also to Trey Billings for helping in manuscript processing and preparation and to Marissa Greif and Nany Kim for preparing the index. Frank Keil also acknowledges support by NIH grant R01-HD23922 for support of the research-related aspects of this project.

Contributors

Woo-Kyoung Ahn
Department of Psychology
Vanderbilt University
Wilson Hall
Nashville, TN 37240
woo-kyoung.ahn@vanderbilt.edu

William F. Brewer
Department of Psychology
University of Illinois—Urbana-
Champaign
629 Psychology Bldg, MC 716
603 E. Daniel
Champaign, IL 61820
wbrewer@s.psych.uiuc.edu

Patricia W. Cheng
Department of Psychology
University of California
1285 Franz Hall
P.O. Box 951563
Los Angeles, CA 90095-1563
cheng@psych.ucla.edu

Clark A. Chinn
Department of Psychology
University of Illinois—Urbana-
Champaign
629 Psychology Bldg, MC 716
603 E. Daniel
Champaign, IL 61820

Andy Clark
Department of Philosophy
Washington University
Campus Box 1073
One Brookings Drive
St. Louis, MO 63130-4899
andy@twinearth.wustl.edu

Robert Cummins
Department of Philosophy
University of California
1238 Social Science and Humanities
Building
One Shields Avenue
Davis, CA 95616-8673
rccummins@ucdavis.edu

Clark Glymour
Department of Philosophy
Carnegie Mellon University
135 Baker Hall
5000 Forbes Avenue
Pittsburgh, PA 15213
cg09@andrew.cmu.edu

Allison Gopnik
Psychology Department
University of California
3210 Tolman Hall #1650
Berkeley, CA 94720-1650
gopnik@socrates.berkeley.edu

Christine Johnson
Psychology Department
University of California, San Diego
9500 Gilman Drive
La Jolla, CA 92093-0109

Charles W. Kalish
Wisconsin Center for Educational
Research
University of Wisconsin, Madison
Educational Sciences 1057
1025 W. Johnson St.
Madison, WI 53706
ckalish@macc.wisc.edu

Frank C. Keil
Department of Psychology
Yale University
2 Hillhouse Avenue
P.O. Box 208205
New Haven, CT 06520-8205
frank.keil@yale.edu

Gregory Murphy
Department of Psychology
University of Illinois—Urbana-
Champaign
629 Psychology Bldg, MC 716
603 E. Daniel
Champaign, IL 61820

Robert N. McCauley
Philosophy Department
Emory University
214 Bowden Hall, Academic Quad
Atlanta, GA 30322
philrnm@emory.edu

Ala Samarpungavan
Department of Psychology
University of Illinois—Urbana-
Champaign
629 Psychology Bldg, MC 716
603 E. Daniel
Champaign, IL 61820

Herbert Simon
Psychology & Computer Science
Departments
Carnegie Mellon University
5000 Forbes Avenue
Pittsburgh, PA 15213
has@cs.cmu.edu

Paul Thagard
Department of Philosophy
University of Waterloo
200 University Ave. West
J. G. Hagey Hall of the Humanities
Waterloo, ON N2L 3G1
Canada
pthagard@watarts.uwaterloo.ca

Robert A. Wilson
Department of Philosophy
University of Illinois
105 Gregory Hall
810 South Wright Street
Urbana, IL 61801
rwilson@uiuc.edu

1

Explaining Explanation

Frank C. Keil and Robert A. Wilson

1.1 The Ubiquity and Uniqueness of Explanation

It is not a particularly hard thing to want or seek explanations. In fact, explanations seem to be a large and natural part of our cognitive lives. Children ask why and how questions very early in development and seem genuinely to want some sort of answer, despite our often being poorly equipped to provide them at the appropriate level of sophistication and detail. We seek and receive explanations in every sphere of our adult lives, whether it be to understand why a friendship has foundered, why a car will not start, or why ice expands when it freezes. Moreover, correctly or incorrectly, most of the time we think we know when we have or have not received a good explanation. There is a sense both that a given, successful explanation satisfies a cognitive need, and that a questionable or dubious explanation does not. There are also compelling intuitions about what make good explanations in terms of their form, that is, a sense of when they are structured correctly.

When a ubiquitous cognitive activity varies so widely, from a preschooler's idle questions to the culmination of decades of scholarly effort, we have to ask whether we really have one and the same phenomenon or different phenomena that are only loosely, perhaps only metaphorically, related. Could the mental acts and processes involved in a three-year-old's quest to know why really be of the same fundamental sort, even if on much smaller scale, as those of an Oxford don? Similarly, could the mental activity involved in understanding why a teenager is rebellious really be the same as that involved in understanding how the Pauli exclusion principle explains the minimal size of black holes? When the domains of understanding range from interpersonal

*[handwritten margin note: No *]*

*[handwritten note at bottom: * cf Piaget + distinction between folk + philosophy !]*

affairs to subatomic structure, can the same sort of mental process be involved?

Surprisingly, there have been relatively few attempts to link discussions of explanation and cognition across disciplines. Discussion of explanation has remained largely in the province of philosophy and psychology, and our essays here reflect that emphasis. At the same time, they introduce emerging perspectives from computer science, linguistics, and anthropology, even as they make abundantly clear the need to be aware of discussions in the history and philosophy of science, the philosophy of mind and language, the development of concepts in children, conceptual change in adults, and the study of reasoning in human and artificial systems.

The case for a multidisciplinary approach to explanation and cognition is highlighted by considering both questions raised earlier and questions that arise naturally from reflecting on explanation in the wild. To know whether the explanation sought by a three-year-old and by a scientist is the same sort of thing, we need both to characterize the structure and content of explanations in the larger context of what they are explaining (philosophy, anthropology, and linguistics) and to consider the representations and activities involved (psychology and computer science). Even this division of labor across disciplines is artificial: philosophers are often concerned with representational issues, and psychologists, with the structure of the information itself. In addition, disciplinary boundaries lose much of their significance in exploring the relationships between explanation and cognition in part because some of the most innovative discipline-based thinking about these relationships has already transcended those boundaries.

Consider five questions about explanation for which a cognitive science perspective seems particularly apt:

How do explanatory capacities develop?
Are there kinds of explanation?
Do explanations correspond to domains of knowledge?
Why do we seek explanations and what do they accomplish?
How central are causes to explanation?

These are the questions addressed by *Explanation and Cognition*, and it is to them that we turn next.

1.2 How Do Explanatory Capacities Develop?

The ability to provide explanations of any sort does not appear until a child's third year of life, and then only in surprisingly weak and ineffective forms. Ask even a five-year-old how something works, and the most common answer is simply to use the word "because" followed by a repetition or paraphrase of what that thing does. Although three-year-olds can reliably predict how both physical objects and psychological agents will behave, the ability to provide explicit explanations emerges fairly late and relatively slowly (Wellman and Gelman 1998; Crowley and Siegler 1999). But to characterize explanatory insight solely in terms of the ability to provide explanations would be misleading. As adults, we are often able to grasp explanations without being able to provide them for others. We can hear a complex explanation of a particular phenomenon, be convinced we know how it works, and yet be unable to repeat the explanation to another. Moreover, such failures to repeat the explanation do not seem merely to be a result of forgetting the details of the explanation. The same person who is unable to offer an explanation may easily recognize it when *recognit-* presented among a set of closely related ones. In short, the ability to *ion vs* express explanations explicitly is likely to be an excessively stringent cri- *recall* terion for when children develop the cognitive tools to participate in explanatory practices in a meaningful way.

This pattern in adults thus raises the question of when explanatory understanding emerges in the young child. Answering this question turns in part on a more careful explication of what we mean by explanation at any level. Even infants are sensitive to complex causal patterns in the world and how these patterns might be closely linked to certain high-level categories. For example, they seem to know very early on that animate entities move according to certain patterns of contingency and can act on each other at a distance, and that inanimate objects require contact to act on each other. They dishabituate when objects seem to pass through each other, a behavior that is taken as showing a violation of an expectation about how objects should normally behave. These sorts of behaviors in young infants have been taken as evidence for the view that they possess intuitive theories about living and physical entities (e.g., Spelke 1994). Even if this view attributes a richer cognitive structure to infants than is warranted, as some (e.g., Fodor 1998; cf. Wilson and Keil, chap. 4, this volume) have argued, some cognitive structure does cause and explain the sensitivity. Thus even prelinguistic children have some concepts of animate and physical things through which they understand how and why entities subsumed under those concepts act as they do. We are suggesting that the possession of such intuitive theories, or concepts, indicates at least a rudimentary form of explanatory understanding.

If this suggestion is correct, then it implies that one can have explanatory understanding in the absence of language and of any ability to express one's thoughts in propositional terms. That early explanatory understanding might be nothing more than a grasping of certain contingencies and how these are related to categories of things in turn implies a gulf between such a capacity in infants and its complex manifestation in adults. Certainly, if any sort of explanatory capacity requires an explicit conception of mediating mechanisms and of kinds of agency and causal interactions, we should be much less sure about whether infants have any degree of explanatory insight. But just as the preceding conception of explanation might be too deflationary, we want to suggest that this second view of one's explanatory capacities would be too *inflationary*, since it would seem to be strong enough to preclude much of our everyday explanatory activity from involving such a capacity.

Consider an experimental finding with somewhat older children and with some language-trained apes. An entity, such as a whole apple, is presented, followed by a presentation of the same entity in a transformed state, such as the apple being neatly cut in half. The participant is then shown either a knife or a hammer and is asked which goes with the event. Young children, and some apes, match the appropriate "mechanism" with the depicted event (Premack and Premack 1994; Tomasello and Call 1997). There is some question as to whether they could be doing so merely by associating one familiar object, a knife, with two other familiar object states, whole and cut apples. But a strong possibility remains that these apes and children are succeeding because of a more sophisticated cognitive system that works as well for novel as for familiar tools and objects acted upon (Premack and Premack 1994). If so, is this evidence of explanatory insight, namely, knowing how the apple moved from one state to a new and different one? Mechanism knowledge seems to be involved, but the effect is so simple and concerns the path over time of a single individual. Is this the same sort of process as trying to explain general properties of a kind, such as why ice expands when it freezes?

One possibility about the emergence of explanation is that young children may have a sense of "why" and of the existence of explanations and thereby request them, but are not able to use or generate them much. There is a good deal of propositional baggage in many explanations that may be too difficult for a young child to assimilate fully or use later, but that is at least partially grasped. Perhaps much more basic explanatory schemas are present in preverbal infants and give them some sense of what explanatory insight is. They then ask "why" to gain new insights, but are often poorly equipped to handle the verbal explanations that are offered.

1.3   Are There Kinds of Explanations?

We began with the idea that explanations are common, even ubiquitous, in everyday adult life. A great deal of lay explanation seems to involve telling a causal story of what happened to an individual over time. One might try to explain the onset of the First World War in terms of the assassination of Archduke Ferdinand and the consequent chain of events. There are countless other examples in everyday life. We explain why a friend lost her job in terms of a complex chain of events involving downsizing a company and how these events interacted with her age, ability, and personality, sometimes referring to more general principles governing business life, but often not. We explain why two relatives will not speak to each other in terms of a series of events that led to a blowup and perhaps even explain why it cannot be easily resolved.

Our ease at generating these sorts of narration-based causal explanations, even when they have many steps, contrasts sharply with our difficulty at providing scientific explanations. Explanations in terms of more general laws and principles comprise vastly fewer steps and are cognitively much more challenging. One possible reason may have to do with the closeness between explanations of individual histories and our ability to construct and comprehend narratives more generally, one of the earliest human cognitive faculties to emerge (Neisser 1994; Fivush 1997). By contrast, it is a fairly recent development that people have offered explanations of kinds in terms of principles. Even explanations of various natural phenomena in traditional cultures are often told as narratives of what happened to individuals, such as how the leopard got its spots or why the owl is drab and nocturnal. Are explanations in science therefore of a fundamentally different kind than in normal everyday practice? The answer is complex, as the essays that follow make clear. It is tempting to think that science does involve the statement of laws, principles, and perhaps mechanisms that cover a system of related phenomena. Yet one must also acknowledge the limits of the deductive nomological model of scientific explanation and the need to conceptualize scientific understanding and practice as something more (or other) than a set of axioms and propositions connected in a deductive pattern of reasoning. In recognizing the limits of the deductive-nomological model of scientific explanation, to what extent do we close the prima facie gap between scientific explanation and the sorts of intuitive explanations seen in young children?

Other sorts of explanations are neither narratives of individual histories nor expositions of general scientific principles. Why, for example, are cars constructed as they are? Principles of physics and mechanics play a role, but so also do the goals of car manufacturers, goals having to do with maximizing profits, planned obsolescence, marketing strategies, and the like. To be sure, these patterns draw on principles in economics, psychology, and other disciplines, but the goals themselves seem to be the central explanatory construct. For another example, we might explain the nature of a class of tools, such as routers, in terms of the goals of their makers. Again such goals interact with physical principles, but it is the goals themselves that provide explanatory coherence. In biology as well, teleological "goals" might be used to explain structure-function relations in an organism without reference to broader principles of biology.

We see here three prima facie distinct kinds of explanation— principle based, narrative based, and goal based—all of which are touched on in the chapters in this book. A key question is what, if anything, all three share. One common thread may involve a pragmatic, coherence constraint that requires that all causal links be of the same sort and not shift radically from level to level. Thus, in a narrative explanation of why Aunt Edna became giddy at Thanksgiving dinner, it will not do to explain how the fermenting of grapes in a region in France caused there to be alcohol in her wine that then caused her altered state. Nor will it do to discuss the neurochemistry of alcohol. It will do to explain the mental states of Edna and those around her that led her to consume large amounts of wine. Similar constraints may be at work in goal-centered and principle-based explanations. We do not yet know how to specify why some set of causal links are appropriate for an explanation and why other equally causal ones are not. We do suggest that common principles may be at work across all three kinds of explanation; at the least, that question is worth posing and investigating.

1.4 Do Explanation Types Correspond to Domains of Knowledge?

Consider whether there are domains of explanation and what psychological consequences turn on one's view of them. At one extreme, we might think that there are many diverse and distinct domains in which explanations operate. There is a social domain, where our "folk psychological" explanations are at home; there is a physical domain, about which we might have both naive and sophisticated theories; there is a religious domain with its own types of explanatory goals and standards, and so on, with the domains of explanation being largely autonomous from one another. At the other extreme, we might think that these domains are interdependent and not all that diverse. For example, some have proposed that children are endowed with two distinct modes of explanation that shape all other types of explanation they come to accept: an intuitive psychology and an intuitive physical mechanics (Carey 1985). In this view, children's intuitive biology emerges from their intuitive psychology, rather than being one distinct domain of knowledge and explanation among others in early childhood.

It seems plausible that the ability to understand and generate explanations in one domain, such as folk psychology, may have little or nothing in common with the same ability in another domain, such as folk mechanics. The nature of the information to be modeled is different, as are the spatiotemporal patterns governing phenomena in both domains. For example, social interactions have much longer and more variable time lags than do most mechanical ones. While an insult can provoke a response in a few seconds or fester for days, most mechanical events produce "responses" in a matter of milliseconds with little variation across repetitions of the event. At the same time, there may also be overarching commonalities of what constitute good versus bad explanations in both domains and how one discovers an explanation. Again, the essays in this volume explore both dimensions to the issue.

Yet explanations may also be interconnected in ways that call into question the idea that domains of explanation are completely autonomous from one another. Consider how the heart works, a phenomenon whose explanation might be thought to lie within the biological domain. If pressed hard enough in the right directions, however, the explainer must also refer to physical mechanics, fluid dynamics, thermodynamics, neural net architecture, and even mental states. Explanations might be thought to fall naturally into a relatively small number of domains but, on occasion, leak out of these cognitive vessels. In this view explanations are constrained by domains in that explanations form domain-based clusters, where each cluster is subject to its own particular principles, even if locating the cluster for specific explanations proves difficult or even impossible. Notoriously, the quest for an explanation of sufficient depth can be never ending. "Why" and "how" questions can be chained together recursively; such chains are generated not only by those investigating the fundamental nature of the physical or mental worlds, but also by young children, much to the initial delight (and eventual despair) of parents.

Although, with domains of explanation, we can avoid the conclusion that to know anything we must know everything, we should be wary of thinking of these domains as isolated atoms. To strike a balance between avoiding a need for a theory of everything on the one hand and excessive compartmentalizing, on the other, is one of the key challenges addressed in several of the chapters that follow. The need for such a balance is also related to whether there might be principles that cut across both domains and kinds of explanations, principles that might tell us when a particular causal chain emanating out of a causal cluster has shifted the level or kind of explanation beyond the cluster's normal boundaries and is thus no longer part of *that* explanation.

1.5   Why Do We Seek Explanations and What Do They Accomplish?

What are explanations for? The answer is far more complex and elusive than the question. It might seem intuitively that we seek explanations to make predictions, an answer that receives some backing from the correspondence between explanation and prediction in the deductive-nomological model of explanation and the accompanying hypothetico-deductive model of confirmation in traditional philosophy of science: the observable outcomes predicted and confirmed in the latter are part of the *explanandum* in the former. Yet in many cases, we seem to employ explanations after the fact to make sense of what has already happened. We may not venture to make predictions about what style of clothing will be in vogue next year but feel more confident explaining why after the fact. If this sort of explanatory behavior occurs with some frequency, as we think it does, a question arises as to the point of such after-the-fact explanations. One possibility, again implicit in many chapters in this volume, is that explanations help us refine interpretative schemata for future encounters, even if prediction is impossible or irrelevant. We may seek explanations from a cricket buff on the nuances of the game, not to make any long range predictions, but merely to be able to understand better in real time what is transpiring on the field and to be able to gather more meaningful information on the next viewing of a cricket match. Here prediction may be largely irrelevant. We may also engage in explanations to reduce cognitive dissonance or otherwise make a set of beliefs more compatible. A close relative dies and, at the eulogy, family members struggle to explain how seemingly disparate pieces of that person fit together. They try to understand, not to predict, but to find a coherent version they can comfortably remember. Simply resolving tensions of internal contradictions or anomalies may be enough motivation for seeking explanations. We suggest here that a plurality of motivations for explanation is needed.

More broadly, we can ask why explanations work, what it is that they achieve or accomplish, given that they are rarely exhaustive or complete. Does a successful explanation narrow down the inductive space, and thus allow us to gather new information in a more efficient fashion? Does it provide us with a means for interpreting new information as it occurs in real time? Given the diversity of explanations, we doubt that there is any single adequate answer to such questions; yet it seems unlikely that a thousand explanatory purposes underlie the full range of explanatory practices. We think that the set of purposes is small and that they may be arrayed in an interdependent fashion. Some explanations might help us actively seek out new information more effectively. Some of those might also help guide induction and prediction. To the extent that we can construct an account that shows the coherence and interrelatedness of explanatory goals and purposes, we can also gain a clearer idea of the unitary nature of explanation itself.

1.6 How Central Are Causes to Explanation?

One final issue concerns the role of the world in general and causation in particular in explanation. At the turn of the century, Charles Sanders

Pierce argued that induction about the natural world could not succeed without "animal instincts for guessing right" (Peirce 1960–1966). Somehow the human mind is able grasp enough about the causal structure of the world to allow us to guess well. We know from the problem of induction, particularly in the form of the so-called new riddle of induction made famous by Nelson Goodman (1955), that the power of brute, enumerative induction is limited. To put the problem in picturesque form, map out any finite number of data points. There will still be an infinite number of ways both to add future data points (the classic problem of induction, from David Hume) as well as connect the existing points (Goodman's new riddle). What might be characterized as a logical problem of how we guess right must have at least a psychological solution because we do guess right, and often.

The idea that we and other species have evolved biases that enable us to grasp aspects of the causal structure of the world seems irresistible. But there is a question as to which of these biases make for explanatory abilities that work or that get at the truth about the world, and how these are related to one another. We might ask whether explanatory devices, of which we are a paradigm, require a sensitivity to real-world causal patterns in order to succeed in the ways they do. Certainly making sense of the world is not sufficient for truth about the world. Both in everyday life and in science, explanations and explanatory frameworks with the greatest survival value over time have turned out to be false. But the sensory and cognitive systems that feed our explanatory abilities are themselves often reliable sources of information about what happens in the world and in what order it happens. Surely our explanatory capacities are doing more than spinning their wheels in the quest to get things right.

While there certainly are explanations in domains where causal relations seem to be nonexistent, such as mathematics or logic, in most other cases there is the strong sense that a causal account is the essence of a good explanation, and we think that this is more than just an illusion. But whether we can specify those domains where causal relations are essential to explanatory understanding, and do so utilizing a unified conception of causation, remain open questions. Philosophers have a tendency to look for grand, unified theories of the phenomena they reflect on, and psychologists often seek out relatively simple mechanisms that underlie complicated, cognitively driven behaviors. Both may need to recognize that the relations between causation and explanation are complex and multifaceted and may well require an elaborate theory of their own.

Many of the questions we have just raised are some of the most difficult in all of cognitive science, and we surely do not presume that they will be answered in the chapters that follow. We raise them here, however, to make clear just how central explanation is to cognitive science and all its constituent disciplines. In addition, we have tried to sketch out possible directions that some answers might take as ways of thinking about what follows. The chapters in this book attempt, often in bold and innovative ways, to make some inroads on these questions. They explore aspects of these issues from a number of vantage points. From philosophy, we see discussions of what explanations are and how they contrast and relate across different established sciences, as well as other domains. From a more computational perspective, we see discussions of how notions of explanation and cause can be instantiated in a range of possible learning and knowledge systems, and how they can be connected to the causal structure of the world. Finally, from psychology, we see discussions of how adults mentally represent, modify, and use explanations; how children come to acquire them and what sorts of information, if any, humans are naturally predisposed to use in building and discovering explanations. More important, however, all of these chapters show the powerful need to cross traditional disciplinary boundaries to develop satisfactory accounts of explanation. Every chapter draws on work across several disciplines, and in doing so, develops insights not otherwise possible.

The thirteen essays in *Explanation and Cognition* have been arranged into five thematic parts. The chapters of part I, "Cognizing Explanation: Three Gambits," provide three general views of how we ought to develop a cognitive perspective on explanation and issues that arise in doing so. Represented here are an information-processing view that adapts long-standing work to the problem of discovering explanations (Simon); a philosophical view on the psychological differences between science and religion (McCauley); and a view that attempts to connect the perspectives of both philosophers of science and developmental and cognitive psychologists on the nature of explanation (Wilson and Keil).

In his "Discovering Explanations" (chapter 2), Herb Simon views explanation as a form of problem solving. Simon asks how it is that we can discover explanations, an activity at the heart of science, and move beyond mere descriptions of events to explanations of their structure. He applies his "physical symbol system hypothesis" (PSS hypothesis) to classes of information-processing mechanisms that might discover explanations, and how computational models might inform psychological ones. He also considers patterns in the history and philosophy of science and their relations to structural patterns in the world, such as nearly decomposable systems and their more formal properties, as well as attendant questions about the social distribution and sharing of knowledge.

Robert McCauley explores the relationships between science and religion, and how explanation is related to the naturalness of each, given both the character and content of human cognition as well as the social framework in which it takes place. McCauley's "The Naturalness of Religion and the Unnaturalness of Science" (chapter 3) draws two chief conclusions. First, although scientists and children may be cognitively similar, and thus scientific thought a cognitively natural activity in some respects, there are more significant respects in which the scientific thinking and scientific activity are unnatural. Scientific theories typically challenge existing, unexamined views about the nature of the world, and the forms of thought that are required for a critical assessment of such dominant views mark science as unnatural. Second, an examination of the modes of thought and the resulting products of the practices associated with religion leads one to view religion, by contrast, as natural in the very respects that science is not. Religious thinking and practices make use of deeply embedded cognitive predispositions concerning explanation, such as the tendency to anthropomorphize, to find narrative explanations that are easy to memorize and transmit, and to employ ontological categories that are easy to recognize. These conclusions may help explain the persistence of religion as well as raise concerns about the future pursuit of science.

Our own chapter, "The Shadows and Shallows of Explanation" (chapter 4), attempts to characterize more fully what explanations are and how they might differ from other ways in which we can partially grasp the causal structure of the world. We suggest that traditional discussions of explanation in the philosophy of science give us mere "shadows" of explanation in everyday life, and that one of explanation's surprising features is its relative psychological "shallowness." We further suggest that most common explanations, and probably far more of hands-on science than one might suspect, have a structure that is more implicit and schematic in nature than is suggested by more traditional psychological accounts. We argue that this schematic and implicit nature is fundamental to explanations of value in most real-world situations, and show how this view is compatible with our ability to tap into causal structures in the world and to engage in explanatory successes. Like Simon, we also consider the importance of the epistemic division of labor that is typically involved in explanatory enterprises.

Part II, "Explaining Cognition," concerns general issues that arise in the explanation of cognition. Its two chapters explore models of explanation used to explain cognitive abilities, locating such models against the background of broader views of the nature of explanation within the philosophy of science. One central issue here is how and to what extent explanation in psychology and cognitive science is distinctive.

Robert Cummins's " 'How Does It Work?' versus 'What Are the Laws?': Two Conceptions of Psychological Explanation" (chapter 5), builds on his earlier, influential view that psychological explanation is best conceived not in terms of the Hempelian deductive-nomological model of explanation but rather in terms of capacities via the analytical strategy of decomposition. While the term *law* is sometimes used in psychology, what are referred to as psychological laws are typically effects, robust phenomena to be explained, and as such are *explananda* rather than *explanantia*. Cummins explores the five dominant explanatory paradigms in psychology—the "belief-desire-intention" paradigm, computational symbol processing, connectionism, neuroscience, and the evolutionary paradigm—both to illustrate his general thesis about explanation in psychology and to identify some assumptions of and problems with each paradigm. Two general problems emerge: what he calls the "realization problem" and what he calls the "unification problem," each of which requires the attention of both philosophers and psychologists.

Andy Clark's "Twisted Tales: Causal Complexity and Cognitive Scientific Explanation" (chapter 6) discusses how phenomena in biology and cognitive science often seem to arise from a complex, interconnected network of causal relations that defy simple hierarchical or serial characterizations and that are often connected in recurrent interactive loops with other phenomena. Clark argues that, despite objections to the contrary, models in cognitive science and biology need not reject explanatory schemata involving internal causal factors, such as genes and mental representations. His discussion thereby links questions about the philosophy of science to the practice of cognitive science.

Essays in Part III, "The Representation of Causal Patterns," focus on the centrality of causation and causal patterns within a variety of explanations, continuing a contemporary debate over how causation is represented psychologically. Traditional philosophical views of causation and our knowledge of it, psychological theories of our representation of causal knowledge, and computational and mathematical models of probability and causation intersect here in ways that have only recently begun to be conceptualized.

In "Bayes Nets as Psychological Models" (chapter 7), Clark Glymour focuses on the question of how we learn about causal patterns, a critical component in the emergence of most explanations. Building on developments in computer science that concern conditional probability relations in multilayered causal networks, Glymour considers how a combination of tabulations of probability information and a more active interpretative component allow the construction of causal inferences. More specifically, he argues for the importance of directed graphs as representations of causal knowledge and for their centrality in a psychological account of explanation. This discussion naturally raises the question of how humans might operate with such multilayered causal networks, an area largely unexplored in experimental research. Glymour turns to work by Patricia Cheng on causal and covariation judgments to build links between computational and psychological approaches and to set up a framework for future experiments in psychology.

Woo-kyoung Ahn and Charles Kalish describe and defend a contrasting approach to the study of causal reasoning and causal explanation, what they call the "mechanism approach", in their "The Role of Mechanism Beliefs in Causal Reasoning" (chapter 8). Ahn and Kalish contrast their approach with what they call the "regularity view," as exemplified in the contemporary work of Glymour and Cheng, and stemming ultimately from David Hume's regularity analysis of causation in the eighteenth century. Ahn and Kalish find the two approaches differ principally in their conceptions of how people think about causal relations and in their positions on whether the knowledge of mechanisms per se plays a distinctive role in identifying causes and offering causal explanations. They offer several examples of how mechanistic understanding seems to affect explanatory understanding in ways that go far beyond those arising from the tracking of regularities.

In "Causality in the Mind: Estimating Contextual and Conjunctive Causal Power" (chapter 9), Patricia Cheng provides an overview of her "Power PC theory", where "power" refers to causal powers, and "PC" stands for "probabilistic contrast model" of causal reasoning, an attempt to show the conditions under which one can legitimately infer causation from mere covariation. Cheng employs her theory to suggest that, by instantiating a representation of the corresponding probabilistic relations between covarying events people are able to infer all sorts of cause-and-effect relations in the world. While Glymour (chapter 7) suggests how to extend Cheng's model from simple, direct causal relations to causal chains and other types of causal networks, Cheng herself offers several other extensions, including the case of conjunctive causes.

Paul Thagard's "Explaining Disease: Correlations, Causes, and Mechanisms" (chapter 10) attempts to show that the distance between the two perspectives represented in the the first two chapters of part III may not be as great as the proponents of each view suggest. Thagard focuses on the long-standing problem of how one makes the inference from correlation to causation. He suggests that some sense of mechanism is critical to make such inferences and discusses how certain causal networks can represent such mechanisms and thereby license the inference. His discussion covers psychological work on induction, examines epidemiological approaches to disease causation, explores historical and philosophical analyses of the relations between cause and mechanism, and considers computational problems of inducing over causal networks.

Although several chapters in part I of the book touch on the relationships between cognitive development and science, the two chapters of part IV, "Cognitive Development, Science, and Explanation," explore this topic more systematically. Indeed, the first of these chapters might profitably be read together with McCauley's chapter on science and religion, while the second has links with Wilson and Keil's chapter.

William Brewer, Clark Chinn, and Ala Samarapungavan's "Explanation in Scientists and Children" (chapter 11) asks how explanations might be represented and acquired in children, and how they compare to those in scientists. They propose a general framework of attributes for explanations, attributes that would seem to be the cornerstones of good explanations in science, but that perhaps surprisingly also appear to be the cornerstones of explanation even in quite young children. At the same time, explanations in science differ from both those in everyday life and from those in the minds of young children, and Brewer, Chinn, and Samarpungavan discuss how and why.

Alison Gopnik addresses the phenomenology of what she calls the "theory formation system," developing an analogy to biological systems that seem to embody both drives and a distinctive phenomenology in her "Explanation as Orgasm and the Drive for Causal Knowledge: The Function, Evolution, and Phenomenology of the Theory Formation System" (chapter 12). In discussing this phenomenology, Gopnik blends together psychological and philosophical issues and illustrates how developmental and learning considerations can be addressed by crossing continuously between these two disciplines. She also brings in considerations of the evolutionary value of explanation, and why it might be best conceived as a drive similar in many respects to the more familiar physiological drives associated with nutrition, hydration, and sex.

In the final part, "Explanatory Influences on Concept Acquisition and Use," two chapters discuss ways in which explanatory constructs influence our daily cognition, either in categorization and concept learning tasks or in conceptual combinations. Explanatory structures seem to strongly guide a variety of everyday cognitive activities, often when these are not being explicitly addressed and when explanations are being neither sought nor generated.

In "Explanatory Knowledge and Conceptual Combination" (chapter 13), Christine Johnson and Frank Keil examine a particularly thorny problem in cognitive science, conceptual combinations. Difficulties with understanding how concepts compose have been considered so extreme as to undermine most current views of concepts (Fodor 1998; cf. Keil and Wilson, in press). Here however, Johnson and Keil argue that framework explanatory schemata that seem to contain many concepts can also help us understand and predict patterns in conceptual combination. The chapter devotes itself to detailed descriptions of a series of experimental studies showing how emergent features in conceptual combinations can be understood as arising out of broader explanatory bases, and how one can do the analysis in the reverse direction, using patterns of conceptual combination to further explore the explanatory frameworks that underlie different domains.

Greg Murphy's "Explanatory Concepts" (chapter 14) examines how explanatory knowledge, in contrast to knowledge of simple facts or other shallower aspects of understanding, influences a variety of aspects of everyday cognition, most notably the ability to learn new categories. Strikingly, an explanatory schema that helps explain some features in a new category has a kind of penumbra that aids acquisition of other features not causally related to those for which there are explanations. Somehow, explanatory structure confers cognitive benefits in ways that extend beyond features immediately relevant to that structure. Murphy argues that this makes sense, given how often, at least for natural categories, many features are learned that have no immediately apparent causal role. Features that fit into explanatory relations are seen as more typical to a category even when they occur much less often than other explanatorily irrelevant features. Such results strongly indicate that explanation does not just come in at the tail end of concept learning. In many cases, it guides concept learning from the start and in ways that can be quite different from accounts that try to build knowledge out of simple feature frequencies and correlations.

Taken together, these essays provide a unique set of crosscutting views of explanation. Every single essay connects with several others in ways that clearly illustrate how a full account of explanation must cross traditional disciplinary boundaries frequently and readily. We hope that researchers and students working on explanation and cognition in any of the fields this collection draws on will be inspired to pursue the discussion further.

Note

Preparation of this essay was supported by National Institutes of Health grant R01-HD23922 to Frank C. Keil.

References

Carey, S. (1985). *Conceptual change in childhood*. Cambridge, MA: MIT Press.

Crowley, K., and Siegler, R. S. (1999). Explanation and generalization in young children's strategy learning. *Child Development, 70,* 304–316.

Fodor, J. A. (1998). *Concepts: Where cognitive science went wrong*. Oxford: Oxford University Press.

Fivush, R. (1997). Event memory in early childhood. In N. Cowan, ed., *The development of memory*. London: University College London Press.

Goodman, N. (1955). *Fact, fiction and forecast*. Indianapolis: Bobbs-Merrill.

Keil, F. C., and Wilson, R. A. (in press). The concept concept: The wayward path of cognitive science: Review of Fodor's *Concepts: Where cognitive science went wrong*. *Mind and Language*.

Mandler, J. M. (1998). Representation. In D. Kuhn and R. S. Siegler, eds., *Handbook of Child Psychology*. 5th ed. Vol. 2, *Cognition, perception and language*. New York: Wiley.

Neisser, U. (1994). Self-narratives: True and false. In U. Neisser and R. Fivush, eds., *The remembering Self*. Cambridge: Cambridge University Press.

Peirce, C. S. (1960–1966). *Collected papers*. Cambridge, MA: Harvard University Press.

Premack, D., and Premack, A. (1994). Levels of causal understanding in chimpanzees and children. *Cognition, 50*, 347–362.

Spelke, E. (1994). Initial knowledge: Six suggestions. *Cognition, 50*, 431–445.

Tomasello, M., and Call, J. (1997). *Primate cognition*. New York: Oxford University Press.

Wellman, H. M., and Gelman, S. A. (1998). Knowledge acquisition in foundational domains. In D. Kuhn and R. S. Siegler, eds., *Handbook of child psychology*. 5th ed. Vol. 2, *Cognition, perception and language*. New York: Wiley.

I

Cognizing Explanations: Three Gambits

2

Discovering Explanations

Herbert A. Simon

At the outset, I will accept, without discussion or debate, the view commonly held by scientists and philosophers alike that the goal of science is to discover real-world phenomena by observation and experiment, to describe them, and then to provide explanations (i.e., theories) of these phenomena. It does not matter which comes first—phenomena or the explanation. As a matter of historical fact, phenomena most often precede explanation in the early phases of a science, whereas explanations often lead to predictions, verified by experiment or observation, in the later phases.

2.1   What Is an Explanation?

In contrast to the general (although not universal) agreement that explanation is central to science, there has been much less agreement as to just what constitutes an explanation of an empirical phenomenon. Explanations are embedded in theories that make statements about the real world, usually by introducing constraints (scientific laws) that limit the gamut of possible worlds. But not all theories, no matter how well they fit the facts, are regarded as explanations; some are viewed as descriptive rather than explanatory. Two examples, one from astronomy and one from cognitive psychology, will make the point.

Examples of Descriptive Theories

From physics we take a celebrated example of a natural law. Kepler, in 1619, announced the theory (Kepler's third law) that the periods of revolution of the planets about the sun vary as the 3/2 power of their distances from the sun. This theory described (and continues to describe) the data with great accuracy, but no one, including Kepler, regarded it as an explanation of the planetary motions. As a "merely descriptive" theory, it describes the phenomena very well, but it does not explain why they behave as they do.

From modern cognitive psychology we take a more modest example of a descriptive law. In 1962, R. B. Bugelski showed that, with presentation rates ranging between about 2 and 12 seconds per syllable, the time required to fixate, by the serial anticipation method, nonsense syllables of low familiarity and pronounceability did not depend much on the presentation rate, but was approximately constant, at about 24 seconds per syllable. That is, the number of trials required for learning a list of syllables varied inversely with the number of seconds that each syllable was presented on each trial. These data can be fitted by a simple equation: Learning time (in seconds) = $30N$, where N is the number of syllables in the list; or Number of trials = $24/t$, where t is the presentation time (in seconds) per syllable. Again, the "theory" represented by these two equations is simply an algebraic description of the data.

What is lacking in these two descriptive theories, Kepler's third law and Bugelski's law of constant learning time, that keeps them from being full-fledged explanations? What is lacking is any characterization of causal mechanisms that might be responsible for bringing the phenomena about, and bringing them about in precisely the way in which they occur. Now I have introduced into the discussion two new terms, *causal* and *mechanism*, that are gravid with implications and at least as problematic as *explanation*. Before attempting formal definitions of these new terms, let me illustrate how they enter into the two examples we are considering.

Examples of Explanatory Theories

Kepler's third law was provided with an explanation when Newton proposed his laws of motion and a law of universal gravitation, asserting that every piece of matter exerts an attractive force on every other piece of matter—a force that is proportional to the product of the masses of the pieces and inversely proportional to the distance between them. Using his newly invented calculus, he then showed deductively that *if* his laws of motion and his law of universal gravitation were valid, the planets would revolve about the sun with the periods described by Kepler's third law. The gravitational force, in the form and with the acceleration-producing intensity that Newton attributed to it, provided the *mechanism* that *causes* the planets to revolve as they do. The gravitational law serves as an *explanation* of why Kepler's third law holds.

Bugelski's description of nonsense-syllable learning as requiring a constant time per syllable was provided with an explanation when Feigenbaum and Simon (1962, 1984) proposed the elementary perceiver and memorizer (EPAM) theory of perception and learning. EPAM is a computer program (in mathematical terms, a system of difference equations) that provides a dynamic model of learning, and that is capable of actually accomplishing the learning that it models. It has two main components. One component (learning) constructs or "grows" a branching discrimination net that performs tests on stimuli to distinguish them from each other; and the other (recognition) sorts stimuli in the net in order to access information that has been stored about them at terminal nodes of the net (e.g., the responses that have been associated with them). The two components have sufficiently general capabilities so that, given appropriate experimental instructions, they can, within the context of the task-defined strategy, carry out a wide range of learning, recognition and categorization tasks.

Both components sort stimuli down the tree to a terminal node by testing them at each intermediate node that is reached and following that particular branch that is indicated by the test outcome. The learning component compares the stimulus with an image at the leaf node that has been assembled from information about previous stimuli sorted to that node. When feedback tells EPAM that it has sorted two or more stimuli to the same leaf node that should not be treated as identical, the learning component adds new tests and branches to the net that discriminate between these stimuli, so that they are now sorted to different nodes. When the task is to respond to stimuli, the learning component also stores information about a response at the leaf node for the appropriate stimulus. The performance component carries out the discriminations necessary to retrieve from the net the associations with the responses to stimuli.

By virtue of the structure of EPAM (which was built before Bugelski's experiments were carried out), the rate at which it learns nonsense syllables (about 8 to 10 seconds is required for each letter in a three-letter syllable) predicts the regularity noticed by Bugelski. The learning and performance components of EPAM constitute the *mechanisms* that *cause* the learning to occur at the observed rate. EPAM serves as an *explanation* of why Bugelski's law holds.

Kepler's third law and Bugelski's law are not isolated examples. It is quite common for phenomena to give birth to descriptive laws, and these laws to be augmented or supplanted later by explanations. In October of 1900, Planck proposed the law bearing his name, which describes variation in intensity of blackbody radiation with wave length, a descriptive law that is still accepted. Two months later, he provided an explanatory mechanism for the law that introduced a fundamental theoretical term, the *quantum*. It was introduced for no better reason than that he found himself able to carry through the derivation only for a discrete, instead of a continuous, probability distribution, and at the time, he attached no theoretical significance to it. Planck's explanation was soon discarded, but the quantum was retained, and new explanatory theories were gradually built around it by Einstein and Ehrenfurst about 1906. Bohr in 1912, in order to explain another purely descriptive law (Balmer's spectral formula of 1883 applied to the hydrogen spectrum), provided yet another and somewhat more satisfactory explanatory quantum theory; but it was not until 1926 that Heisenberg and Schrödinger introduced a still different formulation (in two distinct, but more or less equivalent, versions)—the contemporary theory known as "quantum mechanics."

Relation of Explanatory to Descriptive Theories

From a purely phenomenological standpoint, there are no apparent differences between the descriptive theories in these two examples and the corresponding explanatory theories. In both kinds of theories, a function connects the values of dependent and independent variables. In Kepler's theory, the period of revolution is expressed as a function of the planetary distance; whereas in Newton's, the period of revolution is expressed as a function of the distance, the sun's mass (the mass of the planet, appearing in both numerator as gravitational mass, and denominator as inertial mass, cancels out), and the gravitational constant. The sun's mass provides the cause for the gravitational attraction, and determines the intensity of the cause at any given distance. The gravitational force at the location of a planet causes the planet to accelerate at a rate determined by Newton's laws of motion.

Notice that the gravitational constant is not directly observable: its magnitude is determined by fitting the laws of motion to the observed positions and velocities of the planets. We can recover the descriptive law in its original form simply by absorbing such theoretical terms in the parameters that are estimated in order to predict the observations (as Newton did in his derivation of Kepler's third law). The explanation is superfluous to the description of the phenomena. This is not a special case, but always holds for the relation between a description and its explanation—the explanation calls on theoretical terms, that is, new variables that are not directly observable, and these are absorbed when the descriptive law is deduced from the explanatory one and fitted to the data. (For the way theoretical—not directly observable—terms enter into theories and can be eliminated from them in the derivation of descriptive laws, see Simon 1970, 1983.) We will see later that the explanation generally deals with phenomena at a finer temporal resolution than the original description did.

In the same way, according to Bugelski's theory, learning time is expressed as a function of the number of responses to be learned. In EPAM, syllables are learned by executing certain learning and performance processes, each of which requires a postulated length of time. Because, under the conditions of the experiment, about the same processing is required to learn each response, learning time will be proportional to the number of responses to be learned. The constancy of learning times is explained by the constancy of the mechanisms incorporated in EPAM that cause the learning to occur. Moreover, the EPAM theory predicts, in accordance with the empirical data, that the constancy will disappear if the presentation time is too short (less than about two seconds) or too long (longer than about ten seconds). With too rapid presentation, essential processes will not have time to go to completion, leading to considerable confusion and wasted time. With too slow presentation, the system will sometimes be idle before the next stimulus is presented.

The line between descriptive and explanatory laws is not a sharp one, for we may find all kinds of intermediate cases—especially for qualitative explanations. For example, Kepler proposed that the planetary orbits were caused by a force emanating from the sun that swept them around and that gradually diminished with distance, but he was not able to provide a more precise characterization of the force or its mode of action.

Similarly, Mendel not only described how the characteristics of his sweet peas varied from generation to generation, but also explained the statistical regularities in terms of the inheritance of what we now call "genes"; but it was not until the beginning of the nineteenth century that genes were associated with cellular structures visible under the microscope, providing a description at the next lower level that concretized the earlier explanation.

Taxonomies can also be thought of as mediating between description and explanation, for in nature the separations among sets of things often define natural kinds. The members of a natural kind share commonalities beyond those required to distinguish one kind from another. These commonalities suggest the existence of underlying mechanisms that rationalize the taxonomy. Thus the general greenness of plants (not generally used to formally distinguish them from animals) later finds an explanation in terms of the mechanisms of photosynthesis. The recognition of a natural kind is frequently a first step toward explaining the coexistence of its characteristics.

Why We Want Explanations

If the theoretical terms that appear in explanatory theories are eliminated when descriptive theories are derived from them, what is the point of the explanatory theories? Why do we wish to have them, and why do we tolerate the introduction of terms that do not correspond to observables? Because this question is answered most easily by looking at descriptive laws derived from experimental rather than observational data, we will look again at Bugelski's law of constant learning time.

Prior Beliefs and Evidence   An experiment is not a world in itself. The data it produces must be interpreted in the light of everything we knew before the experiment was run. (This is the kernel of truth in Bayes's rule.) That a certain law fits observed data is more believable if there is some prior reason for believing the law to hold than if it is introduced ad hoc for the sole purpose of fitting the data. In the case at hand, the fact that Bugelski's law would hold in a world in which the EPAM mechanisms operated, combined with the fact that EPAM had previously been shown to account for a number of other known experimental phenomena of memory, gives us strong additional reasons for accepting the law, which now becomes an explanation of the data in terms of the mechanisms of EPAM.

In the same way, Kepler's third law is only one of many descriptive laws that can be deduced from Newton's laws of motion and gravitation. Kepler's first two laws are also inferable from Newton's laws, as are many descriptions of terrestrial phenomena (Galileo's law of falling bodies, for example; and in fact the whole body of phenomena of classical statics and dynamics). Bringing together a wide range of phenomenon under the egis of a small set of explanatory laws is a small price to pay, cognitively or aesthetically, for introducing one or more new theoretical terms.

Laws and Definitions   One further comment on the introduction of theoretical terms is in order, as there has been much confusion about it in the literature. The same laws that define the theoretical terms can also be used to test the explanatory theory: there is no sharp separation between definitions and laws (Simon 1970). For example, Ohm constructed a circuit with a battery, a wire whose length he could vary, and an ammeter to measure the current. Ohm's law explained the level of the current by the ratio of the voltage of the battery to the amount of resistance (measured by the length of the wire). Current (I) and resistance (R) were observables, but voltage (V) was a theoretical term. Is not Ohm's law ($V = I/R$), then, merely a definition of voltage, rather than a prediction of outcomes? If only one observation is made, that is true. But if successive observations are made with different lengths of resistance wire, then the first observation can be used to determine the voltage, and the remaining observations to test whether its defined value is consistent with the new currents and resistances. Ohm's law combines definition and theory in one, and the same can be shown to be true of many other fundamental laws (e.g., $F = ma$).

Unified Theories   In cognitive science, the development of explanatory mechanisms leads in the direction of unified theory, in the sense proposed by Newell (1990). As we move toward a unified theory (whether in the form of Soar, Act-R, or as the kind of combination of EPAM, GPS, and UNDERSTAND that I advocate), we aim to embrace a rapidly growing set of experiments and observations in a gradually larger set of mechanisms. As long as the size and the complexity of the theory (in terms of the number of mechanisms and parameters it contains) grows more slowly than the size and complexity of the phenomena explained, the theory becomes more testable, and more plausible if successful, as it is extended.

There is no reason, by the way, for the psychological mechanisms of a unified theory of the mind to stop at the boundaries of cognition. Indeed, there are already proposals for extending the unified theories to embrace attention, motivation, and emotion as well (Simon 1956, 1967, 1994). In a word, these proposals suggest that attention, which controls cognitive goals and inputs, is the connecting link between cognition, on the one side, and motivation and emotion, on the other.

Extrapolation   There is another, but related, reason besides generality why we seek explanatory laws. If one or more features of a situation change, but the rest remain constant, there is no reason to expect a descriptive law to continue to hold in the new situation. But by extrapolating an explanatory theory to a new situation, we can determine whether the law still holds in its original form or, if it does not, how it must be modified to fit the data in the new situation. For example, the stimuli producing Bugelski's data were nonsense syllables of low pronounceability. Will the same law continue to fit the data if the stimuli are one-syllable words? If EPAM is the correct explanation, than we can deduce that it will continue to hold. Conversely, if the relation continues to hold for the new situation, the hypothesis that EPAM provides the correct explanation becomes more plausible.

Explanations, Mechanisms, and Causes

Structural Equations   In econometrics, equations that simply describe phenomena without explaining them are called "reduced-form equations"; equations that also explain the phenomena are called "structural equations", corresponding to what I have been calling "mechanisms". A particular structural change in the economy (e.g., a change in monetary policy) could be expected to change a particular structural equation or small subset of equations (those incorporating the monetary mechanism), leaving the others unchanged. Hence the effect of the change could be predicted by estimating its effect on the specific structural equations that describe the monetary policy, by solving the system containing the modified monetary equations, and by assuming the others remain unchanged. Structural equations describe component mechanisms. If components of the theory represent such mechanisms, experiments can often be performed on the individual components, or knowledge about them can be used to estimate the component's parameters and to estimate the effects of particular events on them. Hence the use of structural equations in describing and explaining a complex system paves the way toward detailed experiments on components of the system to determine the exact form of the mechanisms they embody.

EPAM and other psychological theories describing information-processing mechanisms are systems of structural equations. A computer program is formally equivalent to a system of difference equations, permitting the state of the system at each point in time to be predicted from its state at the previous moment and the inputs to it at that time; the individual subroutines or productions in the program describe the (hypothesized) processes of particular components of the system. Among the structural components of EPAM are a short-term memory, a discrimination net in long-term memory, processes for sorting stimuli in the net, and processes for adding new tests and branches to the net.

Causation Systems of structural equations and the mechanisms they describe allow us to introduce the language of causation (Simon 1953; Pearl 1988; Spirtes, Glymour, and Scheines 1993; Iwasaki and Simon 1994). If a mechanism connects several variables, change in the value of one of them will produce, that is, will *cause*, a change in another. In which direction the causal arrow will point depends not only on the individual mechanism but on the whole system of structural equations in which the mechanism is embedded. Thus downward movement of a weighted piston in a vertical cylinder that encloses a body of gas at constant temperature will, by reducing the volume of the gas, increase the gas pressure, so that a decrease in volume *causes* an increase in pressure. On the other hand, an increase in the temperature of the gas will *cause* an increase in the pressure, which will, in turn, *cause* the gas to expand, moving the piston outward. The same mechanism (cylinder, piston, and heat source) that directs the causation from volume to pressure in the first case directs the causation from pressure to volume in the second.

Expressing the situation in a system of equations, we will see that the reversal in the direction of causation is determined by taking different variables as exogenously determined. In the first case, volume and temperature are the exogenous variables, and, by the gas laws, they causally determine the pressure. In the second case, temperature and equilibrium pressure—that is the weight of the piston—are the exogenous variables, whence the same gas laws causally determine the volume.

Levels of Explanation

Descriptions are often distinguished from explanations by saying that the former answer the question of how something behaves, the latter the question of why it behaves in this particular way. But as children often remind us, every answer to a "why" question elicits a new "why" question. If gravitational force and the laws of motion explain the "why" of Kepler's laws, why do the former hold? If EPAM explains Bugelski's law of learning, what explains the behavior of EPAM? What are the mechanisms that enable the EPAM net to grow and to discriminate?

Near-Decomposability   It is generally acknowledged that "whys" lead to a potentially infinite regress, whose first members, if we halt the regress, must lack an explanation. The reason that there can be a regress at all is closely tied to the typical architectures of complex systems (Simon 1996, chap. 8). The complex systems we generally encounter in nature do not consist of a symmetrical assemblage of parts without end. On the contrary, they are almost always put together in a hierarchical fashion, each assembly being analyzable into subassemblies, and those into subsubassemblies, and so on. Systems having such levels are called "nearly decomposable" (or "nearly completely decomposable"). They have very strong mathematical properties.

A well-known hierarchy of nearly decomposable systems runs from multicelled organisms to single-celled organisms, to complex DNA and protein molecules, to small organic and inorganic molecules, to atoms, to atomic nuclei, to subatomic particles like the proton and neutron, to quarks—seven levels if we stop at that point. In psychology, a hierarchy of nearly decomposable systems runs from social systems, to behavior of individual organisms, to major cognitive functions (e.g., problem solving, using language, learning), to elementary information processes, to neuronal processes, and thence through the hierarchy described previously.

Nearly decomposable systems can be characterized by two basic properties that have important consequences, both for the behavior of the systems and for our understanding of them. First, most events at each system level occur within a characteristic range of temporal frequencies, the mean frequency increasing, usually by one or more orders of magnitude, as we step down from each level to the next. Thus, in a cognitive system at the problem-solving level, we are mostly concerned with processes having a duration ranging from several hundred milliseconds up to tens of seconds or even more. At the level of elementary information processes, we are mostly concerned with processes ranging in duration from a millisecond up to hundreds of milliseconds; at the neuronal level, with processes ranging from a small fraction of a millisecond to perhaps tens of milliseconds.

Related to this differentiation of levels by the durations of their processes is the fact that there are typically many more interactions among the elements within a given component (at any given level of the structure) than there are among elements belonging to different components at that level. This pattern of interaction can be shown mathematically to imply that, by selecting different temporal frequencies of events for study, the components at any given level of the structure can be described, to a good degree of approximation, independently of their linkage with other components at the next level above, and without attention to details of structure and behavior within each of the subcomponents at the next level below. The subcomponents can be treated essentially as aggregates, for they have time to reach a steady state during the time interval of study; and the supercomponents can be treated as constant environments, for they do not change significantly over the relevant time intervals. (For the relevant considerations that motivate this approach to causal ordering and the underlying mathematics, see Simon 1952; Simon and Ando 1961; Courtois 1977; Rogers and Plante 1993; Iwasaki and Simon 1994; and Simon 1996.)

As a simple example, think of the differences in explaining temperature changes over hours, over seasons, and over geological eras. The hourly differences are heavily influenced by the rotation of the earth, the seasonal differences by the revolution of the earth about the sun, and the longer-term differences by much more subtle causes that are only partially understood. It is important (and fortunate) that an explanatory theory of seasonal changes can limit itself to a couple of levels, ignoring the details of hourly changes and treating the average conditions of the current century as constant.

Similarly, by using observational instruments with very different temporal resolutions, we obtain information about quite different levels of mechanisms of human cognitive processes: for example, single-cell recording in the brain (milliseconds), versus nuclear magnetic imaging (NMI) or verbal protocols (seconds), versus laboratory notebooks (hours or days).

Specialization in Science and Decomposability This partial decomposability of systems has consequences not only for the explanatory theories we can build, but also for the specializations of the scientists who build them. Thus, in the natural sciences, we have organismic biologists, cell biologists, molecular biologists, organic and inorganic chemists, physical chemists, astrophysicists, geophysicists, nuclear physicists, and particle physicists, each studying phenomena at a different system level. Similarly, in our own field, we have sociologists, social psychologists, cognitive psychologists, sensation, perception, and motor psychologists, neuropsychologists, neurobiologists, and so on.

Of course, we must pay attention to the "nearly" in the phrase "nearly decomposable." Each level can be studied independently of the levels above and below only to an approximation, the goodness of the approximation depending on the separation of the frequencies at which the mechanisms at successive levels operate—the greater the separation, the better the approximation. The typical temporal separations between "vertically" adjacent scientific domains are one or two orders of magnitude—like the ratios of seconds to minutes or years to months. Moreover, we will want to aim not only at building a body of descriptive theory for the phenomena at each level in terms appropriate to that level, but also at building the bridge theories that explain the phenomena at each level in terms of the mechanisms at the next level below.

In the case of psychology, as we succeed in building theories of complex cognitive processes, elementary information processes (EIPs) operating on symbols, and neural processes, we will want to build theories that explain how the cognitive processes are explained (i.e., implemented or realized) by systems of EIPs; the EIPs by neural mechanisms; and ultimately, the neural mechanisms by chemical laws. Although today we can explain many complex cognitive phenomena at the level of EIPs, another major advance will have been achieved when we can associate a sequence of neural events with the addition of a symbol to long-term memory, or the retrieval of a symbol from long-term memory and its temporary storage in short-term memory. That day may be near, but it has not yet come.

Levels in Psychology Psychology has only gradually, and rather recently, recognized the need to build its theories in layers in this way. As recently as World War II, or even several decades later, many neuroscientists saw no need for (or perhaps no possibility of) building testable symbolic theories that were not expressed directly in terms of neurological mechanisms. On the other end of the spectrum, the more radical behaviorists saw no need or possibility of building testable symbolic theories that would be expressed in terms of the organismic mechanisms mediating between stimuli and responses. One way of interpreting the "information-processing revolution" in cognitive psychology is that it opened up the important cognitive and informational processing level that lay between gross behavior and neurons, and began to supply and test bodies of explanation at this level. Perhaps the weakest link in the chain today is the general absence of bridging theories between the EIP and neurological levels, although the advent of new laboratory methods and instruments (for example, functional MRI or fMRI) brings with it the hope that the gap will soon begin to narrow.

It cannot be emphasized too strongly that this "layering" of cognitive science is not just a matter of comfort in specialization but reflects the structure and layering of the phenomena themselves and the mechanisms that produce them. Moreover, it leads to a far simpler and more parsimonious body of theory. We can see a striking example of this parsimony in the layering of modern genetic theory from population genetics at the most aggregate level, through classical Mendelian genetics at the level of the species and its members, to the genetics of chromosomes as the bearers of genes, and then to molecular genetics and its detailed chemical explanation of the more aggregated laws.

Reductionism The presence of layers of theory reflecting the near-decomposability of the phenomena does not in principle refute or deny reductionism. It may be possible *in principle* to construct a theory of "everything" in terms of quarks (or whatever may turn up at another level below quarks), although constructing such a theory would be wholly infeasible computationally, and the theory if achieved, wholly incomprehensible to the human mind. It would essentially duplicate the whole book of Nature, and we would have to create a new hierarchical theory, in layers and exploiting Nature's near decomposability, in order to read that book.

2.2 The Discovery of Explanations

The work of science comprises a wide range of disparate activities: finding problems, finding ways of representing phenomena, finding data (by observation or experiment), planning experiments and observations, inventing and improving observational instruments, discovering patterns in data (descriptive laws), discovering explanatory laws, deducing the consequences, especially the observable consequences of systems of laws (this includes making predictions and postdictions), devising new representations. Undoubtedly there are others, but these will serve to indicate the range and variety of tasks that scientists engage in.

There can be a corresponding specialization of scientists, by type of activity as well as by subject matter. In a field like physics, some specialists restrict themselves almost entirely to experimental work, often further specialized by the kinds of instruments and experimental designs they employ. Others are almost pure theorists, seldom involved in observational or experimental work. Some focus on the invention and improvement of instruments and techniques of measurement. In the biological sciences, there is much less specialization: theorists are expected to run experiments to test theories, and experimentalists, to construct lawful descriptions and explanations of their data. Indeed, there are very few biologists who are exclusively theorists. In this respect, psychology resembles biology much more than it resembles physics.

In sections 2.3 and 2.4, I will be concerned with building theories to describe and explain data. Because the invention, construction, and application of new representations for a problem are closely associated with the development of descriptive and explanatory theories, I will also be concerned with representations. And because it turns out that experiments and observations are often causal instigators of theory, I will have to include many aspects of empirical work in my story.

I propose that the basic processes employed in these tasks are essentially the same over all fields of science. I will therefore aim at a general theory, not limited to theory building in cognitive psychology but including some examples drawn from that field. With this inclusion, the proposed theory will be incestuous—a cognitive theory of discovery in cognition (and in every other field of science).

Bottom-Up and Top-Down Science

It will be convenient to maintain the distinction between descriptive and explanatory theories because the development of descriptive theories is more closely tied to specific phenomena and often derives from observation of them, whereas the development of explanatory-theories frequently entails some theoretical activity before data gathering. The reasons for this difference will become evident as we proceed, but its basic cause can be stated quite simply: descriptive theories generally deal with phenomena at a single level of the complex system that is under study; explanatory theories usually account for phenomena at one level by means of mechanisms drawn from the next lower level of the system structure.

This does not mean that science has to build from the bottom up. In point of fact, it quite often is constructed by a skyhook procedure from the top down. An obvious example is the progress of physics from macrophenomena (a swinging pendulum or the moon's motion about the earth) through atoms, nuclei and particles, eventually to quarks, and perhaps someday beyond them. Phenomena at one level call for explanations at the next level below, and mechanisms have to be postulated at that lower level, even beyond what can be observed directly. Thus Mendel postulated genes before the locus of the genetic mechanism was found in the chromosomes, and Planck postulated the quantum of action to account for spectral observations. As we shall see, the distinction between bottom-up and top-down approaches has important implications for the ways in which adjacent levels can most effectively communicate and cooperate.

Discovery as Problem Solving

Among cognitive scientists who have approached discovery from an information-processing standpoint, the view is widely held that discovery is "simply" a form of problem solving. I put "simply" in quotes because no implication is intended that discovery is not difficult—merely that it calls for no basic processes that are qualitatively different from those found in every other kind of problem solving that has been studied.

If scientific discovery is problem solving, then at least three kinds of activities are required: (1) amassing, externally and in memory, large databases of relevant information, richly indexed so as to be evoked when appropriate patterns (cues) are presented by data or theory; (2) constructing representations for the problems to be addressed; and (3) carrying out heuristic (selective) searches through the problem spaces defined by the problem representations. No implication should be drawn from this list that these activities are performed in the order shown, or in any particular order. In fact, all three activities are closely intermingled in the processes of research.

A single problem may require search in more than one problem space. As a simple example, consider Kepler's search for what become his third law. Because there was no prior theory that could assist the search, it was wholly driven by the data. First, there was the space of astronomical observations, from which estimates of the planets' periods of revolution about the sun (P) and distances from it (D) could be obtained. Second, there was the space of possible laws that could be tested against the data. No space of possible problems was required, for the problem had already been posed by Aristotle and others. The space of data was not especially problematic because the distances and periods had already been estimated by Copernicus and others, and color and brightness were almost the only other planetary properties that were known. If a law were proposed—for example, the linear law $P = aD + b$—the parameters a and b could be estimated from estimates of P and D for any pair of planets and the law tested by measuring the goodness of fit of the remaining planets to the law. If the test failed, then a new law could be generated and the test repeated. Success depended on using a generator that would produce the correct function without too much search.

An almost identical procedure applies to the search for Bugelski's law, which also begins with the observed data, having no prior theory for guidance. Once a pair of variables has been picked, the trick is to find the function that links their values. This means searching, in some sense, the space of possible functions, and because this space is not well defined, the real problem focuses on this search. Of course, in the case of Bugelski's law one might suppose that a linear function would almost surely be tried first. What prevented discovery of Bugelski's law for many years was that experimenters on verbal learning typically reported numbers of trials required for learning rather than time per syllable learned. For Kepler's third law, where the answer is $P = aD^{3/2}$, it is less clear what kind of a function generator would arrive at this result, and how quickly it could do so. I will return to this question presently.

The Social Structure of Discovery: The "Blackboard"

Before I begin a detailed analysis of discovery processes, I need to engage in some discussion of the social structure of science. By "social structure," I am not referring to the broader "externalist" societal influences on science, however important they may be in determining careers, budgets, and the interactions between the ideas and attitudes of scientists and the mores and ideologies of the society. Instead, I am referring to the social processes and communication flows internal to the scientific community (and specialized communities of scientists). One central characteristic of scientific work is that its output is written on a public "blackboard" of publication. A piece of work is not complete until it has been written on the blackboard; and the blackboard is open to all to read.

We may imagine scientists as travelers, journeying along long, branching paths. Some of these paths lead nowhere and are abandoned. Others reach destinations that seem to be interesting, and which are then described on the blackboard. Scientists who find descriptions of places of interest written on the blackboard may copy them off and continue along the paths described—or along alternative paths suggested to them by what they read, producing new destinations for inscription on the blackboard.

When a particularly interesting locale is reached, the person who noted it on the blackboard is credited with its discovery. Scientists who are realistically modest are aware that they were responsible for only a short final segment of the path, and indeed that they saw the goal only because they were "standing on the shoulders of giants." If we, the observers, see only the final destination, the idyllic tropical isle that has been found, we will be filled with admiration and wonder at the discovery. Even if we are familiar with the entries on the blackboard that preceded it, we may find the final leap remarkable. Only as we are informed in detail about the intervening steps can we begin to see that each one is rather simple, and can be explained in terms of a small set of simple processes. Because the scientific reports inscribed on the blackboard are not ordinarily written as detailed logs of the journey that led to the destination, it is the task of the theory of scientific discovery to reconstruct this journey—to describe the discovery processes and to demonstrate their sufficiency to account for the discovery.

The existence and use of the blackboard, including the strong motivation to write on it as soon as a new land is found, greatly facilitates specialization in science. Some scientists specialize in constructing theories, descriptive or explanatory as the case may be. Others specialize in performing experiments, and so on. (Of course, as scientific work is more and more carried out by teams, there can also be a great deal of within-team specialization in the course of producing the multiauthor papers that finally show up on the blackboard.)

There is much discussion today in science about the crisis of communications resulting from the vast accumulation of knowledge, specialization, and the burgeoning of journals. The cognitive and information sciences face a challenging task—discovering an explanatory theory that will suggest efficient designs for the blackboard and ways of searching it rapidly with powerful, intelligent filters capable of retrieving the relevant while ignoring the irrelevant.

2.3   Computer Simulation of Discovery

Research of the past two decades has thrown substantial light on the nature of the paths of discovery. The research has taken the form of computer simulations of a variety of discovery processes—testing the computer models against data on historically important scientific discoveries (publications, retrospective accounts, laboratory notebooks, correspondence), data obtained from laboratory experiments with human subjects in discovery situations and data obtained by observation of scientists at work. The computer models constitute, as we saw earlier, theories of the discovery processes in the form of systems of difference equations. Their principal uses have been to predict the time sequences of events in the course of discoveries and the final products.

Up to the present, the largest body of theory building and testing deals with (1) data-driven discovery; and (2) experiments as discovery tools. There has been research, also, on (3) theory-driven discovery; (4) the uses of analogy in discovery and the related use of analogy in forming problem representations; and (5) the invention of scientific instruments. There have even been informal attempts to assemble these pieces of the picture into a somewhat unified theory of discovery that embraces these processes and others (see Langley, et al. 1987, chaps. 1, 9, 10).

Simulation of Data-Driven Search

For the common case of a quest for a law where there is little or no relevant preexisting theory, search is guilded almost solely by the data themselves. This task is addressed by a computer program, BACON, that simulates data-driven discovery processes. To the extent that BACON can account for the discoveries of Kepler, Bugelski, and others, it provides a theory, both descriptive and explanatory, of the processes that lead to at least this kind of discovery. Because Kepler's third law is a descriptive law, BACON provides a theory of the discovery of descriptive laws. Because BACON is a computer program that can discover such laws using symbolic information processes, it proposes mechanisms of discovery, hence is an *explanatory* theory for the discovery of *descriptive* laws.

The key heuristic in BACON is to examine the pairs of values of the two variables that are to be related (in the case of Kepler, the periods and corresponding distances of the different planets) and to test whether both increase together or one increases as the other decreases. If they increase together, BACON takes the ratio of the values of the two variables, $z = x/y$, to determine whether z is approximately a constant. If it is, a new law has been found; if not, a new variable has been found, which can be tested in the same way.

In the case of Kepler's third law, P varies with D. However, P/D is not a constant, but increases with D. Therefore BACON now tries the ratio of these two variables, obtaining a new variable, P/D^2. BACON now finds that P/D varies *inversely* with P/D^2, and *multiplies* them, obtaining P^2/D^3, which is, in fact, a constant (within the limits of error that have been preset). Thus, the third function generated by the system is Kepler's third law, $P = aD^{3/2}$. Notice that the system made no use of the meanings of the variables, hence required no knowledge of the subject matter. Supplied with the appropriate data and without alteration, BACON very rapidly also finds Ohm's law of electrical circuits, Joseph Black's law of temperature equilibrium in liquids, and many other important laws of eighteenth- and nineteenth-century physics and chemistry (Langley et al. 1987).

The laws found in this way will generally be descriptive, although they may, and frequently do, motivate the invention of explanatory mechanisms, primarily by the introduction of theoretical terms. Let us follow Kepler's third law one step further to show how this is accomplished. Suppose, prior to Newton's providing an explanation for the law, it is observed (as, in fact, it was) that a number of satellites revolve around Jupiter. A curious astronomer measures their distances and periods and BACON, provided with these data, finds that Kepler's third law again fits the observations, but with a new constant, b, so that $P = bD^{3/2}$. BACON will now associate the two constants, a and b, with the distinct sets of observations, and, with a little more cleverness than it now possesses, might assign them as properties of the two central bodies, the sun and Jupiter, respectively. The revolutions of the planets can now be viewed as *caused* (i.e., explained) by this property of the central bodies (which we can recognize as inversely related to their masses—the smaller the mass, the longer the period. Further elucidation, and progress toward the inverse square law of gravitational force, would have to await the discovery of the notions of force and acceleration and their mutual relation.

Similarly, we can see how steps can be taken from description to explanation in psychological theories. If, given Bugelski's law, we compare the time taken to learn N three-letter nonsense syllables of low association level with the time taken to learn N three-letter words, we find that the former is about three times the latter. We can provide this relation with meaning by regarding the nonsense syllables as composed of three familiar chunks (letters), and the words as composed of a single familiar chunk. The learning time is now proportional to the number of chunks to be learned, and a basis has been provided for conceptualizing an explanatory mechanism. In fact, EPAM, which provides such a mechanism at the level of more elementary information processes, predicts precisely this 3 to 1 difference between the learning times for nonsense syllables and words.

Laws of Qualitative Structure

Although, thus far, we have been concerned almost wholly with quantitative laws, even rather advanced sciences often also contain qualitative laws of great importance. Consider, for example, the germ theory of disease. The theory identifies a particular kind of observable object—a microorganism in the body—as a causal mechanism for disease. Its claim is entirely qualitative: not only does it not specify an equation relating the quantity (or other properties) of the microorganism to the intensity of the disease, but it does not even claim that all diseases are caused by microorganisms. It is roughly equivalent to the recommendation: "If disease symptoms are present, look for germs; there may be some."

A more elaborate, but still qualitative, hypothesis is the physical symbol system (PSS) hypothesis, which defines a physical symbol system in terms of the elementary processes it is capable of performing, and then claims that thought is produced by systems having these processing capabilities. It is roughly equivalent to the recommendation: "If a system gives evidence of thinking, look for the presence of elementary information processes."

Insofar as it identifies a kind of mechanism, the germ theory of disease is an explanatory theory. Insofar as it simply describes the causative agent without indicating how it works (merely tells you to look for a microorganism), it is not much more than a descriptive theory. Likewise, the PSS hypothesis falls short of being a full explanatory theory because, although it claims that certain processes and only these processes will be observed, it does not specify how the processes are organized to produce the phenomenon. Indeed we might consider both the germ theory of disease and the PSS hypothesis of thinking to be forms of representation rather than full-blown theories. They tell us how to go about the first steps of representing the theory: "Introduce microorganisms," or "Specify appropriate symbolic processes."

This does not mean that we cannot specify a theory beyond a crude qualitatively described mechanism without sacrificing its qualitative character. For example, without creating an actual computer program, we could begin to specify the EPAM theory by describing it as consisting of a discrimination net (a branching tree of tests with terminal nodes for the categories being discriminated), a set of processes for performing successive tests on stimulus features, and a set of processes for creating new tests and branches and inserting them into the tree in response to feedback about confusions between stimuli.

Conversely, we can specify a mathematical representation for a theory without providing a complete specification of processes. For example, we may specify that the theory will be represented by a set of linear differential equations, or by a computer program in the form of a production system written in a list-processing language. Similarly, an equation may describe a learning curve (e.g., the well-known power law) without postulating a particular learning mechanism to account for the shape of the curve. The degree of completeness of a theory is more or less orthogonal to the degree to which it is qualitative or quantitative.

Recalling our earlier discussion of causation, we can view a specification of the causal ordering of a set of variables as a qualitative theory of the mechanisms operating on and among these variables. In this way, we might describe a (much simplified) qualitative theory of vision by **Stim**ulus → **Ret**ina → **Feat**ures → **Rec**ognition → **STM**. Which is say, light arriving at the eye (**Stim**) causes stimulation of the retina (**Ret**), which causes transmission of signals to the brain, where features (**Feat**) are extracted, and where the stimulus is recognized (**Rec**) and held in short-term memory (**STM**). In fact, until recent decades, theories in cognitive psychology generally took some such form, making them quite ambiguous and weak in their predictive powers, but not without content.

Conversion of such theories into computer programs increases their precision and allows many more empirically testable quantitative and qualitative predictions to be made.

Simulation of Theory-Driven Search

We return now to the search for theories, in this case to search that is driven by preexisting theoretical postulates instead of by data. Once we have a theory at hand, especially a rather powerful one like Newton's laws, we may proceed to seek explanations for known phenomena by deductive processes (this is what Thomas Kuhn called "normal science"), or we may make deductions from the theory in order to predict new phenomena, thereby providing tests for the validity of the theory.

In general, the only deductions that can be made from descriptive theories are extensions to phenomena of the same kind as those to which the theoretical function was originally fitted: for example, the extension already discussed of Kepler's third law from the solar system to the satellites of Jupiter. In the same way, a system of functions fitted to past data may be used to predict future observations of the same phenomena.

In the case of an explanatory theory, the opportunities for application to new situations are much broader, as the examples we have discussed already suggest. In either case, however, the term *deduction* must be used with care. Although the derivation of Kepler's laws from Newton's is a deduction, the task of the scientist is to *discover* this derivation, a task that will generally require heuristic search through a problem space. It is therefore an inductive, not a deductive, process. In some cases, there may be a straightforward algorithm that is guaranteed to find the solution: most cases of predicting a future state from the present one with a dynamic mathematical model or a computer program are of this kind. But in other cases, especially in extending the theory to new phenomena, the search for the derivation may be decidedly nontrivial.

The apparent paradox of needing inductive processes to deduce the consequences of a theory can be clarified by a little closer look at the nature of theories. A theory consists of laws that place constraints on the set of possible worlds: only worlds that satisfy the constraints are possible, but there may be many such worlds. The solar system, for example, satisfies the constraints imposed by Kepler's laws, as does the system of Jupiter and its satellites. Both systems also satisfy the constraints imposed by Newton's laws. However, demonstrating that Newton's laws imply Kepler's laws requires the discovery of a proof—a particular path through the space of Newtonian possible worlds that shows that all Keplerian worlds belong to this space—and finding such a proof is an inductive process. (Reproducing this process could be a useful exercise for the reader.)

The representation of chemical reactions as recombinations of atoms into molecules provides a clear example of the use of theory to explain phenomena at one level of description in terms of concepts at a more basic level. The lower-level theory postulates that all chemical substances consist of small bundles (molecules) of more elementary particles (atoms), and that chemical reactions rearrange the atoms from one set of bundles into a new set of bundles. Thus molecules of oxygen and molecules of hydrogen react to form molecules of water; molecules of hydrogen and molecules of nitrogen react to form molecules of ammonia. The lower-level theory further postulates that (1) the number of atoms of each kind of particle input into a reaction is equal to the number of atoms of each kind that is output (conservation of atoms); and (2) in gaseous reactions, the relative volumes of any two species of molecules (at standard temperature and pressure) are proportional to the numbers of those molecules (Gay-Lussac's law).

A computer simulation, DALTON, has been used to show how chemical reactions that have been described at the higher level in terms of the kinds and weights of molecules in the input and output can be explained at the lower level in terms of rearrangement of atoms among molecules. For example, if hydrogen and oxygen are elements, and two volumes of hydrogen and one of oxygen combine to form two volumes of water vapor, then DALTON shows that the simplest explanation of this reaction is that (1) each molecule of hydrogen consists of one atom and each molecule of oxygen, of two atoms; and (2) two molecules of hydrogen and one of oxygen then form two molecules of water, where each water molecule contains one atom of hydrogen and one of oxygen (HO). These, of course, are not today's formulas for water (H_2O) or hydrogen (H_2). However, when DALTON later tries to discover the reaction that synthesizes ammonia from hydrogen and nitrogen, it finds that it must postulate that the hydrogen molecule possesses two atoms. Now it revises the water reaction to read $2H_2 + O_2 = 2H_2O$.

A somewhat different lesson is taught by an experience with EPAM. The chunking mechanism that was used to explain why words are learned much faster than nonsense syllables also provided an explanation for

George Miller's (1956) "magical number seven"—the observed fact that short-term memory (STM) capacity is determined by number of familiar chunks, not by bits or other units. However, later work by Baddeley, Thomson, and Buchanan (1975) demonstrated that the STM capacity varied with pronunciation rate of the material stored, so that fewer two-syllable than one-syllable words could be retained. Zhang and Simon (1985) showed that the EPAM model with a more sophisticated STM structure could approximate the observed data even more closely if account were taken both of time for pronunciation and time to retrieve familiar chunks from memory. Here we see the familiar pattern of a theory explaining an observed regularity, new observations challenging the regularity, and a modification of one mechanism of the explanatory theory to account for both the original and the new data.

Another experience with EPAM led to its extension from verbal learning tasks to classification or categorization tasks (concept attainment). To learn stimulus-response pairs, EPAM must grow a discrimination net that distinguishes each stimulus or response from each other one. The mechanisms that achieve this make many successful predictions of the effects of greater or less similarity among stimuli on the time required for learning. In categorization tasks, in contrast to verbal learning tasks, a key requirement of a successful theory is ability to group together (i.e., *not* to discriminate between) stimuli that belong to the same category. It was observed that, given appropriate reinforcement, the EPAM mechanisms could group stimuli as readily as they could distinguish them, and it has now been shown that, given the appropriate experimental instructions, the same mechanisms that perform the learning task are able to perform the categorization task, with good agreement between theory and experimental data (Gobet et al. 1997).

The fruitfulness of mutual interaction between description and explanatory theorizing is illustrated by the general problem solver (GPS) theory. The earlier logic theorist (LT) theory had been used to demonstrate the problem-solving power of selective search guided by heuristics. Thinking-aloud protocols of human subjects were gathered for the LT task (discovering proofs for theorems in logic) to test the veridicality of the theory. Study of the protocols revealed a mechanism, means–ends analysis, that was not explicitly incorporated in LT, but that has since been found to be common in human protocols over a wide range of tasks. The control of search in the new program, GPS, was built around means–ends analysis, leading to a long line of both theoretical and empirical research to determine the ubiquity of the method, its limitations and variants, and the role it plays in the control of heuristic search in a wide variety of tasks.

These examples may suffice to illustrate some of the characteristics of theory-driven discovery, and the similarities and differences between it and the data-driven discovery mechanisms discussed earlier. All of the examples, both from the natural sciences and from psychology, deal with situations where an explanatory theory was already in place, and ask how that theory can be related to empirical phenomena and higher-level theories that describe those phenomena. In a later section, I will have more to say about the initial discovery of explanatory theories.

Design of Experiments and Instruments

Although the role of experiments in testing theories is well known and has been discussed extensively, the role of experiments in discovering theories has been less fully examined. In fact, it is sometimes claimed that experiments need to be designed in the light of preexisting theories—that experimenting (or observing) without a theory is futile. Some examples of Nobel prize–winning discoveries reached by experimentation that was initiated with little or no prior theory will show how wrong this claim is.

The Curies were seeking to extract radioactive uranium from pitchblende. The radioactivity of pure uranium was known, and the task was to obtain a gradual increase in radioactivity as the pitchblende was purified. To the Curies' surprise, they discovered after a time that the material they were purifying achieved a radioactivity in excess of that of pure uranium. They then built a simple explanatory theory: that the radiation was being produced, not by uranium, but by a hitherto unknown element that they named radium.

Fleming saw bacteria dying in a Petri dish he had neglected to wash, and saw a mold, *Penicillium*, growing near where the bacteria were disintegrating. He formed the hypothesis that the mold was the cause for the deterioration of the bacteria, and proceeded to experiment in two directions: (1) to see what varieties of bacteria could be killed by this means; (2) to look for a substance excreted by the mold that could account for the effect and to find the chemical structure of the substance. His work, followed by that of Florey and Chain (1944) led to the discovery of the first antibiotic, penicillin.

These are just two examples, selected from a much larger number, of situations where an accidental observation, or a surprising phenomenon in an experiment, such as Krebs's discovery of the role of ornithine in urea synthesis (Kulkarni and Simon 1988), led to the construction of an important explanatory theory. The critical conditions for creating a high likelihood that experiments or observation will be fruitful are (1) that the scientist have a large repertory of relevant information that stimulates attention to unexpected events and recognizes their significance (Pasteur observed that "accidents happen to the prepared mind"); and (2) that materials be available from this same repertory of knowledge for constructing explanations of what has been observed. Thus capabilities for recognizing important phenomena based on a large knowledge base, take their place side by side with capabilities for effective heuristic search as major weapons in the scientist's armamentarium.

The invention of new scientific instruments is another important activity of scientists, and it, too, often leads to theoretical discoveries. It has undoubtedly been known since before the dawn of history that hot water can be made cooler, and cold water warmer, by mixing them. The invention by Fahrenheit (and others) of the thermometer, allowed that commonplace observation to be turned into a descriptive law, and then into an explanatory law. The descriptive law predicted that the final temperature of the mixture would be the average of the initial temperatures, weighted by the quantities of hot and cold water. This description led to a new theoretical concept, the quantity of heat: the quantity of substance times the temperature. When dissimilar substances were mixed, another new theoretical term, *specific heat*, was introduced to characterize the heat capacity per unit weight of each particular substance. This still rather simple and descriptive theory of heat (but with new explanatory terms like *quantity of heat* and *specific heat*) was gradually expanded and extended into a theory of thermodynamics that served as the foundation for the invention of steam engines and other power sources. At all stages of the history, there was a close interaction among observations, observing instruments, experiments, and descriptive and explanatory theories—advances in each stimulating progress in the others.

Recognition, Analogy, and Representation

My final topic, already introduced in the previous subsection, is the way or ways in which explanatory theories are discovered. Without pretending to provide a full theory, I should like to propose yet other mechanisms that I believe play an important role in theory construction. One of them, analogy, has been commented on extensively in the literature; the others have been much less discussed. The evidence that will be reported here will be mostly of a historical kind.

Recognition   In mentioning accidental discovery, I have already introduced the notion of recognition as a discovery mechanism. Its key elements are (1) a large body of knowledge held in a memory that is (2) indexed by cues, whose recognition in a situation gives access to relevant information in the memory.

Thus Fleming was an experimental biologist with a vast stock of knowledge about bacteria and many other organisms. Recognition of surprising cues (the dying bacteria) led him to look for conditions that would account for them. Not finding any, he noticed another unusual circumstance: the presence of a mold. His expectations had been violated, thereby fixing his attention on the phenomena, and the phenomena could be fitted into a very broad law of qualitative structure, similar to, but more general than, the germ theory of disease: "If you notice that an organism is dying (or any other surprising event), look for unusual phenomena in its vicinity that could conceivably provide a cause." Another general heuristic that appears to have been available to him was now evoked: "To discover why one organism is causing damage to another, look for a substance being excreted by the former and test it for toxicity." Further heuristics also already available to Fleming could then be evoked and used to guide the process.

The plausibility of this account is enhanced when we find closely similar sequences of events in other cases of "accidental" discovery. I have already mentioned the Curies and Krebs. We can add to this list Faraday, in his search for an explanation of the magnetic induction of electric current; Penzias and Wilson, in their search for an explanation of the low-level background radiation they had detected in space; Einstein, in his search for an explanation for the photoelectric effect and for the anomalies of specific heats of diamond and other substances at low temperatures; Bohr, in his search for an explanation of the spectrum of the hydrogen atom; and many others.

In speaking of "recognition" in these situations, I do not mean that the explanatory theory is already in the discoverer's mind, waiting to be evoked by an act of recognition. What are usually evoked are some possibly relevant facts, often associated with some rather vague and general laws of qualitative structure that provide a framework for further theoretical development. We may, if we wish, think of these as broad analogies—often at a very abstract level—that can be built on and elaborated with the help of other knowledge that is evoked from the store.

Faraday's discovery of magnetic induction of electricity, and gradually, of a semiquantitative theory to explain it, provides many examples of these processes (Magnani 1996). I will mention a few of the salient ones. Because Faraday kept a detailed notebook of his experiments, his work is an extraordinarily rich source for such examples. The initial experiments were motivated by Oersted's discovery, a decade earlier, that an electric current could induce magnetism in a piece of soft iron. Faraday (for reasons unknown) decided that there should be symmetry between electricity and magnetism—that if a current could induce magnetism, a magnet should, under appropriate circumstances, induce an electric current. Following Oersted, he produced a magnet by winding a current-bearing wire around a torus of iron; then he tested a second circuit, incorporating a wire wound around the opposite side of the torus, for current—finding none.

Accidentally, he noticed that when he closed the first circuit, turning on the current, the needle of the ammeter in the second circuit was displaced, but only momentarily. When he opened the circuit again, the ammeter was momentarily displaced in the opposite direction. As the effect was transient and in opposite directions in the two instances, Faraday's first thought was that closing the circuit must have caused a "change in state" in the second circuit, signaled by the transient movement of the ammeter; and that opening the first circuit must have caused the second one to revert to its original state. The notion of change of state was a familiar one to any physicist and chemist of Faraday's time (e.g., in connection with the freezing or evaporation of liquids). His next thought was to find direct evidence of the changed state of the wire. As Faraday had done extensive work with electrolytic decomposition of molecules, he first sought evidences of chemical change. He found no direct evidence of "change of state," chemical or other, but did not then reject the hypothesis that closing the first circuit produced an "electrotonic" state in the second. He produced a name for the event, if not a mechanism.

Some months later, as he continued to work on the problem, Faraday discovered how to produce a steady current (by continuous motion of the magnet relative to the wire, or vice versa). He also recalled his previous familiarity with the "lines of magnetic force" that could be exhibited by scattering iron filings over a magnet and its surround. He found that the current was produced when the motion of the electric circuit caused it to cross the lines of magnetic force, and that the current was greater the denser the lines and the more rapidly they were cut. Putting these observations together, he now had a very concrete model, employing the theoretical (but indirectly visible) lines of magnetic force to serve as a mechanism that explained how a magnet could create a continuous electric current.

These are just two episodes in a much larger story, but they are wholly consistent with the remaining episodes. Noticing phenomena led Faraday to intense efforts to provide a model for interpreting them. The models he created, whether they turned out to be mainly correct or illusory, provided a basis for the design and execution of new experiments. The models themselves were largely crafted out of ideas that were already in Faraday's repertoire and experience (e.g., "change in state," "lines of force"), so that the theory generator was closely tied to observation and experiment. His models were very concrete, occupying space and drawable, usually incorporating the actual geometrical arrangement of his apparatus, and only adding a few "intangibles" like the lines of force—which were also depictable in the same space. Faraday's representations emerged from the devices he was so clever in building for his experiments, for example, devices that permitted continuous motion of a circuit relative to a magnet.

An example of an explanatory theory in cognitive psychology where recognition of pattern in phenomena played a leading role in its discovery is the theory of learning from worked-out examples, based on the notion of adaptive production systems (production systems that can create new productions and add them to their memory stores). This theory describes and explains a powerful learning mechanism that is currently having considerable application in pedagogical experiments. When protocols of students solving simple equations in algebra were examined, it was noticed that the students often proceeded by means-ends analysis, a process that we have seen already incorporated in the GPS theory. They noticed features of the equation that differentiated it from the desired form ("$x =$

a number") and applied appropriate operations for removing these features. (Example: If the equation has a number on the left-hand side, subtract that number from both sides.)

On the basis of such observations, Neves (1978) constructed an adaptive production system—a production system that could construct new productions out of information obtained from means-ends analysis and could then insert these new productions in its memory to enlarge its arsenal of heuristics. Thus, by examining the worked-out steps in the solution of an algebra equation, the system might notice that one step consisted in subtracting the same expression from both sides of the equation, thereby removing a numerical term from the left side, and bringing the equation closer to the desired final form. The system would now combine what it had noticed about the difference between current and desired expressions with the operation that it had observed had been applied to create a new production: "If there is a numerical term on the left-hand side of the equation, subtract that term from both sides." After constructing three or four such new productions, the system was capable of solving linear equations in one unknown.

The theory of learning from examples by the mechanism of an adaptive production system has been applied with great success to the construction of an entire three-year curriculum in algebra and geometry that is being used extensively in Chinese middle schools (Zhu and Simon 1987). The theory is, of course, extremely general, extending far beyond this particular application to skill learning in general.

Analogy There has been much attention to analogy as a source of problem representations. An analogy is itself a representation (of something) that has been stored in memory and is evoked for possible modification into a representation for a new situation. Once its possible relevance is recognized, the analogy is applied with the help of a matching process of some kind that maps it (partially) on the new situation. As an explanation of the novel representation, the analogy, like any answer to a "why" question, raises three new "why" questions of its own: What caused the analogy to be present in memory? What caused it to be evoked as possibly relevant on the occasion of the new problem situation? And how was it used to help find the solution?

An acceptable explanation of why an analogy is stored in memory is that it is part of the collection of representations that are current in the thinker's culture—the general culture, or the culture of a scientific specialty or even of a single laboratory. As in any explanation in a dynamic system, we explain an event (in this case, acquiring an analogy) by referring to previous events, leading simply to another "why" question about an earlier discovery. Thus we need not explain how Newton invented the calculus in order to explain why a nineteenth-century physicist uses the calculus as the basis for representing wave motion. The representation (the analogy) was simply *there* for the latter to use. Nor need we explain how Dalton, in the eighteenth century, could turn to an atomic representation of chemical processes. The analogy had been there at least since Democritus.

The idea of a discrete (quantum) change in energy was acquired by Einstein from Planck's 1900 model of blackbody radiation. For reasons that are largely unkown (although its apparent irreconcilability with classical Maxwellian theory was a major consideration), it impressed him as a very central, if confusing, idea. He evoked it on a number of occasions when he was faced with problems unrelated to blackbody radiation: notably, the photelectric effect in 1905 and anomalous values of specific heat at low temperatures, about 1906.

Explaining why an analogy is evoked on a particular occasion is rarely easy, for the evocation will depend on the precise structure of the mechanisms of both attention and recognition, and on the contents of long-term memory (and their organization). Usually the explanation is finessed by pointing to similarities between the two situations. Thus Bohr compared the hydrogen atom to the solar system (as Nicholson and others had already done) because they both involved a large central mass with one or small masses revolving about it and with the force field of the central mass connecting them. However, the matching process was apparently rather arbitrary and ignored important details: in particular, that the orbital electron would radiate energy, thus causing it gradually to collapse into the nucleus. Bohr then evoked Planck's quantum to "explain" why the orbit could not change gradually, hence could only jump from one discrete state to another. The choice of what to match and what not to match appears quite ad hoc, justified only by its success in explaining the atom's radiation spectrum.

Thus, while there is no convincing explanation of why Bohr used this particular analogy in this particular form and in combination with the quantum hypothesis at this particular time, there is a quite direct

explanation of why the analogy, so used, would lead him to an explanation of the wavelengths in the hydrogen spectrum that had been observed
thirty years earlier and provided with a descriptive theory by Balmer's
curve fitting. There is also a simple explanation of why no one did it much
earlier: the prerequisite knowledge of the structure of the atom only
became known through Rutherford's work in 1911.

For the reasons illustrated by this historical example, we should regard
it as unlikely that we will soon have models of the process of analogy that
will allow us to predict what analogies will be used by whom and when.
However, programs like MERLIN and FERMI (Moore and Newell 1974;
Larkin et al. 1988) have been written that demonstrate how such comparisons can be carried out, so that we have at least a general theory of
the process and mechanisms that actually can and do use analogies effectively. The situation is like that of heart attacks (to use an analogy). Our
knowledge of human physiology allows us to say a great deal about the
mechanisms at work when such attacks occur, but this does not help us
predict them except in the most general way, for example, to show which
conditions of the heart predispose it to attacks. "Heart attacks happen to
the weak heart" is a law of qualitative structure comparable to Pasteur's
"Accidents happen to the prepared mind," quoted earlier.

I have been using the term *analogy* broadly. It is generally used to
compare two things that are at about the same level of concreteness: a
magnetic field and the flow of an incompressible fluid (an analogy used
powerfully by Faraday and Maxwell); an atom and a solar system. I am
suggesting that we broaden the concept of analogy to include a pair consisting of a very general representation (the calculus, atomic theories of
matter, the concept of physical symbol system) and a quite specific instantiation of it (the dynamic equations for a planetary system, the chemical
theories of Dalton or Lavoisier, the general problem solver theory, respectively). Analogies in both the narrower and wider sense play the same role
in the discovery of new representations, employing essentially the same
process: they must be available, they must be evoked, and steps must be
taken to specialize or modify them to fit the new situation. The theory
of analogy would then have much to learn from the general theory of
knowledge transfer in cognition, and vice versa. Indeed, one might say that
they are the same theory, or at least strongly analogical.

The analogies that have been most studied are diagrammatic or pictorial in character. But, of course, an analogy can be verbal, algebraic, or

representable in other modes. The question of modality is not relevant to the present discussion, and will be ignored here.

Representation We have arrived from analogy directly to the topic of representation, and to the key question: Where do representations come from? Part of the answer should already be apparent: most problems are formulated and solved using representations that are already available in memory. The invention of a new representation, or even substantial modification of an existing representation, is an important, but relatively infrequent event in the life of a scientist. Once a month, once a year, once a decade, once in a lifetime? The statistics have not been assembled.

The most general representations undoubtedly have a genetic basis. The eye and subsequent feature-extracting processes already recognize both the continuous and the discrete: continuous expanses of space or matter and their discrete boundaries. There are, almost certainly, built-in mechanisms for detecting symmetries and testing identity of stimuli; a memory that holds list structures will contain a test for the relation of "next" on a list. And it has been shown (Kotovsky and Simon 1973; Simon and Sumner 1968) that complex cognitive tasks (e.g., the Thurstone Letter or Number Series Completion Task and the Raven or the task of detecting pattern in music) require just these kinds of mechanisms and recognition capabilities for their performance.

The UNDERSTAND program (Hayes and Simon 1974) has shown how problem representations can be generated from problem instructions by extracting the objects, relations among objects, and operations on objects that define the problem. Novak's ISAAC program (1977) has shown how representations for particular physics problems can be generated from verbal problem descriptions, using representations of component elements that are already available in memory. Siklossy's ZBIE program (1972) has shown how language can be learned by mapping the analogies between visual images of situations and sentences describing these situations. Thus we can say that we have the beginnings of a theory of how representations can be discovered for new situations.

With respect to representations that provide the basis for explanatory laws, there is a great deal more to be done. Here, we must at present turn mostly to historical material, like the notebooks of Faraday and the other examples we have mentioned previously. In cases that have been studied closely, the representation never emerges suddenly from the head of Zeus, but is created incrementally, usually in quite small steps. I have already spoken of the twenty-six years it took to progress from Planck's serendipitous introduction of the quantum to the matrix mechanics of Heisenberg and the wave mechanics of Schrödinger that constitute modern quantum mechanics. Those twenty-six years were filled with alternative analogies, false starts, hints from new experiments and observations—a long sequence of tiny moves forward, but also backward and sideways. I will just comment briefly on a couple of other examples.

The incremental character of the discovery of the calculus, however solid Newton's claim to be its inventor, is well documented, and has even led some to bestow the name of inventor on one of Newton's predecessors, Isaac Barrow or Fermat. Given the incremental progress toward the calculus, the unique inventor really does not have to be identified—another example of giants standing on giants' shoulders. But if there is a sufficient number of layers of "giants," none of them need be exceptionally tall.

Special relativity creates an especially interesting case, as it led to the substitution of four-dimensional space-time for three-dimensional space, as well as the replacement of the Galilean by the Lorentz transformation. Key elements in this revolution were Einstein's idea that the speed of light might be the same in all coordinate systems, and his (and others') concern that Maxwell's equations were not invariant under Galilean transformations. We have little to guide us as to why the former assumption was not rejected out of hand as "unthinkable," unless it be Einstein's unsuccessful attempt to find a criterion for synchrony of clocks that would be maintained even with movement through space. We might also attribute to him a willingness to follow thoughts wherever the mathematics led them, but that does not provide much of an explanation.

In any event, as others (Fitzgerald, Lorentz, Poincaré) also found the Lorentz transformation while working from the same preoccupations as Einstein's with the invariance of Maxwell's equations, that particular path is understandable enough; and because the others did *not* follow through completely to interpret the transformation of the time coordinates, as Einstein did, we can isolate his uniqueness on that point. Here, the key to Einstein's success (and his particular derivation of the Lorentz transformation) was his taking seriously the concrete task of synchronizing clocks under the assumption of the invariance of the velocity of light. This called for no new representation, but simply for following through on the algebraic consequences of a familiar one (a light emitted from one end of a moving rod and reflected from the other end). Even the basic equations are elementary and familiar: they are identical with the equations of the familiar riverboat round-trip (or airplane round-trip) problems of high school algebra. Only when these equations are combined, to determine the way in which the coordinates are transformed in changing from a stationary to a moving reference system do the surprising new implications of special relativity appear.

Perhaps these examples will evoke at least some skepticism about the appearance of a new representation being typically a sudden and inexplicable event. A better metaphor is that new representations evolve from bending and twisting old representations to fit recalcitrant phenomena. The numerous activities of science do not stand in isolation from each other. Searches in each of the spaces—of phenomena, of explanatory and descriptive theories, of representations, of instruments, of experiments—are motivated by the products, and especially by the unexpected products, of searches in the other spaces.

Representation in Cognitive Science Before we leave this topic, I should like to discuss the discovery of the representation central to contemporary cognitive science: mind and brain as physical symbol system (or, if you prefer, as computer). There is often talk of the "computer metaphor," but the computer is much more than a metaphor, for within the context of the physical symbol system hypothesis, both electronic computer and brain *are* computers: siblings in the family of intelligent systems. Our earlier discussion of levels should make clear that the commonality of computer and brain exists at a particular level: the information-processing level. At the next lower level, of implementation by electronics or neurons, as the case may be, no similarity is implied, beyond some of architecture. This should surprise us no more than that electric energy can be produced by a waterwheel, a gas turbine, or a nuclear reactor. As the concrete evidence compiled over recent decades by computer simulation of thought shows, total dissimilarity at lower levels in no way interferes with the possibility of exquisitely accurate simulation at the higher symbolic level. Conversation about minds and machines that is carried on in disregard of that evidence (as it frequently is) makes absolutely no sense.

But back to the question of the origins of the information-processing theory of thought. Adam Smith is credited with the invention, in 1776, of advances in the representation of a market economy in which an important role was played by the division of labor. By dividing up tasks into very small elements and carrying out these elementary tasks repetitively and with the use of specialized methods and equipment, their cost could be greatly reduced. More than a decade later, a French mathematician, Prony, who was entrusted by the French revolutionary government with the construction of a set of logarithmic and trigonometric tables, despaired of completing the task in the time allotted to him (where failure might cost his head). Chancing on a copy of *The Wealth of Nations*, he found the chapter on the division of labor and saw a solution to his problem. Mathematics, even computation, was then regarded (as it remains today for most of the world's population) a recondite art, requiring the highest mental powers. But by separating it into its elements, even a complex computation could be reduced to a sequence of simple, repetitive steps, any one of which could be performed after a little training by any person of even modest intelligence. Prony conceived of producing his mathematical tables the way Smith had proposed for producing pins.

It was Prony's mass production of mathematical tables that suggested to the English mathematician, Babbage, a generation later, the idea of a mechanical calculating machine. Thus as the human assembly line suggested the routinization of arithmetic, routinization of human arithmetic suggested the automatic calculating machine, and the calculating machine suggested the PSS hypothesis for the representation of thinking. No great leap of the imagination was required at all, just the idea that structures of arbitrary complexity can be assembled by the repetitive combination of a few elementary processes. That is the PSS hypothesis in a nutshell. A whole generation of cognitive psychology has been concerned with beginning to fill this abstract representation with concrete specifications of the compound mechanisms required to perform different acts of intelligence. Specializations and concretizations of the general representation are important: answers to questions about the specialized components that have to be assembled for the system, the seriality or parallelism of these components, the ways they must be fitted together. But all of these refinements are being essayed under the broad canopy of the physical symbol system representation.

2.4 Conclusion

In this chapter, I have undertaken to apply the physical symbol system hypothesis and the theory of human thinking that derives from it to reach an understanding of how explanations for natural phenomena (including the phenomena with which cognitive science is occupied) are discovered. Section 2.1 was devoted to clarifying the concept of explanation, and the differences between descriptive and explanatory theories of natural phenomena. Section 2.2 introduced the thesis that explanations are discovered with the help of the same processes that are used to solve other kinds of problems, and described some of the characteristics of the problem solving that occurs in science. Section 2.3 provided a more detailed picture of the processes of scientific problem solving, and of the use of electronic computers to explicate these processes by simulating them.

In the course of the chapter, although I have made reference to a substantial body of empirical evidence for my thesis, it represents only a small sample of the total mass of evidence now available in the literature. I hope I will be excused for drawing many of the examples from my own work, for that is the work with which I am most familiar, and most of it was undertaken specifically to test and elaborate on the thesis I am expounding here.

I cannot emphasize too strongly the centrality of empirical evidence to that thesis. The question of whether people think in the manner postulated by the physical symbol system hypothesis and its problem-solving elaborations is an empirical question, to be settled by careful observation and experimentation, and not by arguments from the philosopher's armchair. The question of whether electronic computers can be programmed (or can program themselves) to think as humans do is no less an empirical question, which does not yield its answer to a priori reasoning. A very large body of empirical evidence assures us that the answer is yes.

References

Baddeley, A. D., Thomson, N., and Buchanan M. (1975). Word length and structure of short-term memory. *Journal of Verbal Learning and Verbal Behavior, 14*, 575–589.

Bugelski, B. R. (1962). Presentation time, total time, and mediation in paired-associate learning. *Journal of Experimental Psychology, 63*, 409–412.

Courtois, P. J. (1977). Decomposability, queueing and computer system applications, New York: Academic Press.

Feigenbaum, E. A., and Simon, H. A. (1962). A theory of the serial position effect. *British Journal of Psychology, 53,* 307–320.

Feigenbaum, E. A., and Simon, H. A. (1984). EPAM-like models of recognition and learning, *Cognitive Science, 8,* 305–336.

Florey, H., and Chain, E. (1944). The development of penicillin in medicine. Washington, DC: Smithsonian Institution.

Gobet, F., Richman, H. B., Staszewski, J. J., and Simon, H. A. (1997). Goals, representations and strategies in a concept attainment task: The EPAM model. In D. Medin, ed., *Psychology of learning and motivation.* Vol. 37. San Diego, CA: Academic Press.

Hayes, J. R., and Simon, H. A. (1974). Understanding written problem instructions. In L. W. Gregg, ed., *Knowledge and cognition.* Potomac, MD: Erlbaum.

Iwasaki, Y., and Simon, H. A. (1994). Causality and model extraction. *Artificial Intelligence, 67,* 143–194.

Kotovsky, K., and Simon, H. A. (1973). Empirical tests of a theory of human acquisition of concepts for sequential patterns. *Cognitive Psychology, 4,* 399–424.

Kuhn, T. S. (1962). *The structure of scientific revolutions.* Chicago: University of Chicago Press.

Kulkarni, D., and Simon, H. A. (1988). The processes of scientific discovery: The strategy of experimentation. *Cognitive Science, 12,* 139–176.

Langley, P., Simon, H. A., Bradshaw, G. L., and Zytkow, J. M. (1987). *Scientific discovery: Computational explorations of the creative process.* Cambridge, MA: MIT Press.

Larkin, J. H., Reif, F., Carbonell, J., and Gugliotta, A. (1988). FERMI: A flexible expert reasoner with multi-domain inferencing. *Cognitive Science, 12,* 101–138.

Magnani, G. (1996). *Visual representation and scientific discovery: The historical case of the discovery of electromagnetic induction.* Master's thesis, Carnegie Mellon University, Pittsburgh.

Miller, George A. (1956). The magical number seven, plus or minus two: Some limits on our capacity for processing information. *Psychological Review, 63,* 81–97.

Moore, J., and Newell, A. (1974). How can MERLIN understand? In L. W. Gregg, ed., *Knowledge and cognition.* Potomac, MD: Erlbaum.

Neves, D. M. (1978). A computer program that learns algebraic procedures by examining examples and working problems in a textbook. In *Proceedings of the Second National Conference of the Canadian Society for Computational Studies of Intelligence.* Toronto: Canadian Society for Computational Studies of Intelligence.

Newell, A. (1990). *Unified theories of cognition.* Cambridge, MA: Harvard University Press.

Novak, G. (1977). Representations of knowledge in a program for solving physics problems. *International Joint Conference on Artificial Intelligence, 5,* 286–291.

Pearl, J. (1988). *Probabilistic reasoning in intelligence systems,* San Mateo, CA: Kaufmann.

Richman, H. B., Staszewski, J. J., and Simon, H. A. (1995). Simulation of expert memory using EPAM IV. *Psychological Review, 102,* 305–330.

Rogers, D. F., and Plante, R. D. (1993). Estimating equilibrium probabilities for band diagonal Markov chains using aggregation and disaggregation techniques. *Computers in Operations Research*, *20*, 857–877.

Siklossy, L. (1972), Natural language learning by computer. In H. A. Simon and L. Siklossy, eds., *Representation and meaning*. Englewood Cliffs, NJ: Prentice-Hall.

Simon, H. A. (1953). Causal ordering and identifiability. In W. C. Hood and T. C. Koopmans, eds., *Studies in econometric method*. New York: Wiley.

Simon, H. A. (1956). Rational choice and the structure of the environment. *Psychological Review*, *63*, 129–138.

Simon, H. A. (1967). Motivational and emotional controls of cognition. *Psychological Review*, *74*, 29–39.

Simon, H. A. (1970). The axiomatization of physical theories. *Philosophy of Science*, *37*, 16–26.

Simon, H. A. (1983). Fitness requirements for scientific theories. *British Journal for the Philosophy of Science*, *34*, 355–365.

Simon, H. A. (1994). Bottleneck of attention: Connecting thoughts with motivation. In W. D. Spaulding, ed., *Integrative views of motivation, cognition, and emotion*, Lincoln: University of Nebraska Press.

Simon, H. A. (1996). *The sciences of the artificial*. 3d ed. Cambridge, MA: MIT Press.

Simon, H. A., and Ando, A. (1961). Aggregation of variables in dynamic systems. *Econometrica*, *29*, 111–138.

Simon, H. A., and Feigenbaum, E. A. (1964). An information-processing theory of verbal learning. *Journal of Verbal Learning and Verbal Behavior*, *3*, 385–396.

Simon, H. A., and Sumner, K. (1968). Pattern in music. In B. Kleinmuntz, ed., *Formal representations of human judgment*, New York: Wiley.

Spirtes, P., Glymour, C. N., and Scheines, R. (1993). *Causation, prediction and search*. New York: Springer.

Zhang, G., and Simon, H. A. (1985). STM capacity for Chinese words and idioms: Chunking and acoustical loop hypotheses. *Memory and Cognition*, *13*, 193–201.

Zhu, X., and Simon, H. A. (1987). Learning mathematics from examples and by doing. *Cognition and Instruction*, *4*(3), 137–166.

3

The Naturalness of Religion and the Unnaturalness of Science

Robert N. McCauley

Aristotle's observation that all human beings by nature desire to know aptly captures the spirit of "intellectualist" research in psychology and anthropology. Intellectualists in these fields agree that humans have fundamental explanatory interests (which reflect their rationality) and that the idioms in which their explanations are couched can differ considerably across places and times (both historical and developmental). Intellectualists in developmental psychology (e.g., Gopnik and Meltzoff 1997) maintain that young children's conceptual structures, like those of scientists, are theories and that their conceptual development—like the development of science—is a process of theory formation and change. They speculate that our explanatory preoccupations result, at least in part, from a natural drive to develop theories. Intellectualists in the anthropology of religion (e.g., Horton 1970, 1993) hold that, although it may do many other things as well, religion is primarily concerned with providing explanatory theories. They maintain that religion and science have the same explanatory goals: only the idioms of their explanations differ.

The connections between the concern for explanation, the pursuit of science, the persistence of religion, and the cognitive processes underlying each clearly merit further examination. By considering both their cultural manifestations and their cognitive foundations, I hope to clarify not only how science and religion are related but some of the ways their explanatory projects differ.

I shall argue that, despite their centuries' old antagonisms, no development in science will ever seriously threaten the persistence of religion or the forms of explanation religion employs or the emergence of new religions. (I strongly suspect that science will never seriously threaten the persistence of particular religions either, but I only aim to defend the weaker, collective claim here.) In section 3.3, I shall show that religion and its characteristic forms of explanation are a "natural" outgrowth of the character and content of human association and cognition. First, though, I must say a few words about the senses of "natural" I have in mind and note some respects in which religion may seem "*un*natural". The principal aim of section 3.2 will be to show that at least on some fronts science does not come at all naturally to humans.

3.1 Preliminaries

Although science studies the natural world and religion seems concerned with supernatural worlds, I shall argue that, cognitively speaking, it is religion that is natural and science that is largely unnatural. Describing some aspect of human mental life or conduct as "natural" can support a vast number of possible meanings. I shall focus on two.

We say that a belief or action is "natural" when it is familiar, obvious, self-evident, intuitive, or held or done without reflection—when it seems part of the normal course of events. Closing the window is the "natural" thing to do when sitting in a cold draft; expecting a salesperson on the other end of the line is the "natural" thing to think when your telephone rings during dinner. Of course, what counts as the normal course of events depends, in part, on our social and cultural circumstances.

Judgments and actions deemed "natural" in this first sense typically do not require reflection. That they are obvious or self-evident does not, of course, preclude reflection in such domains. For example, people might reflect at length on the principles and preparation that inform their system of etiquette, although provided their elders have successfully imparted to them the social graces, that reflection is unlikely to have much impact on their on-line judgments and behaviors.

The point of calling many features of religion "natural" and many features of science "unnatural" in this first sense is not merely to note that much about religion is so readily available that it does not even prompt reflection, whereas much about science does. The point is also that even when reflection about religious matters occurs, nonreflective habits of mind typically overwhelm its effects in on-line cognitive processing (see, for example, discussion of Barrett and Keil 1996 in section 3.3).

Thoughts or acts can also said to be "natural" in a more restrictive sense, if they have features that rest on what Pascal Boyer (1994) has called "noncultural" foundations. This second sense is more restrictive: things counted as "natural" on the basis of their comparative independence from specific cultural input form a subset of those deemed natural in the first sense, that is, ones that seem familiar, obvious, or self-evident. These aspects of human activity and mental life not only do not require extensive cultural support, often it is not obvious that they require much of any cultural support.

Two considerations bear on "natural" in this second sense. The first, less easily measured consideration concerns the relative superfluousness of particular cultural arrangements for the generation and persistence of the behavioral patterns and cognitive accomplishments in question. The second, more important consideration for the purposes of this chapter is cognitive.

Some cognitive capacities seem to turn neither on any particular cultural input nor, as in the case of face recognition, on any peculiarly cultural input at all. Children's proclivity to acquire language and nearly all human beings' appreciation of some of the basic physics of solid objects, their assumptions about the mutual exclusivity of taxonomic classes in biology, and their abilities to detect and read agents' minds are just some of the proposed candidates for human cognitive capacities that arise independently of any particular cultural input.

These capacities seem in place comparatively early in human development, and their functioning usually seems both automatic and fast. Their operations occasion no conscious searches for evidence, and even if they did, the associated inferences seem woefully underdetermined by whatever evidence might be available. Why, for example, should shifting his weight to his other side and momentarily raising an eyebrow make us so confident that our interlocutor is skeptical of our claim?

Whether such considerations (together with the noncultural status of the underlying cognitive processes and representations) require that these capacities also be innate has been a point of considerable debate over the past thirty years (see, for example, Spelke 1994). The more interesting question, though, is what being "innate" might amount to (see, for example, Karmiloff-Smith 1992). As Jeffrey Elman and his colleagues (e.g., 1996, 369) have noted, some of the representations and processes in question are, quite possibly, the nearly inevitable outcomes of comparatively minor variations on familiar principles guiding learning in neural networks.

In calling religion "natural" and science "unnatural" in this second sense, I am suggesting two things. First, the elaborate cultural institutions surrounding each play a far more integral role in the generation and persistence of science than they do in the case of religion. (Indeed, for some religious systems, for example, among prehistoric hunter-gatherers, such far-reaching cultural institutions have never existed.) Second, most of the cognitive activity underlying religion concerns cognitive processes that rely far less on particular cultural input, particular forms of cultural input, or even peculiarly cultural input than is the case with science.

Such claims about religion are contrary to appearances. Focusing on the idioms in which religion frames its explanations can foster a sense that religion is unnatural. Religious presumptions about superhuman agents who have extraordinary properties and do extraordinary things contribute to the intuition that religion is less natural than science. After all, allegedly miraculous events conflict with almost everyone's common sense. Even the most experienced and sensitive scholars of religion periodically confront alien religious beliefs that strike them as either bizarre or hilarious. The apparent uselessness of rituals also contributes to this impression. Rituals often seem like empty forms at best, but more often, like utterly pointless activities.

Nothing, though, promotes the notion that religion is unnatural more than the practice throughout the field of religious studies of insisting (1) that religion and religious experience, in particular, are unique; and therefore (2) that religion requires special methods of study. Various scholars of religion (see, for example, Farley 1988, 68–69; Cannon 1996, 43; and Paden 1992, 10) maintain that religion's distinctive status sets a singular, principled constraint on the effectiveness of scientific proposals to explain it. They deny that customary forms of explanation in the natural and social sciences will yield *telling* accounts of religious phenomena—holding, in effect, that the modes of study deemed most worthwhile in the investigation of the natural world are especially limited or inadequate when it comes to religious phenomena. Indeed, these putative limitations on scientific methods result from the assumption that religion is unnatural or that it deals with the nonnatural.[1]

My goal in section 3.3. is to shake this impression of religion's "unnaturalness". I shall discuss the respects in which religion (including its principal forms of explanation) can be fairly described as "natural" (in both of the relevant senses). Contrary to the sentiments that inform so much research in the field of religious studies, many features of "religious cognition" are not at all extraordinary, and thus the methods and findings of the cognitive sciences can illuminate them. Consequently, contrary to widespread assumptions in both religious studies and anthropology, gaining insight into related aspects of religious systems may not depend on scrupulous attention to all of the details of cultural contexts. My case turns largely on surveying analyses of religious idioms (concerning both thought and action) and their underlying ontologies that have emanated over the past decade from cognitive accounts of religious phenomena. Those accounts reveal just how "natural" the forms of religion and of religious explanation are—at least in comparison to the explanations science advances.

First, let us turn to respects in which science may be described as "*un*natural" in the two senses at hand. Let me emphasize that I do not intend to portray the comparative naturalness of religion and science as a stark or obvious contrast, but only to suggest that it is religion and not science that has the greater natural appeal.

3.2   The Unnatural Nature of Science

In making my case for the comparative unnaturalness of science relative to religion, I do not aim to undermine arguments of developmental psychologists (Carey 1985; Gopnik 1996; Gopnik and Meltzoff 1997) to the effect that the cognitive maneuvers of children and scientists are similar in many respects. These developmentalists argue (1) that scientists' and children's conceptual structures are theories; (2) that, for children as well as scientists, these theories provide explanations of events in the world; (3) that, like scientists, children are sensitive to the role evidence can play in improving their conceptual structures; and (4) that conceptual development in children is, like scientific change, a process of formulating, evaluating, amending, and sometimes even replacing theories.[2]

In claiming that religion is more natural than science, it does not follow that nothing about science comes naturally. Undoubtedly, some cognitive activities scientists engage in—their formation of hypotheses, their attention to evidence, and their elaboration, modification, and replacement of theories—predate the emergence of distinctively scientific traditions and institutions and probably do constitute fundamental operations in cognitive development.

Intellectualists in the anthropology of religion share with intellectualists in developmental psychology (and Aristotle) the conviction that human beings have basic psychological inclinations to make sense of the world around them. They maintain that the resulting presumptions and concerns about obtaining explanations are natural inclinations of the human cognitive system in the senses at hand. But note that if an intellectualist account of religion is on the right track, then religion is *no less* natural in this respect than science is. Religion, no less than science, expresses this natural inclination in humans to the extent that it deploys conceptual structures ("theories"—in the developmental psychologists' comparatively broad sense of that term) for the purposes of explanation.

If the drive for explanatory theories is a psychologically natural, that is, a noncultural, inclination displayed equally, though differently, in science, conceptual development, and religion, then what is it about science that justifies dubbing it "unnatural" (or quintessentially "cultural") and setting it apart from religion and conceptual development? What distinguishes science is, first, the relative sophistication and systematicity it brings both to the generation of empirical evidence and to the assessment of that evidence's import for explanatory theories and, second, the pivotal roles that social and cultural arrangements—as opposed to our ordinary cognitive predilections—play in those processes (see Gopnik and Meltzoff 1997, 20, 38; Gopnik 1996, 508; and Brewer and Samarapungavan 1991, 222).

This is not to question children's recognition of the importance of collecting evidence. Nor shall I question the religious on this front either, though, that may be unduly charitable, as remarks on memory in section 3.3 will suggest. Rather, the points I wish to make turn on highlighting both the centrality and the difficulty of systematically pursuing, producing, and appraising empirical evidence in science (Brewer and Samarapungavan 1991, esp. 221). The requisite skills neither automatically come to human beings nor automatically become habits of the human mind. This is one of the reasons why science must be *taught* and why so many have such difficulty both learning it and learning how to do it.

It is also a reason why speaking of "the scientist as child" is so apt (Gopnik and Meltzoff 1997, 13–47). Children are not so much like sophisticated little scientists as scientists, their considerable training and expertise notwithstanding, are like children, not only insofar as they exhibit similar explanatory interests and strategies, but also insofar as they exhibit the same cognitive biases and limitations that other human beings do.

Whether as children or educated scientists, human beings seek explanations, generate theories, and consider evidence, but they also operate with
vague hypotheses, perform fallacious inferences, have memory lapses, and
display confirmation bias (see the final paragraphs of this section).

Scientists can get around some of their cognitive limitations by
exploiting a vast array of tools (such as literacy and mathematical
description) and cultural arrangements (such as journals, professional
associations, and the division of labor). Children, by contrast, mostly work
in comparative isolation unaided by these tools, unable to take advantage
of such arrangements, and unacquainted with the enormous bodies of
knowledge to which scientists have access (Brewer and Samarapungavan
1991).

The institution of science does an even better job than either individual scientists or local research teams of getting around cognitive limitations because it is the collective product of an international community
of inquirers for whom prestige, fame, and wealth turn, in no small part,
on their seizing opportunities to criticize and correct each other's work.
Such communal features of the scientific enterprise establish and sustain
norms that govern scientific practice. They also ensure that the *collective*
outcome of the efforts and interactions of mistake-prone individuals and
small research groups with one another in the long run is more reliable
than any of their individual efforts are in the short run. (Contrary to the
intellectualists in anthropology, the divergent idioms in which science and
religion frame their explanatory theories are not the only things that distinguish them.)

Gopnik and Meltzoff (1997, 13) concede that insofar as such social
considerations "are an important part of theory formation and change in
science, whatever the children are doing is *not* science." The creation of
explanatory theories and the insistence that they stand up to empirical
evidence are necessary but not sufficient conditions for science. In addition to these cognitive proclivities, the invention, persistence, and progress
of science depend crucially on developing traditions for extending and
criticizing theories with increasing systematicity and insight. Pursuing that
process is what Thomas Kuhn (1970) called doing "normal science." Developing such traditions is at least indirectly responsible for the huge range
of activities scientists undertake in the course of their work. The pivotal
role of these additional cultural arrangements guarantees that science will
not inevitably erupt *only* from cognitive dispositions to formulate theories

and to care about empirical evidence. (I shall argue in section 3.3 that religion, by contrast, requires far less cultural support.)

Some of the best evidence of science's unnaturalness, that is, evidence of its substantial dependence on cultural arrangements that entail uncommon and comparatively difficult forms of cognition, is its *rarity*. For some, recognizing that rarity may turn on not confusing science with technology. Science and technology are not the same thing—not because science is independent of technology but because technology can be and once was wholly independent of science. Some historical perspective—indeed, some prehistorical perspective—may clarify this point.

First, the connection between basic scientific research and its technological spin-offs is a comparatively recent phenomenon. Before the nineteenth century, the history of technology is mostly unrelated to the development of science (Wolpert 1992). The invention and improvement of agricultural implements and techniques, weaponry, forms of transportation, and even basic household tools until the last few centuries have turned mostly on the practical ingenuity and creativity of workers and craftsmen who regularly faced the relevant problems. Antonio Stradivari made great violins long before anyone could explain the connections between their construction and their exquisite sound. If literacy is a necessary condition for doing and possessing science, then all of the tools that appeared before literacy are obvious illustrations of the potential independence of technological pursuits.

Unlike technology (and religion, for that matter), science originated *within* human history. Our prehistoric ancestors designed and developed a variety of tools, but they did so without the aid of science. In addition, technology, unlike science, is not the exclusive achievement of humans. We now know that other species have produced tools—other species within the genus *Homo*, chimpanzees and, perhaps, some of the Australopithecines (Mithen 1996, 95–98).

Even in the age of modern science, we still possess a rough and ready but sound intuition that inventors of new technologies like Bell or Edison neither had quite the same interests nor pursued quite the same activities as research scientists such as Maxwell or Morgan. The crucial point is that the practical orientation of technology and the abstract theoretical interest in understanding nature that characterizes science are not the same aims, even if they are regularly interconnected now.

Rejecting the relatively firm distinction between science and technology for which I am arguing leaves the problem of explaining important, discontinuous episodes in the history of human thought. According to many historians and philosophers of science, science has existed at least twice in human history—once among the ancient Greeks and a second time beginning in early modern Europe.[3] In both instances, science instituted ongoing exchanges concerning competing theories about the world that turned, at least in part, on the systematic pursuit, accumulation, and assessment of empirical evidence.

Among the huge range of activities scientists undertake, two deserve particular attention when considering the unnaturalness of science:

1. Scientists develop explanatory theories that challenge received views about empirical matters; and
2. Their critical assessment of those theories highly values evidence born of empirical tests.

Most of the puzzle solving of normal science follows on these activities, especially the second. The important point, for now, is that neither the *contents* of scientific theories that dispute received views nor the *forms* of thought required for such critical assessment come to human beings very readily.

The contents of most new, popularly unassimilated scientific theories agree with common sense no more (and often a good deal less) than do the most fantastic religious beliefs. Science and religion concur that the empirical world is not always the way it appears, and both supply proposals about the realities behind the appearances. Moreover, we sometimes have no better accounts of the underlying forces and factors science champions than we do for the entities religious systems proffer. The accomplishments of Newton and Darwin are examples. Both men advanced theories that depended on presumptions (about gravity and inheritance respectively) for which they had no satisfactory accounts nor, in Newton's case, even any hypotheses.

Science challenges our intuitions and common sense repeatedly. With the triumph of new theories, scientists and sometimes even the public must readjust their thinking (Thagard 1993). When first advanced, the suggestions that the earth moves, that microscopic organisms can kill human beings, and that solid objects are mostly empty space were no less contrary to intuition and common sense than the most counterintuitive consequences of quantum mechanics have proved for us in the twentieth century. Although science and religion both change, a central aim of science is to arrive at more penetrating explanatory theories that correct and—sometimes quickly, sometimes slowly—supplant currently prevailing views (McCauley 1986).

Admittedly, in well-developed sciences (e.g., chemistry) the vast majority of practitioners today are not out to uproot fundamental theory. Even in the highly specialized research of most contemporary science, however, this central aim has not changed. It is just that the more penetrating explanations and the improved theories typically concern much narrower domains. The recent upheaval in the theory of ulcers is a fitting illustration (Thagard 1998, 1999).

When compared to the history of religion, the cumulative effect of scientific change seems unnatural on another count. In contrast to religious accounts of nature, the history of science has been marked by increasing restriction of the range of phenomena for which agent causality constitutes an appropriate explanation (Churchland 1989). In one domain after another, science has replaced purportedly exhaustive explanations of natural processes and events in terms of agents' decisions and actions with narrower, more detailed, partial accounts of phenomena in terms of (mostly probabilistic) mechanisms. Nineteenth- and twentieth-century science has purged such agent-oriented explanations from biology, and it is the conviction of most cognitive scientists that the next few centuries will go some way toward doing the same for psychology. (Anticipating a bit—those accomplishments have hardly even dented humans' unreflective, "*natural*" inclinations to adopt the intentional stance indiscriminately in unguarded moments. This includes scientists' tendencies to lapse into intentional and teleological talk when discussing the operations of complex systems. (Dennett 1987))

More generally, scientific descriptions differ considerably from common descriptions of everyday phenomena. Contrast ordinary talk of the weather with the technical vocabulary of meteorology or our customary talk of moods with the biochemical accounts of the underlying neurophysiological mechanisms. Science pursues explanations of increasing theoretical depth. A theory's increasing depth involves not just the distance of its specialized concepts from common concepts but also a larger set of events that fall within its explanatory purview—

yielding a wider range of empirically testable consequences. It searches for accounts of reality that are more comprehensive and discerning and for which the production of evidence requires progressively more rarefied circumstances. The efforts and costs associated with apparatus for producing these exotic environments (e.g., a supercollider) or with getting to them (e.g., launching the Hubble telescope into orbit) are sometimes monumental.

Explanatory theories in science possess increasingly greater theoretical depth because, unlike religion, science is finally concerned with understanding nature for its own sake and not merely for its effects on us. Lewis Wolpert argues that the historical scarcity of inquiries committed to the intrinsic value of understanding nature is evidence not only of the comparative unnaturalness of such inquiries but of the limits of humans' natural curiosity. "The idea that man is innately curious is partial myth: man's curiosity extends only to what affects his conduct" (Wolpert 1992, 54). In their pursuits scientists are not impervious to our practical concerns with nature, but such concerns are not necessary for doing science. Many scientists devote their entire careers to highly esoteric, impractical studies of nature's narrowest corners. Their interests in appraising comparatively detailed, low-level proposals ensure that those theories remain empirically responsible (see Barbour 1980, 242).

In addition to the persistent unnaturalness of scientific proposals, institutionalized science also involves forms of thought and types of practice that human beings find extremely difficult to master. The acquisition of scientific knowledge is a painstaking and laborious process. To become a professional scientist requires at least a decade of focused education and training, and even then, the scientist typically gains command of only one subfield within a single scientific discipline. Not only is scientific knowledge not something that human beings acquire naturally; its mastery does not even guarantee that someone will know how to *do* science. After four centuries of astonishing accomplishment, science remains an overwhelmingly *unfamiliar* activity, even to most of the learned public and even in those cultures where its influence is substantial.

The more felicitous comparison here is not with religion on the hoof but with theology. The pursuit of theology involves many of the same forms of thought (e.g., deductive and abductive inference) in which science engages. Unlike science, though, such sophisticated forms of thought are not necessary for either the occurrence or persistence of religion. Religion can and does thrive *without* theology (Wiebe 1991). In his classic discussion of their religion, Fredrik Barth (1975) insists that the Baktaman of New Guinea are completely unconcerned with theology and that they do not even carry out unsystematic theological reflection.

In science higher-level cultural forces, in contrast to lower-level psychological ones, play a far more significant role in shaping the relevant (explanatory) materials (e.g., the contents of theories as opposed to the contents of myths). The importance of the activities and experiences of a highly trained elite compared with those of an untutored public differs vastly for ensuring the persistence of the two systems in question.

Unlike science, neither the emergence nor the persistence of religion depends on elaborate cultural institutions or the expertise of an esoterically trained elite (either ecclesiastical or theological). Theology as systematic study by either individuals or institutions, although often influential where it does arise, is not at all necessary for the emergence or persistence of religious systems, which occur naturally as reliable by-products of garden-variety features of human cognition and association.

By contrast, science, throughout its history, would not have existed without progressively more sophisticated explanatory theorizing and evidential reasoning and the resulting activities that constitute cutting-edge endeavors. The emergence and persistence of science as a cultural form depend on the coordination—through avenues of professional communication and association—of gifted individuals' invention of new cognitive tools as well as their ongoing refinement of familiar ones, shaping the resulting practices and products along very specific trajectories. These are not activities that come naturally or easily to human beings. Whatever currency scientific knowledge gains within a culture, that knowledge is always the result of determined effort and prolonged reflection of the most esoteric sorts by an intellectual elite.

Scientists, themselves, have produced evidence about the difficulties of doing science. Experimental psychologists (Tweney, Doherty, and Mynatt 1981) have revealed that college-level science students often fail to exhibit the forms of judgment and inference suitable for rational assessment of scientific theories. Even experienced researchers are sometimes prone to erroneous forms of reasoning (Kahneman, Slovic, and Tversky 1982), although they are less likely to make some types of errors when they are operating in areas where they possess expertise.

These sorts of findings have at least two implications. First, over-
coming the cognitive biases and errors to which human beings seem all
too naturally prone requires extensive study and experience, yet even these
provide no guarantee against such shortcomings. Second, it is the comparatively narrow *community* of research scientists that is primarily responsible for maintaining science's critical traditions. Scientific standards, just
like scientific knowledge, depend mostly on the evolution of the expert
scientific community's collective judgment in the long run. Individual
scientists are far too susceptible to such problems as errors in reasoning,
flawed heuristics, and confirmation bias.

The difficulties associated with reasoning properly, judging reliably,
and comprehending esoteric scientific concepts go some way toward
explaining why science progresses so slowly most of the time. These difficulties are also excellent indications of just how *un*natural doing science
is from a cognitive standpoint.

3.3   Religion: Doing What Comes Naturally

In making a case for the relative unnaturalness of science, I looked briefly
at both the practices and modes of thought characteristic of science as
well as the contents of the resulting scientific products. A survey of the
same considerations for religion will disclose just how natural religion is
in these respects. Various large-scale indications suggest that aspects of
religious cognition rely far less on cultural foundations than is typically
presumed. Religion's beginnings are less singular, its changes are (far) less
fundamental, and its scope is more broad than is the case with science. I
will discuss each in turn.

First, the birth of religion is less exceptional. Religion dates from our
prehistoric past. Both the archeological and the anthropological evidence
shows that human religious activities do not depend on keeping chroni-
cles or on inventing writing or even on establishing fixed settlements. If
burial of the dead constitutes sufficient evidence of religious activity, then
Neanderthal burial practices confirm that religion was not even always
confined to a single species (see, however, Mithen 1996).

Second, many religious ideas and forms have recurred throughout
history across a wide array of physical and cultural settings. All religious
systems (including Buddhism as it is popularly practiced) look to agents
and their actions as the critical variables for making sense of both the

social and natural worlds. This is true regardless of whatever more elaborate representations (e.g., the Holy Trinity) a religious elite may impose. Religion—as it is commonly practiced—reliably operates within a framework of commitments to culturally postulated superhuman (CPS) agents, their causal powers as agents, and the ability of our standard theory of mind to make sense of their actions and states of mind.

Although a few scientific ideas (atomism, heliocentricism, continental drift) required extended consideration in more than one era before they eventually prospered, at least so far in the history of science, this seems the exception and not the rule. Science is *uniquely innovative.* Its pursuit has regularly generated new theories and conceptual tools (the calculus, gravity, natural selection, field theory, inferential statistics, quantum theory, antimatter, chaos theory, implicit memory, distributed representation) that have sometimes required reinterpretations of science's most fundamental metaphysical assumptions. In addition, science has not undergone the conservative revolutions that some religious groups have where the explicit aim is not only to overthrow the prevailing states of affairs but to resuscitate earlier forms of religiosity or religious practice *in all of their details* (even when those goals are transparently implausible).

And third, although not every human being is religious, unlike science, religion occurs in *every* human culture. Even when a particular religion becomes extinct, religion itself does not disappear but inevitably reemerges. New religions regularly spring up in human populations (Earhart 1980). If a new religion does not surface quickly enough within a given society, then an existing religious system inevitably invades from without. As Dan Sperber (1996) argues, religious ideas are contagious. Religions propound ideas to which humans seem particularly susceptible.

Thus neither the birth nor the persistence of religion critically depends on any special cultural conditions. (If the experience of the twentieth century is representative, religions persist, as often as not, even in the face of direct suppression.) At least in comparison to interest in scientific ideas, the appeal of religious ideas is in no small part a function of our cognitive predilections.

Analyses of religious phenomena of the sort that I (and others) have advocated elsewhere also point to this conclusion. In contrast to science, religion relies far more fundamentally on our standard cognitive equipment. Much about the contents of religious claims and the modes of religious thought are "natural" in both of the senses I discussed. Compared to science, religion regularly involves assumptions that are more common, materials that are more familiar, and judgments that are more intuitive.

Humans come by the modes of thought religion utilizes far more readily than they come by many of those that science employs. With the exception of a few extraordinary individuals (Faraday comes to mind), becoming a scientific participant virtually always requires extensive formal education. Although considerable education is sometimes a prerequisite for religious activity, this is true only about *some* forms of participation in *some* religious systems.

Science has never arisen in nonliterate cultures. As I argued in section 3.2, its practice and appreciation demand developed intellectual skills, of which the most fundamental are literacy and mathematical fluency. Possessing such forms of intellectual expertise—together with systems of external scientific symbols (Bechtel 1996)—is a key to discerning, retaining, and engaging scientific materials. Standard scientific works—like theological and ecclesiastical works but quite unlike most other religious works—are usually carefully reasoned, tightly constrained by detailed conventions, and couched in relatively dry, antiseptic prose.

The vehicles for imparting religious knowledge and the cognitive capacities on which they depend are far more basic. Typically, religion (in contrast to both science and theology) relies primarily on theater and narrative. (This is not to imply either that rituals are simply plays or that myths are simply stories, but only that the cognitive processes involved in each are essentially the same.) Myth and ritual are essential ingredients in every religion. A fundamental point about myths and rituals is that they are supposed to have been handed down from one generation to the next *without change*. (The invention of writing and reading has mostly encouraged that assumption.)

Religion's explanatory "theories" are usually embedded in or inferred from myths, which take the form of stories. These special religious stories account for arrangements in the natural and social worlds by appealing to the actions, intentions, and mental states of CPS agents, who possess extraordinary properties and who operate both within and beyond the world of everyday experience.

Rituals are actions. CPS agents have allegedly either modeled or prescribed rituals, which participants in the religious system are supposed to repeat. That is also the usual rationale for why participants always do rituals the same way, at least ideally. It is the gods, after all, who have stipulated their forms. Although properly performed rituals either change (or maintain) states of affairs in specifiable ways, only the CPS agents know for sure whether any performance has met all of the requisite criteria. Carrying out these ritual actions provides humans with a means for establishing some order in, and imposing some control over, their natural and social worlds.

Preservation is paramount with such materials; in the absence of literacy particularly, this is no mean feat. Not all religious texts are myths but nearly all of the most memorable ones are. (Even scientists remember stories more readily than they remember theoretical or analytical treatises.) Research in cognitive psychology (Rubin 1995) has demonstrated how narratives like those in myths manipulate a host of variables that appeal to the natural propensities of human memory, including imagery, rhyme, metaphor, and other "literary" devices, as well as basic narrative structures. Narratives are about agents feeling, thinking, and doing things in ways that are causally connected with one another. Events occur in a particular sequence. Actions take place in specific places at specific times, and they have specific consequences that occasion other actions and states of mind in the agents involved. It is difficult for people to remember most human affairs in any other way. In rituals, where the scripted actions do not always hang together in such a familiar way, religions throughout the world enlist other mnemonic aids. Repeated rituals, such as sacrifices, rely primarily on sheer frequency effects to enhance their memorability. Non-repeated rituals, which a normal participant does only once, such as rites of passage, often exploit many of the same variables that underlie "flashbulb memories." (McCauley 1999; Winograd and Neisser 1992).

Each of these considerations imposes constraints on the contents and forms of both rituals and myths; taken together, these constraints can substantially limit the range of viable variation. This is particularly important in nonliterate societies, where religion had its beginnings and where its transmission does not rely on the possession of texts. In these settings especially, religious truths are primarily to be retained and transmitted, rather than reflected on and challenged. The crucial point is that neither comprehension nor retention of religious materials requires development or possession of any of the sort of specialized intellectual skills on which both the acquisition and the progress of science depend.

Religion rests on far more basic cognitive abilities, the most important of which is the ability to distinguish agents and their actions from other things and events in the world. Agents are entities in our environments who merit very different treatment from everything else. Their detection is critical to humans' physical and social survival, and research in developmental psychology (see, for example, Golinkoff 1983, 1986) affirms that children possess this ability in their first year of life.

Events that involve agent causality require representations crucially different from those for events that do not. The cognitive representation of ritual actions depends on a basic action representation system that is "in place" quite early in human development. Indeed, Tom Lawson and I (Lawson and McCauley 1990) have argued that the representational principles and the resulting action structures for religious rituals differ not one whit from those for ordinary actions. Beyond introducing into action representations CPS agents from a religious conceptual scheme, nothing about the cognitive representation of religious rituals differs from the representation of any other action.

By their facility at representing agents and their actions, human beings are thus particularly well prepared to generate, comprehend, recollect, and transmit religious stories, beliefs, and rituals. Where scientific explanations provide progressively more detailed and systematic analyses of complex processes and mechanisms, religion summons CPS agents and their actions for explanatory purposes. At least four types of evidence suggest that the latter approach comes more naturally to the human mind.

First, human beings—children in particular—seem to be inveterate anthropomorphizers. Our cognitive mechanisms for detecting the eyes, faces, and forms of macroscopic organisms that have them, and of human beings in particular, as well as the related mechanisms for attributing agency, mentality, and personality to things in the world, are *profoundly liberal* in their operations, generating false positives at every turn (Guthrie 1993). We not only see faces in the clouds; we routinely talk about our cars' and computers' recalcitrant moods. Advertisers have anthropomorphized everything from cleaning products to vegetables to airplanes. Indeed, superimposing human characteristics on products is probably second only to sex in the advertiser's bag of tricks for grabbing human attention. Attributing agency and psychological properties to various parts of the physical universe—sometimes on the basis of the skimpiest evidence—seems nearly a cognitive compulsion in human beings (see Mithen 1996, 55, 164–167).

In an intriguing set of experiments, Justin Barrett and Frank Keil (1996) have shown that subjects reliably treat deities anthropomorphically in their on-line cognitive processing, regardless of their nonanthropomorphic, "theologically correct" pronouncements about God during more reflective moments. They do so whether they are Catholics, Protestants, Jews, or atheists in the United States or, as subsequent research shows, Hindus, Sikhs, or Jains in India. These findings indicate that a good deal of people's knowledge about how the gods operate does not turn on any specifically cultural content, or at least not on any uniquely religious knowledge.

Second, humans seem to find explanations in terms of agents and their actions more naturally appealing. Social psychologists have discovered telling biases in human judgment on these counts (for discussions, see Gilbert and Malone 1995; Anderson, Krull, and Weiner 1996). Human beings are overwhelmingly predisposed to give accounts of their own and others' behaviors in terms of socially shared theories about agents and their states of mind. Even when experimenters openly manipulate the independent variables that account for the variance in subjects' responses, those subjects typically remain not only unaware of these variables' influence but convinced of the critical role of agents' actions and mental states in determining the outcomes.

Third, religious ontologies and narratives go hand in hand. I have already mentioned mnemonic advantages narratives enjoy, compared to other forms of knowledge organization. The prominence religious systems accord CPS agents and their actions is of a piece with the central role that narratives play in religious thought and practice. Narratives, after all, go nowhere without agents. Agents' actions and states of mind are the underlying engines that drive narratives. Proliferating agents inevitably requires proliferating narratives because every agent has a story. Introducing individual agents raises kinds of questions that only stories can answer. In explaining sequences of individual events, explanations even in the natural sciences may sometimes seem to resemble narratives. But such appearances are misleading. Explaining a mass extinction on the basis of an upheaval in the weather caused by a huge meteor's impact with the earth makes reference neither to actions nor to an agent's states of mind.

Descriptions of chains of efficient or material causes do not constitute a narrative.

Finally, as Boyer (1994) has emphasized, by appropriating such fundamental notions as "agent" (and the conception of causality that accompanies it) for the purposes of characterizing the invisible forces of the universe, religious systems provide participants with a huge amount of information "for free". This last point deserves some elaboration.

Boyer (1999, 2000) argues that religious categories are parasitic on a host of "natural" ontological categories, which even young children readily deploy (see also Keil 1979, 1989). Concomitant with each category are nondemonstrative inferences that provide an army of default assumptions concerning that category's instances. Knowing, for example that a toaster is an *artifact* immediately entitles us to assume that it has a determinate size, shape, and weight, that human beings have had some influence on its current state, but also that it does not respire, contemplate, or copulate. Similarly, knowing that gods are *agents* licenses inferences about their values, preferences, mental states, and actions.

What distinguishes religious from natural ontologies, according to Boyer, is the violation or transfer of some of the intuitive properties associated with entailed superordinate categories. For example, if something is an agent, then (normally) it is also a physical object and possesses all of the associated physical properties. CPS agents may differ from normal agents in that they *violate* the constraints this superordinate category, "physical object," imposes. Thus, they may pass through solid objects or be everywhere at once. CPS agents may violate constraints that other superordinate categories, such as being an organism, impose. So, CPS agents may be eternal, parentless, or capable of recovering from death. On the other hand, the *transfer* of psychological properties appropriate to agents can render artifacts, such as statues or ebony trees, capable of hearing, comprehending, and remembering humans' pleas.

Compared with scientific categories, those in religion lack theoretical depth. Contrary to first impressions, religious accounts of things differ little from everyday accounts. Religious systems import all of our familiar, commonsense psychology about agents' intentions, beliefs, desires, and actions for the explanation of phenomena throughout the natural and social worlds. Whether applied to other drivers on the road or to the rulers of the cosmos, this system performs quite nicely most of the time for understanding and anticipating agents' actions and states of mind. The rationale underlying an explanation of someone's illness as the result of an ancestor's interventions based on that ancestor's displeasure with the victim's conduct is as readily comprehensible to a child as it is to the most experienced religious official.

In the absence of cultural forms that foster the collective growth of humans' critical and imaginative capacities, human beings rely on their natural cognitive dispositions, which often appear to be domain specific and comparatively inflexible in their application. CPS agents, stories about them, and rituals for controlling and appeasing them are the inevitable outcomes of a cognitive system that simultaneously seeks explanations, possesses an overactive agent detector, and, perhaps most important *lacks scientific traditions*. As Daniel Dennett (1998, 122) has remarked, "Until science came along, one had to settle for personifying the unpredictable— adopting the intentional stance toward it—and trying various desperate measures of control and appeasement."

To review: religion occurs in every culture and predates history. On most fronts, religious materials embody assumptions and take forms that are either commonplace, intuitive, or a normal part of cognitive development. The modes of thought and the patterns of explanation that religious systems exploit are usually familiar and uncomplicated. Moreover, religious systems depend fundamentally on an array of cognitive resources that arise early in human development. All of these considerations suggest that religion is cognitively more familiar than science and that religion taps cognitive traits that are more widespread and readily available than those science requires. So, too, does the fact that participants acquire religion more easily than science.

Acquiring the knowledge necessary to participate in a religious system is much more like acquiring a natural language than it is like mastering the knowledge and skills necessary to do serious science. Acquiring religious knowledge often requires little, if any, explicit instruction. Humans are *born into* religious and linguistic communities. Like natural language, religion exploits cognitive dispositions, which seem to arise early in human development.[4] Because so many pivotal religious conceptions have so little theoretical depth, possessing everyday concepts prepares people for the acquisition of religion in a way that it does not prepare them for the acquisition of science.

Since some otherwise normal human beings are not religious, though, the suggestion that the acquisition of religion depends on some domain-specific cognitive mechanism devoted just to it is not at all plausible (despite the underlying uniformities of religious cognition I have emphasized). Still, the evidence I have been surveying is consonant with the proposal that cognitive mechanisms that arose to address very different problems—such as distinguishing basic ontological categories and differentiating actions from other sorts of events—are fundamentally engaged in the generation and acquisition of religion. (I am unconcerned here about how responsible innate factors are for the development and eventual shape of these mechanisms.)

If the acquisition of basic religious competence turns so critically on the possession and operation of such naturally occurring cognitive inclinations, then participation in a religious system should be largely independent of differences in intelligence, and so it seems to be. Indeed, the acquisition of and participation in a religious system seem to turn no more (and, perhaps, even less) on so-called general intelligence than do the acquisition and use of natural language.

Advocates of cognitive modularity, who hold that specific, dedicated neural mechanisms underlie such capacities, argue that one sort of evidence for the existence of mental modules is precisely the fact that these singular mechanisms occasionally get disconnected in a small fraction of the population. Some persons, who might have most other cognitive capacities essentially intact, may, for example, prove severely impaired (either congenitally or as the result of injury) with respect to such things as the recognition of faces, the production of grammatical speech, or the detection of agents. Prosopagnosics are incapable of recognizing faces. Broca's aphasics are incapable of producing grammatical speech. Simon Baron-Cohen (1995; Tomasello, Kruger, and Ratner 1993) argues that autism is precisely the inability to detect agents and to read their minds. The abilities of autistic people to recognize agents and to distinguish actions from other events seem substantially impaired, while their abilities on most other fronts often fall within the normal range.

Oliver Sacks (1995) describes an autistic woman who has learned to manage well enough to earn a Ph.D., teach at the college level, and run her own business. Still, he reports that she does not comprehend many features of even standard social exchange. Baron-Cohen (1995) argues that rather than benefiting from the virtually automatic operation of what he calls our "theory of mind module," such people manage by enlisting their general intelligence for carrying out standard inductions about their social experience. They are destined to possess no more knowledge about human conduct than what the methods of behaviorism can afford. My bet is that, as a result of their disability, religion is something that even autistic persons functioning at such a high level do not readily comprehend or acquire. In this connection, it is worth noting that Sacks (1995, 259) reports that his subject was "bewildered" by myths and drama.

Many primatologists maintain that the abilities to detect agents and read their minds are not the exclusive possessions of modern humans (see, for example, Byrne and Whiten 1988). The archeological evidence about other members of our genus suggests the same. If that is true and if my analysis of the character and origins of our religious proclivities is correct, then religion involves the expression of some of our most basic cognitive inclinations.

If religion is as natural and science is as unnatural as I have argued, science poses no significant challenge to religion. Indeed, if my analysis is correct, it is the preservation of *science* that should concern us—its current prominence notwithstanding. In the global marketplace of ideas, that is, in the transmission of culture, some views have natural disadvantages. Science, with its esoteric interests, its counterintuitive claims, and its specialized forms of thinking, certainly seems to qualify. Those historians and philosophers of science who point to two critical episodes in the history of Western thought hold that science was once lost and had to be reinvented. One consequence of my view is that nothing about human nature would ever prevent its loss again.

Notes

An abbreviated version of this chapter was presented at the University of Minnesota on June 13, 1998, as my presidential address to the Society for Philosophy and Psychology. I wish to express my gratitude to the following individuals for their helpful comments and encouragement: Justin Barrett, Larry Barsalou, William Bechtel, Marshall Gregory, Frank Keil, E. Thomas Lawson, Ulric Neisser, Ilkka Pyysiäinen, Brigitte Schön, James Snyder, Christian von Somm, Rob Wilson, and the members of the 1997 Emory Faculty Seminar.

1. Such claims are regularly asserted but rarely (if ever) argued. How they could be advanced without assuming that religion deals with matters *beyond* the natural realm is difficult to see. But it is just that assumption that has led critics such as Tom Lawson and me (Lawson and McCauley 1990, 1993) to argue that religious studies itself often includes covert religious (or "theological") presumptions.

2. I have argued (McCauley 1987) that adults' conceptual structures are best understood as theoretical, and I have no hesitations about so characterizing children's—I am

far more optimistic now about the ability of connectionist and neural network models to account for our conceptual resources (see Churchland 1989; Barsalou 1999). I am also sympathetic with the view that semantic and conceptual development is usefully construed in terms of changes in theories, though I hasten to note that theoretical progress does not always involve revolutionary changes. Theory development in science and, I suspect, in scientists and children as well is often evolutionary rather than revolutionary (see McCauley 1986).

3. Compare the position of Karl Popper (1992, 136–165), who sees these two cases as discontinuous, and thus sees two separate points of origination for science, with that of Lewis Wolpert (1992, 35), who holds that they constitute a single, continuous tradition.

4. This point seems uncontroversial. The disagreements arise about how elaborated the initial dispositions are (see Elman et al. 1996, 41).

References

Anderson, C. A., Krull, D. S., and Weiner, B. (1996). Explanations: Processes and consequences. In E. T. Higgins and A. W. Kruglanski, eds., *Social psychology: Handbook of basic principles*. New York: Guilford Press.

Barbour, I. (1980). Paradigms in science and religion. In G. Gutting, ed., *Paradigms and Revolutions*. Notre Dame, IN: University of Notre Dame Press.

Baron-Cohen, S. (1995). *Mindblindness: An essay on autism and theory of mind*. Cambridge, MA: MIT Press.

Barrett, J., and Keil, F. (1996). Conceptualizing a non-natural entity: Anthropomorphism in God concepts. *Cognitive Psychology, 31*, 219–247.

Barsalou, L. (1999). Perceptual symbol systems. *Behavioral and Brain Sciences, 22*, 577–660.

Barth, F. (1975). *Ritual and knowledge among the Baktaman of New Guinea*. New Haven: Yale University Press.

Bechtel, W. (1996). What should a connectionist philosophy of science look like? In R. McCauley, ed., *The Churchlands and their critics*. Oxford: Blackwell.

Boyer, P. (1994). *The naturalness of religious ideas*. Berkeley: University of California Press.

Boyer, P. (1999). Cultural inheritance tracks and cognitive predispositions: The example of religious concepts. In H. Whitehouse, ed., *Mind, evolution, and cultural transmission*. Cambridge: Cambridge University Press.

Boyer, P. (2000). Evolution of a modern mind and origins of culture: Religious concepts as a limiting-case, In P. Carruthers and A. Chamberlain, eds., *Evolution and the human mind: Modularity, language and meta-cognition*. Cambridge: Cambridge University Press.

Brewer, W. F., and Samarapungavan, A. (1991). Childrens' theories vs. scientific theories: Differences in reasoning or differences in knowledge? In R. R. Hoffman and D. S. Palermo, eds., *Cognition and the symbolic processes: Applied and ecological perspectives*. Hillsdale, NJ: Erlbaum.

Byrne, R., and Whiten, A. (1988). *Machiavellian intelligence: Social expertise and the evolution of intellect in monkeys, apes, and humans.* Oxford: Oxford University Press.

Cannon, D. (1996). *Six ways of being religious: A framework for comparative religion.* Belmont, CA: Wadsworth.

Carey, S. (1985). *Conceptual change in childhood.* Cambridge, MA: MIT Press.

Churchland, P. M. (1989). *A neurocomputational perspective.* Cambridge, MA: MIT Press.

Dennett, D. C. (1987). *The intentional stance.* Cambridge, MA: MIT Press.

Dennett, D. C. (1998). The evolution of religious memes: Who—or what—benefits? *Method and Theory in the Study of Religion, 10,* 115–128.

Earhart, H. (1980). Toward a theory of the formation of Japanese new religions: A case study of Gedatsu-Kai. *History of Religions, 20,* 175–197.

Elman, J. L., Bates, E. A., Johnson, M. H., Karmiloff-Smith, A., Parisi, D., and Plunkett, K. (1996). *Rethinking innateness: A connectionist perspective on development.* Cambridge, MA: MIT Press.

Farley, E. (1988). *The fragility of knowledge.* Philadelphia: Fortress Press.

Gilbert, D. T., and Malone, P. S. (1995). The correspondence bias, *Psychological Bulletin, 117,* 21–38.

Golinkoff, R. M. (1983). The preverbal negotiation of failed messages. In R. Golinkoff, ed., *The transition from prelinguistic to linguistic communication.* Hillsdale, NJ: Erlbaum.

Golinkoff, R. M. (1986). "'I beg your pardon': The preverbal negotiation of failed messages." *Journal of Child Language, 13,* 455–476.

Gopnik, A. (1996). The scientist as child. *Philosophy of Science, 63,* 485–514.

Gopnik, A., and Meltzoff, A. (1997). *Words, thoughts, and theories.* Cambridge, MA: MIT Press.

Guthrie, S. (1993). *Faces in the clouds.* Oxford: Oxford University Press.

Horton, R. (1970). African traditional thought and Western science. In B. Wilson, ed., *Rationality.* New York: Harper and Row.

Horton, R. (1993). *Patterns of thought in Africa and the West: Essays on magic, religion, and science.* Cambridge: Cambridge University Press.

Kahneman, D., Slovic, P., and Tversky, A., eds. (1982). *Judgement under uncertainty: Heuristics and biases.* Cambridge: Cambridge University Press.

Karmiloff-Smith, A. (1992). *Beyond modularity: A developmental perspective on cognitive science.* Cambridge, MA: MIT Press.

Keil, F. (1979). *Semantic and conceptual development.* Cambridge, MA: Harvard University Press.

Keil, F. (1989). *Concepts, kinds, and conceptual development.* Cambridge, MA: MIT Press.

Kuhn, T. (1970). *The structure of scientific revolutions.* 2d ed. Chicago: University of Chicago Press.

Lawson, E. T., and McCauley, R. N. (1990). *Rethinking religion: Connecting cognition and culture.* Cambridge: Cambridge University Press.

Lawson, E. T., and McCauley, R. N. (1993). Crisis of conscience, riddle of identity: Making space for a cognitive approach to religious phenomena. *Journal of the American Academy of Religion, 61,* 201–223.

McCauley, R. N. (1986). Intertheoretic relations and the future of psychology. *Philosophy of Science, 53,* 179–199.

McCauley, R. N. (1987). The role of theories in a theory of concepts. In U. Neisser, ed., *Concepts and conceptual development.* Cambridge: Cambridge University Press.

McCauley, R. N. (1999). Bringing ritual to mind. In E. Winograd, R. Fivush, and W. Hirst, eds., *Ecological approaches to cognition: Essays in honor of Ulric Neisser.* Hillsdale, NJ: ⟵ GET Erlbaum.

Mithen, S. (1996). *The prehistory of the mind: The cognitive origins of art, religion and science.* New York: Thames and Hudson.

Paden, W. (1992). *Interpreting the sacred.* Boston: Beacon Press.

Popper, K. (1992). *Conjectures and refutations.* London: Routledge.

Rubin, D. (1995). *Memory in oral tradition: The cognitive psychology of epic, ballads, and counting-out rhymes.* New York: Oxford University Press.

Sacks, O. (1995). *An anthropologist on Mars.* New York: Knopf.

Spelke, E. S. (1994). Initial knowledge: Six suggestions, *Cognition, 50,* 432–445.

Sperber, D. (1996). *Explaining culture: A naturalistic approach.* Oxford: Blackwell.

Thagard, P. (1993). *Conceptual revolutions.* Princeton: Princeton University Press.

Thagard, P. (1998). Ulcers and bacteria: 1. Discovery and acceptance. *Studies in History and Philosophy of Science*: Part C., *Studies in History and Philosophy of Biology and Biomedical Sciences, 20,* 107–136.

Thagard, P. (1999). *How scientists explain disease.* Princeton: Princeton University Press.

Tomasello, M., Kruger, A., and Ratner, H. H. (1993). Cultural learning. *Behavioral and Brain Sciences, 16,* 495–552.

Tweney, R., Doherty, M., and Mynatt, C., eds. (1981). *On scientific thinking.* New York: Columbia University Press.

Wiebe, D. (1991). *The irony of theology and the nature of religious thought.* Montreal: McGill-Queen's University Press.

Winograd, E., and Neisser, U., eds. (1992). *Affect and accuracy in recall.* New York: Cambridge University Press.

Wolpert, L. (1992). *The unnatural nature of science.* London: Faber and Faber.

4

The Shadows and Shallows of Explanation

Robert A. Wilson and Frank C. Keil

Explanation is a river that flows through human life. Explanations are ubiquitous, pervading our activities from the most simple and mundane ("Just going to the store to buy some milk") to the most sophisticated and unusual, such as the explanations in science and mathematics. Explanations are found across all cultures and historical time periods (Sperber, Premack, and Premack 1995). For example, in the history of medicine, lay people and medical experts alike have offered rich explanations for various diseases, explanations that were often wrong in many key respects, but that clearly were explanations (Lindberg 1992; Scarborough 1969; Magner 1992). Similarly, in cross-cultural research, despite huge variations in the details concerning mechanisms underlying disease, the search for causal explanations represents a striking commonality amid this diversity (Atran 1996; Maffi 1994).

Despite its pervasiveness and centrality to human life, explanation remains one of the most underexplored topics in the cognitive sciences. In psychology in particular, explanation—how extensive and various our explanatory capacities are, what types of mechanisms underlie those abilities, and how the abilities develop—is a topic that has been mostly discussed only incidentally as researchers have investigated related phenomena such as problem solving, theory formation, text comprehension, concepts, and expertise.

The most developed discussions of explanation are to be found in the philosophy of science, from its twentieth-century inception in positivist models of science—reaching its high point in the extended studies of Hempel (1965) and Nagel (1961)—to the contemporary postpositivist explorations of Salmon (1989) and Kitcher (1989). These discussions have covered a huge array of issues, most notably, the role of laws in explanation; the relationships between causation, explanation, and prediction; and the interplay between the articulation of theories and the growth of explanatory power. As admirable as much of this work is, its focus imposes two mutually reinforcing limitations in understanding explanation from a cognitive science perspective.

First, the concentration in such discussions is on *scientific* explanation. Although the various accounts of explanation offered—from the classic covering-law model to Kitcher's explanation patterns (1989, 1993)— have sometimes made acute observations about explanation in nonscientific contexts, scientific explanation has served as a paradigm even there. And not unreasonably: the sciences have rightly been taken to be the source of our best explanations for a range of phenomena, and the most likely source of good explanations of phenomena currently beyond our ken. Problems arise, however, in extrapolating from explanation in the special institutional and cultural locus of science to explanation in its natural and more common niche: everyday life. Scientific explanation usually works in a community of scholars who rely heavily on public forums for sharing and accessing explanatory insights; and a large set of explanatory standards, both implicit and explicit in many sciences, would seem to guide the generation and growth of explanations in ways that do not occur in everyday life.

Second, due both to peculiarities of positivist approaches to the philosophy of science and to the abstract proclivities of philosophers themselves, questions about the psychological and social realities underlying explanatory phenomena have remained largely unasked (let alone answered) within these approaches. The well-known distinction between the "context of justification" and the "context of discovery," initially drawn by Reichenbach (1938) but prevalent within philosophy of science more generally until the last twenty years, has come to set a boundary between the "logic of explanation"—the province of philosophers of science—and the psychology or sociology of explanation. While recent and various "naturalistic turns" in the philosophy of science reject this dichotomy (see Kitcher 1992), the sort of boundary that it circumscribed around philosophical explorations of science remains largely intact, even if the area enclosed is somewhat more encompassing. Distinctively philosophical concerns persist: a preoccupation with the forms that best represent scientific explanations, with questions about scientific explanation in general, and with the relations between explanation and causation, theoretical knowledge, and modeling. Again, this may be fine insofar as understanding scientific explanation goes, but it constitutes a limitation on the study of explanation in general.

The first two tasks of this chapter are themselves perhaps "distinctively philosophical" in that we will try first to identify and then to locate explanation vis-à-vis a cluster of related notions. Our aim is to do so in a way that both maps this conceptual space and opens it up for more psychologically oriented exploration.

4.1 Identifying Explanation

In its most general sense, an explanation of a given phenomenon is *an apparently successful attempt to increase the understanding of that phenomenon.* As simple as this claim is, it implies a number of features:

1. Explanations are the product of something that we, individually or collectively, do; as the result of our activity in the world, explanations often have intentional and social presuppositions and consequences.
2. Explanations fail when they do not increase the understanding of the phenomenon they purport to explain. For them to be embraced as explanations, however, they must, at least transiently, *appear* to some group to increase understanding.
3. Because they aim to increase understanding, explanations always have a psychological aspect.
4. Because aiming to increase understanding can be done with respect to oneself or with respect to an intended audience, explanations may, but need not, have a communicative and pragmatic aspect.
5. Because success in increasing understanding usually reflects an insight into how the world is, explanations help to create knowledge, to develop better theories and models of how things are, and to explain why they operate as they do.
6. Because any phenomenon is inextricably bound up with many others, any given explanation always has implications for phenomena other that which it initially attempts to explain. Thus explanation increases understanding not just for its target, but inevitably for a larger sphere of often completely unanticipated affairs. (It is this spreading penumbra of insight that, we will argue below, helps account for an important asymmetry between prediction and explanation.)

On its own, this simple list of features of explanation hardly gets to the heart of the concept of explanation. Note, however, that these are the features that have been emphasized by contrasting philosophical approaches to explanation, although each approach has tended to overemphasize some of these features at the expense of ignoring or downplaying the others. This imbalance, in part, is why these approaches give us only what we have chosen to call the *shadows of explanation*. For example, classic positivists (e.g., Hempel 1965; Nagel 1961) have overstated feature 6 in their view of the symmetry between prediction and explanation, and have done so while virtually ignoring features 1 through 4. Pragmatic approaches to explanation (e.g., Bromberger 1966; van Fraasen 1977), by contrast, overstate the point made in feature 4 and to some extent that in feature 2 and thus have little to say about either social and psychological dimensions to explanation (other than those invoked in communicative acts) or the growth of knowledge that explanations can contribute to. Realist approaches to explanation concentrate on what makes feature 5 true, and, apart from feature 6, virtually ignore the rest. Finally, social constructivists, insofar as they have any view of explanation, take feature 1 to represent the central feature of explanation, and have little of interest to say about the remainder of our list.

Explanation, then, might be seen as being characterized by an extensive array of features that, only as a coherent aggregate, can start to take us beyond the shadows. Yet most accounts have avoided such a "family resemblance" approach and tended to try to isolate one single defining criterion. In addition to this excessive focus on just one of many features, there has traditionally been an assumption that all explanations are essentially of the same type, regardless of the *explanandum*. This assumption also seems wrong to us. The structure and very nature of explanations may interact heavily with what sort of thing is being explained. The kinds of causal interactions central to, say, biology may require a very different sort of interpretative knowledge than those central to, say, physics. The canonical explanations in such domains as history, mathematics, mechanics, quantum physics, folk psychology, biology, and economics may all have their own nature. Or perhaps somewhat broader explanatory types, such as statistical, teleological, and intentional explanations, intersect with different facets of these natural domains, sometimes being applied in different ways to the same phenomena to yield very different insights. Although we have questioned the assumption of a simple "explanatory essence" by pointing to various scientific domains, it is perhaps most clearly false when we move to consider both commonsense and scientific explanations together. Your explanation of why you will be late home for dinner and a mathematician's proof of a theorem share very little.

We think that a full characterization of explanation requires an integrated and coherent account incorporating all six of the features listed above. Yet we have said nothing so far about four aspects of explanation that would seem to many to be at the very heart of what explanation is:

1. the role of laws and observation in explanation
2. the relation between causation and explanation
3. the place of measurement and mathematization in explanation
4. the structure of explanation.

These are, of course, issues central to philosophical discussions of scientific explanation, but in trying to cast a wider net, it is appropriate that our starting point be neutral with respect to specific commitments about any of these. For example, laws and quantification certainly do feature in many scientific explanations, but at least prima facie play little role in commonsense explanations outside of science. Working with a conception of explanation that makes a claim about one of these issues would be to assume that scientific explanations are a sort of paradigm of explanation, and we have already suggested that such a view is mistaken, at least in its general form. Understanding the nature of (1)–(4) for any kind of explanation will be important, but the specifics may vary greatly. Even if there are important structural properties to, say, explanation in both scientific physics and folk psychology, these may have little in common with one another.

4.2 Locating Explanation

Although psychologists and other researchers in the cognitive and behavioral sciences have had relatively little to say about explanation, they have had much to say about related concepts. Psychological studies of hypothesis formation and testing, of prediction and discovery, and of reasoning have their own well-worked paradigms. For example, the 2-4-6 paradigm for investigating how people generate and test hypotheses (Wason 1968), and both the Wason card task and the Kahneman-Tversky paradigms (Wason and Johnson-Laird 1972; Kahneman and Tversky 1973) for exploring human inference represent extensively utilized experimental paradigms in psychology that investigate notions related to that of explanation. More recently, Brewer, Chinn, and Samarpungavan (chap. 11, this volume) have explored psychological dimensions to the theory-observation distinction, and the burgeoning literature on the child's theory of mind has created a forum in which the idea of nativist and developmentally unfolding "theories" has been debated (Wellman 1990; Wellman and Gelman 1997). For example, it now appears that preschoolers have considerable difficulties identifying how they came across knowledge and understanding unless it led directly to a novel behavior (Esbensen, Taylor, and Stoess 1997; Taylor, Esbenson, and Bennett 1994). In one especially compelling case four-year-old children were taught essentially the same information either as new facts or as new behaviors, such as the meaning of Japanese counting words (facts) versus how to count in Japanese (behavior). They learned both very well, but had sharply contrasting intuitions about the origins of such knowledge. They claimed they had prior knowledge of the information when it was presented as facts (often saying they had always known it) but were much more likely to see the behavioral version of the information as something they had just learned.

Interestingly but not surprisingly, when psychologists have touched on the broader issues into which these investigations feed, they have often appealed to the literature in the philosophy of science. For example, the idea of the "child as scientist" is familiar from Carey 1985 (and that of the "scientist as child," from Gopnik 1996). Here, developmental psychologists and philosophers have productively exchanged ideas on conceptual change, theoretical knowledge, and the nature of concepts. It is far less clear, however, exactly where explanation fits into this discourse and how it is to be approached in an interdisciplinary manner.   *Explanation*

We consider three central notions: prediction, understanding, and theories. Each has a clear psychological component, although we will suggest that theories are best thought of as psychological only in a derivative sense. We shall consider the idea that these notions form a progression of increasing sophistication and depth, with explanation falling between understanding and theories. Moreover, we can think of these as natural human competencies; that is, we all predict, understand, explain, and theorize as part of our everyday activities, and could not have anything approaching human experience without such competencies. Recognition of them as competencies helps highlight their action component, a theme that will be important in understanding what everyday explanations are all about. To consider the progression, we need to characterize more fully the sense in which prediction and understanding are weaker, and theory stronger, than explanation. We start with prediction.

Prediction

We are all familiar with cases where we can predict that something will happen, even though we are unable to explain why it will. For example, many of us can and reliably do predict that our cars will start when we turn the ignition switch, but few of us are able to explain in any real detail just why this is so. It is not, of course, that we would be without words were we asked "Why?"; rather, it is that the sort of explanation that typically ensues will be likely to do little more than indicate the engine and battery as being connected up to the ignition switch in some way. (With car engines being increasingly electronic and computational, the paucity of our explanations here has become more striking in the last few years.) The same is true of most commonplace gadgets that we use every day.

Correspondingly, there are many cases where prediction is completely barren of any insight or explanatory power; this is especially so for many natural phenomena. You may know that a red sky at night portends good weather the following day without knowing anything more. You may know that one high tide is followed by the other in roughly thirteen hours without any understanding of why. Similarly, many arbitrary social conventions may have nothing more than a predictive component, such as predicting that the fork will be on the left of the plate at dinner. Even complex or unfamiliar artifacts can have a purely predictive component. You might know that your computer tends to crash when you print from a certain program but have absolutely no notion as to why. You might notice than an unfamiliar tool is always at one orientation at one time of day and a different orientation at a different time but again have no notion why.

It is also true, however, that for many of these artifacts, we do have a level of "functional" explanation that can provide some insight to those who are less familiar with the object. Thus we might explain pressing a print key on a computer to a preschooler as telling the computer to send all the words on the screen to the printer, and as telling the printer to put all those words on paper. Even though our understanding of detailed mechanisms may be minimal, we can often provide some explanatory insight at this relatively shallow functional level. Moreover, we can use such functional explanatory knowledge to make predictions, troubleshoot a faulty system, or help evaluate more detailed explanations about how it works. We see this aspect of explanation to be a reflection of our features 1 and 4.

For any phenomenon for which we have an explanation, there seem to be myriad predictions that we can and do make—many of which are confirmed. Suppose that Joe is able to explain to you, in some detail, just why your car starts when you turn the ignition switch. Then Joe will also be able to predict what will happen if various parts of the engine are damaged or removed, or if the conditions under which you try to start your car are varied (e.g., radical temperature shifts). Very likely, he will also be able to predict what will happen in a variety of perhaps apparently unrelated situations (e.g., when you fiddle with bits of your lawnmower). An explanatory ability in a particular case may let you make predictions you could not otherwise have made. After all, predictions typically come in clusters; thus an ability to predict one thing typically carries with it an ability to predict many other things. But whereas explanatory ability seems to provide predictive ability, predictive ability does not provide explanatory ability. It is in this sense that explanation is stronger than prediction— for humans at least, a *psychological* point, though we suspect that it will be true for any predictive-explanatory device.

This intuitive point about the relative ease with which prediction can be generated seems confirmed by the existence of automated predictive devices capable of predicting a range of things, from locations of aircraft to the likelihood a treatment will halt the progression of an otherwise fatal disease. Even powerful and impressive predictions can be generated from correlation and simple inductive strategies of extrapolation. Whether any of these devices can be said to explain the corresponding phenomena seems to us doubtful. The case becomes somewhat more intricate when patterns of covariation are considered (Cheng 1997; Glymour, chap. 7, this volume; Thagard, chap. 10, this volume), but here, too, we doubt that we have explanation.

Although explanatory ability guarantees predictive ability in the sense specified above, it does not always allow us to predict corresponding specific outcomes. Prediction of a specific future state of affairs from a present one may be practically impossible, while a full explanation after the fact might be quite easy. Informally, we are often in situations where we might say that we could never have anticipated that something would happen but that, after the fact, we see exactly how and why it came about. More formally, this effect is related to the difference between physical systems that can be modeled by simple sets of equations and systems that, while fully determinate, cannot be so modeled. In this sense, explanation is easier to come by than prediction, and it provides us with further reason to create some cognitive distance between prediction and explanation. What we have in mind here can perhaps best be conveyed through examples.

In folk psychology, we can often explain why people did what they did after the fact, even though we could not predict ahead of time how they would act. This is not simply because we are not in a position to observe those people sufficiently, but because just how people will behave is influenced by a myriad of interacting variables, the values of which may depend on minute details of the situation. This is surely why so many of our conversations about the minds of others are attempts to make sense of a behavior after the fact rather than to predict it. Such "retrodictive" explanations are not just the province of psychology; they are seen throughout life. The crew of a commercial fishing boat may be completely unable to predict prices for the swordfish they caught when they return to port. Yet they may easily explain how and why the prices dropped when another large boat halfway around the world just checked in to a port before them with a huge cargo of swordfish. Or you may not have any ability to predict the gender of your child, but might well be able, after the fact, to explain how that particular gender occurred. In all of these cases, although anyone in a position to offer an explanation will also be able to make some corresponding prediction (minimally, about what would happen in certain counterfactual situations), explanatory ability here serves a function independent of the generation of predictions.

There has been much attention in recent years to the properties of fully deterministic nonlinear dynamic systems, where extremely minor differences in initial conditions can lead to dramatically different outcomes (e.g., Waldrop 1992). Because we cannot often know such initial conditions to the necessary levels of precision, we are pragmatically unable to make predictions for any future events critically dependent on those initial conditions. Part of our difficulty in being able to predict turns on the time frame of the prediction. We may be able to predict the weather in three hours at levels far above chance but may have not predictive power for three weeks in advance even if, at that time, we can explain how the weather got that way. But often the time frame of most interest is just the one we cannot predict in advance but can explain after the fact. We may be intensely concerned about how a volatile relative, Uncle Jack, will react at an upcoming wedding, but be unsure as to whether Uncle Jack will be extremely enthusiastic about the wedding or profoundly offended. Which behavior emerges may depend on the precise wording of an offhand remark made by another family member, a remark that might be taken as an insult or a compliment, regardless of the speaker's intentions. Uncle Jack's defensiveness may have a hair-trigger sensitivity that makes it impossible to know in advance which way a remark will be taken; yet the ensuing behavior of either type may make perfect sense to those who understand the underlying dynamics of Uncle Jack's personality. In addition, both the explanation and the dynamics may be considered absolutely essential to any real understanding of Uncle Jack's behavior. Thus explanation after the fact may be most powerful just where prediction is weakest and least effective.

Discussions of explanation seem often to underestimate the extent to which most real-world events are nonlinear dynamic systems whose behavior is explained at such a global level that explanation here is accompanied by almost no specific predictions. Yet, if such explanation-without-prediction cases are so common, why do we even engage in explanations in such cases? One possibility is that explanations help sharpen our ability to perceive and respond to events in the future. Consider, for example, what happens if someone provides us with glasses that greatly improve our vision. It would be odd to say that the glasses help us predict events better; but they might certainly help us pick up information more accurately and powerfully. The lenses greatly improve the quality of information gathered in real time, thereby allowing richer and more powerful interpretations of experience and the ability to interact with aspects of the world more effectively. Like lenses, explanations may often serve to sharpen our perceptions of events, to be able to see more clearly what is going on in real time without necessarily being able to make better predictions for longer than a moment or two more in the future. Explanations serve to buttress our overall conceptual frameworks for interpreting and making sense of the world around us.

Consider, as a final example, the case of an avid sports fan who takes a friend unfamiliar with the sport to a hockey game. The fan will certainly make some predictions the friend will not, but much of the time the fan's predictions will be no more accurate than the friend's, even though the fan is vastly better at understanding what has happened and what it meant. So also for the players in the event, who might best know what a particular situation "means" and how best to respond to it, without knowing what the situation will be in a few minutes.

It is not that increasing explanatory insight carries with it no predictive gains; but such gains may often be over a very short term, while the largest explanatory insights may be over a much longer term. The value of that insight over the longer term lies less in prediction and more in the ability to "see" and remember the dynamics of future events more accurately. Explanations thus can provide better lenses on the causal structure of the world.

In short, explanation seems much conceptually richer than prediction and typically entails certain kinds of predictions. But explanation may be functionally important even when it does little to predict the phenomena it explains the best.

Understanding

Subject to the caveat above, understanding entails prediction but also includes accompanying knowledge through inference and memory, and some sense of how and why things happen, even if this remains largely implicit and inarticulate. It is also less articulate and communicative than explanation because one can understand something without being able to explain it to another. The reverse, however, seems impossible.

We want to suggest that understanding, which may otherwise be largely implicit, must be made explicit for either the communication to others or the reflection by oneself that typifies explanation. The existence of an explanatory sense or hunch that is more than understanding but not so explicit as to be propositional supports this suggestion. Thus you might be able to choose appropriately between competing explanations for reasons that are not obvious even to yourself, simply because one explanation just seems to "fit" better.

Our conception, then, is of understanding as a cognitive state that remains largely implicit but that goes beyond merely being able to correlate variables. We think that one chief source for understanding, so conceived, is that as agents in the world, cognizers are often in a position to have some sense of how and why things happen through knowledge of their own actions. Notoriously, we often have know-how, or procedural knowledge, largely implicit and nonreflective understanding that goes beyond simply being able to predict the co-occurrence of two or more variables (Zola-Morgan and Squire 1993). Any of the basic activities of daily life carries with it a sense of the place of that activity within the surrounding causal nexus that is not merely predictive. For example, in walking through a neighborhood park you perceive many things and events familiar to you—dogs being walked, children on swings, trees swaying—each of which you have some understanding of, even though you may not have articulated any thoughts about them. Moving from understanding to explanation involves that further articulation. Note also that the Taylor, Esbenson, and Bennett (1994) study on the development of awareness of knowledge referred to earlier in this section suggests that knowledge that leads to new actions is identified earlier in development as something that one has learned and can be evaluated as such more easily.

Understanding, then, might often have the flavor of procedural knowledge that occurs outside the sphere of conscious thought. You can understand how to tie your shoes without being able to explain it to another. Indeed, this is often the problem when world class athletes are hired as coaches. They might understand perfectly how to execute certain complex moves but be unable to explain them at all to novices.

Theory

The idea that individuals construct theories, or maturationally develop them, and that this is what enables them to engage in explanation of the world around them, underlies much contemporary research in cognitive development and work on the psychology of science. The standard experimental paradigm used to explore this idea provides the participant with a task, the response to which is best explained by that individual's possession of a theory regarding the domain into which the phenomenon investigated by the task falls. For example, when infants preferentially look at an object that violates simple constraints on bounded physical objects, such as not being interpenetratable, it is common to attribute to them a "theory" of the mechanics of objects (e.g. Spelke 1994). Or when four-year-olds attribute distinct sets of causal relations only to living things, one might claim they have a naive theory of biology (Keil 1995). Our view is that this attribution of theories to individuals has been too free and easy, in part because of an overlooked feature of everyday explanations: how *shallow* they are.

We can begin elaborating on what we mean by the "shallows of explanation" by extending the metaphor we began the chapter with: that although explanation flows through nearly all forms of human life, it typically does not run very deep. More concretely, explanations typically stop or bottom out surprisingly early on. To return to one of our earlier examples, although almost any of us who owns a car can give some sort of explanation as to why our car starts (or fails to start) when the key is placed in the ignition and turned, few of us are able to respond with any depth to the follow-up "why" or "how" questions. And the shallowness in this case is the norm: we rarely have ready access to explanations of any depth for all sorts of phenomena for which we are able to offer some sort of explanation. Indeed, we often carry with us an illusion of depth until we are faced with the actual task of explanation. Thus people frequently assume they have vivid, fully mechanistic models of how things work or how things got the way they did, but when forced to make these models explicit by way of explanation, their assumptions of explanatory competence prove groundless. For example, in current research in the second author's laboratory, college students are asked whether they know how various familiar devices work, such as toilets, contact lenses, and derailleurs. Many assert that they have a complete and fully worked out understanding such that they could explain all the necessary steps in any process involving the object. Yet when asked for such explanations, a large percentage of these participants will show striking inabilities to put together a coherent explanation, missing not just a few arbitrary details, but critical causal mechanisms. Until they attempt such explanations, they are often under the illusion that they have a complete, "clockworks," understanding.

We can distinguish two different kinds of shallows, those within a level and those across levels, where we can think of levels either as those in the classic reductionist hierarchy (physics, chemistry, biology, psychology, sociology) or, perhaps more perspicuously, in terms of Simon's nearly decomposable systems (1969). The two different kinds of shallows represent distinct ways in which explanation may be circumscribed or limited. To take an example of the shallows of explanation across levels, while we might have a perfectly detailed mechanistic account of how an electric blender works within a level (gears, blades, motor torques, and the cutting action of the blades on solids at different velocities) our knowledge across levels (how electromagnetism makes a motor work or how the chemical bonds of solids change when they are mechanically sheared) might be extremely limited, and hence our explanations there would be shallow. Conversely, we might also have huge explanatory holes at the primary level of analysis, as with the car starting example or, like most people, when we try to explain the motions of gyroscopes (Proffitt and Gilden 1989), even if we are able to provide detailed explanations across higher and lower levels for particular components of the overall system.

In our view, theories have much more depth than explanations, but this greater depth does not mean that theories must explain everything relevant to a phenomenon. The normal usage of the term *theory* has never required that a theory explain everything. For example, a theory of how the agent for mad cow disease works does not require a regress down to particle physics to be a legitimate theory. Although theories have more scope and systematicity than explanations, they reach a kind of natural boundary when they tie together a wide range of phenomena into one coherent account that links both observables and unobservables (Wilson 1994; Wilson 1995, chap. 8).

Just as the shadows of explanation are a consequence of its ubiquity, the shallows of explanation are a consequence of its frequent occurrence in the absence (or minimal presence) of theory. It is in this sense—precisely what we invoked in arguing that explanation is stronger than (mere) prediction—that explanation is weaker than theory.

Let us make our argument here more explicit:

1. Explanation is typically shallow;
2. Theories allow us to offer explanations with more depth than the shallows of explanation suggest we typically provide; therefore
3. Having a theory about X entails being able to explain X; but
4. Being able to explain X does not entail having a theory about X; thus
5. Explanatory ability is weaker than theoretical ability.

The first premise is, we claim, itself a phenomenon in need of explanation. The second premise is a fact about theories expressed in light of the first premise. The inference from these premises to our conclusion follows provided we can eliminate hypotheses that claim that the shallows of explanation are caused by something other than what we will call the *theoretical abyss.*

4.3 The Shallows and the Theoretical Abyss

We have suggested that, often enough, a theoretical abyss exists between our ability to provide limited explanations that suffice for the purposes at hand and the possession of corresponding, detailed theoretical knowledge that would allow us to provide more satisfying, richer explanations. Because there would be no theoretical abyss if the shallows of explanation were a consequence of something other than the absence of theoretical knowledge, here we will consider why alternatives to the theoretical abyss are not all that plausible. In particular, we will argue that a range of alternatives that appeal to social aspects of explanation and to general processing limitations should be rejected; namely, that the following two hypotheses (and their variants) are false:

H_1. The shallowness of explanation is simply a function of contextual or social features of the practice of explanation; and

H_2. The shallows of explanation stem from a limitation in our abilities, but are a consequence of general processing and access abilities—not of the absence of theoretical knowledge.

H_1 and its variants seek to identify the shallows of explanation as a sort of shortcoming of social performance or the pragmatics of communication (e.g., the maxim of not giving too much information in discourse; see Grice 1989). Personality traits (e.g., shyness) and the level of social comfort will certainly account for some cases of why explanations are shallow. But such hypotheses are implausible in the case of explanation more generally because the shallows of explanation are a feature of both communicative and reflective explanation, where only communicative explanation need involve social performance at all. As for reflective explanation, we may often think about a phenomenon, decide we know how it works, and then file that "explanation" away without communicating it to others. Precisely because we do not explain it to others, we may further entrench the illusion of explanatory depth. Perhaps we even confuse a sense of understanding with having a true explanation, or perhaps we have explanatory fragments that seem so clear that we falsely assume we know all the links between those fragments as well.

Like H_1, H_2 and its variants also view the shallows of explanation as a performance limitation, one that is due to memory and processing limitations. But they are implausible because the shallows of explanation manifest themselves not only in contrived experimental situations or cases where bottlenecks are imposed through task demands; they are pervasive in explanation "in the wild." To insist that we have the theoretical knowledge that would allow us to overcome the shallows of explanation but do not draw on it for, broadly speaking, reasons of cognitive architecture would be plausible were there circumstances under which we did *not* fall into the shallows of explanation. But so far as we can tell, the *only* way of avoiding the shallows is *to learn a theory*, that is, to acquire precisely the web of knowledge that, we claim, is typically missing. In addition, there is every reason to believe that people can and do know causal propositional structures vastly more complicated than those required to escape the shallows of explanation. After all, humans have for millennia shown an astonishing ability to accurately remember lengthy narratives with complex internal causal structures, logical arguments, and entailments, and with carefully laid out presuppositions and assumptions that lead to predictions. Perhaps the overall cognitive demands of explanation are radically different from those of learning a narrative, but we see no signs of such a difference.

Of course, we have only considered two of the more obvious alternatives to the existence of a theoretical abyss as an explanation for the shallows of explanation, and thus would be rightly accused of posing a false dilemma (trilemma, actually) if we were to rest our case here. But we think that the theoretical abyss also comports rather well with some broader features of explanation and the sort of division of cognitive labor it invokes, and it is to these that we now turn.

4.4   The Division of Cognitive Labor

In our explanatory endeavors, we rely extensively on knowledge in others, and we rely on the assumption of knowledge in others to give us a sense of explanatory insight. This division of cognitive labor is a critical, prominent part of everyday explanation, one whose typical omission in discussions of explanation is, we think, a consequence of overlooking the shadows and shallows of explanation.

What do we mean by a "division of cognitive labor"? Putnam (1975) introduced the idea of a linguistic division of labor in his argument that "'meanings' just ain't in the head," and we base our conception on his. Putnam's idea was that while everyday users of natural language are able to apply the terms of that language by knowing what he called "stereotypes" of those terms, it is only "experts" who know the real essences of the referents of those terms. There is thus a sort of division of linguistic labor between everyday folk and various sets of experts, whereby everyday folk make do with relatively superficial referential knowledge but are still able to talk about things because of the knowledge experts have of the "essences" of those things. To take Putnam's most famous example, while everyday folk know that water is a clear, drinkable liquid found in lakes and that water falls from the sky when it rains, it is only experts who know the underlying molecular essence of water, that is, what water *really* is.

We propose that there is a similar division of cognitive labor that underwrites explanatory knowledge. That is, everyday folk know enough about the "nominal essences" of the things that they interact with regularly to be able to offer relatively shallow explanations for the behavior of those things. But there are also experts who have either the within-level or across-levels knowledge that everyday folk typically lack, and who are in a position to offer explanations with more depth. Although we, as individuals, are faced with the theoretical abyss as the norm, the theoretical knowledge we lack exists in others, just not in us. This is to say that explanation and the theories that underwrite its depth, are "wide," that is, they do not supervene on an individual's intrinsic, physical properties.

The extent to which theories and explanation are wide is even more striking than it is for meanings (Putnam 1975) and concepts (Millikan 1998). Explanations are intimately linked to the structure of the world they try to account for and to the broader community of knowledge. Explanations, far more than meanings or concepts, are expected to work in that they should enable us to interact more proficiently with some aspect of the world. For that reason, they must resonate with some aspect of the real world. We assume the following:

1. The structure of the world is organized into clusters with their own distinctive levels and kinds of patternings, causal and otherwise;
2. To be able to get much traction in thinking about those regularities, theories and explanations must be specifically tailored to the structures in each of these clusters of domains;
3. This specialization means that theories and explanations will be different, not just in what they refer to, but in their structure and form as a consequence of what they are trying to explain.

Just as the different sense organs have evolved very different sorts of structures for processing such different patterns as light and sound, theories of biology and physics are different from the bottom up. To understand them and how they work, we must see them as linking a person to the world, not just to an internal mental representation. To handle a variegated perceptual world, we have evolved distinct perceptual modules; to handle a complicated theoretical world, we have enacted a form of distributed cognition in the form of the division of cognitive labor.

How could this division of cognitive labor work? It could not be that we simply have labels for various kinds of experts, such as physicists, chemists, biologists and doctors. We must also have some sort of insightful sense of what goes on in those areas of expertise, that is, of how mental constructs in those experts relate to the things they know so much about. The shallows notion may be the key here because it gives us an ability to know, in a superficial way, what explanations are like in a domain without really knowing much at all in the way of detail. This is far different from the normal sense of distributed cognition (e.g., Hutchins 1995), but it may be the central one to understanding how explanation works in broader social contexts.

We see two complementary ways in which the division of cognitive labor could work: through schematic modes of construal, and through public forms of representation, somewhat like the "blackboards" that Simon (chap. 2, this volume) suggests. The modes of construal allow people to have some sense of what experts know in a domain without knowing the details. The deep reliance of explanatory practices on public forms of representation—from writing systems, to iconic symbols, to video displays—implies that what constitutes or realizes an explanation literally extends beyond the head of the individual (Wilson 2000). We spell out how such notions might work in sections 4.5 and 4.6; both reflect the sense in which explanations are not "in the head."

The shallows notion also suggests a different view of what concepts are and how they fit into explanations. There has been great attention of late to the "concepts in theories" view of concepts (Carey 1985; Gopnik and Wellman 1994; Murphy and Medin 1985). But so much of that discussion has seemed to assume a view of theories as the very kinds of concrete detailed models of reality we have argued are so uncommon, usually impractical, and not useful. Instead, if we think of concepts as embedded in "modes of construal," we start to see that their role in explanations can fit very nicely with the shallows idea.

We have argued that the shallows of explanation are themselves to be explained by the distinction between explanation and theory. This distinction comports nicely with our rejection of a concepts-in-theories view that requires explanations to be explicit, propositional entities (whether spoken, written, or thought) that contain concepts. Precisely what concepts are is a thorny issue on which we do not propose to take a stand here. But we do want to address the extent to which concepts, explanations, and theories all involve irreducible causal mechanistic aspects, and to advance a position that is compatible with our views on the shadows and shallows of explanation.

4.5   Irreducible Causal Explanation and the Shallows

It is striking that the notion of a cause is invoked in almost all everyday explanations, whether directly or via the notions of causal structure, relations, and powers. We find causation almost everywhere in explanation: from explaining why the water boils in the kettle when you turn the stove on, to explaining how trees grow, to explaining why people join a health club. Exceptions include purely mathematical explanations, explanations that appeal solely to logical features of a situation (such as inconsistency), and discussions of some legal and social conventions. We shall concern ourselves here solely with causal explanations, noting that we construe this notion broadly to encompass most explanations that we encounter in both everyday life and science.

How is the pervasiveness of *causal* explanation compatible with the shallows of explanation? After all, if causes are either explicitly or implicitly invoked in everyday explanations, then explanations must have some sort of depth to them, since causes are, often enough, underlying entities, and are, often enough, not themselves observed. In short, to put this more pointedly, causes are often *theoretical* entities, and their postulation thus presupposes the existence of theories of some sort, however impoverished. Given that, the prevalence of causal explanation seems incompatible with the theoretical abyss we have posited in our account of explanation.

Our view is that while causes are invoked in explanation all the time, it is *how* they are invoked and *who* gets to invoke them that is the key to resolving this puzzle, telling us much about the way in which the ubiquity of causal explanation is compatible with the shallows of explanation, and pointing to another partial cause of the shallows. The concept of cause ordinarily appealed to in explanation is not much more than that of "something that brings about, in some way, the phenomena that we seek to explain." It is truly a "we know not what," to use Locke's characterization of substance in *An Essay Concerning Human Understanding*. And those who do know about the nature of the relevant causes are often not the ones offering the causal explanation. The "how" and the "who" here correspond, roughly and respectively, to the two ways the division of cognitive labor functions: via sketchy modes of construal; and via the extended minds that result from cognizing through shared forms of representation.

This feature of our appeal to causes helps explain both the shadows and shallows of explanation. We take the notion of causation itself to be a primitive notion, one that has its own shadows in both reductive accounts of causation (e.g., Humean accounts) and nonreductive accounts that consider causation to be richer but still analyzable in terms of prior notions (e.g., time, powers, properties). Causation, like explanation, is ubiquitous and best understood as a cluster notion; hence philosophical reconstructions of the concept are doomed to a shadowy existence. We can, perhaps, even see the shadows of at least causal explanation as inherited from those of causation itself. But we also appeal to causes even when, in a very real sense, we do not know what these are. We seem almost perceptually built to infer the presence of causes, even if the theoretical understanding necessary to understand the nature of those causes lags far behind. The Humean cues of contiguity and constant conjunction are often sufficient for us to suspect a cause, irrespective of whether we have any conception of the type of mechanism involved or the underlying character of that cause. Given the shallows of causation, it is no wonder that our causal explanations are themselves shallow.

4.6   Shadows, Shallows, and Explanatory Success

The problem we have touched on in the previous section has a general form that we would like to address more fully in this section. We argued in section 4.1 that the shadows of explanation are a reflection of the inherent complexity of explanation and the difficulties of understanding it from any one perspective. Explanations may all share a function of helping their users at least think they understand a phenomenon better, but beyond that very broad functional description, there are a huge array of phenomenological variations: flashes of insights, slow creeping realizations, picking up on a useful analogy, narrowing down alternatives, and so on. The psychological experience of explanation thus itself has a shadowy nature (for an alternative view, see Gopnik, chap. 12, this volume).

This shadowy nature, however, may not reflect a loose family resemblance concept as much as a rich implicit structure to explanations that is not easily translatable into explicit formulations. We think this large implicit structure is also linked to the issue of the "shallows of explanation" discussed in sections 4.2 and 4.3. The shallows represent the surprising extent to which explanations do not explain many phenomena in very many steps.

Why, then, do explanations work for us if they are so shallow, so devoid of detailed mechanisms most of the time? Is there anything systematic about their structure that enables them to work? We argue that there may be several patterns to explanatory knowledge that give a framework that allows us to pick between classes of explanations without knowing much at all about specific mechanisms. And, given that the potential depth for explanations of many natural phenomena is so vast as to approach infinity, it may be a highly adaptive way for humans to gain and use explanatory insight. Here, then, is our general problem: how do we get a handle on the patternings that exist in the world for them to be of any use to us, while not having clear notions of mechanism?

Here are some ways in which we might have an explanatory sense but stay firmly in the shallow end of the explanatory pool:

1. We can have senses of *explanatory centrality* of particular properties in particular domains. Color of an object, for example, figures more centrally in explanations involving most natural kinds of things than it does in explanations involving most artifacts (Keil et al. 1998). Size of an object may tend to impact more on artifacts because it can disrupt function more. These notions would be relatively useless if they had no generality and differed for every small level category. Instead, however, it seems that there are strikingly common patterns at a very high level. Thus all animals tend to have roughly the same sorts of properties as explanatorily central and these will be very different from those for artifacts or nonliving natural kinds (Keil and Smith 1996; Keil et al. 1998).

There is a great deal we need to understand more fully here with respect to different sense of centrality (Sloman et al. 1998). Consider a property's causal potency, that is, the extent to which changing a property causally impacts on other properties of a kind, destabilizes that kind's integrity, and so on. This may be one of the most powerful and intuitive senses of centrality. But there is also the sense of noncausal centrality in terms of a key construct in mathematics or social conventions. One question asks if causal potency works at a more general level than the other forms of potency and centrality.

2. Notions of *causal powers* have been prominent in recent years in the philosophy of science, especially in the philosophy of biology (e.g., talk of gene action, and debates over the units of selection) and in the philosophy of psychology (e.g., the individualism debate, mental causation). These notions too can give an explanatory sense without yielding precise mechanisms. What is troubling here is that the idea of an object's causal powers is used in a loose and often ambiguous way, as one of us has argued previously (Wilson 1995, chaps. 2, 5). What is more pressing in the current context is that we do not have a really clear idea of what notions of causal powers amount to at the psychological level. They seem stronger than notions of causal potency because they can be so specific to particular properties and very low level categories. It might seem that "causal powers" is another expression for a property or object, but the real sense seems more one of an interaction between a kind of thing and the world in which it is situated. Thus we can understand and explain something in terms of its causal powers, which means not just listing its properties as set of things attached to it, but, rather, listing its dispositions to behave in certain ways in certain situations. A hammer has the causal powers to pound in nails and remove them, and thinking of it as a decontextualized "pounder" seems to miss the point. One has to think of a hammer's causal powers in terms of the sorts of things it acts upon. Causal powers then seem often to be conceived of relationally, rather than as intrinsic properties that can be simply abstracted from the contexts in which they are instantiated.

Thus we might well have strong constraints on what count as appropriate explanations in a domain that come from causal powers notions without having specific mechanisms in mind and thereby still remaining in the explanatory shallows. We may know that gold has a wide array of causal powers that are distinctive to it and expect that any explanation involving it must be in accord with those causal powers. But at the same time we may have little or no understanding of why it has those causal powers. Much the same may also be true for attributions of causal powers to people, animals, and artifacts.

3. We have a sense of explanation that is based on notions of *kinds of agency* and *kinds of cause*. Thus we can think that certain kinds of agency and cause are much more likely to be central in one domain than another. Intentional agency is critical to understanding humans but not earthquakes. Teleological agency is more critical to biological kinds. Similarly, we may expect action-at-a-distance to dominate in both psychological and gravitational interactions, but not mechanical ones. The explanatory value of such notions depends critically on how fine grained and reliable they might be, topics that are still hotly under debate; but again, even with rich detail, we could still not really have a clear sense of specific mechanism.

4. Related to kinds of agency and cause are notions about *kinds of causal patternings*. But these are importantly different and need to be understood as such. Independent of kind of agency or cause might be patterns such as whether causal interactions proceed in serial chains or are massively parallel (serial chains being perhaps more common in simple artifacts), or whether many properties converge to support one or diverge from a common source to support many others. There are a large number of such patterns that one can identify and associate with particular domains, but again only as frameworks or guidelines.

We can think of these four aspects of the shallows of explanation, taken together, as yielding modes of construal that help us take an explanatory approach to a problem without knowing all the details. These modes may be what drive not just most lay intuitions but those in science as well (Dunbar 1994). Moreover, they may often be implicit in ways that make them a presupposed background in many scientific discussions.

4.7 The Shallows and Developing Explanation

By looking at how modes of construal and the shallows emerge in all of us, we can understand why they work so well in helping us get an explanatory sense from others' expertise and know-how (including our knowledge of when to access that expertise in greater detail). In particular, it is beginning to appear that even before children have entered elementary school, they have a strong sense of how knowledge is clustered in the minds of experts, and it seems they must do so through navigating the shallows and using modes of construal. For example, preschoolers seem to at least have notions of causal potency or centrality, causal patternings, and kinds of agency, and almost surely of causal powers as well, although that notion has not been investigated systematically (Keil et al. 1998; Wellman and Gelman 1997). Causal potency is seen in preschoolers in their abilities to know that some sorts of properties are likely to be much more central in some domains than others. Again, color is understood as more likely to be central to natural kinds of things than to artifacts (Keil et al. 1998). This has been looked at primarily in terms of the extent to which counterfactual statements are seen as undermining a kind's integrity (e.g., a red-tire-looking-thing is a still a tire, but a red-seagull-looking-thing might well not be a seagull). Ongoing research is now asking how such notions of centrality would influence young children's preferences for some explanations over others.

There is also evidence that young children have senses of different causal patternings in various domains. Thus they seem to know early on that action-at-a-distance is a more reasonable causal pattern for animate than inanimate things (Leslie 1995); or that some patterns of causal homeostasis may fit better with natural kinds than with artifacts (Keil 1995). They also understand that the agency responsible for purposeful movement in plants is different from that in sentient beings. Thus the sunflower follows the sun all day because of a very different kind of agency than that in the human sunbather.

Most recently, research in the second author's laboratory is showing that preschoolers have strong senses about how pieces of explanatory knowledge might be clustered in the minds of others—exactly the sort of understanding that would be central to a working division of cognitive labor. For example, a child might be told that Bill knows all about why two magnets, if turned the right way, stick together; and that John knows all about why a china lamp breaks into pieces if it falls off a table. The child is then asked who knows more about why television screens get all fuzzy sometimes during thunderstorms. Even preschoolers will cluster explanations about electricity and magnetism together to a greater extent than either of those explanation types with mechanics. There is no doubt that they are in nearly full ignorance of any specific mechanisms, yet they have some sense of how some explanations are more likely to be related in the minds of experts. In this example, they may be keying into notions of invisible forces and action-at-a-distance. Our general point, however, is that throughout much of development, and long before formal schooling, framework explanatory schemata are at work and seem to be essential for further theory growth and conceptual change. The need for such structures so early in development may be yet another reason why the skeletal "shallows" format is so psychologically important.

4.8 Conclusions

We have introduced two novel notions—the shadows and the shallows of explanation—in embarking on the larger project of opening up explanation to broader, interdisciplinary investigation. The "shadows of explanation" refers to those philosophical efforts to provide either a conceptual analysis of explanation or in some other way to pinpoint the essence of explanation. The "shallows of explanation" refers to the phenomenon of having surprisingly limited everyday, individual cognitive abilities when it comes to explanation. Explanations are, as we said at the outset, ubiquitous, but they typically are not accompanied by the depth that we might at first expect.

We have attempted to explain the existence of the shadows and shallows of explanation in terms of a theoretical abyss between explanation and richer, theoretical structures that are often attributed to people, and thus suggested that the shadows and shallows of explanation are linked. In particular, if explanations are understood as largely implicit, skeletal notions about causal pattern—causal schemata, if you like—they will lead to both shadows and shallows effects. We see the shallows of explanation not only as compatible with humans' remarkable explanatory successes, including our grasp of causal explanation, but also as a reflection of the shadowy and shallow grasp we all have of causation. It further seems that this implicit skeletal format may be essential for two reasons.

First, it is the only way to cognitively handle the theoretical abyss; and second, it is perhaps the only format that could be mastered by the very young child. For other reasons having to do with how concepts emerge in development, the explanatory schemata are critical early on, and the younger the child the more implausible any explicit fully detailed set of explicit propositions become. But even as adults all of us find tremendous value in not having to master the full causal details in any domain.

Instead, we get along much better by using our modes of construal and our social blackboard of signs and markers to access just the amount of depth we need on each occasion. Thus we have offered an account of the shallows both in terms of shorn-down, internal mental machinery, and in terms of an enriched, public symbolic environment, relative to the currently dominant ways of thinking about cognition and the world.

To carry the shallows metaphor further, we know that we cannot dive infinitely deep or even stay at any depth for very long; but by using appropriate public charts and supporting frameworks, we can make occasional brief and directed dives, sometimes of surprising depth. Thus also, in focused and limited ways, we can go to extraordinary explanatory depths with the help of public charts and frameworks of knowledge. But we could never possibly stay at such depths at all times across all domains.

Note

Preparation of parts of this chapter and some of the studies described therein was supported by National Institutes of Health grant R01-HD23922 to Frank C. Keil. Our thanks to Leon Rozenblitt and Greg Murphy for helpful comments on an earlier draft of this chapter.

References

Atran, S. (1996). From folk biology to scientific biology. In D. R. Olson and N. Torrance, eds., *Handbook of education and human development: New models of learning, teaching, and schooling*. Cambridge: Blackwell.

Bromberger, S. (1966). Why-questions. In R. Colodny, ed., *Mind and cosmos*. Pittsburgh: University of Pittsburgh Press.

Carey, S. (1985). *Conceptual change in childhood*. Cambridge, MA: MIT Press.

Cheng, P. (1997). From covariation to causation: A causal power theory. *Psychological Review, 104*, 367–405.

Dunbar, K. (1994). How scientists really reason: Scientific reasoning in real-world laboratories. In R. J. Sternberg and J. Davidson, eds., *Mechanisms of insight*. Cambridge, MA: MIT Press.

Esbensen, B. M., Taylor, M., and Stoess, C. (1997). Children's behavioral understanding of knowledge acquisition. *Cognitive Development, 12*, 53–84.

Gopnik, A. (1996). The scientist as child. *Philosophy of Science, 63*, 485–514.

Gopnik, A., and Wellman, H. M. (1994). The theory theory. In L. A. Hirschfeld and S. A. Gelman, eds., *Mapping the mind: Domain specificity in cognition and culture*. Cambridge: Cambridge University Press.

Grice, H. P. (1989). *Studies in the ways of words*. Cambridge, MA: Harvard University Press.

Hempel, C. G. (1965). *Aspects of scientific explanation*. New York: Free Press.

Hutchins, E. (1995). *Cognition in the wild*. Cambridge, MA: MIT Press.

Kahneman, D., and Tversky, A. (1973). On the psychology of prediction. *Psychological Review, 80,* 237–251.

Keil, F. C. (1995). The growth of causal understandings of natural kinds. In D. Sperber, D. Premack, and A. Premack, eds., *Causal cognition: A multidisciplinary debate*. Oxford: Oxford University Press.

Keil, F. C., and Smith, W. C. (1996). Is there a different "basic" level for causal relations? Paper presented at the thirty-seventh annual meeting of the Psychonomic Society, Chicago, November.

Keil, F. C., Smith, C., Simons, D., and Levin, D. (1998). Two dogmas of conceptual empiricism. *Cognition, 65,* 103–135.

Kitcher, P. (1989). Explanatory unification and the structure of the world. In P. Kitcher and W. Salmon, eds., *Scientific explanation*. Minneapolis: University of Minnesota Press.

Kitcher, P. (1992). The naturalists return. *Philosophical Review, 101,* 53–114.

Kitcher, P. (1993). *The advancement of science*. Oxford: Oxford University Press.

Leslie, A. (1995). A theory of agency. In A. L. Premack, D. Premack, and D. Sperber, eds., *Causal cognition: A multidisciplinary debate*. New York: Oxford University Press.

Lindberg, D. C. (1992). *The beginnings of Western science: The European scientific tradition in philosophical, religious, and institutional context, 600 B.C. to A.D. 1450*. Chicago: University of Chicago Press.

Locke, J. (1690). *An essay concerning human understanding*. Reprint, Oxford: Oxford University Press, 1975.

Maffi, L. (1994). A linguistic analysis of Tzeltal Maya ethnosymptomatology. Ph.D. diss., Abstract in *Dissertation Abstracts International, 55,* 950–951.

Magner, L. N. (1992). *A history of medicine*. New York: Marcel Dekker.

Millikan, R. G. (1998). A common structure for concepts of individuals, stuffs, and real kinds: More mama, more milk and more mouse. *Behavioral and Brain Sciences, 21,* 55–100.

Murphy, G. L., and Medin, D. (1985). The role of theories in conceptual coherence. *Psychological Review, 92,* 289–316.

Nagel, E. (1961). *The structure of science*. 2d ed. Reprint, Indianapolis: Hackett, 1979.

Proffitt, D. R., and Gilden, D. L. (1989). Understanding natural dynamics. *Journal of Experimental Psychology: Human Perception and Performance, 15,* 384–393.

Putnam, H. (1975). The meaning of meaning. In *Mind, language and reality*. London: Cambridge University Press.

Reichenbach, H. (1938). *Experience and prediction*. Chicago: University of Chicago Press.

Salmon, W. (1989). Four decades of scientific explanation. In P. Kitcher and W. Salmon, eds., *Scientific explanation*. Minneapolis: University of Minnesota Press.

Scarborough, J. (1969). *Roman medicine*. Ithaca, NY: Cornell University Press.

Simon, H. (1969). *The sciences of the artificial*. Cambridge, MA: MIT Press.

Sloman, S., Love, B., and Ahn, W. (1998). "Feature Centrality and Conceptual Coherence". *Cognitive Science*, *22*, 189–228.

Spelke, E. (1994). Initial knowledge: Six suggestions. *Cognition*, *50*, 431–445.

Sperber, D., Premack D., and Premack A. eds. (1995). *Causal cognition*. Oxford: Oxford University Press.

Taylor, M., Esbenson, B. M., and Bennett, R. T. (1994). Children's understanding of knowledge acquisition: The tendency for children to report they have always known what they have just learned. *Child Development*, *65*, 1581–1604.

van Fraassen, B. (1977). The pragmatics of explanation. Reprinted in R. Boyd, P. Gasper, and J. D. Trout, eds., *The philosophy of science*. Cambridge, MA: MIT Press, 1991.

Waldrop, W. M. (1992). *Complexity: The emerging science a the edge of order and chaos*. New York: Simon and Schuster.

Wason, P. C. (1968). Reasoning about a rule. *The Quarterly Journal of Experimental Psychology*, *20*, 273–281.

Wason, P., and Johnson-Laird, P. (1972). *Psychology of reasoning: Structure and content*. London: Batsford.

Wellman, H. (1990). *The child's theory of mind*. Cambridge, MA: MIT Press.

Wellman, H. M., and Gelman, S. A. (1997). Knowledge acquisition in foundational domains. In D. Kuhn and R. Siegler, eds., *Handbook of Child Psychology*. 5th ed., Vol. 2, *Cognition, perception and language*. New York: Wiley.

Wilson, R. A. (1994). Causal depth, theoretical appropriateness, and individualism in psychology. *Philosophy of Science*, *61*, 55–75.

Wilson, R. A. (1995). *Cartesian psychology and physical minds*. New York: Cambridge University Press.

Wilson, R. A. (2000). The mind beyond itself. In D. Sperber, ed., *Metarepresentation*. Oxford: Oxford University Press.

Zola-Morgan, S., and Squire, L. R. (1993). Neuroanatomy of memory. *Annual Review of Neuroscience*, *16*, 547–563.

II

Explaining Cognition

"How Does It Work?" versus "What Are the Laws?": Two Conceptions of Psychological Explanation

Robert Cummins

5.1 In the Beginning

In the beginning, there was the deductive nomological (DN) model of explanation, articulated by Hempel and Oppenheim (1948). According to DN, scientific explanation is subsumption under natural law. Individual events are explained by deducing them from laws together with initial conditions (or boundary conditions), and laws are explained by deriving them from other more fundamental laws, as, for example, the simple pendulum law is derived from Newton's laws of motion.

It is well-known that DN is vulnerable to a wide variety of counterexamples (e.g., Kim 1962; Salmon 1998). As a result, DN is not widely defended. But it is, I think, still widely believed that scientific explanation is subsumption under law. This is something of a scandal. Given DN's miserable track record in spite of spirited defense by many ingenious believers, one is led to ask why so many cleave so faithfully to a doctrine that has proved so indefensible?

There are two factors that work to keep DN in place. First, there is the fact that every experimental paper one picks up involves the explanation of some data by appeal to some hypothesis or other. It is tempting to conclude that philosophers' continued failure to articulate this practice in some defensible way is a point against philosophers, not against DN. And second, there is the fact that there is no widely understood and compelling alternative to DN on the market. If cognitive psychology has taught us anything, it is that no one willingly gives up a well-worn idea without having something to put in its place. I propose to examine these two factors in turn.

5.2 Two Pitfalls

In psychology, DN gets a spurious plausibility from the fact that data are routinely said to be "explained" or "accounted for" by some hypothesis or other. But this is likely to be misleading in at least two ways.

First, when psychologists talk about explaining or accounting for some percentage of the variance, the "hypothesis" in question is that the experimental treatment will have some real effect. One is looking to reject the null hypothesis in favor of its complement, namely, the hypothesis that whatever differences there are between the treatment group and the control group are not due to chance (random variation). But this sort of hypothesis isn't a law or anything like a law. The word "hypothesis" as it is used in statistical analysis, and the word "hypothesis" as it is used to refer to a conjectured theory or law, are little more than homonyms: They share the element of conjecture and little else. While there is nothing wrong with either use of the word, in the present context, we do well to keep the two senses distinct. With this in mind, I will use "proposed law" to refer to a hypothesis in the second sense.

The second way in which talk of explanation in the context of the statistical analysis of data is likely to be misleading is that, even though experimenters sometimes are attempting to test a theory or an hypothesis in the second sense (i.e., a proposed law or regularity), this is an exercise in confirmation, not explanation. We say that a law or theory accounts for or explains the data, but this simply means that the data *confirm* the law or theory. When a law is confirmed by some data set, this is evidence that the law *describes* the data (to some reasonable approximation). The now classic illustration of this is Balmer's formula (Hempel 1966):

$$\lambda = 3645.6 \frac{n^2}{n^2 - 4},$$

This formula specifies the wavelengths of the emission spectrum of hydrogen. Finding spectral lines in the places predicted by the formula confirms the law, but no one thinks the law explains why the lines are where they are.

Defenders of DN concede that Balmer's formula and similar cases are cases in which subsumption under law is not explanatory. They then take their task to be formulating a criterion that will distinguish cases like Balmer's formula from genuinely explanatory laws. There is wide consensus, however, that this has not been done successfully, and the suspicion grows that it *cannot* be done successfully. I think we should take seriously the possibility that it cannot be done because there isn't any difference: No laws are explanatory in the sense required by DN. Laws simply tell us what happens; they do not tell us why or how. Molière, satirizing scholastic appeals to occult properties and "virtues," tweaks the doctors of his time for explaining that opium puts people to sleep because it has a dormitival virtue. But isn't this just what subsumption under law always amounts to? Does the Law of Effect explain why giving a pigeon Pigeon Chow whenever it pecks a key increases the rate of key pecking? Or does it just restate the phenomenon in more general terms? Surely the correct moral to draw here is that the law of effect is an *explanandum*, not an *explanans*.

In science, when a law is thought of as an *explanandum*, it is called an "effect." Einstein received his Nobel prize, not for his work on relativity, but for his explanation of the photo-electric effect. In psychology, such laws as there are are almost always conceived of, and even called, effects. We have the Garcia effect (Garcia and Koelling 1966), the spacing effect (Madigan 1969), the McGurk effect (MacDonald and McGurk 1978), and many, many more. Each of these is a fairly well confirmed law or regularity (or set of them). But no one thinks that the McGurk effect explains the data it subsumes. No one not in the grip of the DN model would suppose that one could *explain* why someone hears a consonant like the speaking mouth appears to make by appeal to the McGurk effect. That just *is* the McGurk effect.

The mistaken idea that accounting for data by subsuming it under law is explanation is also fostered by a confusion between explanation and prediction.[1] A law that predicts a certain data point or data set is said to "explain" it. But prediction and explanation are separable in ways that DN cannot accommodate. It is possible to understand how a mechanism works, and hence to be in a position to explain its behavior and capacities—the *effects* it exhibits—without being able to predict or control its behavior. This is true generally of stochastic or chaotic systems. It is also true of systems whose relevant initial states are unknowable or simply unknown. In possession of a machine table for a Turing machine, I can explain all of its capacities, but, lacking knowledge of its initial state, I may be unable to predict its behavior (Moore 1956). Less interestingly, but just as important, some systems are simply intractable. We can explain the swirling trajectory of a falling leaf, but it would be hopeless to predict it.[2] Finally, many systems are well understood in an idealized form, but their actual behavior cannot be predicted because the relevant boundary conditions are seldom or never realized.

So, systems can be well-understood yet unpredictable. What about the converse? Can a system be predictable without being understood? Certainly. For centuries, the tides have been predicted from tide tables. Their predictability was not improved at all by Newton's successful explanation of them.[3] Consider also the plight of the seventeenth-century scientist confronted with the fact that pounding a nail makes it hot. Caloric theory, the going theory of heat at the time, treated changes in heat as diffusion phenomena. Your coffee cools because the caloric in it diffuses into the surrounding cup and air until equilibrium is reached. The fire reheats it because the caloric in the fire diffuses into the pot and surrounding air, and thence to the coffee, and so on. But pounding a nail will make it hot regardless of the temperature of the hammer.[4] This phenomenon—call it the "Galileo effect" after the man who made it famous—is relatively easy to quantify. You can be in a position to predict what is going to happen, and even be able to quantify those predictions, yet still have no idea *why* it happens. Conversely, once in possession of the mechanical theory of heat, one sees that pounding a nail is like poking a cube of Jell-O: more vibration equals more heat. But this insight does not improve predictability at all; it explains the Galileo effect, but it is the statement of the effect itself that generates the predictions.

5.3   Why the Laws of Psychology are *Explananda*

From the perspective I've been urging, it emerges that a substantial proportion of research effort in experimental psychology isn't expended directly in the explanation business; it is expended in the business of discovering and confirming effects. An effect, I've been arguing, is an *explanandum*, not an *explanans*. In psychology, we are overwhelmed with things to explain, and somewhat underwhelmed by things to explain them with. Why is that?

I want to begin by mentioning a sociological factor just so it can be set to one side. The fact is that it is very difficult to publish a paper that simply offers an explanation of an effect. Most journals want reports of experiments. Explanation, such as it is, is relegated to the "discussion" section, which is generally loose and frankly speculative compared to the rest of the paper. Discussion sections are often not read, and their contents are almost never reported in other articles. The lion's share of the effort goes into the experiments and data analysis, not into explaining the effects they uncover. Any other course of action is a quick route to a plot in Tenure Memorial Park.

This is not mere tradition or perversity. It derives from a deep-rooted uncertainty about what it would take to really explain a psychological effect. What, after all, would a successful explanatory theory of the mind look like?

We can be pretty sure what it wouldn't look like. It wouldn't look like a *Principia Psychologica*. Newtonian mechanics was laid out as an axiomatic system, self-consciously imitating Euclidian geometry, a widely influential paradigm in the seventeenth century, and has since been the dominant paradigm of an explanatory theory in science. It is arguable whether this is a really useful paradigm in any science. Certainly mechanics, even Newtonian mechanics, is never presented that way today. Still, if the goal is to lay out the fundamental principles of motion, the axiomatic approach makes a kind of sense. There are, one might suppose, a small number of fundamental principles governing motion, and these, together with some suitable definitions, might enable the derivations of equations specifying the (perhaps idealized) behavior of any particular mechanical system: a pendulum, a spring, a solar system, and so on. What makes this seem a viable approach is the idea that motion is the same everywhere, whatever moves, wherever and whenever it moves. It is also this sort of idea that grounds the widespread conviction that physics is the most fundamental science.

Conversely, what grounds the idea that psychology and geology are not fundamental sciences is the thought that psychological and geological systems are special. The principles of psychology and geology and the other so-called special sciences do not govern nature generally, but only special sorts of systems. Laws of psychology and geology are laws in situ, that is, laws that hold of a special kind of system because of its peculiar constitution and organization. The special sciences do not yield general laws of nature, but rather laws governing the special sorts of systems that are their proper objects of study. Laws in situ specify effects—regular behavioral patterns characteristic of a specific kind of mechanism.

Once we see that the laws of a special science are specifications of effects, we see why theories in such sciences could not be anything like Newton's *Principia*. Who would be interested in an axiomatic development of the effects exhibited by the liver or the internal combustion engine? What we want is an explanation of those effects in terms of the constitution and organization of the liver or engine. At the level of fundamental physics, laws are what you get because, at a *fundamental* level, all you can do is say how things are. We don't think of the fundamental laws of motion as effects, because we don't think of them as specifying the behavior of some specialized sort of system that behaves as it does because of its constitution and organization. The things that obey the fundamental laws of motion (everything) do not have some special constitution or organization that accounts for the fact that they obey those laws. The laws of motion just say what motion *is* in this possible world. Special sorts of systems, on the other hand, exhibit distinctive characteristic effects. In general, then, it seems that special sciences like psychology should seek to discover and specify the effects characteristic of the systems that constitute their proprietary domains, and to explain those effects in terms of the *structure* of those systems, that is, in terms of their constituents (either physical or functional) and their mode of organization (see Cummins 1983, chaps. 1, 2, for how this kind of explanation applies to psychology).

5.4 Effects and Capacities

What I have been calling "psychological effects" are not the only, or even the primary, *explananda* of psychology. I have been concentrating on effects because I have been criticizing the idea that psychological explanation is subsumption under law, and psychological laws specify effects. The primary *explananda* of psychology, however are not effects (psychological laws) but *capacities*: the capacity to see depth, to learn and speak a language, to plan, to predict the future, to empathize, to fathom the mental states of others, to deceive oneself, to be self-aware, and so on. Understanding these sorts of capacities is what motivates psychological inquiry in the first place.

Capacities are best understood as a kind of complex dispositional property. Standard treatments typically assume that dispositions are specified by subjunctive conditionals along the following lines:

Salt is water-soluble = If salt were put in water, then, ceteris paribus, it would dissolve.

This sort of analysis is valuable because it makes it clear that to have a dispositional property is to satisfy a law in situ, a law characterizing the behavior of a certain kind of thing. Capacities and effects are thus close kin.

For this sort of analysis to work, we have to know what precipitating conditions (putting x in water) generate which manifestations (x dissolves). For many psychological capacities, it is a matter of some substance to specify exactly what they are. The specification of a capacity is what Marr (1982) called the "computational problem." This can be extremely nontrivial. How, after all, should we specify the capacity to understand Chinese? Or it can be relatively simple, as in the case of calculational capacities (the capacity to add or multiply, for example). So one reason we do not think of the capacity to learn a natural language as an effect is just that it is relatively ill specified. As a consequence, the primary *explananda* of psychology—capacities—are not typically specified as laws, nor is it clear that they always can be (see discussion of capacity to play chess under "computationalism" in section 5.6).

But there is a more interesting reason. Many of the things we call "effects" in psychology are in fact incidental to the exercise of some capacity of interest. An analogy will help to clarify the distinction I have in mind. Consider two multipliers, M1 and M2. M1 uses the standard partial products algorithm we all learned in school. M2 uses successive addition. Both systems have the capacity to multiply: given two numerals, they return a numeral representing the product of the numbers represented by the inputs. But M2 also exhibits the "linearity effect": computation is, roughly, a linear function of the size of the multiplier. It takes twice as long to compute $24 \times N$ as it does to compute $12 \times N$. M1 does not exhibit the linearity effect. Its complexity profile is, roughly, a step function of the number of digits in the multiplier.

The "linearity effect" is incidental to the capacity to multiply in M1. It is, as it were, a side effect of the way M1 exercises its capacity to multiply, and that is why we call this fact about computation time an "effect" and the multiplication a "capacity". Of course, the "linearity effect" might be computed. We could design a system M3 that not only computes products, but computes reaction times as well, timing its outputs to mimic a successive addition machine. M3 might be quite difficult to distinguish from M1 on behavioral grounds, though it need not be impossible. The timing function might be disabled somehow without disabling the multiplier. More subtly, computation of the relevant output times might itself be nonlinear, in which case M3 will not be able to fool us on very large inputs (assuming it can process them at all). Or it might be that the "linearity effect" in M3 is cognitively penetrable (Pylyshyn 1982), in which case it cannot be incidental. Thus it can be a matter of substantive controversy whether we are looking at an exercise of a capacity or an incidental effect. This is precisely what is at issue between the friends of imagery and their opponents. Are the rotation and scanning effects (for example) incidental effects of rotating or scanning a picturelike representation, or is it the exercise of a capacity to estimate rotation or scanning times involving real physical objects? (See, for example, Pylyshyn 1979.)

As primary *explananda* of psychological theory, capacities typically do not have to be discovered: everyone knows that people can see depth and learn language. But they do have to be specified, and that, to repeat, can be nontrivial. As secondary *explananda*, effects typically *do* have to be discovered. Much more important, however, is the different bearing that explaining effects as opposed to capacities has on theory confirmation. Given two theories or models of the same capacity, associated incidental effects can be used to distinguish between them. This is important for two reasons. First, it is always possible in principle, and often in fact, to construct weakly equivalent models of the same capacity. To take an extreme case, Smolensky, Legendre and Miyata (1992) have shown that, for any parser written in a LISP-like language called "tensor product programming language" (TPPL), it possible to construct a distributed connectionist network that effects the same parses. With respect to parsing per se, then, there is nothing to choose between the two models. However, they predict very different incidental effects. Second, even when two models are not weakly equivalent, they may be on a par empirically, that is, close enough so that differences between them are plausibly attributed to such factors as experimental error, idealization, and the like. Again, incidental effects that may have no great interest as *explananda* in their own right may serve to distinguish such cases.

We can expect, then, to see a good deal of effort expended in the explanation of incidental effects that have little interest in their own right: no one would construct a theory just to explain *them*. But their successful explanation can often be crucial to the assessment of theories or models designed to explain the core capacities that are the primary targets of psychological inquiry.

5.5   Functional Analysis

A theory may explain a dispositional property by systematic analysis—i.e., analyzing the system that has it, or it may proceed instead by analyzing the disposition itself. I call the application of property analysis to dispositions or capacities "functional analysis."

Functional analysis consists in analyzing a disposition into a number of less problematic dispositions such that programmed manifestation of these analyzing dispositions amounts to a manifestation of the analyzed disposition. By "programmed" here, I simply mean organized in a way that could be specified in a program or flowchart. Assembly line production provides a transparent illustration. Production is broken down into a number of distinct and relatively simple (unskilled) tasks. The line has the capacity to produce the product by virtue of the fact that the units on the line have the capacity to perform one or more of these tasks, and by virtue of the fact that when these tasks are performed in a certain organized way—according to a certain program—the finished product results. Schematic diagrams in electronics provide another familiar example. Because each symbol represents any physical object having a certain capacity, a schematic diagram of a complex device constitutes an analysis of the electronic capacities of the device as a whole into the capacities of its components. Such an analysis allows us to explain how the device as a whole exercises the analyzed capacity, for it allows us to see exercises of the analyzed capacity as programmed (i.e., organized) exercises of the analyzing capacities.

In these examples, analysis of the disposition goes together in a fairly obvious way with componential analysis of the disposed system, analyzing dispositions being capacities of system components. This sort of direct form-function correlation is fairly common in artifacts because it facilitates diagnosis and repair of malfunctions. Form-function correlation is certainly absent in many cases, however, and it is therefore important to keep functional analysis and componential analysis conceptually distinct. Componential analysis of computers, and probably brains, will typically yield components with capacities that do not figure in the analysis of capacities of the whole system. A cook's capacity to bake a cake analyzes into other capacities of the "whole cook." Similarly, Turing machine capacities analyze into other Turing machine capacities. Because we do this sort of analysis without reference to a realizing system, the analysis is evidently not an analysis of a realizing system but of the capacity itself. Thus functional analysis puts very indirect constraints on componential analysis. My capacity to multiply 27 times 32 analyzes into the capacity to multiply 2 times 7, to add 5 and 1, and so on, but these capacities are not (so far as is known) capacities of my components.

The explanatory interest of functional analysis is roughly proportional to (1) the extent to which the analyzing capacities are less sophisticated than the analyzed capacities; (2) the extent to which the analyzing capacities are different in kind from the analyzed capacities; and (3) the relative sophistication of the program appealed to, that is, the relative complexity of the organization of component parts or processes that is attributed to the system. Item (3) is correlative with (1) and (2): the greater the gap in sophistication and kind between analyzing and analyzed capacities, the more sophisticated the program must be to close the gap.

Ultimately, of course, a complete theory for a capacity must exhibit the details of the target capacity's realization in the system (or system type) that has it. Functional analysis of a capacity must eventually terminate in dispositions whose realizations are explicable via analysis of the target system. Failing this, we have no reason to suppose we have analyzed the capacity as it is realized in that system.

5.6   Existing Explanatory Paradigms in Psychology

Here is the territory traversed thus far:

1. Psychological explanation is not subsumption under law.
2. Psychological laws are not general laws of nature, but laws in situ, namely, specifications of effects, not explanatory principles.
3. The primary *explananda* of psychology are capacities.
4. Effects and capacities in special kinds of systems are generally to be explained by appeal to the structure of those systems.
5. Much of the effort in psychology, and almost all of the methodology, is devoted to the discovery and confirmation of effects.

It is striking that, while there is an extensive body of doctrine in psychology about the methodology appropriate to the discovery and confirmation of effects, there is next to nothing about how to formulate and test an explanation.[5] This is not surprising. If you think that explanation is subsumption under law, then you will see the discovery and testing of laws as the same thing as the formulation and testing of explanations. It may be a measure of the ubiquity of DN thinking that the methodology of hypothesis testing is nowhere complemented by a comparably sophisticated methodology of explanation testing. On the other hand, it may be that explanation testing simply does not admit of formulation in an explicit methodology because successful explanation has as much to do with the knowledge and cognitive capacities of the explainers as it does with the logical properties of the explanation, a possibility I will return to below. Whatever the cause, psychologists faced with the task of explaining an effect generally have recourse to imitating one or another of the explanatory paradigms established in the discipline. These are familiar enough, but a brief review in the present context will prove illuminating.

There are five general explanatory paradigms that are influential in contemporary psychology:

1. Belief-desire-intention (BDI) explanations;
2. Computational symbol-processing explanations;
3. Connectionist explanations;
4. Neuroscience explanations;
5. Evolutionary explanations.

Belief-Desire-Intention

This is by far the most familiar explanatory model, and the model of commonsense psychological explanation, Freudian psychodynamics, and a great deal of current developmental, social and cognitive psychology. It is what Dennett praises as "explanation from the intentional stance", and what Churchland deplores as "folk psychology" (Dennett 1987; Churchland 1981). Underlying BDI is a set of defining assumptions about how beliefs, desires, and intentions interact. These assumptions are seldom if ever made explicit, just as one does not make explicit the mechanical assumptions about springs, levers, and gears that ground structural explanations of a mechanical machine. Everyone knows that beliefs are available as premises in inference, that desires specify goals, and that intentions are adopted plans for achieving goals, so it does not have to said explicitly (except by philosophers).

It is truly amazing how powerful this scheme of things is, particularly if unconscious beliefs, desires, and intentions are allowed. But there are problems. The most fundamental of these is something I call "Leibniz's Gap". Here is Leibniz's formulation of the Gap:

Moreover, we must confess that the perception, and what depends on it, is inexplicable in terms of mechanical reasons, that is, through shapes and motions. If we imagine that there is a machine whose structure makes it think, sense, and have perceptions, we could conceive it enlarged, keeping the same proportions, so that we could enter into it, as one enters into a mill. Assuming that, when inspecting its interior, we will only find parts that push one another, and we will never find anything to explain a perception. And so, we should seek perception in the simple substance and not in the composite or in the machine. (Leibniz 1714, sec. 17)

There is, as Liebniz points out in this famous passage, a gap between the concepts of BDI psychology, and those we use to describe the brain. Thus, even if we are convinced that the mind is the brain, or a process going on in the brain, physical observation of the brain seems to give us data in the wrong vocabulary: synapses rather than thoughts. When we look at a brain, even a living brain, we do not see thoughts. Or, not to beg the question, we do not see anything we readily recognize as thoughts. If you had a Newton camera and took a snapshot of a billiard game in progress, you would see vectors with centers of gravity at their tails. If you had a psychology camera and took a snapshot of a living brain, you would, according to BDI psychology, see beliefs, desires, intentions, and their canonical relations. But to build a psychology camera, you would need to somehow bridge Leibniz's Gap by correlating observed brain properties, events, and processes with beliefs, desires, and intentions, and this, at least for now, is beyond us. Thus the wide Leibnizian gap between BDI psychology and the brain is destructive to satisfying psychological explanation. Lacking some precise suggestion about how beliefs, desires, and intentions are instantiated in the brain, we are left wondering whether even the most powerful BDI analysis of some psychological effect might specify a way to achieve the effect, but not *the* way, that is, the way the brain does it. This objection is a "philosophical" objection in that it is independent of how predictively successful BDI analyses turn out to be. If we knew there was only one way to achieve the psychological effects we find in the laboratory and in the field, then the fact that a psychological effect had a satisfactory BDI analysis would constitute evidence that the brain must somehow realize the structure that analysis specified. But, of course, we do not know that there is only one way to design a mind like ours, and, lacking this knowledge, we do not know whether the predictive inaccuracies that accompany any scientific theory are due to the fact that the human mind is not a BDI device or to the fact that our theory is idealized, that measurement is imperfect, and so on.

Another serious conceptual problem with BDI has to do with the nature of the propositional attitudes—belief, desire, intention, and their kin—that are its workhorses. BDI psychology requires a conception of the attitudes that allows for beliefs, desires, and intentions that not only are not conscious, but that cannot be made conscious. Although most philosophers and psychologists find this acceptable, it has not gone unchallenged (Searle 1992). Somewhat more seriously, BDI requires that the attitudes be "atomistic," which is to say, that they be able to exist in relative isolation. In a BDI framework, standard accounts of linguistic or visual processing, for example, require beliefs about phrase structures and zero-crossings in subsystems that are relatively isolated informationally from other aspects of cognition. No psychologist working on concepts and their acquisition would think that merely being able to see, or to understand language, is sufficient for having the concept of a phrase structure or a zero-crossing. Yet having beliefs about phrase structures and zero-crossings seems to require having these concepts. Thus atomism about the attitudes, though it has its defenders (Fodor and Lepore 1992) is by no means uncontroversial (Stich 1983; Block 1986).[6]

Finally, it is not clear that psychological phenomena can generally be reduced to the interaction of propositional attitudes, even if these are broadly construed to include such things as the language processor generating a representation of the phrase structure of the current linguistic input. BDI seems best suited to so-called higher cognition, and in particular, to high-level reasoning and planning. Even here, there are formidable critics. Eliminativists (e.g., Churchland 1981) have argued that BDI, whether it be "folk theory" or grounded in an innate theory of mind, is, in fact, discredited theory.

Computationalism

Computationalism (the brain is a computer and the mind is what it is doing) is just BDI minus some of the baggage. Computationalism is a "top down" strategy. In the hands of the computationalist, that strategy begins by identifying a task or capacity to be explained: the capacity to learn a language, or converse, or solve a problem, etc. It then attempts to specify that capacity as a function or relation: what inputs produce what outputs under what circumstances. Finally, that characteristic function or relation is analyzed into components that have known computational realizations. (In practice, this means analysis into components that can be programmed in LISP or some other standard programming language.)

This strategy involves three assumptions and a precondition that are worth noting:

1. *Psychological functions are computable.* This is actually a rather strong and daring assumption. Most dynamical systems found in nature cannot be characterized by equations that specify a computable function. Even three bodies moving in Newtonian space do not satisfy this assumption. It is very much an open question whether the processes in the brain that subserve cognition can be characterized as the computation of a computable function.

2. Another underlying assumption of top-down computationalism as it is usually characterized (and as I have just characterized it) is that psychological capacities can be specified independently of their analyses. But this is pretty patently false in many cases: There is, for example, no input–output function the computation of which would constitute playing intelligent chess. Or rather, there are a great many. Think of a chess system as a move generator, that is, as a function from board positions (current) to board positions (the move). In a given situation, intelligent chess players might make any number of different moves. Indeed, the same player might make different moves on different occasions. In practice, then, the only way to specify a chess function is to actually write an algorithm for computing it. We cannot, in general, expect to specify a cognitive function before we analyze and implement it, and this introduces a methodological difficulty. If we cannot specify the *explanandum* independently of the *explanans*, how are we to compare competing explanations? We can, of course, determine which theory better predicts whatever observational data there is—that is, we can determine which does a better job predicting whatever known effects there are—but this tells us only which underlying theory is more likely true, not which generates the better explanation. The distinction is important. It is well known that if it is possible to accommodate the data at all, it is possible to accommodate them with a theory that says nothing whatever about the underlying mechanisms or their analysis, that is, in a way that has no explanatory force whatever (Craig 1953; Putnam 1965). This problem is underappreciated because a tendency to focus exclusively on accommodating effects leaves explanatory issues out of the picture from the start.

3. A third underlying assumption of the top-down strategy, closely related to the second assumption, is that we will be able to recognize and characterize the relevant inputs and behaviors antecedently to serious attempts to explain how the later are computed from the former. Here the difficulty is that pre-analytic conceptions of behavior and its causes may seriously misrepresent or distort what is actually going on. Connectionists sometimes complain that there is no reason to think that cognition in the brain is the manipulation of representations that correspond to our ordinary concepts. Top-down strategists therefore run the risk of characterizing the *explananda* in terms that crosscut or that distort the causally relevant categories. This is analogous to the almost irresistible temptation in biology to believe that the morphological traits of importance and interest to us must correspond to our genes in some neat way. Computationalists are wont to reply that what Dennett (1987) calls the "intentional stance"—predicting and explaining behavior in terms of beliefs, desires, and intentions—is enormously successful, and hence that it cannot be fundamentally wrong to characterize cognition in something like these commonsense terms. The same can be said for Ptolemaic astronomy or Newtonian mechanics, however. Considerable explanatory and predictive success is possible with a fundamentally mistaken or even an incoherent theory.

So much for the assumptions. Now for the precondition:

A successful application of the top-down strategy requires that the target explanandum *is analyzable.* Everyone who has ever tried their hand at programming is familiar with this constraint. You cannot write a program that computes bids in bridge or computes square roots if you do not know how to compute bids in bridge or compute square roots. But many psychological capacities are interesting *explananda* precisely because we have no idea how the task is done. This is why artificial intelligence plays such a central role in computationalism. It requires very considerable ingenuity to discover a way—any way—to construct three-dimensional specifications of visual space from retinal images, or to make it happen that, in problem solving, two short sessions are more effective than one long one.

But even with success, there is a problem. Having figured out *a* way to compute a cognitive function, what reason is there to think that that is how our brains do the job? I do not mean to suggest that there is no way of addressing this problem, only that it is a problem that is bound to arise in a top-down framework. Computationalists are thus inevitably left with a narrowed but still substantial Leibnizian gap: the gap between a computational description of psychological processes and a bioneural description of the processes in the brain.[7]

Connectionism

The top-down strategy is *explanandum* driven: you begin with a capacity to explain, and try to find a computational architecture that will have it. The bottom-up strategy is *explanans* driven: you start with a specification of the architecture, and try to find a way to make it do the task.[8] What connectionists have in common is the assumption that cognitive capacities are built out of a stock of primitive process designed explicitly to be rather brainlike. They begin with the building blocks of a simplified and idealized brain, and attempt to create systems that will behave in a recognizably cognitive way. The connectionist thus seeks to narrow the Leibnizian Gap even further to that between a genuinely bioneural description of the brain, and the simplified and idealized "neural networks" that are their stock in trade.

But a much narrowed Gap is not the only payoff. As it happens, it is possible to program connectionist networks to do tasks that the programmer does not know how to do. All that is required is a sufficiently representative "training set"—a set of inputs paired with their correct responses. Thus the precondition of top-down computationalism discussed above can be avoided. You can program a network to do a task you have not the faintest idea how to do. There is a downside to this, however: once you have trained a network, you may still have little if any idea how it does the task. Because studying an artificial network is much easier than studying a living brain, you are still substantially ahead. But you are not home free.

Moreover, it is seldom noticed that one of the lately discussed assumptions required by the top-down approach is also required by bottom-uppers. Training sets must be specified somehow, and the problem of how to conceptualize inputs and behaviors is no easier for connectionists than it is for top-down computationalists. While connectionists need not assume that networks operate on internal representations that correspond to ordinary commonsense concepts, they are no better off than top-down computationalists when it comes to conceptualizing the target *explananda*.

Before we leave the topic of underlying assumptions and enabling conditions, it is worth pausing to note that some of the central enabling assumptions of computationalism are shared by connectionism. Both assume that the mind is basically a cognitive engine and only secondarily a seat of emotion, feeling, and sensation. Both assume that consciousness is inessential to the understanding of cognition. And both assume that cognition does not require a biological brain, let alone an immaterial soul. Both are thoroughly functionalist and materialist. And both are representationalist in that both assume that cognition is to be understood as disciplined transformation over states whose primary function is the representation of information relevant to the cognitive capacity being exercised. The differences that divide computationalism and connectionism are practically invisible against the scale that measures the distance between them and the behaviorism of Watson or Skinner, or the structuralism of Titchner.

Neuroscience

Everyone who is not a dualist believes that mental processes are processes that go on in the brain. If one's goal is a science of the mind, however, observation of the brain seems to yield results on the wrong side of Leibniz's Gap. The computationalist response to this problem is to try to understand cognitive processes in abstraction from the brain or any other "hardware" in which they might occur. The computationalist strategy is first to articulate a computational theory of cognition, and then to inquire into how the implicated computational processes might be carried out in the brain. This strategy has some evident merits. Because no one doubts that computational processes can be physically realized, computationalism is free from any dualist taint. Yet the problem of bridging Leibniz's Gap is conveniently put off until some future date when we will surely know more about both cognitive and neural processes. An evident drawback, however, is that there is no guarantee that cognitive processes are computational processes at all, let alone that cognition in biological brains will turn out to be the kind of processes we are led to investigate by following a strictly top-down approach. Although that approach has had some notable successes, it has also had some notable failures. It would not be unreasonable to conclude that the difficulties faced by Computationalism might be due to insufficient attention being paid to the only processes we know for sure are sufficient to subserve mentality in general, and cognition in particular, namely brain processes. Perhaps we should simply accept the fact that, as things currently stand, studying the brain puts us on the wrong side of Liebniz's Gap, but hope that, as our knowledge increases, the outlines of a bridge over the Gap will eventually appear.

Connectionists attempt to take a middle ground here, starting in the middle of the Gap, as it were, and trying simultaneously to bridge to either side. Most neuroscientists, it seems, are at least tolerant of the connectionist strategy. But they are inclined to argue that connectionist models are such vastly oversimplified models of the brain as to be misleading at best. If we are going to bridge Liebniz's Gap, we are going to have to know a great deal more about the brain than we do now. This much is agreed on all sides. So why not get on with it? And, because the brain is the only known organ of mentality, whether natural or artificial, it seems only sensible to begin by trying to understand how it works. Any other strategy arguably runs the risk of being a wild goose chase, an attempt to make mentality out of stuff that just is not up to the job.

This line of argumentation has been around at least since the seventeenth century, but because there was no very good way to study the brain, it has had few practical consequences until relatively recently. Steady technological progress, however, is beginning to make Leibniz's thought experiment a reality. As a result, the problem he articulated so eloquently is forced upon us anew, for, marvelous as the new technology is, it does not, and cannot, provide "psychology glasses," lenses through which observed brain anatomy and activity emerge as psychological faculties and thought processes.

Technology can take us to the brink of Leibniz's Gap, but only theory can bridge it. There are two conceptions of how neuroscience might contribute to the bridge. According to one approach, concepts generated by neuroscience proper to articulate its data and theory should be used to reconceive the mental from the bottom up, discarding mentalistic concepts that have no clear neuroscientific reconstruction, and simply replacing ones that do (Churchland 1987). Psychology on the mental side of Leibniz's Gap will either be assimilated or perish. Well-confirmed effects remain as *explananda* in this view, with the caveat that the concepts used in their articulation must not be tainted too deeply by concepts that have no acceptable neuroscientific reconstruction.[9] Psychological capacities of the sort that constitute the primary *explananda* of more top-down approaches are viewed with suspicion—guilty (until proven innocent) of not cutting nature at the joints. I call this approach the "strong neuroscience program".[10]

As things stand, the strong neuroscience program is almost impossible to put into practice. Standard descriptions of dissociations, of tasks done during functional magnetic resonance imaging (FMRI), and so on are up to their eyebrows in terminology from the "wrong" side of Leibniz's Gap. A more common and more ecumenical conception of the role of neuroscience treats it as a source of evidence designed primarily to arbitrate among functional analyses formulated in other terms, terms from unreduced psychology residing on the other side of the Gap from "pure" neuroscience. There are serious methodological issues here that are matters of controversy in psychology, neuroscience, and philosophy, but it is clear in a general way how weak neuroscience bears on the issue of psychological explanation: it passes the buck. On this conception, psychological effects and capacities are explained as the effects or capacities of BDI, computationalist, or connectionist systems, and these are assumed to be instantiated somehow in the brain. Neuroscience enters the picture as a source of evidence, arbitrating among competitors, and ultimately, as the source of an account of the biological realization of psychological systems described functionally.

Evolutionary Explanations

Like neuroscience, evolution can be regarded as either a source of psychological explanations or as a source of evidence bearing on one or another non-evolutionary theory that generates its own psychological explanations, and this generates a distinction between a strong evolutionary program and a weak evolutionary program analogous to the distinction between the strong and weak neuroscience programs. The evidential role of evolution is relatively easy to specify. Functional analyses attribute functions to the analyzed systems. A source of evidence that a system really has a given function, or has a component with a given function, is that such a function would have constituted an adaptation, or the likely corollary of an adaptation, for the system's ancestors.[11] Conversely, a functional analysis that proposes functions in a biological system that have no plausible evolutionary rationale are suspect on the grounds that nature is not being carved a the joints. Again, there are important methodological issues here, but they do not bear on the nature of psychological explanation, only on the confirmation of the theories that generate them.

The strong evolutionary program is based on the idea that evolution might actually explain a psychological capacity or effect. This idea is difficult to articulate and assess. At best, it seems that evolution might explain why a certain psychological capacity or effect is pervasive in a given population. It could, to put it crudely, explain *why* we see depth, but not *how*. Thus an evolutionary explanation and an explanation generated by one of the other paradigms would not be direct competitors in the same explanatory game. This is obscured by the fact that evolutionary reasoning could favor some functional analyses over others, which entails that evolutionary explanations could be incompatible with explanations generated by one of the other frameworks (BDI, computationalism, connectionism, neuroscience). But evolutionary explanations do not seek to answer the same question as those generated by the other frameworks. Hence, as long as there is no incompatibility in the functional analyses each postulates, there is no reason why we should have to choose between an evolutionary explanation and, say, a connectionist explanation or a BDI explanation.

5.7   Two Problems for Psychological Explanation

The first three of the familiar frameworks just rehearsed—BDI, computationalism, and connectionism—are, as they should be, *analytical* frameworks. That is, they are frameworks for analyzing (decomposing) complex capacities into more primitive components. The strong neuroscience program aspires to be an analytical framework, and is perhaps well on the way to becoming one. Weak neuroscience and the weak evolutionary program do not pretend to be explanatory frameworks in their own right, hence offer no alternative to the analytical approach. Finally, what I have called the "strong evolutionary program" is, I think, best construed as explaining the prevalence of an effect or capacity in a population, and thus leaves untouched the question of what the mind is and how it works.

Our survey of the currently viable explanatory frameworks thus reveals that, although there is still considerable lip service paid to DN, actual theory building and explanation construction takes place in frameworks that are not designed for the elaboration of laws but rather are designed for the elaboration of functional analyses. The foundational problems for psychological explanation, then, are special versions of the problems that arise for functional analysis generally. If we leave aside strictly epistemological problems, problems about how functional analyses are to be "discovered" or confirmed, and focus solely on how they work as explanations, two central issues emerge.[12] The first might be called the "realization problem". Functional analysis always leaves one with a gap between the functional characterization of a system and the various nonfunctional characterizations that are assumed to apply to the system whose functional analysis is at issue.[13] In psychology, this is what I have called "Leibniz's Gap". The second problem might be called the "unification problem". Functional analyses are usually generated to explain some particular capacity or effect, or a closely related set of them. Researchers concerned with some aspect of vision may be sensitive to the issue of unifying their account with those directed at some other aspect of vision. But they are less likely to concern themselves with making their analyses fit with the analyses of those researching language or emotion or reasoning.

Leibniz's Gap: Intentionality and Consciousness

The realization problem, in the form of Leibniz's Gap, looms for every current explanatory framework surveyed above, with the exception of strong neuroscience, which holds that concepts not proprietary to neuroscience itself need not be taken seriously. While attractive philosophically because it eliminates the Gap, strong neuroscience is, as remarked above, nearly impossible to put into practice as an explanatory strategy simply because the vast majority of the *explananda* are formulated in terms that either explicitly or implicitly draw on concepts that have no known counterparts in neuroscience. Indeed, neuroscience that does honor eliminativist constraints seems, at present anyway, to have little to do with psychology. I propose, therefore, to put the strong neuroscience program aside and concentrate on frameworks that must, in one way or another, face Leibniz's Gap.

There is no special mystery about what counts as a satisfactory solution to realization problems generally. Every time we design an artifact to satisfy a functional characterization and then build it, we solve a realization problem. This shows that there is no special philosophical mystery about what it is to realize a functionally specified system. Difficulties arise, however, in special cases in which there is a fundamental unclarity in one or more of the primitives of the analytical framework. There is deep uncertainty about whether beliefs, desires, and intentions can be computationally realized, not because we do not understand what realization requires, but because we are unclear about beliefs, desires, and intentions. There is no comparable worry about whether a given computationally specified system is realized in the brain. There is uncertainty, of course, but it is a different kind of uncertainty. We know what it takes to realize a computationally specified system, we just don't know if what it takes is in the brain. But we don't know what it takes to realize a belief or desire.[14] Do any of the many sophisticated planners currently in the literature actually have beliefs, desires, and intentions? And if they do not, should we conclude that planning does not require belief, desire, and intention, or should we conclude that computationalist planners are mere imitators of mental activity? Everyone recognizes these as Philosophical Questions, which, in this context anyway, means mainly that everyone recognizes that they are questions that, as things now stand, cannot be addressed experimentally. And, of course, there is an exactly parallel, and perhaps related (Searle 1992), set of problems about consciousness.

It is important to see that the Liebnizian gap between intentional states like belief, desire, and intention, on the one hand, and computationalist, connectionist, or neuroscience concepts, on the other, is not just a problem for BDI. It is a problem for any framework that either characterizes its *explananda* in intentional terms or assumes (tacitly or explicitly) a realization of intentional states in its proprietary mechanisms and processes—whether these be the computational manipulation of data structures, the spread of activation disciplined by connection weights, or synaptic connections and spiking frequencies. I think it is pretty obvious that both kinds of intentionalist taint are ubiquitous, though not universal, in psychology and artificial intelligence. I submit that this is why so much psychological explanation, while it is often compelling and informative, is almost always ultimately unsatisfying. What is more, we do not know whether the problem is just that we do not really understand intentional states, or that, as eliminativists claim, there is nothing to be understood. We never solved the realization problem for entelechies either, but that was a knock on vitalism, not a failure of philosophical analysis.

All of this is old news, of course. But it is worth reminding ourselves that there is nothing wrong with psychological explanation that a solution (or dissolution) of the problem of intentionality and consciousness would not cure.

The Unification Problem

There is, however, a de facto problem that plagues psychological explanation, and that is its evident lack of unification.

The first and most obvious problem is that there are four quite different explanatory frameworks operative in contemporary psychology: BDI, computationalism, connectionism, and (strong) Neuroscience. While the first two and the second two are reasonably close together, it remains true that explanations constructed in one framework are seldom translatable into explanations in another; the gap between BDI and computationalism, on the one hand, and Connectionism and (strong) neuroscience, on the other, is particularly wide and typically competitive.

It is a commonplace in science to attack different problems from the perspective of different explanatory models. To explain the flow of water and wave propagation, one typically models water as a continuous incompressible medium. To explain diffusion and evaporation, one models water as a collection of discrete particles.[15] But it is important to see how this situation differs from the situation that prevails in psychology. The different models of water are brought in to explain different effects. While water cannot be both a continuous incompressible fluid and a cloud of free molecules, each model is directed at a different set of problems. There is no competition between the models concerning the solution of the *same* problem.[16] In contrast, it is notorious that connectionist and computationalist models compete in just this way, a classic example being the explanation of the acquisition of the past tense in English (Rumelhart and McClelland 1986; Pinker and Prince 1989). In this respect, contemporary psychology resembles seventeenth-century mechanics in which Cartesians and Newtonians competed to explain the same phenomena within different frameworks. There is, of course, no way to resolve this kind of competition other than to let the science take its course. In the meantime, however, every explanation in psychology is, to some extent, undermined by the deep disunity that afflicts the field in its current state of development. Until the field is unified in some way—by the victory of one of the current competitors, by the emergence of a new framework, or by a successful realization hierarchy (BDI realized computationally, realized as a connectionist network, realized in the brain)—the suspicion remains that some or all of the explanations currently offered are fundamentally flawed because they are articulated in a fundamentally flawed framework.

In addition to the disunity across frameworks, there is considerable disunity within each framework, particularly within computationalism and connectionism.[17] Both frameworks allow for an enormous variety of models based on very different principles.[18] Attempts at unity are not unknown: in the computationalist camp, Anderson's ACT⋆ (1996) and Newell's SOAR (1990) spring to mind, as does Grossberg's ART (1982) in the connectionist camp. But it is an understatement that these are not widely accepted; the prevailing bewildering diversity of models tends to undermine confidence in any.

Having said all of this, I do not think we should worry much about disunity. The ordinary practice of good science will take care of disunity eventually. There is a far greater danger in forcing more unity than the data warrant. Good experimentation, like good decision making generally, can tell us which of two models is better, but it cannot tell us how good any particular model is. The best strategy, then, is to have a lot of models on offer on the grounds that, other things equal, the best of a large set is likely better than the best of a small one.

5.8   Conclusions

I have been urging that explanation in psychology, like scientific explanation generally, is not subsumption under law. Such laws as there are in psychology are specifications of effects. As such, they do not explain anything, but themselves require explanation. Moreover, though important, the phenomena we typically call "effects" are incidental to the primary *explananda* of psychology, viz., capacities. Capacities, unlike their associated incidental effects, seldom require discovery, though their precise specification can be nontrivial. The search for laws in psychology is therefore the search for *explananda*, for it is either the search for an adequate specification of a capacity or for some capacity's associated incidental effects. Laws tell us what the mind does, not how it does it. We want to know how the mind works, not just what it does.

Capacities and their associated incidental effects are to be explained by appeal to a combination of functional analysis and realization, and the currently influential explanatory frameworks in psychology are all frameworks for generating this sort of explanation. Thus, in spite of a good deal of lip service to the idea that explanation is subsumption under law, psychology, though pretty seriously disunified, is squarely on the right track. Its efforts at satisfying explanation are still bedeviled by the old problems of intentionality and consciousness. This is where psychology and philosophy meet. Psychology need not wait on philosophy, however. The life sciences made a lot of progress before anyone knew how life was realized.

Notes

1. I do not mean to suggest that DN theorists were confused about this. On the contrary, they held that explanation and prediction are just two sides of the same coin. The point is rather that DN conflates explanation and prediction, which are, I claim, orthogonal.

2. Cartwright (1983) denies that we can explain the trajectory of a falling leaf. But all she argues for is that we cannot predict it. She seems to think it follows from this that we have no reason to believe that the laws of mechanics accurately subsume it. A more conservative view is that we understand falling leaves quite well. No one seriously thinks this is an outstanding mystery of nature on a par with the nature of consciousness, say. The problem is just that prediction is intractable.

3. This is an interesting case in a number of ways. Newton's successful explanation in terms of the moon's gravitational influence does not allow prediction, which is done today, as before Newton, by tables. So here we have in a single instance a case where prediction is neither necessary nor sufficient for explanation. Moreover, we have a case where explanation seems to come apart from truth. The Newtonian mechanics on which the explanation is based has been supplanted, yet the explanation is still accepted.

4. Friction was thought to release otherwise bound caloric, but this will not help with a cold hammer and nail.

5. There is hypothetico-deductivism (HD): explanations are "theories", which are tested by deducing from them what effects should be exhibited. Explanations are then tested by determining whether the effects they predict are real.

6. It is interesting that, as the phenomena become more "specialized," intention and desire tend to drop out. There is surely some truth in the idea that the game of life is to form intentions (plans) that will get things moved from the desire box (Desire[I am rich]) to the belief box (Believe[I am rich]). But it is a stretch to think that this is the fundamental loop in language processing or vision.

7. The gap is narrowed relative to BDI because a computational analysis will at least have demonstrated the physical—indeed computational—realizability of the processes they postulate. BDI explanations are always subject to the eliminativist worry that the fundamental processes postulated have no physical realizations at all. Still, it is arguable that many computationalist explanations only make sense on the controversial assumption that beliefs, desires, and intentions have reasonably straightforward computational realizations. I return to this point below.

8. In practice, most computationalists are actually bottom-uppers to some extent. This is because, as a graduate student, you apprentice in a research group that is more or

less committed to a given architecture, and your job is to extend this approach to some new capacity. It is just as well: pure top-downism, as described by Marr (1982), is probably impossible. Computationalist architectures, however, are not well-grounded in the brain, so the problem just rehearsed remains.

9. The history of science is full of effects that were not real in the sense that subsequent science rediagnosed the inevitable failures to fit the data precisely as conceptual error rather than experimental error.

10. The use of "strong" and "weak" to distinguish two conceptions of the role of neuroscience in psychological explanation, and the use of these words to distinguish two analogous conceptions of the role of evolutionary theory in psychological explanation, should not be taken as terms of approbation or abuse. They are modeled after Searle's well-known distinction between strong and weak AI (Searle 1980).

Perhaps I should emphasize as well that I am not here attempting to characterize neuroscience, but only its abstract role in psychological explanation. The same goes for my remarks about evolution in the next section.

11. Corollary: x was an adaptation, and y is a likely precondition or consequence of having x, so whatever evolutionary argument exists for x confers some plausibility on y as well.

I don't mean to suggest that adaptation and selection is all there is to evolution. But non-selectionist scenarios for the evolution of a psychological function are bound to be relatively difficult to construct or confirm.

12. I do not mean to suggest that these problems are trivial or unimportant. Indeed, I think they are many and deep. But these are problems about confirmation, not about explanation. One of the many unfortunate consequences of DN is that it (intentionally) blurs the distinction between confirmation and explanation.

13. As many have pointed out (see, for example, Lycan 1987), the distinction between functional and nonfunctional levels of organization is relative. Realizing systems are seldom characterized in nonfunctional terms. They are rather characterized in terms of functions that differ from those whose realization is at issue. A logic circuit, for example, might be analyzed in terms of AND gates, OR gates, and INVERTERS. The realization of this circuit might then be specified in terms of resistors, transistors, and capacitors. These are themselves, of course, functional terms, but their realization is not at issue, so they count as nonfunctional relative to the gates and invertors whose realization is being specified.

14. Except trivially: a normal brain. All this does is rule out dualism.

15. The example is from Paul Teller, in conversation.

16. I do not mean to suggest that this situation is entirely unproblematic. It is certainly tempting to suppose that there is a deep disunity here—unless both models of water can be treated as acceptable idealizations or simplifications grounded in a deeper single model.

17. Functional analyses tend to proliferate when there are no strong restrictions on the primitives. Computationalism, in principle, allows any computable function as a psychological primitive. Connectionism is somewhat less permissive, but there is still a bewildering variety of network architectures. Strong Neuroscience, insofar as it exists

as an explanatory framework at all, imposes very few constraints on functional architecture beyond those dictated by gross anatomy and (often controversial) dissociation effects (the Classic is Ungerleider and Mishkin 1982).

BDI is probably the most unified of the currently viable explanatory frameworks because it is defined by a choice of primitives. Still, there have been few systematic attempts to make the principles of interaction among these principles explicit. An exception is Freudian psychodynamics. While this is (extended) BDI, most of its fundamental principles—for example, repression—would be regarded as dubious by many BDI researchers.

18. As Smolensky, Legendre, and Miyata (1992) have pointed out, explanation in these frameworks tends to be model based rather than principle based.

References

Anderson, J. (1996). *The architecture of cognition*. Mahwah, NJ: Erlbaum.

Block, N. (1986). Advertisement for a semantics for psychology. In P. French, T. Uehling, Jr, and H. Wettstein, eds., *Studies in the Philosophy of Mind*. Vol. 10 of *Midwest Studies in Philosophy*. Minneapolis: University of Minnesota Press.

Cartwright, N. (1983). *How the laws of physics lie*. Oxford: Clarendon Press; New York: Oxford University Press.

Churchland, P. M. (1981). Eliminative materialism and propositional attitudes. *Journal of Philosophy, 78*, 67–90.

Craig, W. (1953). On axiomatizability within a system. *Journal of Symbolic Logic, 18*, 30–32.

Cummins, R. (1983). *The nature of psychological explanation*. Cambridge, MA: MIT Press.

Dennett, D. (1987). *The intentional stance*. Cambridge, MA: MIT Press.

Fodor, J., and Lepore, E. (1992). *Holism: A shopper's guide*. Oxford: Blackwell.

Garcia, J., and Koelling, R. (1966). The relation of cue to consequence in avoidance learning. *Psychonomic Science, 4*, 123–124.

Grossberg, S. (1982). *Studies of mind and brain: Neural principles of learning, perception, development, cognition, and motor control*. Dordrecht: Reidel.

Hempel, C. (1966). *Philosophy of natural science*. Englewood Cliffs, NJ: Prentice Hall.

Hempel, C., and Oppenheim, P. (1948). Studies in the logic of explanation. *Philosophy of Science, 15*, 135–175.

Kim, J. (1962). On the logical conditions of deductive explanation. *Philosophy of Science, 30*, 286–291.

Leibniz, G. (1714). *The monadology*. In *Leibniz: Basic Works*. Trans. R. Ariew and D. Garber. Indianapolis: Hackett, 1989.

Lycan, W. (1987). *Consciousness*. Cambridge, MA: MIT Press.

MacDonald, J., and McGurk, H. (1978). Visual influences on speech perception processes. *Perception and Psychophysics, 24*, 253–257.

Madigan, S. (1969). Intraserial repetition and coding processes in free recall. *Journal of Verbal Learning and Verbal Behavior, 8,* 828–835.

Marr, D. (1982). *Vision.* New York: Freeman.

Moore, E. (1956). Gedanken experiments on sequential machines. In C. Shannon and J. McCarthy, eds., *Automata studies,* Princeton: Princeton University Press.

Newell, A. (1990). *Unified theories of cognition* Cambridge, MA: Harvard University Press.

Pinker, S., and Prince, A. (1989). Rules and connections in human Language. In R. Morris, ed., *Parallel distributed processing.* Oxford: Oxford University Press.

Putnam, H. (1965). Craig's theorem. *Journal of Philosophy, 62,* 251–259.

Pylyshyn, Z. (1979). The rate of "mental rotation" of images: A test of a holistic analogue hypothesis. *Memory and Cognition, 7,* 19–28.

Pylyshyn, Z. (1982). *Computation and cognition.* Cambridge, MA: MIT Press.

Rumelhart, D., and McClelland, J. (1986). On learning the past tenses of English verbs. In J. McClelland, D. E. Rumelhart, and the PDP Research Group, eds., *Parallel distributed processing.* Vol. 2. Cambridge, MA: MIT Press.

Salmon, W. (1998). *Causality and explanation.* New York: Oxford University Press.

Searle, J. (1980). Minds, brains, and programs. *Behavioral and Brain Sciences, 3,* 417–424.

Searle, J. (1992). *The rediscovery of mind.* Cambridge, MA: MIT Press.

Smolensky, P., LeGendre, G., and Miyata, Y. (1992). *Principles for an integrated connectionist/symbolic theory of higher cognition.* Technical Report 92-08. Boulder, CO: University of Colorado, Institute of Cognitive Science.

Stich, S. (1983). *From folk psychology to cognitive science: The case against belief.* Cambridge, MA: MIT Press.

Ungerleider, L., and Mishkin, M. (1982). Two cortical visual systems. In D. J. Ingles, ed., *Analysis of visual behavior.* Cambridge, MA: MIT Press.

Twisted Tales: Causal Complexity and Cognitive Scientific Explanation

Andy Clark

6.1 Complexity and Explanation

Recent work in biology (e.g., Oyama 1985; Johnston 1988; Gifford 1990; Goodwin 1995), cognitive science (see Thelen and Smith 1994; Elman et al. 1996; Kelso 1994; Port and van Gelder 1995; Steels 1994; Maes 1994; Resnick 1994; and Boden 1996), economics (see esp. Arthur 1990; see also Clark 1997a), cognitive anthropology (see Hutchins 1995), and philosophy (see Varela, Thompson, and Rosch 1991; Griffiths 1992; van Gelder 1995; van Gelder and Port 1995; Sterelny 1995; Dennett 1995, chaps. 5, 8; Godfrey-Smith 1996; and Clark 1997b) displays an increasing sensitivity to what might be termed *complex causation*. Complex causation obtains when some phenomenon of interest appears to depend on a much wider and more tangled web of causal influences than we might have hoped or imagined. Thus, although all causation is arguably complex, it is certainly the case that we can discover that, in a given instance (say, the explanation of mature form in certain biological organisms), the relevant causal web is much broader and more multifactored than it once appeared. Such a web (we shall see examples in section 6.2) may actively involve both internal factors, such as genetic influences, external factors, such as environmental influences and basic laws of form, and extended processes of reciprocal interaction in which some factors both modify and are modified by the action of the others (see Varela, Thompson, and Rosch 1991; van Gelder and Port 1995; and Clark 1997b).

Complex causal webs have, of late, figured in a number of arguments designed to put pressure on familiar explanatory constructs. Target constructs include the notions of "inner programs," "genes for," and "internal representations." Thus Thelen and Smith (1994, xix) argue that action and cognition are not to be explained by reference to genetic blueprints or programs because these emerge from the interactions of multiple forces spanning brain, body, and world; as a result, "there is order, direction, and structure . . . but there is no design [nor] program in the genes." Elman et al. (1996, 351) argue, for similar reasons, that "it is more useful to view genes as catalysts rather than codes or programs"; they go on to promote a multifactor, highly interactionist view as an alternative to the widespread idea that we are born with innate knowledge concerning grammar, physics, theory of mind, and so on (pp. 357–396). Perhaps most ambitiously of all, the multiple and complex interactive relations that characterize real-world, real-time activity have been seen by some as threatening the internal programs and computations in the cognitive scientific explanation of action. The leading idea here is that "the relation between nervous system and environment is one of influence of dynamics rather than specification of state" (Wheeler 1994, 40) may afflict the inner organization itself to the extent that it becomes fruitless or impossible to try to see "the causal interactions between . . . modules as representation-passing communications." Traditional explanatory models, according to these arguments, underrate the extent to which action is structured by the continuous interplay of multiple (inner and outer) forces. Hence the appeal, to many theorists, of the dynamical systems perspective that depict "complexes of parts or aspects . . . all evolving in a continuous, simultaneous and mutually determining fashion" (van Gelder and Port 1995, 13).

There is much that is true and important in all these claims and arguments. Some of the detailed disputes I comment on elsewhere (see, for example, Clark 1997b; Clark and Wheeler 1999). The present focus, however, is much more narrow. I shall examine just one aspect of the arguments, namely, the (putative) tension between explanations that speak of "genes for," "programs for," "codes for," and so on, and the fact (assuming it is a fact) that specific outcomes depend on a multitude of subtly interacting internal and external factors and forces. The appearance of tension, I shall argue, is largely illusory and is fostered by the (explicit or tacit) acceptance of one or both of the following myths:

Myth 1: The Self-Contained Code. If some x is to be properly said to code for, program for, describe or even prescribe some outcome y, then x must constitute a detailed description of y, even when x is considered *independently* of its normal ecological backdrop.

Myth 2: Explanatory Symmetry. If the overall causal web is complex, yet x is to be cited as the cause of y, then x must be the factor that does the *most actual work* in bringing about y. Causal symmetry, by contrast, implies explanatory symmetry.

Both myths are untrue (that is why they are myths), but they are pernicious and exert a clear (often explicit—see sections 6.4 and 6.5) force on our thought and argument. The remedy for the myths is, I think, some reflection on (1) the nature of causal explanation—in particular, on the role of what I shall call the "locus of plasticity" on our intuition about causal pathways; and (2) the notion of the practical information content of a message, code or inscription.

Section 6.2 displays two examples of the kind of causal complexity at issue. Section 6.3 then canvasses some of the more challenging responses to the discovery of such complexity. Sections 6.4 and 6.5 question these responses by undermining the twin myths described above; section 6.6 presents my conclusions.

6.2   Ways of Web Making

To illustrate the kinds of complex causal webs that might confound the unwary explanation giver, our first example is borrowed from Elman et al. 1996 and displays the range of factors and interactions involved in a newly hatched chick's well-known capacity rapidly to "lock on" to, or "imprint on" a mother hen, whereas our second is taken from Thelen and Smith 1994 and involves the development of walking skills in human infants.

Example 1: Imprinting in Chicks
Newly hatched chickens rapidly become attached to the first mobile object they see. This attachment manifests itself as a tendency to follow and attend to the "imprinted" object in preference to all others. In the wild, this process of imprinting leads the chick to attach itself to a mother hen. But in the laboratory, the process can be manipulated so that the chick imprints on some other mobile object such as a moving ball or cylinder (Johnson 1997; reviewed in Johnson and Bolhuis 1991). But how, exactly, does this process work? Is it simply that the chick is "prewired" so as to fixate on the first conspicuous object it sees? That, to

be sure, is a fair description of the outcome. But the process itself turns out to involved "interactions at a number of different levels: organism-environment, brain systems, cellular and molecular" (Elman et al. 1996, 324).

To begin with, the imprinting process seems to involve two quite independent neural systems. The first, called "Conspec" by Johnson and Morton (1991), disposes the chick to prefer stimuli that fir the head and neck configuration of a similar-sized bird and mammals (Johnson and Horn 1988).The second, a learning system called "intermediate and medial hyperstriatum ventrale" (IMHV) and located in that specific region of chick forebrain, develops a representation of the highly attended object that allows the chick to recognize the object despite variations in spatial location and orientation (Johnson 1997, chap. 4; Elman et al. 1996, chap. 6). The presence of these two distinct contributory neural systems is indicated by, for example, lesion studies that show that damage to IMHV impairs preferences acquired by learning (as when a chick imprints on a rotating red box), yet does not affect the general predisposition to prefer broadly henlike stimuli (Johnson and Horn 1986; Johnson 1997, 110).

Given a normal ecological backdrop, the Conspec and IMHV systems collectively yield a powerful and robust attachment to a single attended hen. But how do they actually interact? One simple possibility is that the Conspec system acts as a kind of internal filter that selects the training data "seen" by IMHV. Further investigations, however, have shown that such internal filtering is probably not occurring (Johnson and Bolhuis 1991). Instead, the two system appear to be internally noncommunicating and to interact via a loop that involves the real-world behavior of the whole chick. Conspec, operating in a normal ecological setting, causes the whole organism (the chick) to expose itself to a heavy dose of training inputs targeted in a mother hen. IMHV has additional restrictions on the kinds of things it can learn about, requiring a mobile stimulus of a certain size before it kicks in. The combination of Conspec and IMHV, operating against a natural ecological backdrop, thus leads the chick (via a loop out into the attending behavior of the whole organism) to rapidly and robustly develop a translation-invariant representation of a mother hen.

The learning restrictions of IMHV have been speculatively explored using a connectionist model (O'Reilly and Johnson 1994) in which simple architectural biases focus on mobile stimuli and explain the fluent acquisition of a translation-invariant representation (one able to pick out an object despite variations in viewing angle and spatial operations). Although the details need not detain us (they are nicely laid out in Elman et al. 1996, 327–333, and Johnson 1997, 105–107), they involve the combination of internal positive feedback loops and Hebbian learning. The positive feedback loops cause some units active for an object in position P1 to remain active as the object moves into P2, P3, and so on. The associative learning then allows the development of top-level units that respond to the object (the co-occurring set of features) in whatever spatial location it appears. The system thus develops location-invariant object detectors. In real chicks, this learning process is linked to the expression of a particular gene (c-fos; see McCabe and Horn 1994), and is thus revealed as itself dependent on a variety of molecular level interactions.

As a final note of complexity, the Conspec system is not, in fact, active at birth but instead depends on details of early motor activity. To become active, the Conspec system requires the chick to run about freely at least a small period of time between the ages of 12 and 36 hours. Deprived of such motor activity, Conspec lies dormant and the learning system operates alone, without the benefit of the behavior-based input selection mechanism[1].

Summary Chick imprinting involves the subtle interplay of such diverse factors as the statistical regularities in the chicks visual experience; the presence of motor activity triggering Conspec; the organism-level behavioral effects of Conspec in operation; the genetic bases of IMHV and Conspec; and the nature of the ecologically normally hatching environment (see Johnson 1997, 116; Elman et al. 1996, 332). The "simple" phenomenon of filial imprinting in chicks thus turns on a twisted tale in which "multiple sources of constraints, both from within levels and from other levels (molecular, organism-environment, etc.), ensure a particular outcome: a spatially invariant representation of the mother hen" (Elman et al. 1996, 332).

Example 2: Learning to Walk

Consider the process of learning to walk, a process that now appears to involve a complex series of interactions between neural states, the spring-like properties of leg muscles, and local environmental factors (I address this case in greater detail in Clark 1997b). Learning to walk as "soft assembly" (Thelen and Smith 1994, 60) is contrasted with learning to walk as the temporally staged expression of a prior set of instructions encoded in, for example, a genetically specified central pattern generator or neural control system (Thelen and Smith 1994, 8–20, 263–266). In place of a single, privileged, inner or genetic cause, Thelen and Smith (1994, 17) display a multidimensional interaction process in which "the organic components and the context are equally causal and privileged."

Evidence for the multifactor view comes from a variety of striking experiments in which

• Stepping motions are induced in "nonstepping" infants by holding the baby upright in warm water
• Nonstepping seven-month-olds held upright on a motorized treadmill perform coordinated alternating stepping motions (even compensating for twin belts driving each leg at different speeds)

Such results (see Thelen and Smith 1994, chaps. 1, 4) show that stepping is not under the control of a simple inner variable. Bodily parameters, such as leg weight, which is effectively manipulated by partial immersion in water, and environment factors, such as the presence of the treadmill, also play a role. In the case of the treadmill, further experiments revealed that the crucial factor was the orientation of leg and foot to the treadmill. Infants who made flat-footed contact with the belt exhibited treadmill stepping, whereas those who made only toe contact failed to step. Thelen and Smith (1994, 111–112) hypothesize that the infant leg, when stretched out, acts like a spring. At full back stretch, the spring coils up and swings the leg forward. Flat-footed belt contact may precociously ensure this full back stretch and hence initiate stepping. Relative flexor or extensor tendencies in the legs thus contribute heavily to the emergence of coordinated stepping (p. 113).

Summary Infant stepping behavior depends on the precise balance of interplay of a variety of factors including: the weight of the legs; the "relative flexor (very tight) or extensor (more loose) tendencies of the legs" (Thelen and Smith 1994, 113); and whatever central neural structures are implicated in the motor control process itself. Stepping behavior thus "emerges only when the central elements cooperate with the effectors— the muscles, joints, tendons—in the appropriate physical context" (p. 113).

6.3 Webware: Seeds, Catalysts, Modifiers, and Control Parameters

What kinds of explanatory stories should we tell to make best sense of cases involving complex and heterogeneous causal webs? One widespread negative response goes like this. Whatever stories we tell, they must not involve the isolation of "privileged elements," or give "ontological priority" to any particular strands in the web (see, for example, Thelen and Smith 1994, 17, 580; Elman et al. 1996, chap. 6; van Gelder and Port 1995, 13; for the same claims made in a more purely genetic context, see also Kelso 1995, 183; Goodwin 1995, 119; and Oyama 1985).

The belief that no element in the causal web is in any sense privileged rapidly leads to skepticism concerning types of understanding or model that depict certain elements (be they in the genes or in the actual neural circuitry) as inner programs for the production of certain behaviors. In extreme cases this translates into skepticism concerning the very idea of internal representations (for discussion, see Clark and Toribio 1994; Clark 1997a, 1997b). More obviously, it translates into wariness concerning the idea of (usually inner) elements acting as codes, recipes, blueprints, prescriptions, descriptions, sets of instruments, and so on (see, for example, Thelen and Smith 1994, xix, 9, 33, 83, 112; Elman et al. 1996, 350–352).

Such negativity accrues an obligation. How else are we to comprehend the natural genesis of form and behavior? The general tendency, at this point, is to favor accounts that invoke multiple interactions and biases and that depict form and behavior as emergent properties of the overall causal mesh. The case of genetic determination provides a nice example. The image of the gene (or genes) as directly coding for specific morphological or behavioral outcomes is now universally accepted as a simplification (at best). Genes (as we shall see in greater detail in section 6.5) bring about their effects via an extended sequence of interactive processes. These may include local chemical interactions, basic physical laws governing the emergence of form (see, for example, Goodwin 1995 on "morphogenetic fields") and the complex interplay between development and environ-mental factors (such as the use of ambient temperature to determine the sex of Mississippi alligators, or the more complex and extended example of the chick imprinting mechanism). In such cases, the relation between the genes and the final product is mediated by multiple types and levels of interaction (see esp. Elman et al. 1996, chap. 6). Such mediation, it is argued, works against the notion of the genes as codes, programs, algorithms, descriptions, or prescriptions. Instead, we should think of genes as being more like "catalysts" (Elman et al. 1996, 351), "seeds" (Goodwin 1995, 16), or "modifiers" (Goodwin 1995, 144). In support of the "genes-as-catalysts-not-programs" view, Elman et al. (1996, 351) argue that "programs are (more or less) informationally self-contained. Catalysts, on the other hand, are embedded in an environment of natural laws and processes." A catalyst, they note, is individually inert. Alone, it does nothing. But place it in a certain context (e.g., a vat of chemicals), and it can ensure an outcome that would otherwise not occur. Thus the presence of a gene may produce an enzyme that speeds up a reaction. The gene does not "define the conditions for reaction"—that is left to the laws of biochemistry. Instead, the genes "harness those laws by ensuring that critical components are present at the right time and then nudging the reaction forward" (pp. 351–352).

Why not count the gene as, if not a full blueprint, at least a program—an algorithm for bringing about a certain effect? The reason is that programs are said to be informationally self-contained. Thus Elman et al. (1996, 351) argue that "one can examine a program and—looking only at the code—make a reasonable guess about what it will do. This is not possible with genetic material. The relationship between DNA nase triples and amino acids may be direct; but the assembly of amino acids into proteins, the timing of when specific genes are expressed and the effect of a gene's products are highly context-sensitive."

Genes, on the other hand, are not informationally self-contained. Taken alone, their information content (like that of a catalyst) is zero (p. 351). But taken in context, the information content explodes: it becomes "potentially enormous, embracing whatever 'information' there is in the environment" (p. 351).

This discussion of the "information content" of some part of an extended causal process (in this case, the part is a gene, but that is not essential) is both problematic and revealing. It displays an important widespread confusion centered on the unattainable grail of "informational self-containment." Unraveling this confusion is the task of section 6.4. For the present, however, notice how easily this kind of vision carries over to the developmental cases rehearsed in section 6.2. The neural system Conspec cannot, on its own, account for chick imprinting. But placed in the rich context of the effects of Conspec on whole organism behavior, the learning profile of IMHV and the natural, mother-hen-rich hatching environment, Conspec effectively catalyzes the learning process. By extension, the genetic bases of Conspec function (via a further series of interactions) to ensure that this bias is present and hence—via an extended sequence of environment-exploiting interactions—act to ensure successful imprinting (keeping all the other factors fixed). Thus "dependence on interactions is repeated at successively higher levels of organization" (Elman et al. 1996, 351).

Such dependence on interactions is also at the root of Thelen and Smith's insistence (1994, 17) that (in the stepping example described in section 6.2) there is "no essence of locomotion either in the motor cortex on the spinal cord. Indeed, it would be equally credible to assign the essence of walking to the treadmill [as] to a neural structure. . . ." Much in the spirit of Elman et al.'s notion of the gene as catalyst, Thelen and Smith (1994, 112) argue that flexor tone (the relative tightness or "give" in the infant's legs) is acting as a "control parameter" that acts so as to "engender the shift into stable alternate stepping," and "as a control parameter, flexor tone constrain[s] the interacting elements but [does] not prescribe the outcome in a privileged way."

Finally, consider Elman et al.'s argument (1996) against the idea that innate knowledge underpins our capacities to rapidly learn about grammar, physics, other minds, and so on. In briefest outline, the argument is that nature looks to rely not on detailed prespecifications of "fine-grained patterns of cortical connectivity" (p. 360) but on the provision of a variety of simpler biases involving architecture (neuron types, numbers of layers, connectivity between whole brain regions) and timing (waves of synaptic growth and loss, relative development of sensory systems, etc.; see Elman et al. 1996, table 1.3, p. 35). These biases lead, in environmental and developmental context to the organisms exhibiting specific skills, forms and behaviors, including, for example, the robust acquisition of grammatical knowledge. We are thus innately predisposed to learn a grammar, but in a way that falls short of requiring the innate prespecification of actual grammatical knowledge[2]. Instead, constraints at the levels of timing and architecture, in collaboration with environmental inputs, inexorably nudge the system toward the target knowledge. In such a case, we are told, "the knowledge itself . . . would not be innate and would require appropriate interactions to develop" (Elman et al. 1996, 364).

All these arguments and assertions demand attention in their own right. They all draw our attention to the sheer complexity and hetero-geneity of the causal webs that underlie various phenomena of scientific interest. In the context of the present project, however, I want to focus attention on just one common thread: the tendency to cite causal complexity and the important role of repeated interactions as a reason to eschew talk of specific states or items as prescribing, programming, or coding for specific outcomes. Call this the "inference to egalitarianism." I believe this inference is false, and for two fairly profound reasons. The reasons center first (section 6.4) on the problematic notions of self-containment and informational content, and second (section 6.5) on the difference between invoking a cause and unpacking the workings of a complex system.

6.4   The Myth of the Self-Contained Code

The first reason to be wary (of the inference to egalitarianism) concerns the putative contrast between genuine programs (codes, recipes, etc.) and factors that bring about effects only in the context of a rich backdrop of contributory processes and interactions. The contrast is explicit in Elman et al.'s characterization (1996, 351) of programs as being "(more or less) informationally self-contained." This claim, as far as I can see, is simply false. A program, in any ordinary sense of the word, is far from being a self-contained repository of all the information necessary to solve a problem. Think, for example, of a standard program written in a language such as LISP. LISP lets you store a list (say (*abc*)) then add new items using operators such as cons (concatenate). The input (cons *d* (*abc*)) adds *d* to the head of the list yielding (*dabc*). You can also use functions such as (first) and (rest) to remove items from the lists (see, for example, Franklin 1995, 151, or any LISP textbook).

The point to notice is just that the operation of these functions—on which the success of every real LISP program depends—is by no stretch of the imagination even "more or less" given as part of any actual program written in LISP. Instead, like the operating system firmware the functions work only due to the "ecologically normal" backdrop against which a LISP program brings about its effects. The program—at least as we commonly use the term—does not itself specify exactly how to bring about these effects. Instead, to put it in the kind of terminology used for the cases examined earlier, it constitutes just one factor that (in the special context of a computing device set up to compile or interpret such programs) will reliably lead the overall system to discover a solution to the target problem.

Because ordinary computer programs are not informationally self-contained, the fact that the genes, for example, do not contain all the information needed to describe a biological organism cannot, in and of itself, constitute a reason to reject talk of genes as programming for certain traits, behaviors, or outcomes. Likewise, the fact that neural events are just one factor among many whose combined activity yields stepping behavior cannot, in and of itself, constitute a reason for rejecting the idea of motor programs. In each case, the factor invoked (genes or motor programs) may be regarded as coding for a specific outcome *on the assumption* that such ecologically normal backdrop prevails.

This point is forcefully made by Dennett (1995) in a discussion of the complexities of the genome-organism relation. Dennett notes that DNA constitutes a most indirect manner of "instructing" the process of building a phenotypic body because much of the necessary information is not given in the DNA itself but only in the combination of DNA and a set of environmental conditions. But, Dennett argues, even in the case of a library (universally accepted as being a "storehouse of information") it is "really only libraries-plus-readers that preserve and store information" (p. 197). Likewise DNA codes for organismic features only in the context of an environment capable of "reading" the DNA. The code can do its work only against a certain backdrop. To take a homely example (p. 197): "Every time you make sure that your dishrag gets properly dry in between uses, you break the chain of environmental continuity (e.g., loss of moisture) that is part of the informational background presupposed by the DNA of the bacteria in the dishrag whose demise you seek."

The DNA codes for specific outcomes only in a context that includes both reliable local chemical reactions and wider environmental contingencies (such as moisture). Without this extended "reading system," DNA sequences, Dennett notes, "don't specify anything at all." Yet this rampant presumptiveness should not, he argues, prohibit us from speaking of, say, genes for *x*. For a gene may be "for *x*" in the simple sense that it is a feature whose presence or absence is a difference that makes a systematic (usually population-level) difference to the presence (or absence) of x (see Dennett 1995, 116–117; Dawkins 1982, 23). We shall return to this point in section 6.5.

What, then, of the notion of informational self-containment itself? We are, I think, quite properly pulled in two directions. On the one hand, we might like to say that by keeping a certain ecological backdrop constant, we can legitimately speak of information about biological form being "given in the DNA." This, after all, is no worse than supposing that the books in the library (keeping the human reader constant) contain information about architecture, plumbing, and so on. Nor is it worse than saying that a certain LISP program contains the information needed to solve a given problem. On the other hand, we should not thereby be blinded to how very much the finished product depends on a wider variety of other factors and forces. It is in this sense that, for example, the quantity of information encoded in the genome falls spectacularly short of what would be needed to describe the organism. There is, in short, a conflict between the simple, quantitative measures of information used in information theory and the effective information content that can be carried by a force or structure able to piggyback on (or assume) a certain reading system or a certain context of effect. The apparent mismatch between quantitative information theory and semantics is, of course, well known. What is emerging here is the extent to which that mismatch may be rooted in the way some bearers of content (such as messages) trade on assumptions concerning contexts and readers.

Cohen and Stewart (1994) drive this home using a simple thought experiment. Suppose you are told, "If I don't phone you tonight, Aunt Gertie will be arriving on the 4:10 train from Chattanooga. Take her home." That evening, you receive no phone call. The null event (of your not receiving a call) "conveys a sizable quantity of information with a zero-bit message" (p. 353). Maybe, the authors note, we really have a one-bit message here (one on/off choice). But the moral is unaffected: a complex set of events is reliably set in motion by a sparse signal—a signal that nonetheless effectively conveys a rich content. By contrast, a bare television screen caption that reads "Call 1-800-666-7777" conveys an effective content comprising just 36 bits of information (11 decimal digits). Yet the information-theoretic measure of the television signal is very much higher: it must specify the activity of 100 lines, each involving 1,000 phosphate dots and capable of exhibiting these different colors. The signal thus constitutes (from this perspective) an 800,000-bit message (see Cohen and Stewart 1994, 353).

We are thus led to a contrast between what I am calling the "effective content" of a message and its information-theoretic measure. Effective content, as in the case of the null telephone message, is revealed as a thoroughly context-dependent phenomenon and one that depends on somehow "triggering" the access of information from a specific range of possibilities" (Cohen and Stewart 1994, 353). Information about this range of possibilities lies not in the triggering signal but in the receiver, reader, or environment in which it has its effects. This we have now seen, is true not just of DNA (see Cohen and Stewart 1994, 354, for parallel genetic examples) and neural structures but of words in library books, standard LISP programs—in fact, just about every case where we would talk of one set of items as *coding for* something else. Cohen and Stewart (pp. 354–355) sum it up well:

the meaning in a language does not reside in the code [but] stems from the existence of a shared context. For language, the context is the culture shared by those who speak that language. For the DNA message, the context is biological development . . . all messages in the real world that really are messages happen within a context. That context may be evolutionary, chemical, biological, neurological, linguistic or technological, but it transforms the question of information-content beyond measure. . . .

The observation that chemical factors and rich environmental interactions play a crucial role in bringing about certain effects thus cannot, in and of itself, constitute a good reason to reject the image of genes or inner neural structure as coding for, prescribing, or programming those effects. For rich context dependence is always the rule, even in mundane and unproblematic uses of the notions of program, code, and message. The putative contrast with a fully context-independent way of embodying meaning is misguided: the self-contained code is a myth.

6.5 The Myth of Explanatory Symmetry

The inference to egalitarianism has, however, a second string to its bow. For in designating some factor x as coding for, or programming, an outcome y, we are treating x as somehow special. For we want to say that x codes for y, whereas the ecological backdrop provides the "reading environment" relative to which x bears its effective content. But whence this asymmetry? Could we not equally well depict the environmental factor as coding for y and the other factor (be it genetic or neural) as the backdrop against which these bear the effective contents they do? At which point, the whole value of treating one type of factor as coding for or programming the outcome seems to be called into question. Why not just admit that we are confronting a complex causal web whose combined activity yields the outcome, seek to understand as much as we can of the web itself, and leave it at that? Such, I think, is the thrust of Thelen and Smith's injunctions (1994) against "privileged elements" and of Elman et al.'s suggestion (1996, 321) that we focus attention not on components but on the "complex web of interactions." It is also the explicit moral of Oyama's influential work (1985) on the explanation of biological form, which claims that we must give up the practice of assigning priority to either internal or external factors and forces and instead focus on the interactions themselves as primary objects of study.

I must tread gently here, for I believe that there is something overwhelmingly *right* about these ideas and strictures. If we want to understand how the outcome comes about, the proper explanatory strategy is indeed to confront the complex interactive process as a whole. In the course of such a confrontation, we may sometimes discover that, in terms of actual work done (measured as the degree of control exerted over the final product), the factors that I have been lumping together as the "ecological backdrop" in fact carry the bulk of the explanatory burden. This might be the case if, for example, the production of a certain biological form is heavily determined by basic laws of physics and chemistry and the genetic material simply "seeds" the process (see, for example, Goodwin 1995 on "morphogenesis"; or Kauffman 1993).

But our explanatory attention is not always limited to the project of understanding how the effects come about. Sometimes, at least, we seek to understand *why* they come about. And it is here that we may begin to break the apparent causal symmetry that would depict all factors on an essentially even footing.

Thus consider a paradigmatic case of genetic disease, phenylketonuria, known as PKU disease, which causes mental retardation, shortness of stature, and lack of pigment (Gifford 1990, 333):

the normal gene at the PKU locus produces the liver enzyme phenylalanine hydroxylase, which is requires for the metabolism of the amino acid phenylalanine into tyrosine. Individuals homozygous for the PKU gene cannot produce this enzyme. If one's diet contains the normal amount of phenylalanine, the serum level of phenylalanine rises dramatically. This interferes with the production of myelin, the protective sheath of nerve cells in the brain. But these effects are avoided if a diet low in phenylalanine is provided and this is what is done for therapy.

Gifford notes the interesting consequence: this disease can be avoided or cured by a simple environmental manipulation. Although is a joint effect of the abnormal gene and the diet, PKU disease is classed as a paradigmatic genetic problem. Why? Gifford's suggestion, one endorsed in various forms by both Dawkins (1982, 23) and Dennett (1995, 116), is that we are thereby drawing attention to the fact that the diet is a common factor in the base population, whereas the PKU gene is not. Relative to the base population, it is the *gene* that makes the difference (Dennett 1995, 116), even though the workload (the causal etiology of the disease) is spread between genetic and environmental factors, and even though the outcome is thus fully manipulable by nongenetic means. The answer to the "why" question (Why did that person develop PKU disease?) thus isolates the genetic factors as especially relevant. But the answer to the "how" question (How does PKU disease arise?) implicates genetic and environmental factors essentially on even footing.

The cost of this maneuver is clear enough. Change the normal environmental conditions and what was once a genetic disease becomes an environmentally induced problem. This is because the "why" question is always framed against a fixed background. Gifford thus noted (following Burian 1981) that in the hypothetical case of a population whose normal diet (unlike our own) is low in phenylalanine, the very same causal story would be classed as a case of environmentally induced disease. For the locus of relevant plasticity (as I shall say) then lies not in the genes but in the diet: it would be those (rare) individuals who are both homozygous for the PKU gene and consume high amounts of phenylalanine that fall ill, whereas the genetic factors alone (being homozygous for the PKU gene) would not normally lead—in that population—to the development of the disease. What counts as genetic thus depends "not only on the causal processes in the individual, but also on a fact external to this: the causal factors shared in the population" (Gifford 1990, 334). Such relativity to a contextual baseline is, however, exactly what we should expect given our earlier discussion of the close relation between effective content and an assumed ecological backdrop. The context relativity in no way impugns the correctness (relative to the actual population and environment) of singling out the PKU gene as especially relevant in the production of the disease. What we must not do, of course, is allow this fact to blind us to the full causal picture and hence to the possibility of an environmental cure for the disease itself.

Explanatory priority in a given context thus turns not on what factor, if any, does the greatest amount of actual work but on what *makes the difference* between the cases where the outcome obtains and those where it does not. This is the natural explanatory concomitant of the idea (section 6.4) of detailed effective contents being conveyed by simple (but context-exploiting) physical transactions. In the genetic case, we can take this a step further by noticing that genetic material is naturally "designed" to function as a primary locus of plasticity—it is the *natural* function of the genetic material (relative to an assumed ecological backdrop) to make a specific organism-level difference. In this vein, Sterelny (1995) argues that the genome *represents* developmental outcomes because it is its evolved function to bring about those outcomes. The fact that this bringing about involves multiple gene-environment interactions does not undermine the description of the genome as a representation because "representation depends not on correlation but function" (p. 165). The correlations may be messy and indirect. But the function shines through and is the source of the explanatory asymmetry between genome and environment. Both factors correlate equally with developmental outcomes, but they play asymmetric roles. For example (p. 165):

Snow gums have a different growth pattern in environments in which they are exposed to wind and snow. Both the triggering environment and the snow gum genome are necessary for the gums' response to climatic adversity. But one element of the developmental matrix—the genome—exists only because of its role in the production of the plant phenotype. That is why it has the function of producing that phenotype and hence why it represents that phenotype. So an informational idea of a replicator can be preserved.

The extension of the line on explanatory priority to the case of neural codes and programs is immediate. Here too we should say that a neural structure or process x codes for a behavioral outcome y, if against a normal ecological backdrop, it makes the difference with respect to the obtaining of y. A neural event may thus code for a behavior (say, reaching out an arm) even if the outcome depends equally on a variety of bodily and environmental factors such as the force of gravity and the springlike qualities of arm muscles. For such factors are the ecologically normal backdrop against which the neural state was selected to bring about its effects.[3]

Notice, finally, that this criterion does not simply beg the question in favor of inner or genetic states. Instead, it invites us to keep constant the stabilities and features of the normal ecological backdrop and to focus attention (for the purposes of answering the "why" question) on the locus of plasticity: the place to which differences in the outcome (in the normal context) are best referred. As the extended information-processing resources of biological brains increasingly parasitize and exploit the environment, this primary explanatory locus may sometimes tend to shift outward (see Hutchins 1995; Dennett, 1995; chaps. 12, 13; Kirsh and Maglio 1995). Such complexities, however, are best left for another occasion (see Clark 1997b; Clark (1997c) chap. 10; Clark and Chalmers 1998).

The observation that the real workload involved in bringing about some effect may be evenly spread between allegedly "privileged" factors (genes and neural events) and other influences (environmental, chemical, bodily) cannot, I conclude, in and of itself, constitute a good reason to reject the practice of treating certain factors as special: as coding for, programming, or prescribing the outcome in question. It cannot do so because the relevant asymmetry lies not in the causal chain itself but in the extent to which difference with respect to that outcome, within a baseline population and ecological setting, may be traced to difference in the privileged item. If our goal is to explain those observed differences, we may properly single out a few threads in the complex causal weave. If our project is to understand exactly how the outcome is produced, we must attend instead to the full intricacies of the woven whole.[4]

6.6   Conclusion: Living in Complexity

Life is terrifyingly complex. Things interrelate in deep and often desperately confusing ways. Yet adrift in this dizzying whirlpool of causal flow, we heroically succeed in *making things happen*. When we do so, it is not because we are the self-contained repository of the desired outcome. Nor is it (usually) because we command a detailed description of how to manipulate all the causal chains that link us to our goal. Instead, it is because our strategies have been learned and tuned against a backdrop of culture and physical and social laws and practices. Our strategies take this

complex backdrop for granted and manipulate the flow of events by pig-
gybacking on these unremarked currents in the causal nexus.

In this one respect, at least, life, words, programs, and genes are all
fellow travelers. They all bring about their effects by working within a
complex and extended causal fabric. It is the distinctive virtue of much
recent work in biology, anthropology, and cognitive science (e.g., Goodwin
1995; Hutchins 1995; Elman et al. 1996; Thelen and Smith 1994; Clark
1997c) to begin to recognize the extent and impact of this causal complexity and heterogeneity. Such recognition, however, should not be seen
as a threat to explanatory strategies that invoke notions such as coding for,
programming, or prescribing specific behavioral or morphological outcomes. The illusion of such a threat is, I have argued, linked to the explicit
or tacit endorsement of two (interrelated) myths. The first is the myth of
the self-contained code: the belief that to really code for (or program, or
prescribe) an outcome, an entity must contain within itself a detailed
description of the outcome. This myth is flatly incompatible with any
normal use of the notions of program, code, and message. The second is
the myth of explanatory symmetry: the belief that the practice of treating
certain causal threads using the special terms of codes, programs, and contents cannot be justified if the actual workload is evenly spread between
a wide variety of factors and forces. This belief fails, however, to allow for
the fact that our explanation-giving practice often involves not the simple
measurement of causal work but the (context-and-backdrop-relative)
assessment of the locus of plasticity or differentiation. Which is to say, we
judge that observed differences are best explained by keeping a certain
background fixed and asking what differences then *make the difference*
among the ordinary population.[5] Causal equality at one level (the level of
"work done") may thus coexist with genuine asymmetry at another level
(the level of greatest relevant plasticity). Teleological approaches (such as
Sterelny's story about the snow gum) add a further consideration, namely,
that many privileged loci play the special functional role of existing so as
to support such plasticity. The point, in both cases, is that causal equality
need not imply explanatory symmetry.

Puncturing the twin myths blocks any direct inference from facts
about causal complexity to the rejection of notions such as inner codes,
programs, instructions, or prescriptions.[6] It also casts doubt on arguments
against innate knowledge that depend on contrasting highly interaction-
dependent phenomena with self-contained storehouses of domain-specific

information (see Clark 1998). For it suggests that the basic notion of a state's bearing a specific content is fully compatible with the need to place the state in a rich ecologically context, a context that acts as the assumed backdrop of the original encoding. The same point, substituting "internal representation" for "innate knowledge," can be made against recent attempts to stress organism-environment interactions in (apparent) opposition to reliance on internal representations (see Clark 1997b).

Moving even further afield, the present treatment may perhaps suggest a somewhat conciliatory angle on the internalism-externalism debate in the philosophy of mind (see, for example, Putnam 1975; Burge 1979). For a purely inner state may be said to bear a certain effective content, even thought the actual causal chain that determines what that content is now extends far outside the agent's head. The content is thus referred to the inner state, but its true physical vehicle involves a wide range of additional environmental structures and circumstances. The question of where to locate the "supervenience base" for the content thus admits no straightforward answer. The correct diagnosis is just that the inner state itself bears the effective content but in a way that cannot help but assume an extended ecological backdrop.[7]

There is much that remains unclear and problematic in all these debates, and I do not claim to have done much more than scratch the surface here. The essential point is perhaps this: that the discussion underlines just how badly we still understand the apparently foundational notion of the information content of a physical state and how very hard it is to take ecological context as seriously as we surely must. Yet it is in the balance of these two slippery factors that mind finds its place in the natural world. Like cheap detectives we follow gingerly in its wake.

Notes

1. It is speculated that the motor activity increases testosterone levels, which in turn activate Conspec (see Horn 1985; Elman et al. 1996, 326).

2. There is also a danger of confusing the (clearly correct) observation that the nature of grammatical knowledge was not fully specified in advance of learning with the (more contentious) claim that the innate endowment involves no grammatical knowledge (properly so called) whatsoever. It is not part of the present project to engage the argument at that level (but see Clark 1998).

3. I pursue this case in detail in Clark 1997b using the idea of a partial program: a notion that aims to do justice both to the intuition that effective content trades heavily

on assumed context and that the work directly specified by the neural command may often be substantially less than we had imagined.

4. Elman et al. (1996) are pretty clearly engaged in precisely this latter project. It is not so clear, however, that the ambitions of those who postulate certain forms of innate knowledge are the same. It is for this reason, I believe, that some of the criticisms leveled by Elman et al. tend to miss their mark.

5. This is, of course, related to the old idea of a contrast class underlying causal explanations. For a useful discussion, with a special focus on "why" questions, see van Fraassen 1980, chap. 5.

6. I add the qualification "direct" because I believe other arguments outside the scope of the present treatment do indeed cause trouble for our familiar explanatory styles. See Clark 1997b.

7. Dennett (1995, 409–412) develops an account that looks similar to this. For more on the notion of an extended supervenience base, see Clark and Chalmers (1998).

References

Arthur, B. (1990). Positive feedbacks in the economy. *Scientific American, 92* (February), 99.

Boden, M., ed. (1996). *The philosophy of artificial life.* Oxford: Oxford University Press.

Burge, T. (1979). Individualism and the mental. *Midwest Studies in Philosophy, 4,* 73–122.

Burian, R. (1981). Sociobiology and genetic determinism. *Philosophical Forum, 13,* 43–66.

Clark, A. (1997a). Economic reason: The interplay of individual learning and external structure. In J. Drobak, ed., *The frontiers of the new institutional economics.* San Diego, CA: Academic Press.

Clark, A. (1997b). The dynamical challenge. *Cognitive Science, 21,* 461–484.

Clark, A. (1997c). *Being there: Putting brain, body and world together again.* Cambridge, MA: MIT Press.

Clark, A. (1998). What's knowledge anyway? *Mind and Language, 13,* 571–575.

Clark, A., and Chalmers, D. (1998). The extended mind. *Analysis, 58,* 7–19.

Clark, A., and Toribio, J. (1994). Doing without representing? *Synthèse, 101,* 401–431.

Clark, A., and Wheeler, M. (1999). Genic representation: Reconciling content and causal complexity. *British Journal for the Philosophy of Science 50,* 103–136.

Cohen, J., and Stewart, I. (1994). *The collapse of chaos.* London: Penguin.

Dawkins, R. (1982). *The extended phenotype.* Oxford: Oxford University Press.

Dennett, D. (1995). *Darwin's dangerous idea.* New York: Simon and Schuster.

Elman, J., Bates, E., Johnson, M., Karmiloff-Smith, A., Parisi, D., and Plunkett, K., eds. (1996). *Re-thinking innateness: A connectionist perspective on development.* Cambridge, MA: MIT Press.

Franklin, S. (1995). *Artificial minds*. Cambridge, MA: MIT Press.

Gifford, F. (1990). Genetic traits. *Biology and Philosophy, 5,* 327–347.

Godfrey-Smith, P. (1996). *Complexity and the function of mind in nature.* Cambridge: Cambridge University Press.

Goodwin, B. (1995). *How the leopard changed its spots.* London: Phoenix.

Gray, R. (1992). The death of the gene. In P. Griffith, ed., *Trees of life: Essays in the philosophy of biology.* Dordrecht: Kluwer.

Griffiths, P., ed. (1992). *Trees of life: Essays in the philosophy of biology.* Dordrecht: Kluwer.

Horn, G. (1985). *Memory, imprinting and the brain.* Oxford: Clarendon Press.

Hutchins, E. (1995). *Cognition in the wild.* Cambridge, MA: MIT Press.

Johnson, M. (1997). *Developmental cognitive neuroscience.* Oxford: Blackwell.

Johnson, M., and Bolhuis, J. (1991). Imprinting predispositions and filial preference in the chick. In R. Andrew, ed., *Neural and behavioral plasticity.* Oxford: Oxford University Press.

Johnson, M., and Horn, G. (1986). Dissociation of recognition memory and associative learning by a restricted lesion of the chick forebrain. *Neuropsychology, 24,* 329–340.

Johnson, M., and Horn, G. (1988). The Development of filial preferences in the dark-reared child. *Animal Behavior, 36,* 675–683.

Johnson, M., and Morton, J. (1991). *Biology and cognitive development: The case of face recognition.* Oxford: Blackwell.

Johnston, T. (1988). Developmental explanation and the ontogeny of birdsong: Nature/nurture redux. *Behavioral and Brain Sciences, 11,* 617–663.

Kauffman, S. (1993). *The origins of order.* Oxford: Oxford University Press.

Kelso, J. A. (1995). *Dynamic patterns.* Cambridge, MA: MIT Press.

Kirsh, D., and Maglio, P. (1995). On distinguishing epistemic from pragmatic action. *Cognitive Science, 18,* 513–549.

Maes, P. (1994). Modeling adaptive autonomous agents. *Artificial Life, 1,* 135–162.

McCabe, B., and Horn, G. (1994). Learning-related changes in fos-like immunoreactivity in the chick forebrain after imprinting. *Proceedings of the National Academy of Sciences, U.S.A., 91,* 11417–11421.

O'Reilly, R., and Johnson, M. (1994). Object Recognition and sensitive periods: A computational analysis of visual imprinting. *Neural Computation, 6,* 357–390.

Oyama, S. (1985). *The ontogeny of information: Developmental systems and evolution.* Cambridge: Cambridge University Press.

Port, R., and Gelder, T.V., eds. (1995). *Mind as motion: Dynamics, behavior, and cognition.* Cambridge, MA: MIT Press.

Putnam, H. (1975). The meaning of "meaning." In H. Putnam, ed., *Mind, language and reality.* Cambridge: Cambridge University Press.

Resnick, M. (1994). *Turtles, termites and traffic Jams: Explorations in massively parallel microworlds.* Cambridge, MA: MIT Press.

Steels, L. (1994). The artificial life roots of artificial intelligence. *Artificial Life, 1,* 75–110.

Sterelny, K. (1995). Understanding life: Recent work in philosophy of biology. *British Journal for the Philosophy of Science, 46,* 155–183.

Thelen, E., and Smith, L. (1994). *A dynamic systems approach to the development of cognition and action.* Cambridge, MA: MIT Press.

van Fraasen, B. (1980). *The scientific image.* Oxford: Clarendon Press.

van Gelder, T. (1995). What might cognition be, if not computation? *Journal of Philosophy, 92,* 345–381.

van Gelder, T., and Port, R. (1995). It's about time: An overview of the dynamical approach to cognition. In R. Port and T. van Gelder, eds., *Mind as motion: Explorations in the dynamics of cognition.* Cambridge, MA: MIT Press.

Varela, F., Thompson, E., and Rosch, E. (1991). *The embodied mind.* Cambridge, MA: MIT Press.

Wheeler, M. (1994). From activation to activity. *Artificial Intelligence and the Simulation of Behavior Quarterly, 87,* 36–42.

III

The Representation of Causal Patterns

7

Bayes Nets as Psychological Models

Clark Glymour

7.1 Narrowing the Topic

What people want to know in answer to "why" questions, what satisfies them as an explanation, is hopelessly contextual. Explanatory satisfaction depends on beliefs, interests, moral sensibilities, topic, on just about everything. Why did President Kennedy die? Because brain tissue necessary for life was destroyed by a bullet, answers the autopsy; because he wanted to overthrow Castro, answers the conspiracy theorist; because his assassin was insane, answers another; because for political reasons Kennedy insisted on an open car parade, says the pundit; because God willed it, answers the theist; because he deserved to die, says the Kennedy hater. And they all might be right, although I doubt it.

Because most explanations are causal, most of the information offered in explanation is about what caused what, or more generally about what sorts of things cause other sorts of things. But human judgment about causes is as contextual as explanation. With adults, at least, judgments about which event is "the cause" of another event are loaded with topicality, interest, background knowledge about normal cases, and with moral implications. Tell someone that Suzie was killed in an accident while John was driving her home, and then ask what further information is needed to decide whether John's actions caused her death. People want to know John's condition, the detailed circumstances of the accident, including the condition of the roadway, of John's car, of the other driver if there was one, and so on (Ahn and Bailenson 1995; Ahn et al. 1996). Their judgments about causation have a moral aspect and an aspect that depends on an understanding of normal conditions and deviations from the normal, which vary with culture, background, and circumstance.

Scientific progress always reduces contextuality. When we generalize from particular anecdotes; when in experimentation we isolate systems from particular causes; when we break a complex system into parts studied separately; when we randomize treatments—in all these instances, contextuality is reduced. How, then, can we reduce the contextuality of explanatory judgments?

The knowledge of causation we need to get around in the natural and social world is more specialized than the kind of knowledge we need to say whether one event is "the cause" of another. What we need in the first place is knowledge of the effects of our own and others' actions. We need to know what to expect, in various circumstances, when something is done. The first place to look for an appropriate setting for this sort of learning is developmental psychology. Four times now I have watched the following amazing process. Start with a baby, a thing that does little more than suck and cry. Care for the baby and in several months you have a creature who recognizes people and stuffed pandas and pets and knows to expect different things from them, knows when crying will bring food or comfort, and when it will not, knows which directions things go when thrown or pushed or pulled, understands simple physical principles, can turn the television or a light switch on and off, open and close doors, and more; wait three or four more years, and you have a person who knows her way around, who can predict the consequences of her own actions and the consequences of others' actions, an agent, in other words, who knows a good deal about the causal structure, both physical and psychological, of the everyday world. Developmental psychologists, who watch more carefully than I, tell us that aspects of this process are close to invariant; children learn certain physical regularities at about the same age; they learn psychological regularities at about the same age; and so on (see Gopnik and Meltzoff 1998). The regularities suggest a constancy of method across individuals.

Small children observe the world when nothing much is done, they observe what follows when they act, and they observe what follows when others act. Judged by their expanding power to control and anticipate their environment, the conclusions children draw from these observations are causal. Children's competence at control and prediction may develop apace with linguistic competence, but verbalization is not required, and is not the test of their causal knowledge. To become competent, a child must learn (1) how to categorize (the categorization problem); (2) how to select from the myriad features those relevant to any action (the frame problem); (3) the causal relations among relevant features (the discovery problem); (4) what to expect if no action is taken (the prediction problem); and (5) what action to take to bring about or prevent some desired state (the control problem).

A satisfactory theory of how all of this is done should be fully algorithmic and should agree with relevant experimental data. An almost fully algorithmic theory already exists in the artificial intelligence literature for discovery, prediction, and control, and the theory suggests some approaches to the categorization and frame problems. This chapter is an introduction to that theory—the theory of causal Bayes nets—and what (slim) evidence there is for it as a psychological model.

The evidence is slim because the relevant experiments are missing from the psychological literature. Except about categorization, there are, so far as I can tell, no relevant experimental data on young children.[1] One can try to approximate the circumstances of the child's discovery of the causal structure of the world by giving adults inference problems in novel situations, where they have little or no previous knowledge, where moral issues are not suggested, where the data are observations—either passive or from observed manipulations and interventions—and where the responses are indications of control or power over the environment. There are serious practical difficulties to informative experiments testing how children or adults learn about causal relations from such data, but the big initial difficulties with psychological inquiry into learning causes are as much conceptual as experimental. Doing the right psychological experiments requires framing the right psychological hypotheses, and, when it comes to causation, that has not happened (see chapter appendix).

7.2   A Toy Introduction to the Markov Condition

Both social and developmental psychologists have noted that in life a complex mixture of data occur. Children acquire information about what happens when they do nothing but observe events, and about what happens when they take particular kinds of actions, and about what happens when others take particular kinds of actions; they may do one thing and observe a chain of consequences. A child may pull a blanket and find two toys move with it; pull the first engine in a toy train and find the tender and the caboose come along; pull an electric cord and find the light and the television go off; clap loudly at grandmother's house and find the TV and the light come on; scream at night and find the light goes on and a parent appears.

Consider some experiments one might do at grandmother's house:

Interventions	TV	Light
None	Off	Off
Clap	On	On
Don't clap, turn light switch on	Off	On
Don't clap, turn TV switch on	On	Off
Clap, turn TV switch off	Off	On
Clap, turn light switch off	On	Off

In sufficient ignorance one might wonder whether the clapping causes the TV and light to come on by independent mechanisms; whether the clapping causes the TV to come on, which causes the light to come on; or whether the clapping causes the light to come on, which causes the TV to come on.

The experiments establish the first account. Clapping and then turning off the light leaves the TV on. Clapping and then turning off the TV leaves the light on. If the TV is off, turning the light on without clap-ping does not turn the TV on, and if the light is off, turning the TV on without clapping does not turn the light on. In practical terms, that is the entire content of the claim that clapping causes the TV and light to come on by different mechanisms.

The same inferences could be made without intervening to turn the TV on or off or to turn the light on or off, separately from clapping. With some provisions, it suffices to observe that conditional on whether or not a clapping has occurred, the state of the TV and the state of the light are independent (in frequency) of one another. The provisions are that the TV does not always respond to the clapping and the light does not always respond to the clapping. Here is the principle:

1.   If A, B, C are associated, and A is prior to B and C, and A, B, C are not deterministically related, B and C are independent given A, and there are no common causes of A and B or of A and C, then, other things being equal, A influences B and C through separate mechanisms.

I will elaborate on the "other things being equal" conditions later (see the discussions of faithfulness under "Discovery" in section 7.5 and of causal sufficiency in section 7.3).

Consider a different example, the toy train. And, for the purpose of illustration, ignore the information about causal information that the spatial arrangement of engine, tender, and caboose may give. Here are the results of some experiments one might do:

Intervention		State of Motion	
None	Engine at rest	Tender at rest	Caboose at rest
Pull caboose	Engine moves	Tender moves	Caboose moves
Pull engine	Engine moves	Tender moves	Caboose moves
Disconnect tender from engine and pull tender	Engine at rest	Tender moves	Caboose moves
Disconnect tender from engine and pull engine	Engine moves	Tender at rest	Caboose at rest
Disconnect tender from caboose and pull tender or engine	Engine moves	Tender moves	Caboose at rest
Disconnect tender from caboose and pull Caboose	Engine at rest	Tender at rest	Caboose moves

The state of motion of the engine is independent of the state of motion of the caboose given the state of motion of the tender. If the caboose is pulled or left at rest without pulling the engine, the state of motion of the engine is independent of the state of motion of the caboose given the state of motion of the tender. In practical terms, that is what it means to say that the motion of the engine influences the motion of the caboose, or conversely, only through the motion of the tender.

If the couplings between cars were unstable (as they always were with my toy trains), so that the cars sometimes separated of themselves when the engine was pulled or when the caboose was pulled, the same inferences to causal structure could be made without ever intervening to directly fix the state of motion of the tender. If only the engine is pulled directly, the motion of the caboose is independent of the motion of the engine given the motion of the tender; if only the caboose is pulled, the same independence holds. The principle is this:

2. If states of A, B, C are all associated, and the state of A is independent of the state of C given the state of B, then, other things being equal, the state of A influences the state of C only through the state of B.

The independencies in all of these cases are about (idealized) frequencies. For example, principle 2 could be stated more explicitly as

If for some values of A, B, C fr(A,B) ≠ fr(A)fr(B) and fr(A,C) ≠ fr(A)fr(C) and fr(B,C) ≠ fr(B)fr(C) and fr(A,B,C) ≠ fr(A) fr(B) fr(C), and for all values of A, B, C, fr(C | B,A) = fr(C | B), and A, B, C are not deterministically related, then, other things being equal, the state of A influences the state of C only through the state of B.

Here is the point. Causal structures in everyday life manifest themselves by dependencies and independencies upon various interventions or actions, and these causal structures can also manifest themselves by dependencies and independencies without interventions, or with a limited set of interventions. Different structures may result in different patterns of dependence and independence, and so inferences about causation—about what would happen if an intervention or action were taken—can sometimes be made from data in which no such intervention occurs. Thus, without intervening to keep the tender from moving, it can be determined that if someone kept it from moving, the motion of the engine would not influence the motion of the caboose.

7.3   The Causal Markov Condition

The connections between causal structure and independence or conditional independence illustrated in principles 1 and 2 of section 7.2 have a more general formulation, which is almost standard in computer science nowadays, and increasingly common in statistics. The formalism, developed over the last twenty years, is used as a method for data analysis in the sciences and engineering, not as a psychological model at all, although its psychological roots are evident in one of its sources—the elicitation from human experts of probabilities for computerized expert systems. The formalism is part of a general representation of causal claims; that representation permits algorithms for inferring aspects of causal structure from appropriate observational data. The representations are often called "Bayes nets," or sometimes "directed graphical causal models." For causal features that are linearly related, the representations are isomorphic to structures variously called "path models" or "structural equation models." The latter are familiar to some psychologists in the form of "LISREL models," but their causal significance, their isomorphism to Bayes nets, and the existence of sound search algorithms much superior to those in standard statistical packages, seem to be unfamiliar. The best single reference, is Spirtes (2000).

Let us represent a possible causal structure by a directed graph—an object with nodes (hereafter, vertices) and arrows between some of the them. The vertices will represent features or variables, and a directed edge between two variables, $X \to Y$, will mean that for some values of all of the other variables represented, an action that varies X will cause variation in Y. Thus the representation of grandmother's appliances would be

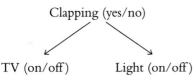

Clapping (yes/no)

TV (on/off)   Light (on/off)

and the representation of causal connections when only the engine is pulled would be

Engine $\longrightarrow$ Tender $\longrightarrow$ Caboose
(moving/not)   (moving/not)   (moving/not)

Factors that do not vary in the data under study are not represented. Thus, for example, if the electric power is always on, it has no corresponding vertex in the representation for grandmother's appliance system. If the power supply did vary, the representation would instead be

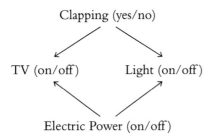

Clapping (yes/no)

TV (on/off)   Light (on/off)

Electric Power (on/off)

Suppose the power supply did vary in the cases at grandmother's house. Then the associations among clapping, TV state, and light state would not be fully explained by the causal relations of these variables with one another, because a *common cause* of the TV state and the light state would have been omitted. If no common causes are omitted from a set of variables, the set is said to be "causally sufficient."

The graph must be acyclic—that is, there is no path of arrows in the same direction that enters and exists the same vertex. Therefore, necessarily, in every graph some of the vertices have no edges directed into them. A vertex with no edge directed into it is said to have "zero indegree" (in graph-theoretic terms), or to be "exogenous" (in econometric terms), or to be an "independent variable" (in psychological terms). (To avoid confusion with probabilistic independence, I will say "exogenous" or "zero indegree.").

The structure of the directed graph encodes probabilistic independence and conditional independence relations among the variables, relations that are claimed to hold (ideally) in *every* (sufficiently large) frequency distribution that can be generated by varying the exogenous variables independently (in the probabilistic sense). The connection assumed between the causal structure represented by the directed graph, and probabilistic independence and conditional independence is given by the

Causal Markov Condition.   Let X be any variable in a causally sufficient set **S** of variables or features whose causal relations are represented by a directed acyclic graph, G, and let **P** be the set of all variables in **S** that are direct causes of **X** (i.e., parents of X in G). Let **Y** be any subset of **S** such that no variable in **Y** is a direct or indirect effect of **X** (i.e., there is no path in G from X to any member of **Y**). Then X is independent of **Y** conditional on **P**.

The causal Markov condition says that in the toy train graph, the motion of the caboose is independent of the motion of the engine conditional on the motion of the tender. It says that in grandmother's house, the state of the TV is independent of the state of the light conditional on whether or not there is a clapping.

The causal Markov condition implies that the joint probability of any set of values of a causally sufficient set can be "factored" into a product of conditional probabilities of the value of each variable on its parents. For example, according to the toy train graph, the probability that the engine moves, the tender moves, and the caboose moves is

prob(caboose moves | tender moves) · prob(tender moves | engine moves) · prob(engine moves)

and in grandmother's house, the probability that there is a clapping and the TV is on and the light is off is

prob(light is off | clapping) · prob(TV is on | clapping) · prob(clapping)

The causal Markov condition has several justifications, but one is this. Consider any system whatsoever whose causal relations are described by a directed acyclic graph in such a way that the probability of any value of any represented variable is determined by (any function of) the values of its parents in the graph. *If the exogenous variables are independently distributed, then the graph and the joint probability distribution must satisfy the causal Markov condition.*

7.4   Causal Bayes Nets

A directed graph and the causal Markov condition do not themselves determine a unique probability distribution; they only impose a restriction on any probability distribution appropriately associated with the graph. Specialized families of probability distributions can be associated with a graph by specifying parameters that determine how the probability of any value of a variable depends on the values of its direct causes, its parents in the graph. Then a particular probability distribution can be specified by assigning values to the parameters. Specifying parameters whose values give a probability distribution that satisfies the causal Markov condition for the graph is called "parametrizing" the graph.

There are many ways to "parameterize" a graph, and which way is appropriate depends on the subject matter. Some parameterizations determine familiar statistical models—linear regression, logistic regression, factor analytic, "structural equation," and so on—and others do not. For grandmother's house, for example, where each variable has but two values, a joint probability distribution can be specified by giving a numerical value to each of

prob(light is x | clapping is z)
prob(TV is y | clapping is z)
prob(clapping is z)

for each choice of x = (on/off), y = (on/off), z = (clap/no clap). The idea is just to use the factorization noted previously.

Sometimes variables are thought to have some explicit functional dependence on one another. Here is another way to parameterize the same graph. Assume that the state of the light is determined by the state of clapping and some unobserved parameter that is either on or off; and similarly, the state of the TV is determined by the state of clapping and another unobserved parameter that is either on or off. Thus we have equations

$L = f(p, \text{Clap})$

$TV = g(q, \text{Clap})$.

Because each variable (or parameter) takes only two values, f and g must be Boolean functions. For example, f and g might be multiplication, or Boolean addition, or one might be multiplication and the other addition. Now specify any probability distribution for which p, q, and Clap are independent for all possible assignments of their values. The result is a probability distribution over L, TV, and Clap that satisfies the causal Markov condition.

For another example of a parametrization with an explicit functional dependence, consider a "structural equation model" of the relations between college academic ranking, average SAT percentiles of entering students, and dropout rate. The equations might look like this:

$\text{SAT} = a + b\text{Rank} + e$

$\text{Drop} = c + d\text{SAT} + f$,

where a, b, c, d are real-valued parameters and e and f are unobserved "noises" and are assumed to be independent. The model corresponds to a parametrization of a family of probability distributions corresponding to a directed graph:

$\text{Rank} \rightarrow \text{Sat} \rightarrow \text{Drop}$

or, if the noises are explicitly represented:

$$\text{Rank} \rightarrow \text{Sat} \rightarrow \text{Drop}$$
$$\uparrow \qquad \uparrow$$
$$e \qquad f$$

A *Bayes net* is a directed acyclic graph and an associated probability distribution satisfying the Markov condition. If the graph is intended to represent causal relations and the probabilities are intended to represent those that result from the represented mechanism, the pair are a *causal Bayes net*.

A great many of the causal models deployed in psychology and the social sciences are some kind of Bayes net. Even feedforward neural networks are Bayes nets. Many recurrent neural nets are examples of a generalization of Bayes nets that allows cyclic graphs with a generalization of the causal Markov condition (d-separation). Unrecognized, Bayes nets and causal Bayes nets are lurking almost everywhere.

7.5 The Utility of Causal Bayes Nets

The value of a representation lies entirely in what can be done with it. With causal Bayes nets what can be done is this:

1. Control: Bayes nets can be used to calculate the value (or probability) of any represented variable that results from any combination of interventions that fix the values of other variables but do not otherwise alter the causal structure.
2. Prediction: Bayes nets can be used to calculate the value of any represented variable conditional on any set of values of any other represented variables.
3. Discovery: Bayes nets—or features of them—can be discovered from observations, experiments and background knowledge.

It is at least interesting that these three functions are among the five capacities any agent—a child, for example—would presumably need to learn for causal competence in everyday life. It seems unlikely that the best computer algorithms, designed for maximal reliability and efficiency with minimal prior information, are implemented in people, but at the very least the computer algorithms show what is possible with Bayes net representations. The points bear illustration.

Control

If the causal structure and the probability distribution are known, the probability of any value of any represented variable upon an intervention that forces specified values on other variables can be calculated from the corresponding "factorization" of probabilities. Suppose, for example, that it were known that genotype (G) causes smoking (S) and lung cancer (L), and that smoking also directly causes lung cancer. Then

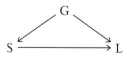

The probability distribution can be written

prob(S, G, L) = prob(L | G, S) prob(G) prob(S | G).

Suppose an odd new law is enforced. A random device decides who will and who will not smoke. What is the probability of lung cancer, given that you smoke, that results? The trick is that the intervention breaks the influence of genotype on S, so that after the intervention the causal structure is

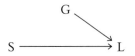

The intervention makes G and S independent, but, ideally, it should leave all other conditional probabilities unchanged. (That, by the way is one of the two principal reasons for randomization in experimental design.) So the probability distribution after the intervention is

probafter(S, G, L) = prob(L | G, S) prob(G) probnew(S).

The last factor on the right changes. If the policy simply prevented smoking, probafter(S = yes,G,L) would be zero for all values of G and L, and the probability of any pair of values of G, L would simply be probafter(S = no, G, L).

In cases where not all of the probabilities are known, the theory of interventions on causal Bayes nets shows what interventions are necessary to find them. Suppose some causal structure is thought to have the form

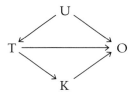

Suppose the joint probability distribution of T and O is known, and U is unobserved. The aim is to discover the influence T has on O, by which we mean the dependence in probability of T on O if T were manipulated and did not influence O through K, but the structure and conditional probabilities were otherwise unchanged. The theory says that probability can be estimated by intervening to fix (or randomize) the value of T, while intervening to fix or hold constant the value of K. The resulting structure is

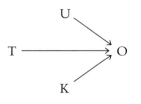

and the probabilities of interest are estimated from the association of O and T then observed.

These simple illustrations correspond almost exactly to our judgments about control in good scientific method. We randomize treatments because we want to disable any possible common causes of treatment and the outcome under study. We blind and double-blind studies because we want to block certain lines of influence so that we can correctly estimate others.

Not all of the consequences of the theory of interventions on causal Bayes nets are so banal. Suppose you knew that the following graph described the causal relations among the variables:

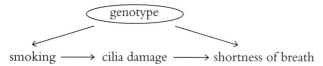

Suppose, further, associations involving genotype are not observed. The association of smoking and shortness of breath is therefore confounded. Nonetheless, the influence of smoking on shortness of breath can be estimated from the observed associations of the other variables, where, once more, by "influence," I mean the conditional probability distributions of shortness of breath that would result from interventions to fix (or randomize) values of smoking. (For a nice presentation of the theory of interventions in Bayes nets, see Pearl 1995.)

Prediction

The Bayes net specifies the joint distribution of the variables as a product of conditional probability distributions. It is not surprising that using the representation, by various techniques the conditional probability of any variable can be computed from specifications of the values of any other set of variables. Various algorithms have been developed to make such computations efficient.

There are, however, somewhat surprising consequences. The smallest set $B(X)$ of variables conditional on which all other variables are independent of X is called the "Markov blanket" of X. The Markov blanket of a variable consists of its parents, its daughters (the variables it effects directly), and the *parents of its daughters*. The italicized set is unintuitive and easily neglected; for example, the widely used backpropagation algorithm for adjusting weights in neural nets overlooks the parents of daughters.[2]

Discovery

We have already seen that distinct causal structures may, either by themselves or with other information, imply distinct independence and conditional independence facts. These differences can be exploited in discovery procedures. For example, for 3 variables there are 25 distinct acyclic graphs belonging in 11 distinct equivalence classes; all of the graphs of the same class imply the same independencies and conditional independencies; any two graphs belonging to distinct classes imply distinct sets of independencies and dependencies. Graphs of the same class are said to be "Markov equivalent." The graphs in each equivalence class are listed in columns below, with the set of independencies and conditional independencies characteristic of the class at the top of each column. "A ⫫ C | B" means, for all values of A, B, C, A is independent of C conditional on B.

A ⫫ C | B	B ⫫ C | A	B ⫫ A | C	None
A → B → C	B → A → C	B → C → A	B ⟶ A ⟵ C (diagram)
A ← B → C	B ← A → C	B ← C → A	
A ← B ← C	B ← A ← C	B ← C ← A	

B ⫫ C	A ⫫ B	A ⫫ C	A ⫫ C, C ⫫ B
B → A ← C	B → C ← A	A → B ← C	A → B C
			A ← B C

B ⫫ A, C ⫫ A	B ⫫ A, B ⫫ C	A ⫫ B, B ⫫ C. A ⫫ C
B → C A	B A → C	A B C
B ← C A	B A ← C	

Provided one assumes that all independencies and conditional independencies are due to causal structure alone, depending on the associations or lack of associations that are found, something can be inferred about the causal structure. The italicized assumption is sometimes called "faithfulness," and is essentially a simplicity postulate, although there are various justifications for it. For example, for several parametrizations of a graph, it is almost certain that a probability distributions will be faithful to the graph.

On the faithfulness assumption, if the only independence relation is $B \perp\!\!\!\perp C \mid A$, then the causal relations are one of the three in the first column. If, in addition, one knows (as with clapping at grandmother's house) that neither B nor C cause A, then the structure $B \leftarrow A \rightarrow C$ is uniquely determined.

The example assumes that $\{A, B, C\}$ is causally sufficient, but inferences can also be made from independence and conditional independence when a set of variables is not causally sufficient—indeed, sometimes it can be discovered from associations that a set of variables is not causally sufficient, because the set of independencies and conditional independencies that hold among those variables alone is incompatible with the causal Markov condition. But we are getting too deeply into details. Suffice to say that there are efficient algorithms that will extract all of the information about causal structure that can be obtained from independencies, conditional independencies, and background knowledge about what does or does not cause what. The chief difference between the performance of these algorithms (in the large sample limit) on causally sufficient and causally insufficient sets of variables is that less causal information can be extracted from insufficient variable sets.[3]

7.6   The Proposal

I think causal Bayes nets are in many—not all—contexts a good normative model. Or to put it another way, causal Bayes nets seem to provide the right norms for most causal judgments. But I also think that, imaginatively used, causal Bayes nets are a good candidate for a substantial part of the framework of an adequate descriptive account of the acquisition and exercise of causal knowledge. They cannot possibly be the whole story, but the features of discovery, prediction and control discussed above suggest they may be a big part. We will see later how other bits of the theory can be applied to other psychological problems.

I have almost no evidence for the proposal. There are almost no psychological experiments that test, or test the limits of, causal Bayes nets as a descriptive model. From a Bayes net perspective, the literature on human judgment of causation is either focused on irrelevant contextual issues, on disputes over the correct parameterization of a tacit network, or on disputes over what features of a tacit Bayes net subjects are reporting when they give verbal assessments of "efficacy" or "causal strength." There are no experiments, to my knowledge, that deliberately test whether subjects form causal judgments in agreement with the Markov condition in simple cases with appropriate data.[4] Imagining such experiments is not particularly hard. If a subject can manipulate feature A, and observe the frequencies of B and C that follow, then the causal Markov and faithfulness conditions distinguish among the following structures:

1. $A \rightarrow B \rightarrow C$
2. $A \rightarrow C \rightarrow B$
3. $C \leftarrow A \rightarrow B$

Assuming the influences are all positive, if structure 2 were the case, then intervening to bring about C would increase the chances of bringing about B, and intervening to prevent C would decrease the chances of bringing about B; in the other structures, manipulating C would have no influence on B. Do people make these inferences? Do animals? There are any number of possible experiments of this sort. To the best of my knowledge, not one has been done deliberately. At least one has been done inadvertently.

7.7   Overshadowing

Baker et al. (1993) report the following experiment, designed to show that in the presence of causes with a large influence on an outcome variable, human subjects underestimate the influence of less important causes. The greater influence "overshadows" the smaller influence.

Subjects played computer games in which they tried to move a tank icon through a minefield. By pushing or not pushing a button, the subjects had the power to camouflage or not camouflage the tank on each trial. Sometimes an airplane icon would appear after the decision about camouflage had been made. In the first experiment reported, the computer arranged things so that the following probabilities obtained, where S represents getting safely through the minefield, C is camouflage, P is appearance of the plane:

$P(S \mid P) = 1$

P(S | ~P) = 0

P(S | C) = .75

P(S | ~C) = .25

After each game, which consisted of 40 trials, subjects were asked to estimate, on a scale from −100 to +100, "the effectiveness of the camouflage" (p. 417).

Baker et al. assume that the correct, normative, measure of the influence of a cause *c* on an effect *e* is the "contingency," Δ*P*, measured by

$$\Delta P = \text{Prob}(e \mid c) = \text{Prob}(e \mid \sim c).$$

"The crucial finding of this experiment," the authors write, "concerns the effect of the high-plane contingency on the estimates of the effectiveness of the camouflage. A high plane contingency sharply reduced estimates of the effectiveness of both the positive (= 0.5) and the zero camouflage contingencies" (p. 418). For example, in the experiment with the probabilities specified above, the mean subject assessment of the "effectiveness" of camouflage was .06 (that is, 6 on the −100 to +100 scale) rather than Δ*P* = 0.5 (50 on the −100 to +100 scale).

The experimenters' understanding was that, normatively, the subjects should have reported the efficacy of the camouflage for reaching safety as a number approximately equal to

100 · [prob(safety | camouflage) − prob(safety | no camouflage)] = 50

In fact, subjects concluded the efficacy of the camouflage was approximately zero. Where Baker et al. see another triumph of irrationality, I see experimental confirmation of the causal Markov condition.

The picture that the experimenters seem to believe the subjects had in the experiment is

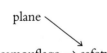

button → camouflage → safety

In such a causal structure, if safety is a Boolean function of plane appearance and camouflage, under the assumptions in the experiment, Δ*P* can be justified as a measure of the probability that turning camouflage on is necessary and sufficient for reaching safety (see Pearl 1998).

The experimental setup had consequences the authors did not note. In the experiment, camouflage/not camouflage and plane appearance/absence are statistically dependent, and camouflage/not camouflage is *independent* of passing/not passing through the minefield *conditional* on appearance/absence of plane. What the subjects should learn about associations over forty trials is then approximately

1. Camouflage $\parallel$ safety | plane
2. No other independencies or conditional independencies hold

Given the cover story and order of appearance of events, the possible causal pictures the subjects might have entertained are

button $\rightarrow$ camouflage $\rightarrow$ safety   plane

button $\rightarrow$ camouflage   safety $\leftarrow$ plane

button $\rightarrow$ camouflage $\rightarrow$ safety $\leftarrow$ plane

button $\rightarrow$ camouflage $\rightarrow$ safety $\rightarrow$ plane

button $\rightarrow$ camouflage $\rightarrow$ plane   safety

button $\rightarrow$ camouflage   plane   safety

button $\rightarrow$ plane $\longrightarrow$ safety   (with camouflage above, button $\rightarrow$ camouflage $\rightarrow$ safety)

button $\rightarrow$ plane   safety   (with camouflage above, button $\rightarrow$ camouflage $\rightarrow$ safety)

button $\rightarrow$ plane $\longrightarrow$ safety   (with camouflage above, button $\rightarrow$ camouflage)

button $\rightarrow$ camouflage $\rightarrow$ plane $\rightarrow$ safety

Only the last two of these structures are consistent with the information given the subjects, the associations and conditional independence noted, the causal Markov and faithfulness conditions, and the assumption that the set of variables considered is causally sufficient. In the next to last structure, camouflage has no effect, and the subjects' response as reported is just about optimal. For the last structure, if the subjects understood their task to be to estimate the "efficacy" of the camouflage without the plane, then again their answer is just about optimal (see also Spellman 1996).

7.8   Causal Bayes Nets Hidden Away in Psychological Models

The model Baker et al. (1993) assume on their subjects' behalf is a simple Bayes net, but unfortunately very likely the wrong one. Patricia Cheng's influential model (1997) of human judgment of "causal power" is also a causal Bayes net model.

Cheng considers experiments in which C is a potential cause of E and there may be other unobserved causes, A of E, that are independent of C, and from observations of frequencies of C and E subjects are asked to estimate the power of C to bring about E. Cheng's model of the subject's model is this: C, if it occurs, has a capacity to bring about E, and that capacity is a probability (although it is *not* prob(E | C)). Similarly for A.

E may be caused by C alone, or by A alone, or it may be overdetermined and caused by both. E will therefore occur if C occurs and C causes E, or if A occurs and A causes E, where the disjunction is not exclusive. The rule for probabilities for inclusive disjunctions is prob(X or Y) = prob(X) + prob(Y) − prob(X,Y). Thus

(⋆) Prob(E) = prob(C) · power of C + prob(A) · power of A − prob(C)
        · power of C · prob(A) · power of A.

Cheng's model is a causal Bayes net with the graph

C → E ← A

and the parametrization is given by the equation

(⋆⋆) E = A · $p_{e,a}$ ++ C · $p_{e,c}$,

where $p_{e,a}$ and $p_{e,c}$ are parameters that take values 0 or 1, and ++ is Boolean addition, one of the parameterizations of Bayes nets described in section 7.3. Taking probabilities of both sides in (⋆⋆) and assuming the independence of the exogenous variables and parameters gives Cheng's equation (⋆). The particular structure and parametrization is known in the computer science literature as a "noisy or gate." The striking originality of Cheng's theory is in the causal interpretation and in noting that the model implies that prob($p_{e,c}$) = prob(E | C, ~A), and can be estimated without observing A.

Cheng also considers circumstances in which a cause tends to prevent an effect. Suppose all unobserved causes U of E are facilitating, and there is an observed candidate preventing cause F of E. Cheng's equation is

$$\text{prob}(E = 1) = \text{prob}(p_{e,u} \ U = 1) \cdot \text{prob}(1 - p_{e,f} \ F = 1).$$

Assuming independence of U and F and of the parameters, she shows that

$$\text{prob}(p_{e,f} = 1) = -\Delta P_f / \text{prob}(E \mid F = 0).$$

The last equation shows that the parameter $\text{prob}(p_{e,f} = 1)$ can be estimated from observations of F, E alone, even in the presence of other unrecorded facilitating causes of E, so long as they are independent of F. Cheng proposes that when, in such circumstances, subjects report their estimates of the power of F to prevent E, they are reporting an estimate of $\text{Pr}(q_{e,f} = 1)$. Her account of judgments of facilitating and preventing causes is justified by an extensive review of the literature in experimental psychology on human judgment of causal power.

Arbitrarily complex combinations of sequences of facilitating and preventing causes can be constructed, each corresponding to a causal Bayes net with a special parametrization. Some small mathematics applied to the representation leads to a number of predictions, none of which, so far as I know, has been tested. For example:

1. If there is an unobserved preventing cause, the causal powers of observed causes cannot be estimated. Hence, in appropriate experimental situations, subjects should be uncertain of the power of a facilitating cause when they have reason to think a preventing cause is acting. Further, subjects using Cheng models should have differential confidence in judgments of causal power when they know there is an unobserved preventing cause of one of two observed facilitating causes.
2. A facilitating cause of a preventive cause of an effect is itself a preventive cause of the effect. Subjects using Cheng models should so judge. (These and a number of other implications are given in Glymour 1998.)

Cheng's theory postulates that when two or more causal factors co-occur, the causal power of any one of them, say A, to produce effect E is sometimes estimated by conditioning on cases in which other factors are absent. But she does not specify when such conditioning is appropriate and when it is not. Cheng also shows that for various combinations of presentations of causal factors ("cues" in the psychological literature), the Rescorla-Wagner (1972) model has asymptotic values for causal strength that require conditioning on values of all co-occurring factors. The search algorithms of the Bayes net representation of causal relations implicitly contain an unambiguous recipe for when, and when not, to condition on co-occurring factors. These features lead to possible "crucial tests" of the Bayes net representation of causal relations against the Rescorla-Wagner model of learning.

Suppose the true structure is as follows:

$$B \longleftarrow A$$
$$\nearrow$$
$$U \longrightarrow E$$

where A, B are "cues" for E and U is unobserved by the subject. In such a system A and E are independent in probability, but are *dependent* conditional on E.

Given sufficient data about A, B, and E, standard Bayes net search algorithms will find that A is not a cause of E, and that B and E have an unobserved common cause (whether B also has an influence on E is undetermined.) If, at least in simple cases, human subjects use Bayes net representations and search procedures appropriate for Bayes nets then for sufficient data from appropriate parameterizations of this structure they should judge that A has no influence on E. But the Rescorla-Wagner model requires the influence of A on E be judged from their association conditional on a value of B, and thus leads to the prediction that subjects should take A to influence E.

7.9 Imitation, Intervention, and Learning

The simple distinctions between associations and causal relations, and between interventions and other events, distinctions fundamental to the theory of causal Bayes nets, are essential in sorting out aspects of learning. Psychology has two traditional models of learning, classical and operant conditioning. In classical conditioning an agent learns the association of features, food and bell ringing in Pavlov's famous example, provided the features meet various conditions, such as proximity of time of occurrence. Measured by drops of saliva, Pavlov's dogs learned to expect food from bell ringing, and I count that as learning an association, but they did not learn anything about causation—they did not learn the effects of any intervention; for example, how to bring about or to prevent either the presentation of food or the ringing of the bell.

Some associations between a prior feature and a subsequent feature hold because the occurrence of the first feature caused the occurrence of the second feature, and some associations hold for other reasons—often because some third feature caused both the first and the second: Pavlov (or his assistants) caused both the bell to ring and the food to appear. By contrast, in operant conditioning an agent learns both an association and at least a fragment of a causal relation. Skinner's pigeons learned that pecking a target is associated with the appearance of food pellets, and they learned at the same time how to control or influence the appearance of food pellets—by pecking the target. That partial causal knowledge was evidenced by an acquired skill, a competence at bringing about the presence of food by appropriate pecking, and of course not by anything linguistic. Skinner and his assistants arranged the mechanism, but given that mechanism each bird learned a causal conditional: if it pecks, food appears.

The causal knowledge acquired in operant conditioning may be radically incomplete if it is confined to implicit knowledge of the effects of the learner's own actions, and not generalized to yield an understanding of the effects of other sources of intervention. It is one thing to know that if I peck on the target, a food pellet will appear, another to know that if there is a blow on the target, from whatever source, a food pellet will appear. A full causal understanding separates events that are subject to a system of causal relations from interventions that alter them, and implies a general grasp of the relevant interventions.

Learning by imitation seems to indicate a more complete causal understanding. Meltzoff and Moore (1977) showed that very young babies imitate some of the actions of others, and of course older children and adults imitate all the time. Imitation can be for its own sake, from which useful consequences may later be discovered, or may be acquired along with knowledge of the consequences of the act imitated. In the latter case, imitation is the manifestation of an efficient way of acquiring causal knowledge, a way that identifies an act as a generic kind, that recognizes the causal power of the kind, and that recognizes the agent's own action as an instance of the kind, no matter how different from the observed action of another one's own action may look or feel to oneself. There is, of course, a reverse inference, from observation of the consequences of one's own actions to knowledge of the consequences of like actions by others.[5]

Learning causal relations from observations of others' actions is essential for the accretion of causal knowledge that constitutes culture. It is, therefore, interesting that recent studies suggest that nonhuman primate modes of learning by imitation may be seriously limited in comparison with humans, either because they do not imitate, or do not learn from observations of others the consequences of imitated actions.

7.10 Categorization

Whatever the biological constraints and imperatives concerning the formation of concepts of kinds, it seems likely that humans and perhaps other creatures also have the capacity to fashion kinds to suit their environments. Adults certainly fashion many categories to discriminate causal powers, and presumably children do as well. There may be many ways that causal roles influence categorization, but consider just one of the ways suggested by network representations.

From the point of view of Bayes nets, fashioning kinds is fashioning variables, deciding when perceptual or historical differences should be used to separate things into distinct kinds, and when they should be ignored. The "should be" has to do with whatever promotes causal understanding, prediction, and control.

Simon has often insisted that intelligence works best in an "approximately decomposable" world, a world where not everything is hooked up to everything else, and the influences of causes are approximately separable. One of the morals of computational research on Bayes nets is that their utilities are only available when the domain is structured so that the networks are sparse. If every variable is in fact dependent on every other variable, conditional on every other set of variables, little about causal structure can be learned from the data short of a complete set of randomized experiments, and, were such a complex causal structure to be known, prediction and control would be infeasible to compute with it. But knowledge of a causal structure is useful in prediction and control only if the structure is not completely empty, only if some features influence other features. Causal knowledge from fragmentary observations, possible when the causal structure is sparse, is useful only when some things influence others, but the structure is still sparse.

Whether the causal relations in a domain are sufficiently sparse to be tractable and sufficiently dense to aid prediction and control depends in part on how the variables are specified—on the kinds. Dense causal structures are sometimes resolved into sparser causal structures by introducing new kinds.

Suppose in population 1, features X and Y are independent, and in population 2, X and Y are also independent, but the probabilities are different in the two populations. Then if the populations are not distinguished as different kinds, X and Y will be dependent in the combined population. The world looks sparser if a new kind is recognized.

Suppose X, Y, and Z are all associated and conditionally associated. Any graph representing hypothetical causal relations to account for the associations will be complete, with an edge between every pair of variables. Now suppose a new feature is noted, conditional on values of which X, Y, and Z are independent. If the new feature is causal, the world looks sparser.

Suppose X causes Y, and Y causes Z, and there are no other causal connections between X and Z. The world looks sparse but sufficiently structured for control. But if X is imperfectly measured—if mismeasured Xs are classified as Xs—and similarly for Y and for Z, then mismeasured X and mismeasured Y and mismeasured Z will all be associated and conditionally associated, and the world will look more complex than it need be.

That sparseness and connection sufficient for prediction and control influence the categories we form seems a hypothesis at least worth investigation.

7.11   The Frame Problem

The frame problem is this. How can a computational agent anticipate the consequences of an action? (That is not what the frame problem originally was, but what it has become.) The problem for artificial intelligence is not chiefly about how an android might know all the causal relations in the world (the programmer, after all, can put in a list), but rather about how that knowledge can feasibly be used to predict the consequences of actions in real time. If the right thing must be done quickly to avoid a disaster (in an example of Dennett's, a bomb goes off) it will not do to go through an endless list of causal connections, most of which are irrelevant; it will not do to check every feature in long-term memory, most of which have nothing to do with the possible actions at hand.

While the android is checking, the bomb goes off. Nor will simpleminded heuristics do.

If babies and children and adults are computational agents, then the frame problem is a problem for them as well, and perhaps still more difficult if the programmer input a learning procedure rather than a list of causal relations. The effects of any action can be feasibly computed in a sparse Bayes network: it is, as it were, prestructured for computing the relevant and only the relevant features. And for frequently consulted relationships, the effects can be precompiled.

And similarly for whatever aspect of the frame problem has to do with learning what variables, what features to include in one's causal theory of everything. Discovering the causal structure of the world is not a one-shot problem. It would make sense for children to assume that what they know about is causally sufficient until experience tells them otherwise, and to expand and reformulate only then. That is what the new developmentalists say children do when learning about the world. I only suggest that a good part of what they learn is the causal structure of the world.

Appendix: Objections to "Decontextualizing" the Study of Causal Inference

Objection 1: The Ecological Fallacy

Most causal judgments do not draw in any direct way on the data of association and action; they draw on what one already knows about causation and the structure of the world, on analogy, on specializations of general principles. There are psychologists who object to studies of causal inference in situations where that sort of information is not available because the circumstances are not typical. But while faithfulness to the complexity of natural settings produces endless research (because natural settings are endlessly varied) and sometimes produces useful technology or policy, it has never, in any science, produced an understanding of fundamental mechanisms. In natural settings, the fundamental mechanisms, whether physical or psychological, are endlessly confounded with one another and cannot be sufficiently separated to reveal their several structures, effects, and interactions.

Sometimes confounding seems a deliberate in the design and interpretation of psychological experiments, including experiments on causal judgment, for example, when an effect E found in condition C is claimed to be refuted after some further feature is added to C, and D does not result. Imagine the history of physics if the same methodology had been used. Bodies in a vacuum near the surface of the earth fall at a constant velocity with distance universally proportional to the square of the elapsed time, you say? Not if you add water.

Objection 2: Association and Causes

Psychology has two traditional models of learning, classical and operant conditioning. In classical conditioning an agent learns the associations of the features, food and bell ringing in Pavlov's famous example, provided the features meet various conditions, such as proximity of time of occurrence.

Quite possibly the model of learning most influential in psychology is the Rescorla-Wagner model (Rescorla 1968) of classical conditioning, essentially a linear network model. It has been championed as an account of learning causal relations, where it is simply a nonstarter. From the association of Pavlov's bell rings and the appearance of food, no model of classical conditioning can learn whether the bell ringing caused the appearance of food or something else (Pavlov, in fact) caused both. What Rescorla-Wagner models can account for is, at best, learning associations, and in special cases the strength of the association in the model will correspond roughly to what people judge the "strength" or "efficacy" or "power" of causes to be. The abstract of David Shanks's Experimental Psychology Society Prize Lecture (1995) illustrates the same confusion: "We can predict and control events in the world via associative learning. Such learning is rational if we come to believe that an associative relationship exists between a pair of events only when it truly does." Although among animals and very young humans, causal relations must somehow be discovered *from* associations, associations are not causes. Nothing good can come of confusing the two ideas. Nothing good has.

Objection 3: Hume and Plato

David Hume argued that we can obtain no conception of causal necessity from experience, hence no knowledge of causal necessities. From that, it seems to follow that such judgments must issue from innate principles. The conclusion, which seems to be given some credence in psychology, (witness the response to Gopnik and Meltzoff) is that what goes on in developing an understanding of the causal structure of the world is maturation, not learning. Absent talk of souls, that is Plato's theory in the *Meno*.

The argument proves too much. Hume's argument is ancient skepticism is the language of eighteenth-century psychology. The skeptical argument of the *Meno*, later elaborated by Sextus Empiricus, is not about causality per se; it is about learning *any* universally quantified hypothesis whatsoever. If the skeptical argument is endorsed, it works for any hypothesis that covers an unbounded collection of cases: give up learning anything except particular facts.

Hume's, Plato's, and Sextus's arguments all presuppose that learning requires a procedure that yields the truth (and nothing but) in every logically possible world. There is no reason to suppose that human learning is so ambitious. We do not think that human children can learn every logically possible syntax, no more should we think that they emmind discovery procedures that work in every logically possible world.

Objection 4: Misguided Norms

Since work on human judgment about uncertainty became popular in psychology, a finger-wagging genre has developed around several topics, including causal judgement. Psychologists make normative assumptions about causation and, interpreting experiments in light of those assumptions, conclude that human judgment is irrational in one or another respect. These assessments are only interesting provided the psychologists have correctly described the relevant information they have explicitly or implicitly given to their subjects, and provided they have correctly described rational norms of inference and judgment. Often neither is the case.

Notes

1. And even relevant experiments on categorization are few and recent. See Gelman and Wellman 1991 and Gopnik and Sobel 1998.

2. The connection with backpropagation seems first to have been noted by Michael Jordan.

3. This remark requires technical qualification in view of unpublished work by Jamie Robins, Peter Spirtes, and Larry Wasserman. If a set is causally sufficient and a time order is known, there are search procedures that uniformly converge to the true structure as the sample size increases without bound—meaning that one could construct a

kind of confidence interval for the estimated structure. Absent those assumptions, the procedures can only converge nonuniformly, meaning that eventually any particular alternative to the truth can be rendered arbitrarily improbable, but there will always exist, for any finite sample, alternatives that are not improbable.

4. Added in proof: Alison Gopnik and her collaborators have recently completed experiments showing that three- and four-year-olds make some causal judgments in accord with the Markov assumption.

5. Language learning is a peculiar and interesting case: the act of naming (as in "milk") has no regular, observed consequences and, when imitated, produces no regular observed consequences, but has instead a complex and irregular association with the presence of the liquid.

References

Ahn, W., and Bailenson, J. (1996). Causal attribution as a search for underlying mechanisms: An explanation of the conjunction fallacy and the discounting principle. *Cognitive Psychology*.

Ahn, W., Kalish, C. W., Medin, D. L., and Gelman, S. A. (1995). The role of covariation versus mechanism information in causal attribution, *Cognition, 54*, 299–352.

Baker, A. G., Mercier, P., Vallée-Tourangeau, F., Frank, R., and Pan, M. (1993). Selective associations and causality judgments: The presence of a strong causal factor may reduce judgments of a weaker one. *Journal of Experimental Psychology: Learning, Memory, and Cognition, 19*, 414–432.

Cheng, P. W. (1997). From covariation to causation: A causal power theory. *Psychological Review, 104*, 367–405.

Gelman, S., and Welmann, H. (1991). Insides and essence: Early understandings of the non-obvious. *Cognition, 38*, 213–244.

Glymour, C. (1998). Psychological and normative models of causal judgement and the probabilities of causes. In *Proceedings of the Fourteenth Conference on Uncertainty in Artificial Intelligence.* Madison, WI.

Gopnik, A., and Meltzoff, A. (1998). *Words, thoughts and theories.* Cambridge, MA: MIT Press.

Gopnik, A., and Sobel, D. (1998). Detecting blickets: How young children use information about causal powers in categorization and induction. Preprint. Berkeley: University of California, Department of Psychology.

Meltzoff, A., and Moore, M. (1977). Imitation of facial and manual gestures by human neonates. *Science, 198*, 75–78.

Pearl, J. (1995). Causal diagrams for empirical research, *Biometrika, 82*, 669–709.

Pearl, J. (1998). *Probabilities of causation.* Technical Report R-260. Los Angeles: University of California at Los Angeles, Cognitive Systems Laboratory.

Rescorla, R. A. (1968). Probability of shock in the presence and absence of CS in fear conditioning. *Journal of Comparative and Physiological Psychology, 66*, 1–5.

Rescorla, R. A., and Wagner, A. R. (1972). A theory of Pavlovian conditioning: Variations in the effectiveness of reinforcement and nonreinforcement. In A. H. Black and W. F. Prokasy, eds., *Classical conditioning II: Current theory and research*. New York: Appleton-Century-Crofts.

Shanks, D. R. (1995). Is human learning rational? *Quarterly Journal of Experimental Psychology, 48A,* 257–279.

Spellman, B. A. (1996). Conditionalizing causality. In D. R. Shanks, K. J. Holyoak, and D. L. Medin, eds., *The psychology of learning and motivation.* Vol. 34, *Causal learning.* San Diego, CA: Academic Press.

Spirtes, P., Glymour, C., and Scheines, R. (2000). *Causation, prediction, and search.* 2nd Edition, Cambridge, MA: MIT Press.

8

The Role of Mechanism Beliefs in Causal Reasoning

Woo-kyoung Ahn and Charles W. Kalish

8.1 Characterizing the Questions of Causal Reasoning

This chapter describes the mechanism approach to the study of causal reasoning. We will first offer a characterization of the central issues in human causal reasoning, and will discuss how the mechanism approach addresses these issues. In the course of this presentation, we will frequently compare the mechanism approach with alternative accounts based on analyses of covariation, or what is often termed the regularity view. The aims of this chapter are to explain why covariation and mechanism are different, to discuss why such a distinction is actually a useful tool for our understanding of causal reasoning, and to explicate the complementary nature of the two approaches. We need first to describe the domain or problem itself: namely, what are these alternative approaches to?

Although there are a number of different ways of characterizing the study of causal reasoning, we depict it as an attempt to examine how *people* think about causal relations and identify causes. That is, our focus is descriptive. Hence, in this chapter, we do not try to provide a normative account of how people should think about causes. Nor, do we try to describe how people are able to reason under exceptional circumstances. Glymour (1998) has argued that proponents of a mechanism view commit an "ecological fallacy" by concentrating on what people do most often, most typically, or perhaps, most naturally. We would argue that ecological validity is among the virtues of a focus on mechanism. Adopting a descriptive perspective is a reasonable and valuable approach for psychologists interested in characterizing how people actually carry out the task of causal reasoning.

There are two parts to the question of how people identify causal relations. First, what do people mean when they identify a relation as causal? Second, by what process do people identify a relation as causal? These two questions roughly correspond to the distinction made by Rey (1983) with regard to categorization. On the one hand, argues Rey, there are metaphysical questions of categorization. What do people think makes something a member of one category rather than another? Given our focus on causation, we may ask what people think distinguishes a causal relation from a noncausal one, a question that has to do with the *definition* of cause. In addition to metaphysical questions, Rey points out that we are often interested in epistemic questions. What do people do to decide whether or not something is a member of a category? Again, with respect to causation, we may ask what people do when they are trying to decide whether a relation is causal or not or to determine what is a cause in a given situation, a question that has to do with *methods of identifying* causes. Although these two questions are clearly linked, an answer to one does not necessarily provide an answer to the other. There may be aspects of a definition that are not (typically) used in identification and means of identifying instances that are only tenuously connected to definitions.

Most work in causal reasoning has focused on epistemic questions (e.g., how people identify a relation as causal). The mechanism approach is most centrally a claim about people's definitions or conceptions of causality, although one claim of this approach is that people's strategies for identifying instances of causal relations typically derive from their beliefs about the nature of causation.

In presenting the mechanism view, we will first describe its claims about people's conceptions of causation and then derive hypotheses regarding the process of causal identification. In describing the definitional and process aspects of the mechanism approach, it will often be useful to contrast our view with covariation approaches in order to highlight important characteristics of the mechanism approach. Given recent accounts of conflict between covariation and mechanism approaches, we will conclude by considering some of the relations between covariation and mechanism in causal reasoning.

8.2   Definition of Causation

Mechanism View

We believe that the core component of the idea of "cause" is a sense of force. If A causes B, then A makes B happen, or B had to happen given

A. It was no accident. It is this sense of necessity that distinguishes genuine causal relations from mere correlations.

While this characterization is probably universally accepted, the mechanism approach suggests that there is usually more to people's notions of cause. We argue that when people say A causes B, they believe that there is a process that took place between A and B in which a force or causal power was transmitted. Borrowing from Salmon's example (1984), imagine a spotlight placed in the middle of the ceiling of a dome. The spotlight is a cause for the light projected on the wall because a pulse of light travels from the spotlight to the wall. Now imagine that the spotlight rotates so that the light moves around the wall. Even though there is a regular and reliable succession such that the position of the light at time T1 is always followed by a new position at time T2, we do not say that the position at T1 causes the position at T2 because we know that causal power is not transmitted from one spot of the wall to the other spot of the wall (see also Harré and Madden 1975; Shultz 1982 for a similar proposal).

The first claim of the mechanism approach is thus that people believe that there is a more basic process underlying the cause-and-effect relation. In other words, when people conceive of cause-and-effect relations, there is a basic assumption of mechanism, namely that, underlying two causally linked events, there is a system of connected parts that operate or inter-act to make or force an outcome to occur. Consider getting sneezed on and getting sick. If people think the sneeze is the cause, then they also believe that there must have been a basic process or mechanism by which the sneeze forced the illness to come about. In modern Western cultures, we typically understand the mechanism to be infection; getting sneezed on infects you with germs that make you sick. A relatively elaborated notion of the mechanism might include the ideas that germs possess the causal power of making a person sick, that the person's immune system has causal power to counteract germs, and that the person's immune system can be weakened by lack of sleep.[1]

The second claim of the mechanism view is that mechanism is framed at a different level of analysis than are the cause and the effect. That is, mechanisms involve theoretical constructs, constructs that are removed from and underlying the evidential phenomena themselves (Gopnik and Wellman 1994). Thus in the example above, "germ" is part of a theoreti-cal vocabulary that is described at a level different from "sneezed on" and "sick."

Of course this leads to a problem of potentially infinite regress. For instance, in explaining why John had a traffic accident, one might refer to a mechanism of drunk driving. In explaining why drinking causes a traffic accident, one can further explain that a person's reaction time is slower when drunk, and so on. Ultimately, this process bottoms out at the point where objects must have their causal powers "essentially," with no other more basic process responsible (Harré 1988). When the issue of essential properties does arise, it is typically dealt with in a nonintuitive, theoretical manner. For instance, accounts of the ultimate or final level of causal relation, beyond which we can no longer pursue questions of mechanism, are typically couched in highly theoretical terms (e.g., quantum theory) or exist within the province of theological explanations (e.g., the uncreated Creator). While this infinite regress may be a scientific or philosophical problem, we argue that commonsense causal reasoning is rarely faced with the consequences of this kind of regress. What is essential in the commonsense conception of causal relations is the belief that there is some process or mechanism mediating this relation, whether understood in detail or not.

To summarize, we suggest that people's beliefs about causal relations include (1) a notion of force or necessity; (2) a belief in a causal process that takes place between a cause and an effect; and (3) a set of more or less elaborated beliefs about the nature of that mechanism, described in theoretical terms. Our emphasis on mechanism beliefs as a fundamental component of the conception of cause contrasts with analyses of causation framed primarily in terms of covariation. In describing the mechanism approach, it is useful to contrast these two views of causal concepts.

Regularity View

The basic tenet of the "regularity view," is that our knowledge of a causal relation arises "when we find that any particular objects are constantly conjoined with each other" (Hume 1777, 27). For instance, a person might observe that whenever she eats shellfish, she gets sick. Then, the person might want to conclude that eating shellfish causes her to get sick. In one of the most elaborate psychological models taking the regularity view, Cheng (1997; Cheng and Novick 1992) proposes that causal strength is a function of a covariation index, $\Delta P = P(E \mid C) - P(E \mid \neg C)$, where $P(E \mid C)$ is the probability of obtaining the target event in the presence of a causal candidate and $P(E|\neg C)$ is the probability of obtaining the target event in the absence of the causal candidate.

Psychological theories and models based on the principle of covariation have generally focused on how people identify causes and how people induce novel causal relations, rather than what it means (or what people think it means) for a relation to be causal. Nonetheless, such theories may contain at least implicit characterizations of causal concepts. We will first examine the conception of causal mechanisms based on the notion of covariation, and discuss how it departs from the mechanism view. We will then discuss how the two views differ in their emphasis on specific instances versus patterns or collections of cases.

Recently, the covariation approach has focused on representing causal mechanisms in terms of a complex web of covariation, or more specifically, as a directed graph in which nodes representing variables are connected with arrows indicating causal directions (Glymour, chap. 7, this volume; Glymour and Cheng 1998; Pearl 1996; Waldmann and Martignon 1998). Glymour (1998, 41–42), for instance, uses the following example from Baumrind (1983) to illustrate this point: "The number of never-married persons in certain British villages is highly inversely correlated with the number of field mice in the surrounding meadows. [Marriage] was considered an established cause of field mice by the village elders until the mechanisms of transmission were finally surmised: Never-married persons bring with them a disproportionate number of cats."

Glymour proposes that B is a mechanism for a correlation between A and C, if, conditional on B, the correlation of A and C goes to zero. In the above example, one observes that as the number of unmarried persons increases, the number of mice in town decreases. Conditional on the number of cats, however, the covariation between the number of unmarried persons and the number of mice would be greatly reduced. Therefore, cats are a mechanism underlying the covariation between marriage and the number of mice. Glymour represents the causal mechanism underlying this contingency as follows:

unmarried persons → # cats → # mice

That is, single people bring in cats, which leads to reduction in the number of mice.

To give another example by Glymour (1998), consider the correlation between yellow fingers and the later occurrence of lung cancer.

Having yellow fingers is not a direct cause of lung cancer because this correlation disappears conditionalized on smoking. The mechanism behind the covariation is a common cause: smoking caused yellow fingers and smoking caused lung cancer. The claim is that causal mechanisms can be represented in terms of conditional probabilities. For this reason, Glymour (1998; see also Glymour and Cheng 1998) argues that separating mechanisms and covariations is implausible.

In one respect, we would agree with this claim. People's ideas about mechanisms may support or produce expectations about patterns of association; these expectations could be used to test hypotheses about potential mechanisms. Thus if people believe that getting sneezed on causes illness via the mechanism of the transmission of germs, they should expect that the covariation between sneezing and illness is conditional on the transmission of germs. Observing a different pattern of associations might lead them to revise their hypothesis about the mechanism of illness causation.[2] Thus, too, we argue that association is related to mechanism as evidence is to theory; that is, mechanism explains association as theory explains evidence.[3]

The point of disagreement, however, is that Glymour argues that because patterns of covariation are mechanisms, and not just evidence for them, "the separation of mechanisms and associations is very odd and implausible, and, to the contrary, it seems that an important part of learning causes might very well be learning mechanisms from associations" (Glymour 1998, 43). By contrast, we argue that the core of the concept of mechanism is a belief in the transmission of causal influence, a belief not fully captured by the formalisms of covariation theories of causal reasoning.

To illustrate our point, let us go back to the previous example of the relations among the number of singles, mice, and cats. The proposal is that cats are a mechanism mediating between singles and mice because conditional on the number of cats, the relation between the number of singles and the number of mice is independent. One possible interpretation of this formulation is that *any* pattern of association in which the third factor "screens out" a correlation between two factors is a mechanism. However, there are identical patterns of data that do not involve mechanisms. Consider the variable "number of rodents." Conditional on the number of rodents, there is no relation between the number of singles and the number of mice. Yet the number of rodents is not a mechanism because the elements of a causal relation must be logically distinct. Although it is simple enough to modify the covariation account to stipulate that causes (mechanisms) and effects must be logically independent, the significance of this example is that conditionalized covariance is not sufficient to identify or define mechanism.

For a second example, consider the volume of cat food sold in a community. There would be a strong negative correlation between the volume of cat food sold and the number of mice, and there would be a strong positive correlation between the volume of cat food sold and the number of singles in town. Furthermore, conditional on cat food sales, the number of singles is independent of the number of mice. If the idea is that *any* pattern of association in which a covariation is screened out by the third factor is a mechanism, then volume of cat food should be also considered a mechanism underlying the relation between the number of single people and the number of mice. Yet few people would agree.

We would argue that the same kind of evidence leads to the conclusion that cats are a mechanism but cat food is not, because we understand something of the causal powers of cats and cat food. Likewise, we judge that "number of rodents" is not the right sort of thing to serve as a mechanism. We argue that patterns of association and covariation are interpreted in light of beliefs about mechanisms and causal powers that are fundamental elements of conceptions of causal relations. That is, not all conditionalized covariations are considered mechanisms.

Of course it is often possible to imagine further covariation information that would rule out spurious mechanisms such as the ones we just discussed. Perhaps the positive correlation between the volume of cat food sold and the number of single people is novel information, and for that reason, people might want to look more carefully for other covariates. For example, we could see that cat food sale is not a true mechanism between the number of mice and the number of single people because it could be screened out by another variable, namely, the number of cats. The problem, however, is that determining how to explore current covariations would be impossible without any appeal to prior knowledge about mechanisms. That is, without prior background knowledge, this process would take unlimited computing time because it could be achieved only through an exhaustive covariational analysis over all objects in the world. Using a purely correlational approach, we would not know where to look for significant covariations. If the covariational analyses are incomplete, the choice between models (i.e., determining which pattern of association is a mechanism and which one is not) cannot be based *solely* on covariation information.

Glymour (1998) also hints at the need for existing knowledge in selecting the right models among all possible ones. If we need existing knowledge to begin with, however, the covariation account faces something of an infinite regress: some biases or predispositions must be needed to get things going. Proponents of the covariation approach often complain that the mechanism approach does not provide any account of where mechanism knowledge comes from in the first place (e.g., Cheng 1997). But as we have shown, the same shortcoming applies to the covariation approach. Furthermore, our claim is stronger than that existing causal mechanism knowledge helps. It is that such knowledge does essentially all the work. We suggest that much of the disagreement between mechanism and covariation approaches stems from the accounts of the background knowledge people bring to bear in reasoning about a new case. Does prior knowledge represent beliefs about mechanisms or the results of previous covariation analyses?

A second way in which the covariation account departs from the mechanism view is that according to the former, cause is primarily defined over samples of multiple events (henceforth referred to as "general cause"). In contrast to this, we argue that it is the conception of the individual or specific case that is fundamental for commonsense conceptions of cause because the sense of transmission of causal power in an individual instance is essential.

Take the case of the live polio vaccine (known as the "oral polio vaccine," which is given as drops in the mouth). In most cases, the vaccine prevents polio. In others, the live vaccine fails and leaves a person unprotected, and in still others, the vaccine, because it is alive, actually causes the disease. Assume these outcomes occur randomly. If a person gets polio after receiving the vaccine and being exposed to the virus, it seems to be a matter of fact whether the vaccine caused the disease, or merely failed to prevent it. That is, two potential mechanisms of a causal outcome are distinct in this case. In one mechanism, causal power is transmitted from the vaccine, and in the other, it is transmitted from the virus the person was exposed to after the vaccine. Yet, from the perspective of the correlation between vaccine and disease outcome, there seems to be no difference. No pattern of covariation could distinguish which of the two mechanisms was responsible in this specific case.[4]

Salmon (1984) gives another example. Suppose a golfer tees off. The shot is badly sliced, but by accident, it hits a tree branch, and drops into the hole for a spectacular hole-in-one. Hitting a tree branch usually prevents a ball from going in the hole. Hence, based on a covariation analysis, hitting a tree would not be identified as a cause of successful golf shots. However, in this specific case, we have no trouble accepting that this player made a hole-in-one because the ball hit the branch.

Of course, the way to address the problem of "low-probability" causes is to transform the representation of the event into a "high-probability" cause. In the golf example, it could be argued that people are really reasoning about the causal consequences of one object hitting another. From past experience, we know that "a small object hitting a large one at angle θ causes the smaller to rebound at angle θ'." Thus it is easy to see the tree as the cause of the ball's traveling in a particular direction, which just happens to be the direction of the hole. As in the cat food example above, the reinterpretation requires positing both that people focus on just the correct piece of covariation information while ignoring misleading data and that they have access to the right sort of prior knowledge. Again, it is not clear which one comes first, the covariational analysis or the access to the mechanism knowledge. The critical difference between a mechanism account and a covariation account seems to lie in the importance each attaches to people's prior knowledge.

Before addressing the issue of prior knowledge, it is worthwhile to mention a different sort of argument for the individual nature of causal relations. Searle (1983, 118) argues that an ascription of intentional cause need not involve any belief that the relation holds generally:

For example, suppose I am thirsty and I take a drink of water. If someone asks me why I took a drink of water, I know the answer without any further observation: I was thirsty. Furthermore, in this sort of case it seems that I know the truth of the counterfactual without any further observations or any appeal to general laws. . . . And when I said that my being thirsty caused me to drink the water, was it part of what I meant that there is a universal law? . . . Part of my difficulty in giving affirmative answers to these questions is that I am much more confident of the truth of my original causal statement and the corresponding causal counterfactual than I am about the existence of any universal regularities that would cover the case.

Similarly, we argue that the core of the idea of cause in laypeople's conception is that a particular factor influences outcomes or transmits causal powers in particular cases. Whether a causal relation held in one occasion will do so in the future is a secondary inference that is conceptually distinct from the original belief in cause.

In the mechanism account, the belief that A caused B consists of the notion that there was some influence or transfer between the two entities or events—something particular happened. We suggest that a covariation approach characterizes the belief that A caused B to be *primarily* an expectation about a general pattern of covariation between A and B. We have tried to show, through some examples, that people may have strong intuitions about causes even in the absence of good evidence or expectations about patterns of covariation about general cases. The covariation rejoinder to these examples is that what we are calling "individual" or "particular" causal relations are really just instances of previously learned patterns of covariation. According to them, to believe that A caused B is to believe that there is a consistent relation between events of type A and events of type B. If beliefs about causal relations must be based on patterns of covariation, then clearly the only empirical questions surrounding causal reasoning concern whether people are sensitive to particular sorts of covariation information and how they choose between, or how they weight, different patterns. Thus we suggest that the covariation position relies heavily on a particular account of the origins of causal beliefs, namely, covariational analysis. In advancing the mechanism approach we want to take issue with the claim that all of a person's causal beliefs are based, in any psychologically significant sense, on covariation.

8.3   Identifying Causal Relations

From a discussion of how people conceptualize causal relations, we now turn our attention to the other aspect of causal reasoning: how people identify or discover that two things or events are causally related. As Rey (1983) points out in his discussion of categorization, there are typically many varied ways of identifying an instance of a category. We believe the same holds true for identifying instances of causal relations. In this section, we will consider two means by which people might identify causal relations: induction and abduction. Inductive methods are often held up as the method by which causes are identified. We will consider the basis of these claims and will argue that induction is usually inappropriate as an account of how people ordinarily identify causes. Instead we will offer an account of causal reasoning based on abduction or "inference to the best explanation." After comparing induction and abduction, we will discuss the role of mechanism and covariation information in induction and abduction, and will end by revisiting the debate between the mechanism and covariation views.

How Inductive Reasoning Works

In the broad sense, induction is any inference made under uncertainty, or any inference where the claim made by the conclusion goes beyond the claim made by the premises (Holland et al. 1987). In this sense, induction subsumes abductive and analogical reasoning, or any nondeductive reasoning. In the narrow sense, induction is limited to inference to a generalization from its instances (Josephson and Josephson 1994; Peirce 1955). For instance, given that all A's observed thus far are B's, one might expect that in general all A's are B's.

We will use the narrow sense of induction, as in existing models of causal induction (e.g., Cheng 1997). In a typical causal induction model, the input to the system is a set of specific instances and its output is an abstract causal rule. In a nutshell, the basic inductive learning mechanism in these models is to tabulate frequencies of specific cases in which a target effect does or does not occur in the presence or absence of a candidate cause, and to calculate causal strengths based on the contingency. This way, causal induction models can account for how causal beliefs originate from noncausal data.

How Abductive Reasoning Works

Causal induction is not the whole story in causal reasoning. People not only attempt to induce novel causal relations from specific cases, they also attempt to explain why something happened in a specific case by applying known causal rules. Peirce (1955), who first described abductive inference, explains this process as follows. Given an observation d and the knowledge that h causes d, it is an abduction to conclude that h occurred. For example, a detective trying to determine the cause of someone's death would proceed by generating hypotheses and assessing their fit with the existing evidence. The detective might first consider whether the victim was shot (knowing that gunshots often cause death). The absence of an external wound would tend to impugn this hypothesis. Or the detective might consider whether the victim was poisoned, gathering data both consistent (the victim was eating before death) and inconsistent (other people who ate the same food did not die) with this hypothesis. Eventually, perhaps after several rounds of hypothesis generation and evidence collection, the detective might decide that only one possible cause of death matches the facts of the case. Thus abduction is often called the "inference to the best explanation," because in general, there are several hypotheses that might account for the evidence, and out of these, the best one is selected. Note that in abductive reasoning, the pattern of data alone does not warrant the inference. The abductive conclusion is only reached by using the data to decide among a set of alternatives generated based on existing knowledge.

The conclusion drawn as the result of an abduction (h in the above illustration) contains a vocabulary not used to describe the data (d). For instance, a patient with jaundice might be diagnosed with hepatitis, from the vocabulary of diseases and not from the vocabulary of symptoms. Because of this, abductions are often considered as "leap from observation language to theory language" (Josephson and Josephson 1994, 13). Naturally, the mechanism view is compatible with abductive reasoning. Our existing knowledge about causal mechanisms is used to determine the best explanation for a given situation, just as a theory explains evidence.

Abductive reasoning is not deductively valid. It is actually an example of the classical fallacy of "affirming the consequent." Although normative criteria have been proposed for causal induction (e.g., Glymour and Cheng 1998), no such framework can be proposed for abduction. Still, uses of abductive reasoning are manifold (e.g., Harman 1965). Examples can be found in medical diagnosis (e.g., Peng and Reggia 1990), legal decision making (e.g., Pennington and Hastie 1986), and even vision (e.g., Charniak and McDermott 1985). Unfortunately, the issue of abductive reasoning has rarely been studied in cognitive psychology.

Generally, it is thought that judgment of the best explanation will be based on considerations such as which explanation is simpler, which is more plausible, which explains more, which fits more coherently with existing knowledge, and so on (see also Brewer, Chinn, and Samapapungavan, chap. 11, this volume). However, the criteria for judging a good explanation need not be explicitly represented nor theoretically motivated. Peirce suggests that abduction may at times be guided simply by "aptitudes for guessing right." Unlike induction, the quality of competing explanations also directly influences abductive reasoning (Josephson and Josephson 1994). In causal induction, the role of competing hypotheses is indirect. For instance, in the power PC theory (Cheng 1997), alternative causal candidates influence induction only by changing the conditional probability of the target effect in the absence of the causal candidate, and one does not even need to know what these alternative candidates are. However, abduction is more like decision making in that a reasoner makes explicit comparisons among alternative explanations in order to select the best one.

The process of abduction is one of trying out alternative explanations and seeing which one best fits the data. There are clearly two parts to this process. One is elaborating and refining existing explanations to improve the fit to existing data. The other is collecting more data in the hope of achieving a better fit to existing explanations. Thus other decisions to be made in abduction include how much effort one should put into data collection versus explanation adaptation. For example, if there is a big cost to guessing wrong, the reasoner would probably want to focus on data collection. On the other hand, if the pressure is to try something quickly, the reasoner would probably be inclined to choose the first best explanation to the data and act on it.

To summarize, the reasoning processes underlying abduction are different from those underlying induction. While causal induction is for learning general or universal causal laws from noncausal data, abduction involves collecting evidence and making decisions about a specific case. We now consider the conditions under which each kind of reasoning would be invoked.

Induction or Abduction?

Induction has the virtue of describing how causal knowledge may be inferred from noncausal data. That is, given experience that does not contain information about causal relations, how do we arrive at causal beliefs? Clearly, if our goal is to give a reductive account of how causal beliefs may arise from noncausal data, induction is our preferred choice. For this reason, induction is often taken as a normative approach to causal reasoning. Indeed, there are now accounts of powerful procedures for deriving causal inferences from correlational data (e.g., Spirtes, Glymour, and Scheines 1993). The relevance of these procedures to the question of human causal inference is where there may be some debate. One focus of research is whether people are able to apply these inductive methods. Research from a number of psychological studies (e.g., Cheng 1997; Cheng and Novick 1992; Spellman 1996) suggests that people can carry out inductions that satisfactorily conform to normative principles. A different perspective on causal reasoning asks whether this is actually how people *typically* reason. Although we might be able to construct scenarios in which people perform (as if they were making) inductions, how ecologically valid are these scenarios?

In our earlier work (Ahn et al. 1995), we gave undergraduate subjects descriptions of events. These varied widely from descriptions of normal everyday activities (e.g., "The customer paid for the bill after eating at a restaurant") to nonsense sentences (e.g., "The tove gyred the mimble"). The subjects' task was to ask the experimenter questions in order to explain the events. Even for nonsense sentences, participants rarely asked for information necessary for causal induction. That is, they did not engage in the process of selecting a causal candidate and collecting the information needed for a covariational analysis. Instead, most responses seemed to reflect an attempt to figure out which known causal mechanism best fit the given situation. For instance, participants frequently introduced new theoretical constructs not mentioned in the descriptions of the events. They also asked whether preconditions for a hypothesized mechanism were satisfied even for nonsense sentences (e.g., "Was the tove mad at the mimble?"). That is, they seemed to be making causal abductions—inferences to best explanation, or inferences to mechanisms (see also Lalljee et al. 1984; Major 1980; White 1989 for similar results).

Sometimes, we have no choice but to apply existing causal knowledge, rather than collecting data necessary for causal induction. Most notably, this often happens when we need to discover what caused an individual event. By definition, covariation information requires multiple instances. At the very least, we need to observe the consequences of the presence and absence of a causal candidate. However, with only a single specific case, even this minimum requirement cannot be met. For instance, a covariational analysis can establish that cigarette smoking causes lung cancer in general. However, it cannot establish whether cigarette smoking caused a *particular* lung cancer, because we cannot observe what would have happened if the person did not smoke cigarettes.

Even with general cases, there are other reasons to believe that abduction is preferred over induction. The normative way of inducing causal relations from covariation assumes that people have a sufficiently large number of representative samples. But in real life, covariation information is not presented all at once in a prepackaged form. Rather, each observation is made one at a time in a sequential manner. Clearly, it is difficult for a reasoner to determine a priori how many observed instances make up a representative sample. Hence we often must make causal attributions on-line as the observations are made. Indeed, Dennis and Ahn (1997) demonstrated that people are willing to make causal attributions based on a small set of cases before waiting to see the whole array of examples. As a result, they exhibit a strong order effect depending on the type of instances they encounter first (see also López et al. 1998 for another example of the order effect in causal induction). Using data as they come in and not assuming unrealistic representational capacities can be also thought of as characteristic of evolutionarily plausible reasoning strategies (Gigerenzer and Goldstein 1996).

The second reason why causal induction might be less prevalent than abduction in real life is that some evidence necessary for calculating conditionalized covariations is impossible to obtain. Recall the previous example of correlation between increase in the amount of cat food sold and decrease in the number of mice. To determine whether cat food sales directly cause the number of mice, we might want to calculate the contingency between these two factors while holding the number of cats constant. Practically speaking, however, such evidence would be impossible to obtain. Indeed, there are numerous other factors (e.g., cat stomachs, cat tails, etc.) whose covariations are (practically) impossible to observe while holding the number of cats constant. In fact, in real-life situations, reasoners normally do not have the luxury of obtaining all the evidence they would like to see before making inductive conclusions.

Although nobody has explicitly claimed that causal induction is the only way people identify causes, the current focus of causal reasoning models gives the impression that causal induction is more important and fundamental than abduction. Contrary to this, we claim that abduction may be the most pervasive and natural means of identifying causes. One might discount this point by saying that it is obvious that once causal knowledge is induced, one might as well use it rather than trying to learn new knowledge afresh (Glymour and Cheng 1998). However, our claim goes beyond this. In explaining why abduction might be more prevalent than induction, we alluded to the problems that are inherent in causal induction. That is, abduction is preferred to induction, not simply because of cognitive efficiency, but because most of the time a complete covariation analysis (not guided by prior mechanism beliefs) is impossible.

Learning

Abduction does not answer the question of the origins of causal beliefs. However, it should be noted that causal induction is only a single (though important) aspect of learning new causal relations. That is, we should not identify causal induction with the question of how people acquire new causal beliefs or how people identify causes. Some causal knowledge is innate; nobody has to teach a baby the consequence of sucking behavior. Some causal knowledge can be acquired through analogical reasoning. For instance, Read (1983) has demonstrated that people make causal predictions even from a single example, especially when the causal rule is complex. Of course, the most common and efficient way of acquiring causal knowledge would be through direct instruction or communication (see Sperber 1996 for more detailed discussion of these processes). There are also more dubious ways to arrive at the conclusion that one thing caused another, such as dreams or visions. As with any other type of belief, people may come to causal beliefs in a host of ways.

In some respects, one might argue that noninductive accounts for learning are circular. In saying that causal knowledge is the result of communication, how did the person who transmits the belief come to have it in the first place? If one traces back to the origin of basic causal beliefs, do they not come from a covariational analysis? As we already discussed, it is not difficult to think of origins other than covariational analyses. Some causal beliefs could be innate. Some could have been fabricated. On the other hand, the covariation-based induction method might actually be most responsible for the creation of new causal beliefs. Even in that case, however, it is not clear what bearing it has on the transmission of causal beliefs. For example, person A might acquire from person B the belief that unprotected sex is a cause of AIDS. The basis for person B's belief, be it an analysis of covariation or a particular religious conviction, may be completely unknown to A. In this case it would seem odd to suggest that the bases of B's beliefs have any significance for A. Thus the premise that induction might account for the origin of causal beliefs does not undermine the argument that noninductive learning methods are prevalent in most situations of learning new causal relations.

Summary
This section described two distinct reasoning processes used to identify causes: induction and abduction. It presented empirical results for our claim that abduction is more prevalent than induction in everyday causal reasoning, along with a theoretical analysis of why this should be the case. Acknowledging that there is some truth to the counterargument that abductive reasoning cannot explain the learning of novel causal relations, we argued that learning new causal relations can be carried out through means other than causal induction.

8.4 Role of Covariation and Mechanism Information in Abduction and Induction

Traditionally, the covariational models have focused on causal induction while the mechanism view has focused on abduction. However, we do not argue that covariational information is useless in abductive reasoning. At the same time, although the mechanism view has often been criticized for lacking an account of the origins of mechanism knowledge (Cheng 1997), we believe that mechanism information is indispensable in induction. In this section, we discuss how covariation information contributes to abduction and, more importantly, how mechanism information contributes to induction.

Use of Covariation Information in Abduction
Covariation information is certainly useful in abduction, although not necessary. Suppose John Doe has lung cancer and there are three possible explanations for this case: (1) he smoked; (2) his family has a history of lung cancer; and (3) he worked in a stressful environment. In determining which one is the best explanation, the base rate (or some kind of covariation-based index) of these candidate factors in the general population would certainly be useful. It should be noted, however, that covariation evidence is only one type of data in abduction. Another important type of data would be the fit between hypothesized mechanisms and specific cases. In the above example, we might also want to know how much

Doe smoked, how close to him was his relative with lung cancer, and so on. Sometimes, these other kinds of evidence can outweigh the evidence provided by covariation, as in the case of base rate neglect due to representativeness heuristics (Kahneman and Tversky 1973). Thus although covariation information is beneficial, it is neither sufficient nor essential for abduction.

Use of Mechanism Information in Induction

There is now a consensus that inductive reasoning requires constraints because of computational complexity (e.g., Keil 1981; see also the special issue of *Cognitive Science*, 1990, devoted to this issue). Clearly, the principle of association is one of the most fundamental learning mechanisms. But the need for additional constraints has been thoroughly recognized in various domains, including language acquisition (e.g., Chomsky 1965), concept learning (e.g., Murphy and Medin 1985), and even learning of covariation per se (e.g., Alloy and Tabachnik 1984). We reintroduce this rather widely accepted idea here because it has not been specifically discussed in the context of causal reasoning. Furthermore, the recently developed covariation-based approach to causal mechanisms seems to be neglecting this issue. Our main claim is that while covariation-based learning of new causal rules is essential, induction is almost impossible without our existing knowledge of causal mechanisms because there are simply too many possibilities.[5] The following are specific ways mechanism information can guide learning new causal rules.

Determinants of Causal Candidates   To determine causal candidates for covariational analyses, one must start out with some understanding of causal mechanisms because, otherwise, one soon runs into a computational explosion (see also Peirce 1955). This is often called the "frame problem" in artificial intelligence. The reason why a normal person would not even think about the possibility that wearing red socks might cause Alzheimer's disease in their later life is precisely because we cannot think of any plausible mechanisms for how this might occur. To quote Popper (1963, 46);

The belief that we can start with pure observations alone, without anything in the nature of a theory is absurd. . . . Twenty-five years ago I tried to bring home the same point to a group of physics students in Vienna by beginning a lecture with the following instructions: Take a pencil and paper; carefully observe, and write down what you have observed. They asked of course, what I wanted them to observe. . . . Observation is always selection. It needs a chosen object, a definite task, an interest, a point of view, a problem.

We do not deny the possibility of starting out with observations of unexplained correlations and then imposing causal interpretations on them. However, this type of purely bottom-up covariational analysis seems extremely rare in real-life situations. As described in the previous section, we have observed it to be a rare exception in our earlier work (Ahn et al. 1995). A true discovery of new mechanisms from observations can only be achieved by a few scientists whose job is devoted to this kind of task. In most everyday reasoning, people start out with hypotheses on causal candidates that are generated from their existing mechanism knowledge.

Relevancy of Data   Even after we select a manageable set of causal candidates to test for a covariational analysis, a reasoner still has to decide which events are relevant for the analysis. In a typical covariational analysis, four pieces of information are needed, crossing presence and absence of the causal candidate with presence and absence of the target effect. The difficulty of a covariational analysis arises in particular when one needs to decide what counts as the absence of an event. The worst possible case would be the joint absence of the causal candidate and the target effect (Einhorn and Hogarth 1986). As discussed in the famous "ravens paradox," although "All ravens are black" is logically equivalent to "All nonblack things are nonravens," our observation of a purple flower does not strengthen our belief that all ravens are black. For any covariational analysis, there is an infinite possible number of joint absent cases, but they cannot possibly all strengthen our causal beliefs. Only some of them seem relevant to increasing our causal beliefs.

Salmon (1966) discusses the problems that accompany this arbitrariness of probabilities. The idea is that the larger the reference class, the more reliable—but the less relevant—the statistics. For instance, in estimating the likelihood that Michael Jordan will catch a cold this winter, we might estimate the frequency of colds based on all the people in the world over the entire history of humankind. Although these statistics might be reliable, it might be more relevant if the estimate were based on male basketball players just during winter, and perhaps just for this year because the dominant type of cold virus changes yearly. Note that as we determine the relevancy, causal interpretation is already starting to creep in (Josephson and Josephson 1994). That is, without constraints from existing causal mechanism knowledge, probability information can be vacuous and inapplicable.

Interpretation of Data   Wisniewski and Medin (1994) convincingly demonstrated that people's domain theories determine how features are interpreted in categorizing objects. In this study, participants received children's drawings that were described as belonging to two different categories. Participants' interpretation of features was heavily dependent on the category labels provided to the drawings. For instance, a circular configuration of lines in a drawing was described as a "purse" when participants were told that a "city child" had drawn it. But when other participants were told that the same drawing was done by a "creative child," the same feature was described as a "pocket" and was interpreted as evidence that the drawer paid attention to detail. Similarly, a single observation can lead to different causal conclusions depending on the underlying beliefs (including beliefs about mechanism) that determine how the given observation is perceived and interpreted. For example, suppose one observes that the common cold was cured every time she had chicken soup. Depending on prior beliefs, she can interpret these observations as support for a hypothesis that eating something warm cures the common cold, or as support for an alternative hypothesis that special ingredients in chicken soup cure the common cold.

When Do We Doubt Correlations?   Covariations cannot be equated with causal relations. To deal with this problem, a recent approach is to calculate causal strengths based on conditionalized covariations, as implemented in the power PC theory (Cheng 1997). For instance, one might notice that birth defects tend to occur among mothers who use computers. But if the contingency is recalculated holding alternative factors constant, the previously positive contingency might disappear. For instance, if one calculates covariation between birth defects and use of computers in the absence of job-related stress, the covariation might become near zero. In that case, the contingency between birth defects and the use of computers is considered a spurious correlation and not a causal relation. However, covariation of a real cause will not be screened out conditional on alternative causes. For instance, if the covariation between birth defects and job-related stress remains positive in the absence of high alcohol consumption (or any other alternative causes), we can conclude that job-related stress is indeed a cause of birth defects. Therefore, according to the power PC theory, "covariation does imply causation when alternative causes are believed to occur independently of the candidate" (Cheng 1997, 374).

An important question that has not been answered is, how do people know a priori which correlations might be spurious, that is, under what conditions would they be forced to calculate further conditional covariations? Sometimes an observed correlation is readily accepted as a causal relation without having to calculate conditional covariations, but sometimes it is not. For instance, there has been a report of a positive correlation between who wins the Superbowl (AFC or NFC) and whether the stock market goes up or down, but no one would draw a causal link between these two. On the other hand, a report on a correlation between the use of aluminum foil and Alzheimer's disease created quite a stir several years ago. The critical difference between these two examples seems to be whether or not people can conjecture a plausible mechanism underlying the correlation.

Sometimes, one might even dismiss correlation data per se because the reasoner cannot think of any plausible mechanisms. For instance, consider the following statistics (Gauquelin 1967). There are more schizophrenics born in winter months than in summer. Children born in May, June, September, and October have higher IQ scores than those born in other months. Those who were born immediately after the rise and culmination of Mars and Saturn are more likely to be physicians. Most people educated under modern science would dismiss such findings, let alone draw causal links. Now, consider that it has further been discovered that it is not just the children's but also the parents' birth dates that are correlated with the children's careers. (Indeed, these are all "real" correlations reported in Gauquelin 1967.) No matter how many more complex covariation patterns we discover, however, most well-educated people would dismiss these findings because they do not believe there could be a mechanism linking planets to personality.

However, Gauquelin (1967) presents an intriguing mechanism-based explanation for these correlations. There are three elements to this mechanism. First comes the proposition that personality (and hence career) and intelligence are genetically determined. Second is the suggestion that the human fetus is sensitive to subtle gravitational forces (for example, marine animals show exquisite sensitivity to minute tidal forces caused by celestial bodies). Finally, add the fact that the fetus precipitates labor, and you have the beginnings of an account. Fetuses with particular personality attributes signal labor in response to particular tidal forces. Once some causal mechanism has been provided, the correlations begin to warrant serious consideration in a way that no additional amount of data would.[6]

Induction of Causal Mechanism   Thus far, the discussion has been limited to the role of mechanism information in induction of single-layer or one-step causal links. Little is known about whether people can actually learn multilayered mechanisms only from covariation. The only empirical study known to us gives a pessimistic picture. Hashem and Cooper (1996), generated nine sets of relatively simple causal networks (e.g., A $\rightarrow$ B $\rightarrow$ C, or A $\leftarrow$ B $\rightarrow$ C) instantiated as diseases. Twenty second- and third-year medical students were instructed to ask for any conditional probabilities among the three variables in each network, and to estimate the causal strength between B and C after receiving answers to their questions. Even from these simple causal networks, their estimates significantly deviated from the normative answers. Although exploratory, the results suggest the need for additional constraints for learning causal networks from the bottom up. Indeed, Waldmann and Martignon (1998), who make use of a Bayesian network to represent mechanism knowledge, admit that it is improbable that humans learn such networks bottom-up, as instantiated in some computational models (e.g., Spirtes, Glymour, and Scheines 1993).

8.5   The Covariation versus Mechanism Debate Revisited

Various issues have been discussed throughout this chapter. In this final section, we compare the covariation-based and the mechanism-based approaches once again and summarize their points of agreement and disagreement.

Both views agree that our prior background knowledge about causal relations plays a role in causal reasoning. Neither approach denies abductive reasoning. The major discrepancies between the two views lie in their differing conceptions of how people think about causal relations and causal mechanisms, and in their differing emphasis on the role of mechanism knowledge in identifying causes. The regularity view does not consider people's beliefs in a necessary force or causal power, and in its current form, it proposes that conditionalized covariations imply causality. We argue (1) that conditional covariations are not what people think of as causal relations; and (2) that calculating conditionalized covariations is not how people typically identify causal relations. The pattern of covariation alone cannot determine which model is a causal mechanism. In real-life situations, induction is impossible without the guide of existing mechanism knowledge. Hence, even if one could develop the most accurate and normative model of causal induction, which could learn complex causal mechanisms from scratch, there still would be a tremendous gap between such a model and a psychological model of everyday causal reasoning.

Our discussion of the significance of mechanism information in induction should not be taken as a direct refutation of covariation-based models of causal induction. Some of these problems (e.g., how to determine causal candidates) have been explicitly acknowledged as issues outside the realm of causal induction models. We do not attempt to dismiss the value of causal induction models. Indeed, the development of models to represent the conditions under which covariations can be equated with causality constitutes an impressive accomplishment of the regularity view.

At the same time, it is also important to realize limits of the inductive models. Glymour (1998, 43) argues that separating mechanism knowledge from covariations "puts everything on a false footing." We believe rather, that it is the normative approach to everyday causal reasoning that puts everything on a false footing. As our discussion has shown, human cognitive capacity and the surrounding environment simply do not provide the circumstances necessary for such a normative model to operate in the real world.

Notes

We would like to thank Lawrence Barsalou, Martin Dennis, and Douglas Medin for their helpful comments on an earlier version of this chapter. We also would like to thank Jennifer Amsterlaw for her thorough proofreading of the manuscript. This work was supported by National Science Foundation grant NSF-SBR 9515085 and by National Institute of Mental Health grant RO1 MH57737 to Woo-kyoung Ahn, and by Agency for Health Care Policy and Research grant RO3 HS09556 to Charles W. Kalish.

1. As in this example, a mechanism usually consists of multiple factors, each possessing causal power. Pragmatic constraints would determine which one of the many

interconnected parts in the mechanism is "the" cause and which ones are preconditions. These pragmatic constraints would include conversational maxims (Hilton 1995), contrast or focal sets (Cheng and Novick 1991; McGill 1989), abnormality of the factors (Hilton and Slugoski 1986), and so on.

2. Of course whether they see the evidence as forcing a revision and how they might revise their conception (e.g., abandoning the idea of germs, postulating a third variable) is undetermined by the data. See Koslowski 1996 following Quine 1969.

3. Cheng (1997) proposes a measure called "causal power," which is a contingency between two observed factors in the absence of all alternative causes. She claims that the relation between this conditionalized contingency and the observed contingency (which is not conditionalized over all alternative causes) is like the one between a theory and a law. We view this relation instead as one between a law and data. A law specifies regularity among factors in the absence of all confounding variables, hence is like the conditionalized contingency, or what Cheng calls "causal power." The observed contingency would be like observed data, which always contain potential confounds.

4. It may be that there are ways to distinguish the two scenarios (e.g., by determining whether there is polio virus in the environment, whether the strain causing the illness is the same as the vaccine strain, etc.). Note, however, that we contend there are different mechanisms driving our expectations that there are some distinct patterns of covariations, not the other way around. The central point is that despite any pattern of past covariations, it is what happened in this particular instance that determines the cause. This is the same point illustrated in the golf example below.

5. This statement should not be taken as the claim that "people do not learn causes from associations" or that "causes have nothing to do with associations," as Glymour (1998, 41) misconstrues it. Our claim (in this chapter, as well as in our previous work) is that associations alone are insufficient for learning causal knowledge, and that there are many ways of learning causal knowledge other than by associations.

6. Note the proposal of a mechanism suggests the kinds of relevant covariation data. In particular, given this account, we would like to see whether the effects are conditional on natural or caesarian birth.

References

Ahn, W., Kalish, C. W., Medin, D. L., and Gelman, S. A. (1995). The role of covariation versus mechanism information in causal attribution. *Cognition, 54*, 299–352.

Alloy, L. B., and Tabachnik, N. (1984). Assessment of covariation by humans and animals: The joint influence of prior experience and current situational information. *Psychological Review, 91*, 112–149.

Baumrind, D. (1983). Specious causal attributions in the social sciences: The reformulated stepping-stone theory of heroin use as exemplar. *Journal of Personality and Social Psychology, 45*, 1289–1298.

Charniak, E., and McDermott, D. (1985). *Introduction to artificial intelligence.* Reading, MA: Addison-Wesley.

Cheng, P. W. (1997). From covariation to causation: A causal power theory. *Psychological Review, 104,* 367–405.

Cheng, P. W., and Novick, L. R. (1991). Causes versus enabling conditions. *Cognition, 40,* 83–120.

Cheng, P. W., and Novick, L. R. (1992). Covariation in natural causal induction. *Psychological Review, 99,* 365–382.

Chomsky, N. (1965). *Aspects of the theory of syntax.* Cambridge, MA: MIT Press.

Dennis, M., and Ahn, W. (1997). Order of confirmatory evidence affects judgment of causal strength. Poster presented at the thirty-eighth annual meeting of the Psychonomic Society, Philadelphia.

Einhorn, H. J., and Hogarth, R. M. (1986). Judging probable cause. *Psychological Bulletin, 99,* 391–397.

Gauquelin, M. (1967). *The cosmic clocks: From astrology to a modern science.* Chicago: Regnery.

Gigerenzer, G., and Goldstein, D. G. (1996). Reasoning the fast and frugal way: Models of bounded rationality. *Psychological Review, 103,* 650–669.

Glymour, C. (1998). Learning causes: Psychological explanations of causal explanation, *Minds and Machines, 8,* 39–60.

Glymour, C., and Cheng, P. W. (1998). Causal mechanism and probability: A normative approach. In M. Oaksford and N. Chater, eds., *Rational models of cognition.* New York: Oxford University Press.

Gopnik, A., and Wellman, H. M. (1994). The theory theory. In S. A. G. Lawrence and A. Hirschfeld eds., *Mapping the mind: Domain specificity in cognition and culture.* New York: Cambridge University Press.

Harman, G. H. (1965). The inference to the best explanation. *Philosophical Review, 74,* 88–95.

Harré, R. (1988). Modes of explanation. In D. J. Hilton, ed., *Contemporary science and natural explanation: commonsense conceptions of causality.* Brighton, U.K.: Harvester Press.

Harré, R., and Madden, E. H. (1975). *Causal powers: A theory of natural necessity.* Totowa, NJ: Rowman and Littlefield.

Hashem, A. I., and Cooper, G. F. (1996). Human causal discovery from observational data. In *Proceedings of the 1996 Symposium of the American Medical Informatics Association.*

Hilton, D. J. (1995). The social context of reasoning: Conversational inference and rational judgment. *Psychological Bulletin, 118,* 248–271.

Hilton, D. J., and Slugoski, B. R. (1986). Knowledge-based causal attribution: The abnormal conditions focus model. *Psychological Review, 93,* 75–88.

Holland, J. H., Holyoak, K. J., Nisbett, R. E., and Thagard, P. R. (1987). *Induction.* Cambridge, MA: MIT Press.

Hume, D. (1777). *An enquiry concerning human understanding.* Reprint, Oxford University Press, 1975.

Josephson, J. R., and Josephson, S. G. (1994). *Abductive inference*. Cambridge: Cambridge University Press.

Kahneman, D., and Tversky, A. (1973). On the psychology of prediction. *Psychological Review, 80*, 237–251.

Keil, F. C. (1981). Constraints on knowledge and cognitive development. *Psychological Review, 88*, 197–227.

Koslowski, B. (1996). *Theory and evidence*. Cambridge, MA: MIT Press.

Lalljee, M., Lamb, R., Furnham, A. F., and Jaspars, J. (1984). Explanations and information search: Inductive and hypothesis-testing approaches to arriving at an explanation. *British Journal of Social Psychology, 23*, 201–212.

Lopéz, F. J., Shanks, D. R., Almaraz, J., and Fernández, P. (1998). Effects of trial order on contingency judgments: A comparison of associative and probabilistic contrast accounts. *Journal of Experimental Psychology: Learning, Memory, and Cognition, 24*, 672–694.

Mackie, J. L. (1974). *The cement of the universe: A study of causation*. London: Oxford University Press.

Major, B. (1980). Information acquisition and attribution processes. *Journal of Personality and Social Psychology, 39*, 1010–1023.

McGill, A. L. (1989). Context effects in judgments of causation. *Journal of Personality and Social Psychology, 57*, 189–200.

Murphy, G. L., and Medin, D. L. (1985). The role of theories in conceptual coherence. *Psychological Review, 92*, 289–316.

Pearl, J. (1996). Structural and probabilistic causality. In D. R. Shanks, D. L. Medin, and K. J. Holyoak, eds., *Psychology of learning and motivation*, Vol. 34, *Causal learning*. San Diego, CA: Academic Press.

Peirce, C. S. (1955). Abduction and induction. In J. Buchler, ed., *Philosophical writings of Peirce*. New York: Dover.

Peng, Y., and Reggia, J. A. (1990). *Abductive inference models for diagnostic problem solving*. New York: Springer.

Pennington, N., and Hastie, R. (1986). Evidence evaluation in complex decision making. *Journal of Personality and Social Psychology, 51*, 242–258.

Popper, K. R. (1963). *Conjectures and refutations: The growth of scientific knowledge*. New York: Harper and Row.

Quine, W. V. (1969). Natural kinds. In W. V. Quine, ed., *Ontological relativity and other essays*. New York: Columbia University Press.

Read, S. J. (1983). Once is enough: Causal reasoning from a single instance. *Journal of Personality and Social Psychology, 45*, 323–334.

Rey, G. (1983). Concepts and stereotypes. *Cognition, 15*, 237–262.

Salmon, W. C. (1966). *The foundations of scientific inference*. Pittsburgh: University of Pittsburgh Press.

Salmon, W. C. (1984). *Scientific explanation and the causal structure of the world.* Princeton: Princeton University Press.

Searle, J. R. (1983). *Intentionality.* NY: Cambridge University Press.

Shultz, T. R. (1982). Rules of causal attribution. *Monographs of the Society for Research in Child Development, 47,* 1–51.

Spellman, B. A. (1996). Acting as intuitive scientists: Contingency judgments are made while controlling for alternative potential causes. *Psychological Science, 7,* 337–342.

Sperber, D. (1996). *Explaining culture: A naturalistic approach.* Oxford: Blackwell.

Spirtes, P., Glymour, C., and Scheines, R. (1993). *Causation, prediction, and search.* New York: Springer.

Waldmann, M. R., and Martignon, L. (1998). A Bayesian network model of causal learning. In *Proceedings of the Twentieth Cognitive Science Conference.* Hillsdale, NJ: Erlbaum.

White, P. A. (1989). A theory of causal processing. *British Journal of Psychology, 80,* 431–454.

Wisniewski, E. J., and Medin, D. L. (1994). On the interaction of theory and data in concept learning. *Cognitive Science, 18,* 221–281.

9

Causality in the Mind: Estimating Contextual and Conjunctive Causal Power

Patricia W. Cheng

I would like to argue that humans, and perhaps all species capable of flexibly adaptive goal-directed actions, are born with a conviction that they use for inferring cause-and-effect relations in the world. This conviction—that entities and events may have causal powers with respect to other entities or events—provides a simple framework that enables reasoners to incrementally construct a picture of causal relations in a complex world. In the reasoner's mind, causal powers are invariant properties of relations that allow the prediction of the consequences of actions regardless of the *context* in which the action occurs, with "context" being the background causes of an effect (those other than the candidate causes) that happen to occur in a situation. The reasoner's goal is to infer these powers. The causal power scheme, however, is coherent only if the inferred powers can be tested in contexts other than the one in which they are inferred. When predictions based on simple causal powers fail, reasoners may be motivated to evaluate conjunctive causal power. All conventional statistical measures of independence, none of which is based on a causal power analysis, contradict measures of conjunctive causal power (Novick and Cheng 1999).

As Hume (1739) noted, because causal relations are neither deducible nor observable, such relations (unless innately known) must be inferred from observable events—the ultimate source of information about the world. (Observable input includes introspection as well as external sensory input.) This constraint poses a problem for all accounts of causal induction, the process by which reasoners come to know causal relations among entities or events: observable characteristics typical of causation do not always imply causation. One salient example of this type is *covariation*—a relation between variations in the values of a candidate cause and those in the effect (for critiques of the covariation view of untutored causal induction, see Cheng 1993, 1997; and Glymour and Cheng 1998). For example, the fact that a rooster's crowing covaries with sunrise (the sun rises more often soon after a rooster on a farm crows than at other times of the day when the rooster does not crow) does not imply that the crowing causes sunrise. Nor does the *absence* of covariation between a candidate cause and an effect, even when alternative causes are controlled, imply the lack of causal power of the candidate. Consider an experiment testing whether a candidate cause prevents an effect. Suppose alternative causes of the effect are controlled, and the effect occurs neither in the presence of the candidate cause nor in its absence, so that there is no covariation between the candidate cause and the effect. For example, suppose headaches never occur in patients who are given a potential drug for relieving headaches (those in the experimental condition of an experiment) or in patients who are given a placebo (those in the control condition). The reasoner would not be able to conclude from this absence of covariation that the candidate cause does not prevent the effect—that the drug does not relieve headaches.

9.1 Scope

This chapter concerns the discovery of causal relations involving candidate causes and effects that are represented by binary variables (or by other types of variables that can be recoded into that form); in particular, for variables representing candidate causes, those for which the two values respectively indicate a potentially causal state (typically, the presence of a factor) and a noncausal state (typically, the absence of the factor). An example of a causal question within this domain is, does striking a match cause it to light?

All analyses presented here address causal strength (the magnitude of the causal relation), separating it from statistical reliability (reason for confidence in the estimated magnitude) by assuming the latter. This chapter is consistent with, but does not address, the influence of prior causal knowledge on subsequent causal judgments (e.g., as in the rooster example; for an account of such judgments, see Lien and Cheng forthcoming; for the debate regarding whether such influence contradicts the covariation view, see Ahn and Kalish, chap. 8, this volume; Bullock, Gelman, and Baillargeon 1982; Cheng 1993; Glymour, chap. 7, this volume; Glymour and

Cheng 1998; Harré and Madden 1975; Koslowski 1996; Shultz 1982; and White 1995).

9.2 The Power PC Theory

To solve the problem of inferring causation from observable input, I proposed the power PC theory (Cheng 1997)—a causal power theory of the probabilistic contrast model (Cheng and Novick 1990)—according to which reasoners interpret covariation between two variables, one perceived to occur before the other, in terms of a probably innate a priori framework that postulates the possible existence of general types of causes (cf. Kant 1781). In this framework, covariation (a function defined in terms of observable events) is to causal power (an unobservable entity) as a scientist's observed regularity is to that scientist's theory explaining the regularity. The theory adopts Cartwright's proposal (1989) that causal powers can be expressed as probabilities with which causes influence the occurrence of an effect.

According to this theory, to evaluate the causal power of a candidate cause i to influence effect e, reasoners make a distinction between i and the composite of (known and unknown) causes of e alternative to i, which I label a, and they explain covariation defined in terms of observable frequencies by the unobservable powers of i and a. For example, when e occurs at least as often after i occurs as when i does not occur, so that

$$\Delta P_i = P(e \mid i) - P(e \mid \bar{i}) \geq 0,$$

reasoners entertain whether i *produces* e; $P(e \mid i)$ is the probability of e given that i occurs and $P(e \mid \bar{i})$ is that probability given that i does not occur. Both conditional probabilities are directly estimable by observable frequencies, and ΔP_i is the probabilistic contrast between i and e, a measure of covariation. To evaluate whether i produces e, reasoners assume that i may produce e with some probability, and explain $P(e \mid i)$ by the probability of the *union* of two events: (1) e produced by i; and (2) e produced by a if a occurs in the presence of i. That is, they reason that when i is present, e can be produced by i, *or* by a if a occurs in the presence of i. Likewise, they explain $P(e \mid \bar{i})$ by how often e is produced by a alone when a occurs in the absence of i.

For situations in which $\Delta P_i \leq 0$ (e occurs at most as often after i occurs as when i does not occur), there are analogous explanations for evaluating preventive causal power. The only assumption that differs in the preventive case is that reasoners assume that i may *prevent* e, rather than produce it, with some probability. This difference implies that when they evaluate whether i prevents e, they explain $P(e|i)$ by the probability of the *intersection* of two events: (1) e produced by a if a occurs in the presence of i; and (2) e not stopped by i. That is, they reason that when i is present, e occurs only if it is both produced by a and not stopped by i. These explanations yield equations that result in the estimation of the power of i in terms of observable frequencies under a set of assumptions, and account for a diverse range of intuitions and experimental psychological findings that are inexplicable by previous accounts (see Buehner and Cheng 1997; Cheng 1997; Wu and Cheng 1999). Such phenomena include some intuitive principles of experimental design.

The assumptions underlying these explanations of covariation in terms of causes producing or preventing effects are

1. i and a influence e independently;
2. a could produce e but not prevent it;
3. the causal powers of i and a are independent of their occurrences (e.g., the probability of a both occurring and producing e is the product of the probability of a occurring and the power of a); and
4. e does not occur unless it is caused.

When a and i do not occur independently (i.e., when there is confounding), then ΔP_i may be greater than, less than, or equal to the causal power of i, and therefore does not allow any inference about i. (See chapter appendix A for a specification of the conditions under which ΔP_i is greater or less than the power of i.) But (Cheng 1997), if

5. a and i do occur independently (i.e., when there is *no* confounding), then equation 9.1 gives an estimate of q_i, the *generative* power of i, when $\Delta P_i \geq 0$:[1]

$$q_i = \frac{\Delta P_i}{1 - P(e|\bar{i})},\tag{9.1}$$

and equation 9.2 gives an estimate of p_i, the *preventive* power of i, when $\Delta P_i \leq 0$:[2]

$$p_i = \frac{-\Delta P_i}{P(e|\bar{i})}.\tag{9.2}$$

Note that the right-hand sides (RHSs) of equations 9.1 and 9.2 require the observation of i and e only, implying that q_i and p_i can be estimated *without* observing a.

The theory "deduces" when to induce, and provides a normative justification for when and why covariation implies causation. Because equations 9.1 and 9.2 obtain only if there is "no confounding," these results show that "no confounding" is a boundary condition for causal inference, explaining the principle of control in experimental design. In addition, equation 9.1 explains why experiments should be designed to avoid a ceiling effect: when something else is always producing e anyhow (i.e., $P(e \mid \bar{i}) = 1$), q_i is undefined. And equation 9.2 explains a tacit preventive analogue: when $P(e \mid \bar{i}) = 0$, p_i is undefined, as illustrated in the headache relieving drug example earlier. This unspoken principle of avoiding contexts in which e never occurs in the absence of a candidate cause in tests of its preventive power is uniformly obeyed in experimental design (see Wu and Cheng 1999 for the use of the last two principles by untutored reasoners).[3] These principles have corresponding analogues in everyday causal inference.

9.3   Two Related Limitations of the Theory

The power PC theory concerns the discovery of *direct, simple* causal relations that consist of a single link between a candidate cause and an effect, in which the causes and effects can each be represented as a single binary variable. Glymour (1998; chap. 7, this volume) has extended this theory in various cases to indirect causes—causal chains and other causal networks. Although this theory accounts for a diverse range of intuitions and findings that are inexplicable by previous accounts of causal inference, one limitation of the theory thus far is that it does not cover *conjunctive* causes—causes that consist of a conjunction of multiple factors. This limitation is serious in that most causes in the real world are likely to be conjunctive. For example, striking a match per se does not cause it to light—there must be oxygen in the environment, the match must be dry, and so on. Likewise, cigarette smoke per se does not cause lung cancer—the smoke has to be inhaled, and the smoker has to be susceptible (only about one in ten heavy cigarette smokers eventually develop lung cancer). The susceptibility itself is probably in turn specified by multiple causal factors. How are conjunctive powers estimated?

If a causal structure of interest in fact involves conjunctive causes, then a related limitation of the power PC theory is that the evaluation of simple power requires the assumption that the candidate cause i influences e independently of all alternative causes of e (assumption 1). For a reasoner who attempts to estimate the simple causal power of candidate i when i in fact interacts with other factors to influence e, what would be the consequences of the unwarranted assumption of *independent influence*? How would the reasoner's estimate go wrong, or not go wrong?

It is important to understand the consequences of the violation of this assumption for several reasons. Sometimes, reasoners may have no choice but to assume independent influence because they lack information about what interacts with i to produce e. For example, they may not be able to observe oxygen or know anything about it at all when evaluating whether striking a match causes it to light. The estimation of conjunctive power is possible only if the components of the conjunction are observable. Even if such information is available, it seems that due to limitations in time and resources, reasoners would start with the simplest representation of the causal world, and add complications only when necessitated by evidence; thus their causal picture of the world can only be incrementally constructed. Finally, as will become clear, an analogous assumption is logically required for some set of candidate causes and causes alternative to them as part of the procedure for inferring whether that set of candidates interact to influence e. Thus even departure from the independent influence assumption requires the use of this very type of assumption with regard to a different partitioning of the set of causes of e. In short, this assumption is necessary. But an account of causal power that makes this assumption cannot explain why inferences apparently regarding simple power such as "Striking a match causes it to light" and "Smoking causes lung cancer" seem justified, even though the candidate causes involved do interact with other factors to influence the effect. What *is* inferred in such cases? What justification is there, if any, for such inferences? And how would reasoners recover from their error, if they erred?

In section 9.4, I generalize the power PC theory by dropping the independent influence assumption and examining what is inferred by a reasoner who attempts to estimate simple causal power when this assumption is violated. I show that, provided causal hypotheses can be tested under a range of contexts, including those other than the one in which a causal hypothesis was inferred, a generalized theory permitting interactive influence supports a justified inductive system that allows reasoners to sketch an increasingly fine-grained picture of the causal structure of the world starting with simple powers. Such tests may reveal failures of the estimated simple power, which may occur when the simple power of candidate cause i opposes a conjunctive power that involves i.[4] Only i and e are assumed to be observed, as would be required for estimating the simple power of i to influence e.

My generalization makes use of the concept of the power of a conjunctive cause (Novick and Cheng 1999). Section 9.5 illustrates Novick and Cheng's approach to the evaluation of conjunctive power. There two candidate causes, i and j, are assumed to be observed, as would be required for the estimation of the *conjunctive power* of i and j.

9.4 What an Attempted Estimate of Simple Causal Power Means When An Alternative Cause May Interact with the Candidate Cause to Influence e

A reasoner who attempts to estimate the simple causal power of i would use equations 9.1 or 9.2. For simple generative or preventive power, respectively, their estimates would be the RHS of equation 9.1, $\left(\dfrac{\Delta P_i}{1 - P(e \mid \bar{i})} \right)$, or the RHS of equation 9.2, $\left(\dfrac{-\Delta P_i}{P(e \mid \bar{i})} \right)$. In this section, I consider what these estimates would mean (i.e., what would replace the simple powers on the left-hand sides of these equations) if not all causes other than i influence e independently of i. In addition to dropping the independent influence assumption, I consider situations in which alternative causes may prevent—or produce—e (i.e., I drop assumption 2). The focus of my analyses is to examine the generalizability of the estimates across contexts.

I keep the same representation of the reasoner's causal world as in the power PC theory, except that I now complicate this representation by one addition: j, a composite of all variables that influence e only in combination with candidate cause i. $P(j)$ is the probability that all components of j are present. Recall that j need not be observed; to the reasoner, i is the only candidate cause.

Contextual Causal Power of a Potentially Generative Candidate Cause i

When j interacts with i to influence e, depending on whether (1) a produces e or prevents e, and (2) j interacts with i to produce e or prevent e, there are four types of situations. In each situation, the reasoner may have the goal of estimating either the generative or preventive power of i. This section summarizes the results for the situations in which generative power is estimated (cases 1 through 4); chapter appendix B presents the results for the directly analogous situations in which preventive power is estimated (cases 5 through 8).

For all my derivations in this section, I assume that

1. when a generative cause x occurs, it produces e with probability q_x (i.e., q_x is the generative power of x); when a preventive cause x occurs, it prevents (an otherwise occurring) e with probability p_x (i.e., p_x is the preventive power of x);

2. all causes alternative to the candidate causes i and j are represented by a composite a, so that no simple cause other than (possibly) i, j, and a influences the occurrence of e;

3. the interaction between i and j can be represented by a separate conjunctive power, p_{ij} or q_{ij}; this power can occur *only* when i and j both occur, but is otherwise treated just like *all* other causal powers;

4. all causal powers (including conjunctive ones) are independent of each other;

5. all causes influence the occurrence of e with causal powers that are independent of how often the causes occur;

6. i, j, and a occur independently of each other; and

7. e does not occur unless it is caused.

Case 1: Does i Cause e, when a May Cause e and j May Interact with i to Cause e?

In this case, e can be generated by i, a, or the interaction between i and j. Given the independence assumptions above, and making use of the idea that e generated by at least one of the three potential causes (the union of e produced by each of the three) is the complement of e failing to be generated by any of the causes (i.e., the complement of the intersection of the failures), it follows that

$$P(e) = 1 - [1 - P(i) \cdot q_i] \cdot [1 - P(a) \cdot q_a] \cdot [1 - P(i) \cdot P(j) \cdot q_{ij}]. \tag{9.3}$$

Therefore

$$P(e \mid \bar{\imath}) = P(a) \cdot q_a \tag{9.4}$$

and

$$P(e \mid i) = 1 - (1 - q_i) \cdot [1 - P(a) \cdot q_a] \cdot [1 - P(j) \cdot q_{ij}]. \tag{9.5}$$

Subtracting equation 9.4 from equation 9.5 yields

$$\begin{aligned}
\Delta P_i &= P(e \mid i) - P(e \mid \bar{\imath}) \\
&= q_i + P(j) \cdot q_{ij} - P(e \mid \bar{\imath}) \cdot q_i - P(e \mid \bar{\imath}) \cdot P(j) \cdot q_{ij} - P(j) \cdot q_i \cdot q_{ij} \\
&\quad + P(e \mid \bar{\imath}) \cdot P(j) \cdot q_i \cdot q_{ij} \\
&= [q_i + P(j) \cdot q_{ij} - P(j) \cdot q_i \cdot q_{ij}] \cdot [1 - P(e \mid \bar{\imath})].
\end{aligned}$$

Rearrangement yields

$$\frac{\Delta P_i}{1 - P(e \mid \bar{\imath})} = q_i + P(j) \cdot q_{ij} - P(j) \cdot q_i \cdot q_{ij}. \tag{9.6}$$

Equation 9.6 shows that in this case, the RHS of equation 9.1 gives an estimate of what I call the "contextual power" of i and j (the RHS of equation 9.6)—the power of the union of i and the interaction between i and j to produce e, to the extent that j occurs in the context. Notice that there are no a terms in the equation. Because powers are *invariant* properties attached to entities by assumption, the only context-dependent term on the RHS of equation 9.6 is $P(j)$. Candidate j may occur with varying probabilities in different situations. But if $P(j)$ happens to be stable within a context, then a reasoner who attempts to estimate the simple power of i would arrive at a useful estimate for predicting the consequences of interventions with i within that context. In other words, the contextual power of i gives an estimate of how introducing i would influence the occurrence of e. This estimate holds regardless of any causes of e other than i and j that happen to occur in the context (as long as they occur independently of i), as implied by the absence of a terms in the equation.

Returning to the match example, let i represent the striking of the match. We know that the simple power of i is 0 (i.e., $q_i = 0$) with respect to e, the lighting of the match, because other factors such as oxygen are necessary for lighting to occur. An attempt to estimate q_i according to the RHS of equation 9.1 nonetheless gives a useful estimate of the consequences of striking a match because, according to equation 9.6, the RHS of equation 9.1 gives an estimate of $P(j) \cdot q_{ij}$, the probability of e generated by the conjunctive cause that includes the striking. Given a context (e.g., striking a match on the surface of the earth indoors or on a sunny day) in which the enabling conditions of i (e.g., oxygen, dryness of the surrounding air) are stable, this estimate should be useful for predicting the lighting of the match when it is struck in that context.

In the special case where $q_i = 0$ and $q_{ij} = 1$, the RHS of equation 9.1 estimates $P(j)$. For example, suppose one's goal is to estimate the probability with which smoking causes lung cancer. One might instead be estimating the proportion of a population who have the genetic factors that leave them susceptible to lung cancer if smoking certainly causes lung cancer in those who are susceptible (cf. the interpretation of the RHS of equation 9.1 in Khoury et al. 1989). In this case, the estimate would be generalizable to other populations if, but only if, $P(j)$ is stable across populations.

Case 2: Does i Cause e, when a May Cause e and j May Interact with i to Prevent e?

In this case, e occurs when (1) it is generated by i, a, or both; and (2) it is not prevented by the interaction between i and j. Therefore

$$P(e) = \{1 - [1 - P(i) \cdot q_i] \cdot [1 - P(a) \cdot q_a]\} \cdot [1 - P(i) \cdot P(j) \cdot p_{ij}]. \tag{9.7}$$

A derivation analogous to that in case 1 shows that

$$\frac{\Delta P_i}{1 - P(e|\bar{i})} = q_i \cdot [1 - P(j) \cdot p_{ij}] - \frac{P(j) \cdot p_{ij} \cdot P(e|\bar{i})}{1 - P(e|\bar{i})}. \tag{9.8}$$

Equation 9.8 shows that unless $q_i = 0$ or $P(j) \cdot p_{ij} = 0$, the RHS of equation 9.1 gives an estimate of a complex expression that is not an enduring property generalizable to other contexts; the estimate would not be useful for predicting the consequences of interventions with i. To see this clearly, note that equation 9.8 implies that $\Delta P_i \geq 0$ if and only if

$$q_i \geq \frac{P(j) \cdot p_{ij} \cdot P(e|\bar{i})}{[1 - P(j) \cdot p_{ij}] \cdot [1 - P(e|\bar{i})]}. \tag{9.9}$$

From this relation between the value of ΔP_i and equation 9.9, it can be seen that even the *direction* of influence of the simple and conjunctive powers of i on e does not generalize across levels of $P(e|\bar{i})$, the reflection of how frequently a produces e in a context. Assigning different values to

$P(e \mid \bar{i})$ on the RHS of this inequality can lead to ΔP_i being positive or negative, that is, manipulating i can increase or decrease the occurrence of e depending on the value of $P(e \mid \bar{i})$. Likewise, it can be seen that the direction of influence also does not generalize across variations in the relative magnitudes of q_i and $P(j) \cdot p_{ij}$. The basic problem is that a conflated estimate of generative and preventive powers, such as the first product on the RHS of equation 9.8, is useless for generalization:generative and preventive powers combine to influence e in different ways with other influences on e. As explained earlier, generative powers combine their influences by forming a union; preventive powers do so by forming an intersection. The same problem arises for the preventive analogue of equation 9.8 with regard to the RHS of equation 9.2, as will be seen. Thus, for the RHSs of equations 9.1 and 9.2 to give useful estimates of causal power, dropping the independent influence assumption requires the introduction of the weaker assumption that there is no conjunctive power involving a candidate cause that opposes its simple power. (The latter assumption is weaker in that the independent influence assumption implies it, whereas even if it is not violated independence may be.)

This requirement might seem to carry a devastating implication—causal discovery is doomed! For any observed ΔP_i, there are no constraints on which kind (generative or preventive) of causal power of i it might indicate. Unless one already knows that there is no conjunctive power of i and j that opposes a simple power of i, one would not know which equation to use for assessing the simple power of i. Even if one does select the right equation by good luck, the causal power estimated when there are oppositional powers is worthless, and the reasoner may not have evidence to rule out this case.

When there is *no testing* of causal inferences in contexts other than the one within which a causal relation was inferred (or more generally, when no information pertaining to the hypothesized causal relations is available in these contexts), so that there is no revision of the hypotheses, the unjustifiability of causal inference from observations alone seems inescapable. A reasoner who starts by estimating simple powers could be stuck with meaningless estimates, and would not know which of the estimates obtained are meaningless. Given that the RHSs of equations 9.1 and 9.2 can sometimes fail as estimates of causal power, to exclude situations in which they fail, these situations must first be identified. To do so requires assessing all possible interactions between i and every variable other than *i*—an infeasible task (not only are there indefinitely many variables, but some of these variables may be unknown to the reasoner).

Other theorists have come to a similar conclusion of doom: causal inference is not justifiable based on observations alone. Cartwright (1989), for example, proposes the slogan "No causes in, no causes out." Pearl (1996) agrees. (For a contrasting position, see Spirites, Glymour, and Scheines 2000.)

My analysis gives a causal-power explanation of the impasse, pointing to the remedy at the same time it identifies the problem. Tests of simple causal powers estimated using the RHS of equations 9.1 or 9.2 may succeed or fail. If they succeed across a wide range of contexts, then it could *only* be by exceptionally bad luck that those estimates are composites of oppositional powers. Otherwise (if tests of plausible simple powers all fail), their failure would suggest the violation of the independent influence assumption, and hence the need for knowledge regarding conjunctive power. An inductive system cannot induce what is logically impossible given the information available. Thus hypothesis testing in different contexts allows thorny situations such as the one in case 2 to be separated from unproblematic ones, allowing justifiable causal discovery to proceed based on observations alone. The disconfirmed hypotheses can be revised or refined to incorporate conjunctive power, although of course there can be no guarantee of success.

I now return to the situations in which $q_i = 0$ or $P(j) \cdot p_{ij} = 0$. These are the two special situations under case 2 in which the simple and conjunctive powers of i do not influence e in opposite directions. If $p_{ij} = 0$ or $P(j) = 0$, conjunctive power is irrelevant, and equation 9.8 reduces trivially to equation 9.1. If $q_i = 0$, equation 9.8 simplifies to

$$P(j) \cdot p_{ij} = \frac{-\Delta P_i}{P(e|\bar{i})}. \tag{9.10}$$

The RHS of equation 9.10 (the same as that of equation 9.2) gives an estimate that would be useful for prediction as long as the value of $P(j)$ is stable within the scope of generalization. In the special case of this equation in which $p_{ij} = 1$, the RHS of equation 9.2 gives an estimate of $P(j)$. Although these estimates are not as generalizable as the simple power of i, they are nonetheless useful for predicting interventions involving i when $P(j)$ is stable.

Does *i* Cause or Prevent *e*, when *a* May Prevent *e* but Influences *e* Independently of *i*?

Before considering cases 3 and 4, let us first consider the simpler case in which *i* does *not* interact with anything to influence *e*. Notice that when *a* may prevent *e* but not produce it, $P(e|\bar{i})$ will be 0; it follows that the RHS of equation 9.2 is undefined, and $\Delta P_i \geq 0$. Therefore only the RHS of equation 9.1 needs to be considered. As Glymour (1998) notes, in this case (which is not discussed in Cheng 1997), my derivation of equation 9.1 does not hold. This is because the preventive power of *a*, unlike its generative power, cannot be estimated by making use of $P(e|\bar{i})$: in the absence of *i*, *a* is the only cause that could be present, and its preventive power cannot be revealed when *e* is never produced by any generative cause. Thus only a single equation results, with two unknown powers, q_i and p_a:

$$P(e|i) = q_i \cdot [1 - P(a) \cdot p_a]. \tag{9.11}$$

There is therefore no unique solution for q_i in general.

Although the derivation does not hold, it turns out that the RHS of equation 9.1 nonetheless provides a conservative, and hence useful, estimate for predicting interventions with *i*. But the assumption that *a* does not completely cancel the influence of *i* on *e* is required if $P(e|i) = 0$ (recall that *a* is unobserved).[5] Without this assumption, a reasoner would be unable to infer that $q_i = 0$ from the observation that $P(e|i) = 0$ because it is possible that $P(a) \cdot p_a = 1$ in equation 9.11. But, if $P(e|i) > 0$, one can infer from this equation that $q_i \geq P(e|i)$, because $1 > P(a) \cdot p_a \geq 0$. The same inferences regarding $P(e|i)$ can be made regarding the RHS of equation 9.1 in this case: because $P(e|\bar{i}) = 0$, this RHS reduces to $P(e|i)$. Therefore

$$\frac{\Delta P_i}{1 - P(e|\bar{i})} = q_i \cdot [1 - P(a) \cdot p_a], \tag{9.12}$$

allowing the inference that if the RHS of equation 9.1 is positive, q_i must be at least as large.

Anticipating cases 3, 4, 7, and 8, the reader should note that even if *j* interacts with *i* to produce *e*, when *a* may prevent *e* but not produce it, ΔP_i cannot be negative: in the absence of *i*, no interaction between *i* and *j* could occur, leaving $P(e|\bar{i}) = 0$. For all these cases then, only equation

9.1 is relevant. That is, when *a* may prevent *e* but not produce it, a reasoner who attempts to assess the simple power of *i* would only be assessing its generative power.

Cases 3 and 4: Does *i* Cause *e*, when *a* May Prevent *e*, and *j* May Interact with *i* to Cause *e* (Case 3) or Prevent *e* (Case 4)?
Under the condition that *a* may prevent *e*, when *j* may interact with *i* to *generate e* (case 3), because $P(e|\bar{i}) = 0$,

$$\frac{\Delta P_i}{1 - P(e|\bar{i})} = [q_i + P(j) \cdot q_{ij} - q_i \cdot P(j) \cdot q_{ij}] \cdot [1 - P(a) \cdot p_a]. \tag{9.13}$$

Likewise, when *j* may interact with *i* to *prevent e* (Case 4),

$$\frac{\Delta P_i}{1 - P(e|\bar{i})} = q_i \cdot [1 - P(j) \cdot p_{ij}] \cdot [1 - P(a) \cdot p_a]. \tag{9.14}$$

Notice that the last two equations have the same form as equation 9.12 except for the replacement of the simple power of *i* with the contextual power of *i*. Thus the same conclusions regarding the simple power of *i* estimated by the RHS of equation 9.1 in the preceding subsection can analogously be drawn about the contextual power of *i* in these cases. In particular, if the RHS of equation 9.1 is positive, then the generative contextual power of *i* (e.g., the first term in square brackets on the RHS of equation 9.13) must be at least as large because $0 < 1 - P(a) \cdot p_a \leq 1$. And for the special case when this RHS is equal to 0 due to $P(e|i) = 0$, the assumption that *a* does not completely cancel the influence of *i* on *e* is required for inferring noncausality.

We saw earlier that an estimate of conflated generative and preventive power given by the RHS of equation 9.1 is not useful in situations where *a* produces *e*. The same point applies to cases 3 and 4 if the generalization contexts might become generative, as this change in context would mean that case 4 becomes case 2. (Recall that the reasoner typically would not know which case obtains.) When *a* could only prevent *e* in the learning context, however, such an estimate is useful under the limited condition that *a* could only prevent *e* in the application contexts under consideration. Then the RHS of equation 9.1 can be at worst a conservative estimate of a potentially generative contextual power. (See cases 5 through 8, in which the reasoner attempts to evaluate the simple preventive power of *i*, in chapter appendix B.)

Summary

If and only if the simple power of i does not oppose a conjunctive power of i and j would (1) the RHS of equation 9.1 always give at worst a conservative estimate of the generative contextual power of i and j when $\Delta P_i \geq 0$; and (2) the RHS of equation 9.2 always give at worst a conservative estimate of the preventive contextual power of i and j when $\Delta P_i \leq 0$. Powers estimated under this condition are applicable in contexts where $P(j)$ is stable, regardless of whether any causes other than i and j occur. Thus, for the RHS of equation 9.1 or 9.2 to provide useful estimates of causal power, the independent-influence assumption can be replaced with the assumptions that no conjunctive power involving a candidate cause opposes its simple power and $P(j)$ is stable. The testing of causal estimates may reveal violations of these assumptions, which may motivate the evaluation of conjunctive causal power.

The assumption that a does not prevent e is required for obtaining optimal estimates of causal power. But if conservative estimates are allowable, dropping this assumption nonetheless requires replacing it with the weaker assumption that a does not completely prevent e for the special case in which $P(e|i) = 0$. In this case, the RHS of equation 9.1 having a value of 0 would not imply that i has no causal power if a completely prevents e. Violations of these assumptions may be detected by testing an estmate in a context where the power of a differs from that in the learning context.

9.5 Assessing Conjunctive Causal Power

When simple and conjunctive powers are oppositional, or more generally when predictions are less accurate than desired even given reliable assessments of simple powers, a reasoner may be motivated to construct a finer-grained picture of the causal world by assessing conjunctive causal power. Novick and Cheng (1999) extended the power PC theory to the evaluation of the conjunctive causal power of two binary variables. We complicated the reasoner's representation of the causal world one more step, by allowing two candidate causes, i and j, to *each* have simple power and jointly have conjunctive power. That is, we modified assumption 2 in section 9.4 to state, "all causes alternative to the candidate causes i and j are represented by a composite a, so that no simple cause other than (possibly) i, j, and a influences the occurrence of *e*." The other six assumptions, except for being applicable to *j* now, remain unchanged. In particular, these include the assumption that the composite *a* occurs independently of *i* and *j*. Allowing *i*, *j*, and their conjunction to have either generative or preventive power, assuming *a* to be potentially generative (recall that there is no unique estimate of generative power if *a* is preventive), and treating *i* and *j* as equivalent (e.g., so that *i* being generative and *j* being preventive is treated as an equivalent situation as *i* being preventive and *j* being generative), there are six possible cases reflecting the various combinations of these powers. We derived an equation for assessing the conjunctive power of *i* and *j* in each of these six cases. I illustrate our approach by reporting two of these analyses below.

Our concept of independent influence (no interaction) is identical to that adopted in Cheng 1997. Figure 9.1 illustrates the independent influence of two causes on a set of entities by the superimposition of the influence of each. Unlike in Figure 9.1, which presents God's view of causality, in our analyses the simple powers of *i* and *j* must be estimated from observable frequencies. They are estimated from frequencies of *e* conditional on the absence of the other candidate, so that the conjunctive power is controlled in the equations explaining the observable frequencies, and equations 9.1 and 9.2 appropriately apply. All causes alternative to a candidate are controlled, as a precondition for the application of these equations.

Case 1: Do *i* and *j* Interact to Cause *e*, When *i*, *j*, and *a* May Each Have Simple Generative Power?

First, consider the case in which *i* and *j* each produces *e*, as illustrated by the example in figure 9.1. Novick and Cheng (1999) reason that, given the assumptions as stated above, if *i* and *j* do *not* interact to generate *e*, then $P(e|ij)$ can be estimated by how often *i*, *j*, and *a* independently produce *e* (because *a* is assumed to occur independently of *i* and *j*, $P(a|ij) = P(a)$):

$$\tilde{P}(e|ij) = 1 - (1 - q_i) \cdot (1 - q_j) \cdot [1 - P(a) \cdot q_a], \tag{9.15}$$

with $\tilde{P}$ denoting an estimated probability given no interaction between the candidate causes to influence *e*. According to equation 9.15, the estimated probability of *e* occurring in this case is the complement of the probability that *e* is not produced by *i*, *j*, or *a* (i.e., the complement of

NO INTERACTION between Causes i and j

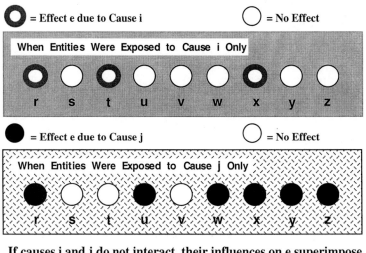

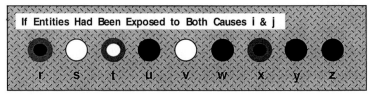

Note: Letters r, s,..., z label individual entities.

Figure 9.1
A theoretical characterization of the independent influence of two causes on a set
of entities.

the probability of the intersection of three events: *e* is not produced by *i*;
e is not produced by *j*; and *e* is not produced by *a*).

Now, if *i* and *j* do interact to generate *e*, the observed $P(e|ij)$ would
be explained by how often *e* is produced by *i*, *j*, their conjunction, or *a*
when it occurs in the presence of *i* and *j*:

$$P(e|ij) = 1 - (1 - q_i) \cdot (1 - q_j) \cdot (1 - q_{ij}) \cdot [1 - P(a) \cdot q_a]. \tag{9.16}$$

Therefore, if

$$\Delta P_{ij} = P(e|ij) - \tilde{P}(e|ij) > 0, \tag{9.17}$$

then $q_{ij} > 0$; that is, if the observed $P(e|ij)$ is larger than the estimated probability of e assuming the independent influence of i and j, then one would infer that i and j interact to produce e.

It follows that

$$q_{ij} = \frac{P(e|ij) - \{1 - (1 - q_i) \cdot (1 - q_j) \cdot [1 - P(a) \cdot q_a]\}}{(1 - q_i) \cdot (1 - q_j) \cdot [1 - P(a) \cdot q_a]} \tag{9.18}$$

$$= \frac{\Delta P_{ij}}{1 - \tilde{P}(e|ij)}. \tag{9.19}$$

The analogy to equation 9.1 should be clear.

Equation 9.19 contains the theoretical term $\tilde{P}(e|ij)$. To express this equation in terms of only probabilities directly estimable by observable frequencies, first consider the RHS of equation 9.18. Each of the three terms involving power, q_i, q_j, and $P(a) \cdot q_a$, is estimable from observable frequencies according to the power PC theory. For q_i, instantiating equation 9.1 conditional on j being absent as explained earlier yields

$$q_i = \frac{P(e|i\bar{j}) - P(e|\bar{i}\bar{j})}{1 - P(e|\bar{i}\bar{j})}. \tag{9.20}$$

Likewise,

$$q_j = \frac{P(e|\bar{i}j) - P(e|\bar{i}\bar{j})}{1 - P(e|\bar{i}\bar{j})} \tag{9.21}$$

and

$$P(a) \cdot p_a = P(e|\bar{i}\bar{j}). \tag{9.22}$$

Replacing q_i, q_j, and $P(a) \cdot q_a$ on the RHS of equation 9.18 according to equations 9.20–22, yields

$$q_{ij} = 1 - \frac{P(\bar{e}|ij) \cdot P(\bar{e}|\bar{i}\bar{j})}{P(\bar{e}|\bar{i}j) \cdot P(\bar{e}|i\bar{j})}. \tag{9.23}$$

Equation 9.23 gives the estimate of q_{ij} based on observable frequencies.

Case 2: Do i and j Interact To Prevent e, When i, j, and a May Each Have Simple Generative Power?

Analogously, if i and j interact to prevent e, the observed $P(e|ij)$ would be explained by

$$P(e|ij) = \{1 - (1 - q_i) \cdot (1 - q_j) \cdot [1 - P(a) \cdot q_a]\} \cdot (1 - p_{ij}). \tag{9.24}$$

$\tilde{P}(e|ij)$ remains as in equation 9.15. Now, one would infer that $p_{ij} > 0$ (i.e., i and j interact to prevent e) if

$$\Delta P_{ij} = P(e|ij) - \tilde{P}(e|ij) < 0. \tag{9.25}$$

It follows that

$$p_{ij} = \frac{-\Delta P_{ij}}{1 - (1 - q_i) \cdot (1 - q_j) \cdot [1 - P(a) \cdot q_a]} \tag{9.26}$$

$$= \frac{-\Delta P_{ij}}{\tilde{P}(e|ij)}. \tag{9.27}$$

The analogy to equation 9.2 is clear. In this case, rewriting in terms of "observable" probabilities yields

$$p_{ij} = \frac{[1 - P(e|ij)] \cdot [1 - P(e|\bar{i}\bar{j})] - [1 - P(e|\bar{i}j)] \cdot [1 - P(e|i\bar{j})]}{[1 - P(e|\bar{i}\bar{j})] - [1 - P(e|\bar{i}j)] \cdot [1 - P(e|i\bar{j})]}. \tag{9.28}$$

Each of the other four cases yields a pair of "theoretical" and "observable" equations, with some overlapping ones across the six cases. As can be seen from the above examples, just as the measures for evaluating simple power vary depending on the type of power being evaluated (generative or preventive) and the value of power is a function of the probability of e due to causes other than the candidate cause, the measures for evaluating interaction between two causes likewise vary depending on the type of conjunctive power being evaluated and the value of conjunctive power is a function of the probability of e due to causes other than the conjunctive candidate cause. These equations for evaluating conjunctive powers, just as those for evaluating simple powers, yield the various intuitively correct boundary conditions for causal inference for the various cases.

Consider the application of equation 9.23 to the example in figure 9.1, assuming that e does not occur in any of the individual entities in the figure when no causes of e occurs. Estimating the conditional probabilities in equation 9.23 with the frequencies in this figure, one obtains

$$q_{ij} = 1 - \frac{\frac{2}{9} \cdot \frac{9}{9}}{\frac{6}{9} \cdot \frac{3}{9}} = 0.$$

That is, causes i and j produce e completely independently, in accord with intuition.

The conjunctive power measures derived by Novick and Cheng (1999) differ from measures of interaction effect size in conventional statistics (see, for example, Fienberg 1980; Rothman and Greenland 1998; Wickens 1989). The choice of tests of main effects or interactions in conventional statistics does not depend, for example, on which direction an observed statistic deviates from the null hypothesis. I believe that for tests of causal hypotheses involving candidate causes that are represented by binary variables for which one value is potentially causal and the other noncausal, one implication of Novick and Cheng's analyses is that conventional statistics contradict intuitions, in particular, the compelling intuitions that underlie experimental methodology (no wonder statistics is hard).

This is not news in that conventional statistics, which is prevalently used to justify causal inferences with the aid of experimental design, is normally taken to be *overridden* by the principles of experimental design. When a relevant principle of experimental design is violated for a certain set of data, the resulting statistics based on that set have no causal interpretation. (In contrast, measures of causal power *incorporate* basic principles of experimental design such as "controlling for extraneous variables" as inherent mathematical results of the theory.) What may be more surprising is that even when no principle of experimental design is violated, conventional statistics may still yield conclusions that contradict those based on causal power measures. For example, if applied to sufficiently many entities with the same pattern of outcomes as in figure 9.1 (e.g., entities other than those in the figure exposed to only cause i also show that e occurs with a probability of 1/3), *all* conventional statistical measures of independence for categorical data (those for assessing reliability as well as those for assessing effect size, for example, the X^2, the G^2, the odds ratio, and log linear models) would unanimously indicate that causes i and j interact to influence e, contradicting the conclusion based on equation 9.23 and intuition. Given that causal power measures incorporate experimental methodology, differences between the two approaches raise the issue, are conventional statistical measures inappropriate for testing causal hypotheses?

9.6   Empirical Implications

What is the psychological reality of these mysterious notions of causal power in the reasoner's head? An interesting contrasting concept was proposed by Pearl (1998), who showed that, under weaker assumptions than in my derivations for generative power, the RHS of equation 9.1 is "the probability of sufficiency" (PS), the counterfactual probability that the candidate cause i would produce e if it were made present in a situation in which i and e are in fact absent. (Note that PS is restricted to apply to the learning context alone.) Pearl's derivation drops my assumption that alternative causes may produce e but not prevent it, and replaces the independent influence assumption with the assumption of monotonicity (i.e., that i never prevents e in any individual in the population in question). Notions of causal power are not required for the causal probability PS, which is therefore a more general interpretation of the RHS of equation 9.1 than is contextual power, in turn a more general intepretation than simple causal power. A more general interpretation of a causal property is one inferred under less stringent assumptions. Notice that the more general the interpretation of a property, the less that property is generalizable to other contexts. These cases suggest why, seemingly paradoxically, scientists conduct experiments with highly contrived specific conditions so as to infer causal relations that are maximally generalizable (Cartwright 1989).

I have cited some previous evidence for the psychological reality of causal powers; I list below a few examples of new questions yet to be investigated:

1. The interpretations of the RHS of equation 9.1 as simple causal power, contextual causal power, and PS are not mutually exclusive. All of these probabilities are counterfactual, with PS requiring fewer assumptions than notions of power. Because the interpretations imply different degrees of generalizability to other contexts, reasoners' interpretations can be measured by their willingness to generalize. For example, when the causal status of i is inferred in a context where there is specific knowledge that all causes alternative to i produce e and that they do so independently of i (with a probability of less than 1), then only simple causal power would predict that reasoners would be willing to apply their inference about i based on this context to a context in which all alternative causes are now known to prevent e instead. If q_i, the simple power of i, is indeed the quantity inferred in the learning context, and $P(a) \cdot p_a$ is the known preventive influence on e due to a in the novel context, then the reasoner could make use of q_i to infer that $P(e \mid i) = q_i \cdot (1 - P(a) \cdot p_a)$ in the novel context. (See Glymour and Cheng 1998 for another example of the

generalizability of inferred causal powers.) In contrast, reasoners using a PS interpretation should be unwilling to generalize to this context.

2. Given that exclusive-or relations are notoriously difficult to learn (Bruner, Goodnow, and Austin 1956), it seems that the reasoner's default assumption is that conjunctive powers that oppose its constituent simple powers do not occur. This default assumption may in itself support the PS and contextual power interpretations. To further test the adoption of these interpretations, if reasoners are given evidence that a conjunctive power involving a candidate opposes its simple power, would reasoners realize that causal judgments regarding the candidate cause cannot be made? PS and contextual power would both predict that they should.

3. The boundary conditions for inference about simple causal power that follow from equations 9.1 and 9.2 are compelling (Wu and Cheng 1999). Are the directly analogous boundary conditions for inference about conjunctive causal powers also intuitive to untutored reasoners? No account of causal discovery other than the power PC theory, its close relative PS, and its extensions to conjunctive power predicts these boundary conditions.

Appendix A: Why Causal Power Is Not Estimable When There Is Confounding

Equation 4 in Cheng 1997, which states that

$$\Delta P_i = [1 - P(a|i) \cdot q_a] \cdot q_i + [P(a|i) - P(a|\bar{i})] \cdot q_a,$$

implies that ΔP_i is not interpretable as an estimate of q_i if a, the composite of all causes alternative to i, does not occur independently of i—it could be equal to, larger than, or smaller than q_i. Below, I derive the situations under which these three possibilities respectively hold.

Case A: $\Delta P_i = q_i$
If and only if $\Delta P_i = q_i$, $\Delta P_i - q_i = 0$.

From Cheng's equation 4, it follows that

$$q_i - q_i \cdot P(a|i) \cdot q_a + P(a|i) \cdot q_a - P(a|\bar{i}) \cdot q_a - q_i = 0.$$

Rearranging yields

$$q_a \cdot [P(a|i) - P(a|\bar{i}) - q_i \cdot P(a|i)] = 0.$$

Therefore, if $q_a > 0$,

$P(a|i) - P(a|\bar{i}) - q_i \cdot P(a|i) = 0$.

That is, if $q_a > 0$, then if $P(a|i) \cdot (1 - q_i) = P(a|\bar{i})$,

$\Delta P_i = q_i$.

Case B: $\Delta P_i > q_i$

Replacing every "=" with ">" in the derivation in case A shows that if $q_a > 0$, then if

$P(a|i) \cdot (1 - q_i) > P(a|\bar{i})$, then $\Delta P_i > q_i$.

Case C: $\Delta P_i < q_i$

Analogously, if $q_a > 0$, then if $P(a|i) \cdot (1 - q_i) < P(a|\bar{i})$, then $\Delta P_i < q_i$.

Appendix B: Contextual Causal Power of a Potentially Preventive Candidate Cause *i*

Analogously as cases 1 through 4 in section 9.4, I now keep the same representation of the causal world as in the derivation of equation 9.2, except for complicating it by adding *j*, the composite of all variables that influence *e* only in combination with *i*. As before, *j* and *a* are not observed.

Case 5: Does *i* Prevent *e*, when *a* May Cause *e* and *j* May Interact with *i* to Cause *e*?

As in case 2, the simple and conjunctive powers may be oppositional in this case. Assuming that *j* produces *e* together with *i* *after* *i* has prevented *e* resulting from *a*, it can be shown that

$$\frac{-\Delta P_i}{P(e|\bar{i})} = p_i + P(j) \cdot q_{ij} - P(j) \cdot p_i \cdot q_{ij} - \frac{P(j) \cdot q_{ij}}{P(e|i)} \qquad (9.29)$$

Equation 9.29 implies that $\Delta P_i \leq 0$ if and only if

$$p_i \geq \frac{P(j) \cdot q_{ij} \cdot [1 - P(e|\bar{i})]}{P(e|\bar{i}) \cdot [1 - P(j) \cdot q_{ij}]}. \qquad (9.30)$$

The implications for this case are directly analogous to those for case 2. Unless background variables, those related to causes other than *i*, can be assumed to be stable, no predictions are justifiable based on the RHS of equation 9.2.

There are two special situations under this case in which the simple and conjunctive powers of i are not oppositional. If $q_{ij} = 0$ or $P(j) = 0$, equation 9.29 reduces to equation 9.2. And if $p_i = 0$, equation 9.29 reduces to

$$\frac{\Delta P_i}{1 - P(e|\bar{i})} = P(j) \cdot q_{ij}. \tag{9.31}$$

As can be seen, in this case the RHS of equation 9.1 gives a useful causal estimate if the value of $P(j)$ is stable. In the special case where $q_{ij} = 1$, it gives an estimate of $P(j)$.

Case 6: Does i Prevent e, When a May Cause e and j May Interact with i to Prevent e?
In this case,

$$\frac{-\Delta P_i}{P(e|\bar{i})} = p_i + P(j) \cdot p_{ij} - p_i \cdot P(j) \cdot p_{ij}. \tag{9.32}$$

As can be seen, the RHS of equation 9.2 gives the contextual preventive power of i and j. The implications for preventive power in this case are directly analogous to those in case 1 for generative power.

Cases 7 and 8: Does i Prevent e, When a May Prevent e and j May Interact with i to Cause e (Case 7) or Prevent e (Case 8)?
Case 8 involves the trivial situation in which all causes are preventive, so that e never occurs and no causal powers can be estimated. When a may prevent e, and j may interact with i to generate e (case 7), the conclusions are directly analogous to those for case 3. Regardless of whether the interaction comes before or after the prevention, if $P(e|i) > 0$, one can infer that

$$\frac{\Delta P_i}{1 - P(e|\bar{i})} \leq P(j) \cdot q_{ij}.$$

Thus, when the only contexts of generalization are ones in which a prevents e, regardless of the type of simple or conjunctive power (case 3, 4, or 7), the RHS of equation 9.1 gives at worst a conservative estimate of a potentially generative contextual power involving i.

Notes

The preparation of this chapter was supported by National Science Foundation grant 9729726. It benefited from illuminating conversations with Phillip Bonacich, who informed me that the definition of independent influence I adopt diverges from those in standard statistical measures; with Clark Glymour, who made me think about my assumptions; with Judea Pearl, who gave me tutorials on his functional causal network approach and inspired me; and with Tom Wickens, who helped me understand differences between Novick and Cheng's measures of interaction and some standard statistical measures. I thank Deborah Decarvalho, John Hummel, and Frank Keil for their very helpful comments on an earlier draft. Mistakes are of course mine.

1. Equation 9.1 was first derived from similar assumptions by Sheps (1958), who referred to it as "relative difference," and was subsequently proposed as a measure of susceptibility to exposure to candidate causes by Khoury et al. (1989). It was also derived by Pearl (1998) under a weaker set of assumptions, with a different interpretation.

2. The solutions for causal powers are unique. Although the transparency of the covariation measures as estimates of causal power differs, explaining other covariation measures leads to the same solution for q_i; likewise, for p_i.

3. It is not the typical "floor effect," which concerns situations in which some enabling conditions of a candidate cause for generative—rather than preventive—power are missing, so that i does not increase the frequency of e.

4. This corresponds to Pearl's "monotonicity" assumption (1998) and is a generalization of the assumption of "no prevention" often made in epidemiology (e.g., Angrist, Imbens, and Rubin 1996).

5. This is a special case of the "faithfulness" assumption in Spirtes, Glymour, and Scheines 2000.

References

Angrist, J. D., Imbens, G. W., and Rubin, D. B. (1996). Identification of causal effects using instrumental variables (with comments). *Journal of the American Statistical Asociation, 91* (434), 444–472.

Bruner, J. S., Goodnow, J. J., and Austin, G. A. (1956). *A study of thinking.* New York: Wiley.

Buehner, M. J., and Cheng, P. W. (1997). Causal induction: The power PC theory versus the Rescorla-Wagner model. In the *Proceedings of the Nineteenth Annual Conference of the Cognitive Science Society,* 55–60. Hillsdale, NJ: Erlbaum.

Bullock, M., Gelman, R., and Baillargeon, R. (1982). The development of causal reasoning. In W. J. Friedman, ed., *The developmental psychology of time.* New York: Academic Press.

Cartwright, N. (1989). *Nature's capacities and their measurement.* Oxford: Clarendon Press.

Cheng, P. W. (1993). Separating causal laws from casual facts: Pressing the limits of statistical relevance. In D. L. Medin, ed., *The psychology of learning and motivation*. Vol. 30, New York: Academic Press.

Cheng, P. W. (1997). From covariation to causation: A causal power theory. *Psychological Review*, *104*, 367–405.

Cheng, P. W., and Novick, L. R. (1990). A probabilistic contrast model of causal induction. *Journal of Personality and Social Psychology*, *58*, 545–567.

Cheng, P. W., Park, J-Y., Yarlas, A. S., and Holyoak, K. J. (1996). A causal-power theory of focal sets. In D. R. Shanks, K. J. Holyoak, and D. L. Medin, eds., *The psychology of learning and motivation*. Vol. 34, *Causal learning*. San Diego: Academic Press.

Fienberg, S. E. (1980). *The analysis of cross-classified categorical data* (2nd edition), 1989. Cambridge, MA: MIT Press.

Glymour, C. (1998). Psychological and normative theories of causal power and the probabilities of causes. In G. F. Cooper and S. Moral, eds., *Uncertainty in artificial intelligence*. San Francisco: Kaufmann.

Glymour, C., and Cheng, P. W. (1998). Causal mechanism and probability: A normative approach. In M. Oaksford and N. Chater, eds., *Rational models of cognition*. Oxford: Oxford University Press.

Harré, R., and Madden, E. H. (1975). *Causal powers: A theory of natural necessity*. Totowa, NJ: Rowman and Littlefield.

Hume, D. (1739). *A treatise of human nature*. 2d ed. Reprint, Oxford: Clarendon Press 1987. Also contains "An Abstract of *A Treatise of Human Nature*."

Kant, I. (1781). *Critique of pure reason*. Reprint, London: Macmillan, 1965.

Khoury, M. J., Flanders, W. D., Greenland, S., and Adams, M. J. (1989). On the measurement of susceptibility in epidemiologic studies, *American Journal of Epidemiology*, *129*, 183–190.

Koslowski, B. (1996). *Theory and evidence: The development of scientific reasoning*. Cambridge, MA: MIT Press.

Lien, Y., and Cheng, P. (Forthcoming). Distinguishing genuine from spurious causes: A coherence hypothesis. *Cognitive Psychology*.

Novick, L., and Cheng, P. (1999). Assessing interactive causal influence. Vanderbilt University, Nashville.

Pearl, J. (1996). In D. R. Shanks, K. J. Holyoak, and D. L. Medin, eds., *The Psychology of Learning and Motivation*, Vol. 34: *Causal learning*. San Diego: Academic Press.

Pearl, J. (1998). *Probabilities of causation: Three counterfactual interpretations and their identification*. Technical Report R-261. Los Angeles: University of California at Los Angeles, Department of Computer Science. Forthcoming, *Synthese*.

Rothman, K. J., and Greenland, S. (1998). *Modern epidemiology*. Philadelphia: Lippincott-Raven.

Sheps, M. C. (1958). Shall we count the living or the dead? *New England Journal of Medicine*, *259*, 1210–1214.

Shultz, T. R. (1982). Rules of causal attribution. *Monographs of the Society for Research in Child Development, 47*, no. 1.

Spirtes, P., Glymour, C., and Scheines, R. (2000). *Causation, prediction, and search.* 2nd revised edition. Cambridge, MA: MIT Press.

White, P. A. (1995). Use of prior beliefs in the assignment of causal roles: Causal powers versus regularity-based accounts. *Memory and Cognition, 23*, 243–254.

Wickens, T. D. (1989). *Multiway contingency tables analysis for the social sciences.* Hillsdale, NJ: Erlbaum.

Wu, M., and Cheng, P. W. (1999). Why causation need not follow from statistical association: Boundary conditions for the evaluation of generative and preventive causal powers. *Psychological Science, 10*, 92–97.

10

Explaining Disease: Correlations, Causes, and Mechanisms

Paul Thagard

Why do people get sick? Consider the case of Julia, a fifty-year-old lawyer who goes to her doctor complaining of stomach pains. After ordering some tests, the doctor tells here that she has a gastric ulcer. If this were the 1950s, the doctor would probably tell her that she needs to take it easy and drink more milk. If this were the 1970s or 1980s, Julia would probably be told that she suffered from excessive acidity and be prescribed Zantac or a similar antacid drug. But because this is the 1990s, her well-informed doctor tells her that she probably has been infected by the newly discovered bacterium *Helicobacter pylori* and that she needs to take a combination of antibiotics that will eradicate it and cure the ulcer.

The aim of this chapter is to develop a characterization of disease explanations, such as the explanation that Julia got her ulcer because of a bacterial infection.[1] Medical explanation is highly complex because most diseases involve the interplay of multiple factors. Many people with *H. pylori* infection do not get ulcers, and some people have ulcers without having an infection. I will offer a proposal that a disease explanation is best thought of as a *causal network instantiation*, where "causal network" describes the interrelations among multiple factors, and "instantiation" consists of observational or hypothetical assignment of factors to the patient whose disease is being explained. Explanation of why members of a particular class of people (women, lawyers, and so on) tend to get a particular disease is also causal network instantiation, but at a more abstract level.

Section 10.1 discusses the inference from correlation to causation, integrating recent psychological discussions of causal reasoning with epidemiological approaches to understanding disease causation. I will use the development since 1983 of the bacterial theory of ulcers and the evolution over the past several decades of ideas about the causes of cancer, particularly lung cancer, to illustrate disease explanation. Both of these developments involved progression from observed correlations to accepted causal hypotheses (bacteria cause ulcers, smoking causes cancer), followed by increased understanding of the mechanisms by which the causes produce the diseases. Section 10.2 shows how causal mechanisms represented by causal networks can contribute to reasoning involving correlation and causation. Section 10.3 presents the causal network instantiation (CNI) model of medical explanation, while section 10.4 discusses the model and its applications.

10.1   Correlation and Causes

Explanation of why people get a particular disease usually begins by the noticing of associations between the disease and possible causal factors. For example, the bacterial theory of ulcers originated in 1982 when two Australian physicians, Barry Marshall and J. Robin Warren, noticed an association between duodenal ulcer and infection with *Helicobacter pylori*, a previously unknown bacterium that Warren had microscopically discovered in biopsy specimens in 1979 (Marshall 1989; Thagard 1999). Marshall and Warren (1984, 1314) were aware that their study, which looked for relations between presence of the bacteria and various stomach elements in 100 patients who had had endoscopic examinations, did not establish a cause-and-effect relation between bacteria and ulcers. But they took it as evidence that the bacteria were etiologically related to the ulcers and undertook studies to determine whether eradicating the ulcers would cure the bacterial infection. These studies (Marshall et al. 1988) were successful, and by 1994, enough additional studies had been done by researchers in various countries that the National Institutes of Health Consensus Development Panel (1994) concluded that bacterial infection is causally related to ulcers and recommended antibiotic treatment.

A similar progression from correlation to causation has taken place with various kinds of cancer. Over two thousand years ago, Hippocrates described cancers of the skin, stomach, and breast, among other tissues, and held that cancer is caused, like all diseases, by an imbalance of bodily humors, particularly an excess of black bile. In the eighteenth century, rough correlations were noticed between cancers and various practices: using snuff and nose cancer, pipe smoking and lip cancer, chimney sweeping and scrotum cancer, and being a nun and breast cancer (Proctor 1995, 27–28). The perils of causal reasoning are shown by the inferences of the Italian physician Bernardino Ramazzini, who concluded in 1713 that the increased incidence of breast cancer in nuns was caused by their sexual abstinence, rather than by their not having children. Early in the twentieth century, it was shown that cancers can be induced in laboratory animals by radiation and coal tar.

Lung cancer rates increased significantly in Great Britain and the United States during the first half of the twentieth century, correlating with increase in smoking, but carefully controlled studies did not begin to appear until the 1950s (Hennekens and Buring 1987, 44). In one classic study conducted in England, 649 male and 60 female patients with lung cancer were matched to an equal number of control patients of the same age and sex. For both men and women, there was a strong correlation between lung cancer and smoking, particularly heavy smoking. By 1964, when the U.S. surgeon general asserted a causal link between lung cancer and smoking, there had been 29 controlled studies performed in numerous countries that showed a high statistical association between lung cancer and smoking. Although the exact mechanism by which smoking causes cancer was not known, over 200 different compounds had been identified in cigarette smoke that were known carcinogens.

To grasp how disease explanations work, we need to understand what correlations are, what causes are, and how correlations can provide evidence for causes.[2] Patricia Cheng's "power PC" theory (1997) of how people infer causal powers from probabilistic information provides a useful starting point. Cheng proposes that when scientists and ordinary people infer the causes of events, they use an intuitive notion of causal power to explain observed correlations. She characterizes correlation (covariation) in terms of probabilistic contrasts: how much more probable is an effect given a cause than without the cause. The association between an effect e and a possible cause c can be measured by $\Delta P_c = P(e/c) - P(e\,|\sim c)$, that is, the probability of e given c minus the probability of e given not-c. In contrast to a purely probabilistic account of causality, however, she introduces an additional notion of the *power* of a cause c to produce an effect e, p_c, the probability with which c produces e when c is present.[3] Whereas $P(e/c)$ is an observable frequency, p_c is a theoretical entity hypothesized to explain frequencies, just as theoretical entities like electrons and molecules are hypothesized to explain observations in physics. In Cheng's account, causal powers are used to provide theoretical explanations of correlations, just as theories such as the kinetic theory of gases are used to explain laws linking observed properties of gases (pressure, volume, temperature).

According to Cheng, a causal power p_c is a probability. But what kind of probability? Although philosophers have debated whether probabilities are frequencies, logical relations, or subjective states, the interpretation of probability that seems to fit Cheng's view best is a propensity, that is, a dispositional property of part of the world to produce a frequency of events in the long run. The causal power p_c cannot be immediately inferred from the observed frequency $P(e/c)$ or the contrast, ΔP_c, because the effect e may be due to alternative causes. Celibate nuns get breast cancer more than nonnuns, but it is nonpregnancy rather than celibacy that is causally related to breast cancer. To estimate the causal power of c to produce e, we need to take into account alternative possible causes of e, designated collectively as a. If there are no alternative causes of e besides c, then $P(e/c)$ $= p_c$, but they will normally not be equal if a is present and produces e in the presence of c, that is, if $P(a/c)*p_a > 0$, where p_a is the causal power of a to produce c. In the simple case where a occurs independently of c, Cheng shows that p_c can be estimated using the equation

$$p_c = \Delta P_c / 1 - P(a) * p_a.$$

The causal relation between e and c can thus be assessed by considering positively the correlation between e and c and negatively the operation of other causes a. When these alternative causes do not occur independently of c, then ΔP_c may not reflect the causal status of c.

Cheng's characterization of the relation between correlations and causal powers fits well with epidemiologists' discussions of the problem of determining the causes of diseases.[4] According to Hennekens and Buring (1987, 30), a causal association is one in which a "change in the frequency or quality of an exposure or characteristic results in a corresponding change in the frequency of the disease or outcome of interest." Elwood (1988, 6) says that "a factor is a cause of an event if its operation increases the frequency of the event." These statements incorporate both ΔP_c, captured by the change in frequency, and the idea that the change in frequency is the result of the operation of the cause, that is, a causal power. Further, epidemiologists stress that assessing whether the results of a study reveal a causal relation requires considering alternative explanations of the observed association, such as chance, bias in the design of the study, and confounding alternative causes (see also Evans 1993; Susser 1973). Thus the inference from correlation to cause must consider possible alternative causes, p_a.[5]

Hennekens and Buring (1987) summarize their extensive discussion of epidemiologic studies in the framework reproduced in table 10.1. Questions A1–A3 reflect the need to rule out alternative causes, while questions B1 and B3 reflect the desirability of high correlations' ΔP_c. Cheng's account of causal reasoning captures five of the eight questions relevant to assessing causal power, but the remaining three questions lie beyond the scope of her model, which is restricted to induction from observable input. Hennekens and Buring (1987, 40) state that "the belief in the existence of a cause and effect relationship is enhanced if there is a known or postulated biologic mechanism by which the exposure might reasonably alter the risk of the disease." Moreover (p. 42), "for a judgment of causality to be reasonable, it should be clear that the exposure of interest preceded the outcome by a period of time consistent with the proposed biological mechanism." Thus, they find, epidemiologists do and should ask mechanism-related questions about biologic credibility and time sequence; this issue is discussed in the next section. Finally, their last question concerns the existence of a dose-response relationship, that is, the observation of a gradient of risk associated with the degree of exposure. This relation is not just ΔP_c, the increased probability of having the disease given the cause, but rather the relation that being subjected to more of the cause produces more of the disease, for example, heavy smoking leads more often to lung cancer than does light smoking.

Table 10.1
Framework for the Interpretation of an Epidemiologic Study

A. Is there a valid statistical association?
   1. Is the association likely to be due to chance?
   2. Is the association likely to be due to bias?
   3. Is the association likely to be due to confounding?
B. Can this valid statistical association be judged as cause and effect?
   1. Is there a strong association?
   2. Is there biologic credibility to the hypothesis?
   3. Is there consistency with other studies?
   4. Is the time sequence compatible?
   5. Is there evidence of a dose-response relationship?

Source: Hennekens and Buring 1987, 45.

Hennekens and Buring show how answers to the questions in table 10.1 provide a strong case for a causal connection between smoking and lung cancer. Many studies have shown a strong association between smoking and cancer, with a nine- to ten-fold increase in lung cancer among smokers (B1, B3), and the high statistical significance of the results makes it unlikely that the association is due to chance (A1). The conduct of the studies ruled out various sources of observation bias (A2), and researchers controlled for four potential confounding factors: age, sex, social class, and place of residence (A3). By 1959, cigarette smoke was shown to contain over 200 different known carcinogens, providing possible mechanisms that establish the biologic credibility of hypothesis that smoking causes cancer (B2). Moreover, there was evidence of a temporal relationship between smoking and cancer, because people obviously get lung cancer after they have been smoking for a long time, and people who stop smoking dramatically drop their chances of getting cancer (B4). Finally, there is a significant dose-response relationship between smoking and lung cancer, in that the risk of developing lung cancer increases substantially with the number of cigarettes smoked per day and the duration of the habit.

The development of the bacterial theory of ulcers can also be interpreted in terms of Cheng's theory of causality and Hennekens and Buring's framework for epidemiologic investigation. In 1983, when Marshall and Warren first proposed that peptic ulcers are caused by bacteria, specifically, *Helicobacter pylori* bacteria, most gastroenterologists were highly skeptical. They attributed the presence of *H. pylori* in Warren's gastric biopsies to contamination, and they discounted the correlation between ulcers and bacterial infection as likely the result of chance or incorrect study design. Moreover, an alternative explanation that ulcers are caused by excess acidity was widely accepted because of the success of antacids in alleviating ulcer symptoms. But attitudes toward the ulcer hypothesis changed dramatically when numerous other researchers observed *H. pylori* in stomach samples, and especially when other research teams replicated Marshall and Warren's finding that eradicating *H. pylori* usually cures ulcers.

The key question is whether *H. pylori* causes ulcers, which requires attributing to it the causal power to increase the occurrence of ulcers. Initial evidence for this attribution was the finding that people with *H. pylori* bacteria more frequently have ulcers than those without, *P(ulcers/ bacteria)* > *P(ulcers/no bacteria)*, but the early studies could not establish causality because they did not address the question of possible alternative causes for the ulcers. Whereas lung cancer investigators had to use case control methods to rule out alternative causes by pairing up patients with lung cancers with similar patients without the disease, ulcer investigators could use the fact that *H. pylori* can be eradicated by antibiotics to perform a highly controlled experiment with one set of patients, comparing them before eradication and after. The results were striking: the frequency of ulcers dropped substantially in patients whose bacteria had been eliminated, and long-term recurrence rates were also much lower. These experiments thus showed a very high value for ΔP, $P(ulcers/bacteria) - P(ulcers/no\ bacteria)$, under circumstances in which no alternative causal factors such as stress, diet, and stomach acidity were varied.

Dose-response relationship has not been a factor in the conclusion that *H. pylori* bacteria cause ulcers because it is not easy to quantify how many *H. pylori* bacteria inhabit a given patient's stomach. Time sequence is not much of an issue because the common presence of *H. pylori* in children implies that people get the bacteria well before they get ulcers.[6] But biologic credibility, concerning the mechanism by which bacterial infection might produce ulcers, has been the subject of much investigation, as I will discuss in section 10.2.

Thus much of the practice of physicians and epidemiologists in identifying the causes of diseases can be understand in terms of Cheng's theory that causal powers are theoretical entities that are inferred on the basis of finding correlations and eliminating alternative causes. But mechanism considerations are also often relevant to assessing medical causality.

10.2 Causes and Mechanisms

What are mechanisms and how does reasoning about them affect the inference of causes from correlations? A mechanism is a system of parts that operate or interact like those of a machine, transmitting forces, motion, and energy to one another. For millennia humans have used simple machines such as levers, pulleys, inclined planes, screws, and wheels. More complicated machines can be built out of these simple ones, all of which transmit motion from one part to another by direct contact. In the sixteenth and seventeenth centuries, natural philosophers came more and more to understand the world in terms of mechanisms, culminating with Newton's unified explanation of the motion of earthly and heavily bodies.

His concept of force, however, went beyond the operation of simple machines by direct contact to include the gravitational interaction of objects at a distance from each other. In the history of science, progress has been made in many sciences by the discovery of new mechanisms, each with interacting parts affecting each other's motion and other properties. Table 10.2 displays some of the most important of such mechanisms. The sciences employ different kinds of mechanisms in their explanations, but each involves a system of parts that change as the result of interactions among them that transmit force, motion, and energy. Mechanical systems are organized hierarchically, in that mechanisms at lower levels (e.g., molecules) produce changes that take place at higher levels (e.g., cells).

Medical researchers similarly are highly concerned with finding mechanisms that explain the occurrence of diseases, for therapeutic as well as theoretical purposes: understanding the mechanism that produces a disease can lead to new ideas about how the disease can be treated. In

Table 10.2
Sketch of Important Mechanisms in Science

Science	Parts	Changes	Interactions
Physics	Objects such as sun and planets	Motion	Forces such as gravitation
Chemistry	Elements, molecules	Mass, energy	Reactions
Evolutionary biology	Organisms	New species	Natural selection
Genetics	Genes	Genetic transmission and alteration	Heredity, mutation, recombination
Geology	Geological formations such as mountains	Creation and elimination of formations	Volcanic eruptions, erosion
Plate tectonics	Continents	Motion such as continental drift	Floating, collision
Neuroscience	Neurons	Activation, synaptic connections	Electrochemical transmissions
Cell biology	Cells	Growth	Cell division
Cognitive science	Mental representations	Creation and alteration of representations	Computational procedures

cancer research, for example, major advances were made in the 1970s and 1980s in understanding the complex of causes that lead to cancer (Weinberg 1996). There are over a hundred different kinds of cancer, but all are now thought to result from uncontrolled cell growth arising from a series of genetic mutations, first in genes for promoting growth (onco-genes) and then in genes for suppressing the tumors that are produced by uncontrolled cell growth. The mechanism of cancer production then con-sists of parts at two levels—cells and the genes they contain—along with changes in cell growth produced by a series of genetic mutations. Muta-tions in an individual can occur for a number of causes, including hered-ity, viruses, and behavioral and environmental factors such as smoking, diet, and exposure to chemicals. Figure 10.1 sums up the current understand-ing of the mechanisms underlying cancer. This understanding is currently generating new experimental treatments based on genetic manipulations such as restoring the function of tumor suppresser genes (Bishop and Weinberg 1996).

Ulcer researchers have also been very concerned with the mecha-nism by which *Helicobacter pylori* infection produces ulcers. Figure 10.2 dis-plays a mechanism similar to one proposed by Graham (1989) that shows some of the interactions of heredity, environment, infection, and ulcera-tion. Research is underway to fill in the gaps about these processes (e.g., Olbe et al. 1996).

Recent psychological research by Woo-kyoung Ahn and her col-leagues has found that when ordinary people are asked to provide causes for events, they both seek out information about underlying causal mech-anisms and use information about correlations (Ahn et al. 1995; Ahn and

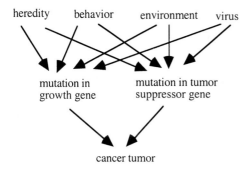

Figure 10.1
Mechanism of cancer production.

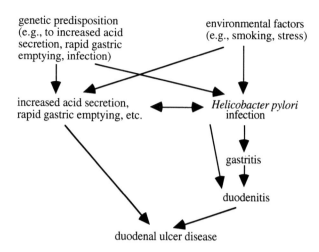

Figure 10.2
Possible mechanism of duodenal ulcer production. Modified from Graham 1989, 51. Gastric ulcer causation is similar.

Bailenson 1996). For example, if people are asked to state the cause of John's car accident, they will not survey a range of possible factors that correlate with accidents, but will rather focus on the process underlying the relationship between cause and effect, such as John's being drunk leading to erratic driving leading to the accident. Whereas causal attribution based on correlation (covariation) alone would ignore mechanisms connecting cause and effects, ordinary people are like medical researchers in seeking mechanisms that connect cause and effect.

As Cheng (1997) points out, however, the emphasis on mechanism does not by itself provide an answer to the question of how people infer cause from correlation: knowledge of mechanisms is itself knowledge of causally related events, which must have somehow been previously acquired. Medical researchers inferred that bacteria cause ulcers and that smoking causes cancer at times when little was known about the relevant causal mechanisms. Reasoning about mechanisms can contribute to causal inference, but is not necessary for it. In domains where causal knowledge is rich, there is a kind of feedback loop in which more knowledge about causes leads to more knowledge about mechanisms, which leads to more knowledge about causes. But in less well understood domains, correlations and consideration of alternative causes can get causal knowledge started in the absence of much comprehension of mechanisms.

To understand how reasoning about mechanisms affects reasoning about causes, we need to consider four different situations in science and ordinary life when we are deciding whether a factor *c* is a cause of an event *e*:

1. There is a known mechanism by which *c* produces *e*.
2. There is a plausible mechanism by which *c* produces *e*.
3. There is no known mechanism by which *c* produces *e*.
4. There is no plausible mechanism by which *c* produces *e*.

For there to be a known mechanism by which *c* produces *e*, *c* must belong to a system of parts known to interact to produce *e*. Only very recently has a precise mechanism by which smoking causes cancer become known through the identification of a component of cigarette smoke (Benzo[a]pyrene) that produces mutations in the tumor suppresser gene p53 (Denissenko et al. 1996). As we saw above, however, there has long been a *plausible* mechanism by which smoking causes lung cancer.

When there is a known mechanism connecting *c* and *e*, the inference that *c* causes *e* is strongly encouraged, although information about correlations and alternative causes must still be taken into account because a different mechanism may have produced *e* by an alternative cause *a*. For example, drunk driving often produces erratic driving, which in turn produces accidents, but even if John was drunk, his accident might have been caused by a mechanical malfunction rather than his drunkenness. Similarly, even though there is now a plausible mechanism connecting *H. pylori* infection and ulcers, we should not immediately conclude that Julia has the infection because approximately 20% of ulcers are caused by use of nonsteroidal antinflammatory drugs (NSAIDs) such as aspirin. But awareness of known and plausible mechanisms connecting *c* and *e* clearly facilitates the inference that *c* causes *e*, in a manner that will be more fully spelled out below. Another way in which the plausibility of a mechanism can be judged is by analogy: if a cause and effect are similar to another cause and effect that are connected by a known mechanism, then it is plausible that a similar mechanism may operate in the first case. There was a plausible mechanism by which *H. pylori* caused stomach ulcers because other bacteria were known to produce other sores.

Sometimes causal inference from correlation can be blocked when there is no plausible mechanism connecting the event and its cause, that is, when possible mechanisms are incompatible with what is known. When

Marshall and Warren first proposed that bacteria cause ulcers, the stomach was widely believed to be too acidic for bacteria to survive for long, so that there was no plausible mechanism by which bacteria could produce ulcers. Later it was found that *H. pylori* bacteria produce ammonia, which by neutralizing stomach acid allows them to survive, removing the implausibility of the bacteria–ulcer mechanism. Similarly, when Alfred Wegener proposed continental drift early in this century, his theory was rejected in part because the mechanisms he proposed for continental motion were incompatible with contemporary geophysics. Only when plate tectonics was developed in the 1960s was it understood how continents can be in motion.

The two cases just mentioned are ones in which the implausibility of mechanisms was overcome, but there are many cases where rejection of causal relations remains appropriate. Even though there is some correlational evidence for ESP, it is difficult to believe that people have such powers as telepathy and telekinesis, whose properties of being unaffected by spatial and temporal relations conflict with known physical mechanisms. Similarly, homeopathic medicine using minute doses of drugs violates established views concerning the amounts of substances needed to be chemically effective. An even more extreme case is the theory of Immanuel Velikovsky that the planet Venus swung close to earth on several occasions, causing among other things the parting of the Red Sea for Moses. Because such planetary motion is totally incompatible with Newtonian mechanics, there is no plausible mechanism by which Venus's motion could have the claimed effect.

How can medical researchers and ordinary people combine information about mechanisms with information about correlations and alternative causes to reach conclusions about cause and effect? Recall Cheng's view that causes are theoretical entities to be inferred on the basis of correlations and alternative causes. Elsewhere (Thagard 1992), I have argued that the justification of scientific theories including their postulation of theoretical entities is a matter of explanatory coherence, in which a theory is accepted because it provides a better explanation of the evidence. Explanatory coherence of a hypothesis is a matter both of the evidence it explains and of its being explained by higher-level hypotheses. For example, Darwin justified the hypothesis of evolution both in terms of the biological evidence it explained and in terms of evolution being explained by the mechanism of natural selection. Moreover, he explicitly compared the explanatory power of his theory of evolution by natural selection with the explanatory limitations of the dominant creation theory of the origin of species. These three factors—explaining evidence, being explained by mechanisms, and consideration of alternative hypotheses—are precisely the same considerations that go into evaluation of a causal hypothesis.

Figure 10.3 shows how the inference that c causes a disease d can be understood in terms of explanatory coherence (for the full theory of explanatory coherence and its implementation in the computional model ECHO, see Thagard 1989, 1992). When medical researchers collect data having a correlation between c and d, that is, a high value for $P(d/c)$ − $P(d/{\sim}c)$, there are several possible explanations for these data. That there really is a correlation in the relevant population between d and c is one possible explanation, but experimenters must rule out chance and experimental bias as alternative explanations.[7] Careful experimental designs involving such techniques as randomization and double-blinding help to rule out bias, and appropriate techniques of statistical inference tend to rule out chance, leading to the acceptance of the hypothesis that there is a real correlation between c and d. However, before researchers can conclude that c *causes* d, they must have reason to believe that this hypothesis is a better explanation of the correlation than other confounding causes

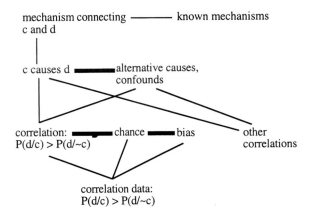

Figure 10.3
Inferring a cause c from correlation data about a disease d. That there is a correlation between d and c must be a better explanation of the observed correlation and other correlations than alternative confounding causes. The existence of a mechanism connecting c and d provides an explanation of why c causes d. Thin lines are explanatory relations, while thick lines indicate incompatibility.

that might have been responsible for it. Again careful experimental design that manipulates only c or that otherwise controls for other potential causes is the key to concluding that c causes d is the best explanation of the correlation. In addition, the existence of a known or plausible mechanism for how c can produce d increases the explanatory coherence of the causal hypothesis. On the other hand, if all mechanisms that might connect c with d are incompatible with other scientific knowledge, then the hypothesis that c causes d becomes incoherent with the total body of knowledge. Evans (1993, 174) offers as one of his criteria for causation in medicine that "the whole thing should make biologic and epidemiologic sense." As Hennekens and Buring (1987) suggest, a major determinant of whether a causal hypothesis makes sense is whether it comes with a plausible underlying mechanism.

Figure 10.3 points to a synthesis of Cheng's ideas about causal powers, probabilities, and alternative causes with considerations of mechanism. Mechanisms are not a necessary condition for causal inference, but when they are known or plausible, they can enhance the explanatory coherence of a causal hypothesis. Moreover, causal hypotheses incompatible with known mechanisms are greatly reduced in explanatory coherence. Inference to causes, like inference to theoretical entities in general, depends on explanatory coherence as determined by evidence, alternative hypotheses, and higher-level hypotheses.

Inference to medical causes is similar to legal inference concerning responsibility for crimes. In a murder case, for example, the acceptability of the hypothesis that someone is the murderer depends on how well that hypothesis explains the evidence, on the availability of other hypotheses to explain the evidence, and on the presence of a motive that would provide a higher-level explanation of why the accused committed the murder. Motives in murder trials are like mechanisms in medical reasoning, providing nonessential but coherence-enhancing explanation of a hypothesis.

This section has discussed how knowledge of mechanisms can affect inferences about causality, but it has passed over the question of how such knowledge is obtained. There are three possibilities. First, some knowledge about basic physical mechanisms may be innate, providing infants with a head start for figuring out the world. For example, it is possible that infants are innately equipped to infer a causal relation when one moving object bangs into another object that then starts moving. Second, some of the links in the causal chains that constitute a mechanism may be learned by induction from observed correlations, as described in Cheng's power PC model. For example, we can observe the relations among pressure, temperature, and volume changes in gases and infer that they are causally connected. Third, sometimes mechanisms are abduced, that is, posited as a package of hypothetical links used to explain something observed. For example, in cognitive science we posit computational mechanisms with various representations and processes to explain intelligent behavior. Darwin abduced the following causal chain:

variation + competition → natural selection → evolution of species.

The difference between abductive and inductive inference about mechanisms is that in inductive inference the parts and processes are observed, whereas in abductive inference they are hypothesized. Knowledge about mechanisms involving theoretical (nonobservable) entities must be gained abductively, by inferring that the existence of the mechanism is the best explanation of the results of observation and experiment. Different domains vary in the extent to which knowledge about mechanisms is innate, induced from correlations, or abductive.

10.3 Disease Explanation as Causal Network Instantiation

The above description of the interrelations of correlations, causes, and mechanisms provides the basis for an account of the nature of medical explanation. We can eliminate a number of defective alternative accounts of explanation, including that explanation is essentially deductive, statistical, or involves single causes.

1. *Explanation is not deductive.* The deductive nomological model of Hempel (1965), according to which an explanation is a deduction of a fact to be explained from universal laws, clearly does not apply to the kinds of medical explanation we have discussed. Deductive explanations can be found in other fields such as physics, in which mathematical laws entail observations. But there are no general laws about the origins of ulcers and cancer. As we saw, most people with *H. pylori* do not get ulcers, and many people without *H. pylori* do get ulcers because of NSAIDs. Similarly, most smokers do not get lung cancer, and some nonsmokers do get lung cancer. The development of ulcers, like the development of cancer, is far too complex for general laws to provide deductive explanation.

2. *Explanation is not statistical.* Statistics are certainly relevant to developing medical explanations, as we saw in the contribution of P(*ulcers/bacteria*) − P(*ulcers/no bacteria*) to the conclusion that bacteria cause ulcers. But correlations themselves have no explanatory force because they may be the result of confounding alternative causes. As we saw in figure 10.3, the conclusion that there is a causal and hence an explanatory relation between a factor and a disease depends on numerous coherence considerations, including the full range of correlations explained, the applicability of alternative causes, and the availability of a mechanism by which the factor produces the disease. A medical explanation need not show that a disease was to be expected with high probability because the probability of getting the disease given the main cause may well be less than 0.5, as is the case for both ulcers/bacteria and lung cancer/smoking.

3. *Explanation is not in terms of single causes.* Although it is legitimate to see bacteria as the major causal factor in most ulcers and smoking as the major causal factor in most lung cancers, it is simplistic to explain someone's ulcer only in terms of bacterial infection, or someone's lung cancer only in terms of smoking. As figures 10.1 and 10.2 displayed, ulcer causation and cancer causation are complex processes involving multiple interacting factors. Medical researchers increasingly stress the multifactor nature of disease explanations. Adult-onset diabetes, for example, is now understood as arising from a complex of factors including heredity, obesity, and inactivity, all contributing to glucose intolerance, possibly because of a mechanism that involves a protein that reduces glucose uptake.

I propose instead that medical explanation should be thought of as causal network instantiation (CNI; for recent work on causal networks, see Glymour et al. 1987; Iwasaki and Simon 1994; Pearl 1988; and Shafer 1996). For each disease, epidemiological studies and biological research establish a system of causal factors involved in the production of a disease. The causal network for cancer is a more elaborate version of figure 10.1, and the causal network for ulcers is a more elaborate version of figure 10.4, which expands figure 10.2. Crucially, the nodes in this network are connected not only by conditional probabilities, P(*effect/cause*), but also by causal relations inferred on the basis of multiple considerations, including correlations P(*effect/cause*) − P(*effect/~cause*), alternative causes, and mechanisms. We then explain why a given patient has a given disease by instantiating the network, that is, by specifying which factors operate in that patient. To go back to the Julia case, the physician can start to instantiate the network in figure 10.4 by determining whether Julia takes large quantities of NSAIDs, for example, because she has arthritis. Different instantiation can take place on the basis of tests, for example, endoscopy or a breath test to determine whether her stomach is infected with *H. pylori*. Some instantiation will be abductive, making hypotheses about the operation of factors that cannot be observed or tested for.[8] The physician might make the abduction that Julia has a hereditary inclination to excess acidity, which would explain why she, unlike most people with *H. pylori*, has an ulcer; the hereditary abduction would be strengthened if her parents and other relatives had ulcers. Similarly, to explain patients' lung cancers, we instantiate a causal network with information about their smoking, their other behaviors, their heredity, and so on.

Instantiation of a causal network such as the one in figure 10.4 produces a kind of narrative explanation of why a person gets sick. We can tell several possible stories about Julia, such as

1. Julia became infected with *H. pylori* and because of a predisposition to excess acidity she got an ulcer.
2. Julia took a large number of aspirin for her arthritis, which produced so much acidity in her stomach that she got ulcers.

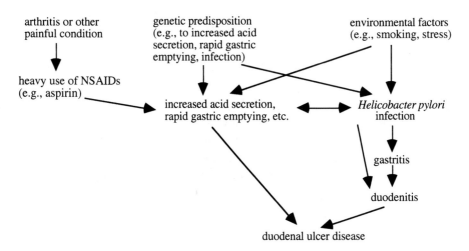

Figure 10.4
General causal network for duodenal ulcers, expanding figure 10.2.

But medical explanation is not just storytelling because a good medical explanation should point to all the interacting factors for which there is both causal evidence and evidence of relevance to the case at hand. Although a narrative may be a useful device for communicating a causal network instantiation, the ensemble of statistically based causal relations is more crucial to the explanation than the narration.

Causal networks provide an explanatory schema or pattern, but they differ from the sorts of explanatory schemata and patterns proposed by others. Unlike the explanatory patterns of Kitcher (1981, 1993), causal networks are not deductive. Deductive patterns may well have applications in fields such as mathematical physics, but they are of no use in medicine, where causal relationships are not well represented by universal laws. Unlike the explanation patterns of Schank (1986), causal networks are not simple schemata that are used to provide single causes for effects, but instead describe complex mechanisms of multiple interacting factors. My account of medical explanation as causal network instantiation, although compatible with the emphasis on mechanistic explanations by Salmon (1984) and Humphreys (1989), provides a fuller specification of how causal networks are constructed and applied.

Explanation of why a group of people is prone to a particular disease is also a matter of causal network instantiation. People in underdeveloped countries are more likely to have gastritis than North Americans, because poorer sanitation makes it more likely that they will acquire the *H. pylori* infections that produce ulcers. Nuns are more likely to get breast cancer than other women, because women who do not have full-term pregnancies before the age of 30 are more likely to get breast cancers, probably because of some mechanism by which pregnancy affects breast cell division. When we want to explain why a group is more likely to get a disease, we invoke the causal network for the disease and instantiate the nodes based on observations and abductions about the disease factors possessed by members of the group. Thus CNI explanations of both individual and group disease occurrence are structurally identical.[9]

10.4   Conclusion

This chapter has shown how correlations, causes, and mechanisms all figure in the construction of causal networks that can be instantiated to provide medical explanations. The main criterion for assessing a model of disease explanation is whether it accounts for the explanatory reasoning of medical researchers and practitioners. We have seen that the causal network instantiation model of medical explanation fits well with methodological recommendations of epidemiologists such as Hennekens and Buring, and with the practice of medical researchers working on diseases such as ulcers and lung cancer. Additional examples of the development and application of causal networks could easily be generated for other diseases such as diabetes. My account of medical explanation as causal network instantiation gains further credibility from the fact that its assumptions about correlations, causes, and mechanisms are consistent with (and provide a synthesis of) Cheng's and Ahn's psychological models of human causal reasoning.

I make here no claims about the application of the CNI model beyond the field of medicine. For fields such as physics, the existence of universal laws and mathematical precision often make possible explanations that are deductive. On the other hand, in fields such as economics, the lack of causal knowledge interrelating various economic factors may restrict explanations to being based on statistical associations. I expect, however, that there are many fields such as evolutionary biology, ecology, genetics, psychology, and sociology in which explanatory practice fits the CNI model. For example, the possession of a feature or behavior by members of a particular species can be explained in terms of a causal network involving mechanisms of genetics and natural selection. Similarly, the possession of a trait or behavior by a human can be understood in terms of a causal network of hereditary, environmental, and psychological factors. In psychology as in medicine, explanation is complex and multifactorial in ways well characterized as causal network instantiation.

Notes

For research support, I am grateful to the Natural Sciences and Engineering Research Council of Canada and the Social Sciences and Humanities Research Council of Canada. My thanks to Patricia Cheng, Herbert Simon, and Rob Wilson for comments on earlier drafts.

1. This chapter is not concerned with the diagnostic problem of finding diseases that explain given symptoms, but rather with finding causes of diseases that patients are known to have. On medical diagnosis, see, for example, Peng and Reggia 1990.

2. Terminological note: I take "correlation" to be interchangeable with "covariation" and "statistical association." Correlations, however, are not always measured by the statistical formula for coefficient of correlation, which applies only to linear relationships.

3. Similarly, Peng and Reggia (1990, 101f.) use "probabilistic causal models" that rely, not on conditional probabilities of the form $P(effect/disease)$, but on "conditional causal probabilities" of the form $P(disease\ causes\ effect/disease)$. Both probabilistic and causal power ideas have a long history in philosophy. On probabilistic causality, see, for example, Suppes 1970; Eells 1991; and Shafer (1996). On causal powers, see, for example, Cartwright 1989; and Harré and Madden (1975).

4. Cheng's characterization also fits with the view of Chinn and Brewer (1996) that data interpretation is a matter of building mental models that include alternative explanations.

5. Is the consideration of alternative explanations in causal reasoning descriptive or prescriptive? Both: I am offering a "biscriptive" model of medical reasoning—one that describes how people make inferences when they are in accord with the best practices compatible with their cognitive capacities (Thagard 1992, 97).

6. The correlation between ulcers and bacteria might be taken to suggest that ulcers cause bacterial infections, rather than the other way around. But the presence of bacteria is too widespread for this to be plausible: $P(bacteria/ulcers) - P\ (bacteria/no\ ulcers)$ is not high because the bacteria are quite common, infecting up to 50% of the population. Moreover, *H. pylori* bacteria were not found to be prominent on gastric ulcer borders, suggesting that the ulcers were not responsible for bacterial growth.

7. Mayo (1996) provides a thorough discussion of the use of statistical tests to rule out errors deriving from chance and other factors. Another possible source of error is fraud, when the observed correlations are based on fabricated data.

8. Abductive inference is inference to explanatory hypotheses. See, for example, Thagard 1988 and Josephson and Josephson 1994.

9. Note that I have not attempted to define *cause* in terms of explanation or *explanation* in terms of cause. Causes, mechanisms, explanations, and explanatory coherence are intertwined notions.

References

Ahn, W., and Bailenson, J. (1996). Causal attribution as a search for underlying mechanism: An explanation of the conjunction fallacy and the discounting principle. *Cognitive Psychology, 31*, 82–123.

Ahn, W., Kalish, C. W., Medin, D. L., and Gelman, S. (1995). The role of covariation versus mechanism information in causal attribution. *Cognition, 54*, 299–352.

Bishop, J. M., and Weinberg, R. A., ed. (1996). Scientific American *molecular oncology*. New York: Scientific American Books.

Cartwright, N. (1989). *Nature's capacities and their measurement.* Oxford: Clarendon Press.

Cheng, P. W. (1997). From covariation to causation: A causal power theory. *Psychological Review, 104*, 367–405.

Chinn, C. A., and Brewer, W. F. (1996). Mental models in data interpretation. *Philosophy of Science, 63* (proceedings supplement), S211–219.

Denissenko, M. F., Pao, A., Tang, M., and Pfeifer, G. P. (1996). Preferential formation of Benzo[a]pyrene adducts at lung cancer mutational hotspots in p53. *Science, 274*, 430–432.

Eells, E. (1991). *Probabilistic causality.* Cambridge: Cambridge University Press.

Elwood, J. M. (1988). *Causal relationships in medicine.* Oxford: Oxford University Press.

Evans, A. S. (1993). *Causation and disease: A chronological journey.* New York: Plenum Press.

Glymour, C., Scheines, R., Spirtes, P., and Kelly, K. (1987). *Discovering causal structure.* Orlando, FL: Academic Press.

Graham, D. Y. (1989). *Campbylobacter pylori* and peptic ulcer disease. *Gastroenterology, 96,* 615–625.

Harré, R., and Madden, E. (1975). *Causal powers.* Oxford: Blackwell.

Hempel, C. G. (1965). *Aspects of scientific explanation.* New York: Free Press.

Hennekens, C. H., and Buring, J. E. (1987). *Epidemiology in medicine.* Boston: Little, Brown.

Humphreys, P. (1989). *The chances of explanation.* Princeton: Princeton University Press.

Iwasaki, Y., and Simon, H. (1994). Causality and model abstraction. *Artificial Intelligence, 67,* 143–194.

Josephson, J. R., and Josephson, S. G., eds. (1994). *Abductive inference: Computation, philosophy, technology.* Cambridge: Cambridge University Press.

Kitcher, P. (1981). Explanatory unification. *Philosophy of Science, 48,* 507–531.

Kitcher, P. (1993). *The advancement of science.* Oxford: Oxford University Press.

Marshall, B. J. (1989). History of the discovery of *C. pylori.* In M. J. Blaser, ed., *Campylobacter pylori in gastritis and peptic ulcer disease.* New York: Igaku-Shoin.

Marshall, B. J., Goodwin, C. S., Warren, J. R., Murray, R., Blincow, E. D., Blackbourn, S. J., Phillips, M., Waters, T. E., and Sanderson, C. R. (1988). Prospective double-blind trial of duodenal ulcer relapse after eradication of *Campylobacter pylori. Lancet, 2,* 1437–1441.

Marshall, B. J., and Warren, J. R. (1984). Unidentified curved bacilli in the stomach of patients with gastritis and peptic ulceration. *Lancet, 1,* 1311–1315.

Mayo, D. (1996). *Error and the growth of experimental knowledge.* Chicago: University of Chicago Press.

National Institutes of Health Consensus Development Panel. (1994). *Helicobacter pylori* in peptic ulcer disease. *Journal of the American Medical Association, 272,* 65–69.

Olbe, L., Hamlet, A., Dalenbäck, J., and Fändriks, L. (1996). A mechanism by which *Helicobacter pylori* infection of the antrum contributes to the development of duodenal ulcer. *Gastroenterology, 110,* 1386–1394.

Pearl, J. (1988). *Probabilistic reasoning in intelligent systems.* San Mateo, CA: Kaufman.

Peng, Y., and Reggia, J. (1990). *Abductive inference models for diagnostic problem solving.* New York: Springer.

Proctor, R. N. (1995). *Cancer wars: How politics shapes what we know and don't know about cancer.* New York: Basic Books.

Salmon, W. (1984). *Scientific explanation and the causal structure of the world.* Princeton: Princeton University Press.

Schank, R. C. (1986). *Explanation patterns: Understanding mechanically and creatively.* Hillsdale, NJ: Erlbaum.

Shafer, G. (1996). *The art of causal conjecture.* Cambridge, MA: MIT Press.

Suppes, P. (1970). *Probabilistic theory of causality.* Atlantic Highlands, NJ: Humanities Press.

Susser, M. (1973). *Causal thinking in the health sciences.* New York: Oxford University Press.

Thagard, P. (1988). *Computational philosophy of science.* Cambridge, MA: MIT Press.

Thagard, P. (1989). Explanatory coherence. *Behavioral and Brain Sciences, 12,* 435–467.

Thagard, P. (1992). *Conceptual revolutions.* Princeton: Princeton University Press.

Thagard, P. (1999). *How scientists explain disease.* Princeton: Princeton University Press.

Weinberg, R. A. (1996). *Racing to the beginning of the road: The search for the origin of cancer.* New York: Harmony Books.

IV

Cognitive Development, Science, and Explanation

11

Explanation in Scientists and Children

William F. Brewer, Clark A. Chinn, and Ala Samarapungavan

In examining explanations as used by scientists and by children, this chapter provides a psychological account of the nature of explanation and the criteria people use to evaluate the quality of explanations. We first discuss explanation in everyday and scientific use, then analyze the criteria used by nonscientists and scientists to evaluate explanations, describing the types of explanations commonly used by nonscientists and scientists. Finally, we use the framework we have developed to discuss the development of explanation in children.

Intended as a naturalist approach to the philosophy of science (Giere 1985; Kornblith 1994), our account of explanation is descriptive rather than normative. Our evidence comes from the use of explanations by adult nonscientists and children, on the one hand, and by contemporary and historical scientists, on the other.

11.1 What Is Explanation?

As a fundamental intellectual construct, explanation itself is very difficult to explain. It seems to us, however, that people have relatively clear intuitions about what is or is not an explanation and that these intuitions serve as the foundation of most discussions of explanation (cf. Friedman 1974). Most philosophical accounts of explanation begin with examples about which the writer has strong intuitions and proceed to develop a theory of explanation consistent with these examples (see the review of philosophical theories of explanation given in Salmon 1990). Psychologists have tended to treat explanation as a primitive construct without analyzing it. Our account of explanation is intended to be very broad, to capture our linguistic and conceptual intuitions about what an explanation is, and to distinguish explanations from other conceptual processes such as description or evaluation.

The Nature of Explanation in Everyday Use

We hypothesize that, in everyday use, an explanation provides a conceptual framework for a phenomenon (e.g., fact, law, theory) that leads to a feeling of understanding in the reader or hearer. The explanatory conceptual framework goes beyond the original phenomenon, integrates diverse aspects of the world, and shows how the original phenomenon follows from the framework. Three general types of conceptual frameworks often used in giving explanations are (1) causal or mechanical; (2) functional; and (3) intentional.

It seems to us that placing a phenomenon in some larger conceptual framework is the conceptual core of people's everyday use of explanation. For example, suppose someone asks, "Why did this balloon expand when placed in the sun?" Statements that do not place the phenomenon in a larger conceptual framework, such as "I saw it get bigger" or "I like balloons," simply do not constitute explanations, whereas statements such as "It contains a gas, and gases expand when they are heated" or "The gas in the balloon is composed of molecules, and they strike harder against the sides of the balloon when they are heated" are canonical examples of explanations.

Placing a phenomenon in a larger conceptual framework reduces the arbitrariness of the phenomenon (Woodward 1989). After being given the explanation of why the balloon expanded, the questioner knows that other balloons would behave the same way and knows why the balloon could not have stayed the same size or contracted. An explanatory framework shows how the phenomenon to be explained follows from the framework, typically in a causal manner. Thus, from an understanding of the idea that there are many very small particles beating against the sides of an elastic balloon and that they hit harder when heated, it follows that the balloon should expand when heated. Providing a framework typically integrates diverse phenomena (Friedman 1974; Kitcher 1981); for example, the account of why the balloon expanded also allows an understanding of why automobile tires contract (seem deflated) in the winter. For something to be an explanation, the framework has to go beyond the original phenomenon. Thus a response that the balloon expanded because it was "expandable" does not provide a larger conceptual framework and does not seem to have explanatory force.

Finally, we have included the experiential process of "understanding" in our account. It is this experience of understanding that gives rise to people's intuitions about what is and what is not an explanation. A desire to achieve this understanding may underlie people's motivation to construct explanations (Gopnik 1996).

The Nature of Explanation in Science

We think that there is much overlap between the form of everyday explanations used by nonscientists and explanations used by scientists. Although discussions of the nature of scientific explanations by philosophers of science and by scientists show a rather strong diversity of opinion, over the last forty years (cf. Salmon 1990), there has been a shift in opinion in the general direction of the view that we hold. More specifically, we hypothesize that scientific explanations are like everyday explanations in that they (1) provide a theoretical or conceptual framework for a phenomenon; (2) go beyond the original phenomenon; (3) integrate a range of phenomena; (4) show how the original phenomenon follows from the framework; and (5) provide a feeling of understanding.

In addition to these shared characteristics, we think that scientific explanations have one very important additional attribute—they must be, in principle, testable. For example, evolutionary biologists have argued that creationism is unscientific because it is untestable—there is no observation that could possibly disconfirm it (Futuyma 1983). It seems to us that this requirement for testability is the one new addition to the core conception of explanation that derives from the scientific revolution.

11.2 Quality of Explanations

Quality of Explanations for Nonscientists

When one is given an explanation of a phenomenon there appears to be a natural human tendency to evaluate the quality of the explanation. Although this issue is clearly open to empirical investigation, we are not aware of any systematic studies of it. Therefore our discussion will include attributes we think are important on general theoretical grounds and data from several empirical studies that can be reinterpreted as relevant to the issue of the judged quality of explanations.

Empirical Accuracy   One of the strong determinants of the perceived quality of an explanation is the degree to which it is consistent with empirical evidence. A study by Brewer and Chinn (1994) supports the idea that nonscientists prefer theories that are consistent rather than inconsistent with the empirical evidence. In this experiment undergraduates were presented either with evidence supporting the theory that dinosaurs were cold-blooded or with evidence for the theory that dinosaurs were warm-blooded. Then they were asked to rate their belief in both theories. The undergraduates showed a very strong preference for the theory that was supported by the evidence they had read.

Scope   A related issue is the scope of an explanation. We think that non-scientists prefer explanations that account for a greater range of phenomena. There are several studies that support this hypothesis. Chinn and Brewer (1992) presented undergraduates with explanatory theories (e.g., the meteor impact theory of mass extinctions at the end of the Cretaceous period) and manipulated the range of data explained by the theory. They found that undergraduates gave higher belief ratings for the theory that could explain the wider range of data. Schank and Ranney (1991) have also shown that undergraduates prefer theories with wider empirical scope.

Consistency   We think nonscientists prefer explanations that are internally consistent to those that have inconsistencies. Once again, there are studies that lend indirect support for this hypothesis, but we do not know of direct tests with adults of this aspect of the quality of explanations.

Simplicity   We consider one explanation to be simpler than another if it accounts for a phenomenon with fewer assumptions or hypotheses than a rival explanation. We are not sure that simplicity should be included in a list of criteria for everyday explanations. Although we are unaware of any systematic studies showing that adults prefer simple to complex explanations when such factors as empirical accuracy and scope are held constant, explanations produced by adults tend to be, if anything, overly simple rather than overly complex (D. Kuhn 1991). Thus we hypothesize that adults are sensitive to the criterion of simplicity.

Plausibility Another important determinant of the quality of an explanation is its plausibility—the degree to which the particular explanation is consistent with an individual's larger background beliefs. Given the wide range of background beliefs that individuals hold about matters of theory and data, there clearly will be wide individual differences in the judgments of the plausibility of a given explanation. We do not know of any direct tests of this hypothesis, but there is some indirect evidence. Chinn and Brewer (1998) carried out a study of undergraduates' responses to anomalous data. They found two categories of responses that consisted of holding on to a particular theory and rejecting anomalous data because it was implausible. For example, one student rejected data purporting to show that a meteor impact would cause eighteen months of complete darkness by saying that these scientists had not taken into account global winds that would disperse the dust.

"Irrational" Beliefs We see a tension between our position on the evaluative criteria used by nonscientists and the fact that a large number of individuals in our society hold apparently irrational beliefs (e.g., creationism, presence of aliens on earth). We are, in fact, concerned by this apparent inconsistency and in future work intend to speak to this issue in greater detail. We see several lines of argument. First, one can appeal to individual or situational differences in the application of the criteria we have proposed. Perhaps most individuals apply the criteria in most situations, but there is a subset of individuals who rarely use them. Additionally, even those individuals who usually apply the criteria in most situations may fail to apply them in particular contexts (e.g., in emotionally-laden situations). Second, we think the gradual decline in the role of supernatural explanations in Western culture could be taken as evidence for the increase in the application of these criteria. Third, it is possible that individuals who believe in ghosts or ESP apply the quality metrics we have described, but differ in their standards of evaluation of the quality of evidence or in the amount of evidence to which they have been exposed. Clearly, this is an area for theoretical and empirical investigation.

Quality of Explanations for Scientists

We hypothesize that the criteria used by scientists to judge the quality of scientific explanations include most of those used by nonscientists to judge everyday explanations plus a number of additional criteria. More specifically, we think that *empirical accuracy, scope, consistency, simplicity* and *plausibility* are used in evaluating both scientific and everyday explanations (the first four are explicitly listed in the criteria used for evaluating scientific theories given in Kuhn 1977 and Thagard 1992). The criterion of *plausibility* (consistency with background theory and data) is not explicitly listed in the accounts of scientific explanation referred to above but is implicitly considered an important criterion by most writers on these issues. Although both scientists and nonscientists share these criteria, we think that scientists typically apply these criteria much more severely. For example, scientists tend to respond very negatively to internal inconsistency in scientific explanations (cf. Laudan 1977), whereas psychologists have often assumed that nonscientists are fairly tolerant of some inconsistencies in their beliefs (e.g., Reif and Larkin 1991).

Precision   We believe that scientists value explanations that make very precise predictions. Indeed, it seems to us that one of the major driving forces in the development of physics and chemistry has been a stronger and stronger application of the criterion of precision to the evaluation of explanations. Scientists in these areas have come to value explanations that produce precise quantitative predictions.

Formalisms   We think that explanations that can be expressed in mathematical form are valued by most scientists over those expressed in more qualitative, discursive form.

Fruitfulness   Finally, we believe that scientists value explanations that provide guidance for future research and that open up new areas of research (Kuhn 1977).

Criteria Changes   Toulmin (1961) and other writers have made strong arguments that the criteria used by scientists to evaluate explanations have changed over time. We take the list above to be based on the evaluative behaviors of contemporary working scientists.

Nature of Explanations versus Quality   It seems to us that scientists discussing proposed explanations sometimes confuse the criteria used to decide whether an assertion is a scientific explanation with the attributes used to evaluate the quality of explanations. For example, when faced with an explanation that involves ESP or perpetual motion, scientists often say these explanations are "unscientific." We think the problem here is that the criteria of empirical support and plausibility are so strong that the scientists are led to conclude that the proposed explanation is simply not an explanation. We want to hold to the distinctions we have outlined above and say that explanations involving ESP or perpetual motion *are* scientific explanations, but poor ones on the criteria of empirical support and plausibility. This distinction is important for us because when we come to section 11.4, on the development of explanations in children, we want to make a clear distinction between children's accounts that are not explanations and children's accounts that show the core explanatory pattern but that are inadequate in terms of empirical support or plausibility.

11.3   Types of Explanations

A core assumption in our account of explanation is that explanations provide a conceptual framework for a phenomenon. These conceptual frameworks involve some of the most general systems of organization of the human intellect such as *causality* and *intentionality*.

We think that there are a large number of conceptual frameworks, which vary widely in scope, from the very general, such as *causality* and *intentionality*, to the more specific, such as the belief that everyday objects are composed of invisible atoms.

Common Types of Everyday Explanations

Causal or Mechanical   Probably the most fundamental form of everyday explanation is causal or mechanical. For example, "Why didn't the light come on?—Because it wasn't plugged in."

Functional   This important form of everyday explanation can involve the function of human artifacts: "Why do lights have light switches?—So people can turn lights on and off." Or it can involve the function of biological kinds ("teleological"): "Why do fish have gills?—So they can take in oxygen."

Intentional   Everyday explanations of human behavior typically make use of an intentional framework: "Why did you cut off the light?—Because I intended to go to sleep."

Types of Scientific Explanations

We think that the conceptual frameworks used in scientific explanations (see Nagel 1961) typically include many of the types used by nonscientists, such as those listed above, although we realize that historically some scientists (e.g., Watson 1919) have rejected the use of intentionality as a framework for scientific explanations.

In addition to the conceptual frameworks listed above, scientists also use *formal* or *mathematical* forms of explanations. "Why does this emission line of hydrogen have this frequency?—Because of Balmer's formula." Although formal or mathematical forms of explanation are the preferred form of explanation in some of the most highly developed sciences, historically there has been a tension in physics between those who prefer causal mechanistic explanations ("models") and those who prefer formal or mathematical explanations (see Campbell 1957; Hesse 1967).

In the history of science, there have been changes both in the criteria used to evaluate explanations and in the preferred conceptual frameworks. In particular, there have been large shifts in the beliefs of scientists about which domains are appropriately explained by which conceptual frameworks. Thus scholars in the Aristotelian tradition thought it appropriate to use intentional or functional (teleological) forms of explanation for various aspects of the physical world, whereas contemporary scientists do not.

11.4   The Development of Explanation in Childhood

In this section we use the analysis of explanation that we have developed to guide our examination of the question of the development of explanation in children. Although there has been little work focused directly on the issue of the development of explanation, it is possible to use research designed for other purposes to begin to explore this topic. In particular, research designed to explore children's naive models of the natural world (Driver, Guesne, and Tiberghien 1985) provides direct evidence on some of the issues raised in the first part of this chapter. The typical methodology of research in this area is to pick a restricted domain of the natural world (e.g., light, heat, electricity) and ask children a structured set of questions designed to reveal the children's theories about phenomena in that domain. In this research paradigm, an attempt is made to avoid asking questions that presuppose the adult scientific theory. This approach has led to a fascinating set of findings. It has shown that, across a range of domains, children behave as "little scientists" and develop their own naive theories of the natural world. This work is directly relevant to the issue of explanation because, in the course of trying to understand children's theories of the natural world, the children are frequently asked "why" or "how" questions about the domain. The children's responses to these questions allow us to explore some aspects of the development of explanation in children because adults usually respond to such questions by giving explanations. Each of the authors of the current chapter has carried out research on the topic of naive theories: observational astronomy (Vosniadou and Brewer 1994); biological evolution (Samarapungavan and Wiers 1994, 1997); and chemical reactions and states of matter (Chinn 1997). We will use selected examples from our research to try to give some preliminary answers to the issues of the development of explanation in children.

In addition to the literature on naive theories, there are a few studies directly on some of the topics discussed in the earlier sections of this chapter. In particular, Samarapungavan (1992) has carried out a direct study of some aspects of children's evaluations of the quality of explanations. Young children were presented with two explanations that differed with respect to a particular attribute and asked which explanation they preferred. We will also discuss the findings from this study.

Development of Explanation

Do children give explanations of natural phenomena that have the characteristics we described in our account of the nature of explanations? The following sets of questions by experimenters (E) and answers by children (C) contain three different children's accounts of the disappearance of the sun at night taken from Vosniadou and Brewer 1994.

Kristie (grade 1)   E: "Where is the sun at night?" C: "Gone in space." E: "How does this happen?" C: "When it get dark it goes way into space."
Karen (grade 3)   E: "Where is the sun at night?" C: "Well, it goes under the earth to China. See, while we have day China has night and while China has night, we have day." E: "How does this happen?" C: "Well the moon and sun trade places every [12 hours]."
Cindy (grade 3)   E: "Where is the sun at night?" C: "On the other side of the earth. Because when night comes over here the sun goes onto

the other side of the earth and it's day on there." E: "How does this happen?" C: "The earth turns around." E: "Does the earth move?" C: "Yeah." E: "Does the sun move?" C: "No."

It seems to us that each of these examples shows that young children produce full-blooded explanations. Each of these accounts places the phenomenon to be explained in a conceptual framework, although each child uses a somewhat different instantiation of a causal or mechanical framework.

Each explanation goes beyond the original regularity. Kristie introduces the concept of space in her explanation and also an implicit corollary that objects far away are not visible. Both Karen's geocentric explanation and Cindy's heliocentric explanation go on to give an account for the day/night cycle on the other side of the earth, thus showing that their explanations have the power to give an account of phenomena far beyond that asked for in the initial question.

Each explanation integrates a range of phenomena. Almost all children who explained the disappearance of the sun at night by having it move away in space also used the same mechanism to account for the disappearance of the moon. In the example quoted above, Karen uses her explanatory framework to give an integrated account of the day/night cycle on both sides of the earth.

Each of these accounts shows how the phenomenon in question can be derived from the postulated conceptual framework. This aspect of explanation was made very explicit in later research on this topic. Samarapungavan, Vosniadou, and Brewer (1996) asked children about the day/night cycle and provided the children with models to help them articulate their accounts. The children were quite good at manipulating the models to show how their theory would generate the day/night cycle.

These studies provide no data on the issue of whether or not the children's accounts gave them a feeling of understanding the phenomenon; however, we think it is highly likely that they do. In fact the desire to understand the diverse phenomena of the natural world may well have been what motivated these children to construct their own theories of the day/night cycle. (Unlike scientists, children are not paid to construct theories!)

Scientific Explanations   In our discussion of the nature of scientific explanations we argued that scientific explanations incorporate all of the attributes of general explanations and add an additional requirement of testability. We think it is quite likely that children are not sensitive to this aspect of explanation and may well be content with explanations that could not be empirically tested. There is indirect evidence on this issue in the literature on children's naive theories. For example, some of the children in the study by Samarapungavan and Wiers (1997) gave creationist accounts of the origin of life—an explanation that one assumes is untestable. Note, however, that most explanations for natural phenomena given by children are potentially testable, like the three astronomy explanations given above. Perhaps the strong preference children show for explanations involving "touch causality" (Andersson 1986; Reiner, Chi, and Resnick 1988) indirectly leads to empirically verifiable explanations.

Child versus Scientist   Our overall analysis suggests that children's explanations for the physical world show the same essential structure as those used by scientists, except that scientists include a requirement that explanations be potentially testable.

Development of Criteria of Quality of Everyday Explanations

Empirical Support   There is considerable evidence that children prefer theories that have empirical support. Samarapungavan (1992) carried out a direct test of this issue, presenting children with two theories, one of which was supported by empirical evidence and the other of which was disconfirmed. Children (even those in the first grade) showed a strong preference for the empirically supported explanation. In addition, the literature on children's naive theories offers much indirect support for the hypothesis that children are sensitive to the issue of empirical support. The studies in this area show that the theories children develop tend to give a good account of the empirical evidence known to the child (the three astronomy examples given above show this characteristic).

    Does the finding that children prefer explanations with better empirical support imply that children also prefer testable explanations? We have argued that children are probably unlike scientists in that they do not require explanations to be testable. Yet a preference for explanations with empirical support may also imply a preference for explanations that can be tested with empirical evidence. However, we do not think there is necessarily an inconsistency here. First, it is the case that many untestable "explanations" can account for all relevant empirical evidence (e.g., it was willed by a Supreme Being) and thus might appear attractive to children who favor explanations with apparent empirical support. Second, note that in the Samarapungavan experiment children were asked to choose, not between a testable explanation and an untestable explanation, but between two testable explanations. We think that a child given such a choice might say that the explanations are equally good or that there is no way to decide between the theories, but would not deny that the untestable explanation was an explanation. We think that a scientist, by contrast, would say that the untestable explanation is not even an explanation. This is an important issue for further investigation.

Scope   The evidence that children prefer theories that account for a wider range of data is more limited. Samarapungavan (1992) carried out an explicit test of this hypothesis and found that children did, in fact, prefer a theory that accounted for a broader set of data to one that accounted for only a subset of that data.

Consistency   The question of whether children's explanations are rigorously consistent is more difficult to answer. It appears that in the domains of the earth's shape (Vosniadou and Brewer 1992), the day/night cycle (Vosniadou and Brewer 1994), and speciation (Samarapungavan and Wiers 1997), children as young as first graders develop coherent explanatory models. In the case of the earth's shape and the day/night cycle, many children form fully consistent models across the two explanatory domains. Levin et al. (1990) have also found that when children with somewhat inconsistent views have the inconsistency pointed out to them, most change one of the explanations to make them consistent. These results suggest that children have the capacity to achieve considerable consistency in their explanations. However, Chinn (1997) has reported that most children's explanations in the domains of matter, states of matter, and chemical reactions were not highly consistent. Researchers in the area of naive mechanics (e.g., diSessa 1988) have argued that adult nonscientists as well as children give explanations that do not cohere with each other very well. We think that further research is needed on this important topic. On one hand, it does appear that nonscientists often tolerate considerable inconsistency in their various explanations. On the other hand, in the early stages of theory development, scientists may also exhibit considerable inconsistency, and it is only through the collective efforts of many scientists that inconsistencies are resolved (cf. Brewer and Samarapungavan 1991).

Simplicity   We are not certain whether children apply a criterion of simplicity in evaluating theories, but we think there is indirect evidence that they do. Samarapungavan (1992) included a condition in which she compared one theory with another theory that had an ad hoc component. She found that older children (grade 5) tended to prefer the theory without the ad hoc component. One can interpret this condition as contrasting a simpler with a more complex theory, and under this interpretation, the study shows that older children prefer simpler theories to more complex ones. There is also indirect support for a simplicity metric in the literature on children's naive models: in the area of observational astronomy, Vosniadou and Brewer (1994) found that children showed a strong tendency to use the same mechanism to explain the disappearance of the sun and the disappearance of the moon; Vosniadou and Brewer used this finding to argue that children apply a simplicity metric in their construction of theories in the area of observational astronomy.

Plausibility   Although there is little direct research on the issue of whether children prefer theories that are consistent with their background beliefs, it seems to us that the indirect evidence is very strong. One of the core findings in the literature on children's theories of the natural world is that children find many scientific explanations very difficult to accept; most of these explanations appear to contain components that are implausible from the child's point of view. For example, the investigations of children's beliefs about the shape of the earth (Vosniadou and Brewer 1992) show that children who hold a flat earth view find the concept of a spherical, rotating earth to be very implausible. From the flat earth point of view the spherical account is inconsistent with background beliefs, such as that the earth looks flat and that people on the bottom of a sphere would fall off. Thus we think it likely that plausibility is one of the important criteria that children apply in judging the quality of explanations.

Development of Criteria of Quality of Scientific Explanations

In this section, we will examine the issue of children's appreciation of the special criteria that scientists apply in theory evaluation.

Precision   Samarapungavan (1995a) has investigated the issue of whether children value precision in theory evaluation. She found that young children were as likely to prefer a theory that made less precise predictions (e.g., more people will get better with treatment X) as they were to prefer one that made more precise predictions (e.g., 9 out of 10 people will get better with treatment X). Samarapungavan found that, in general, children do not become sensitive to the precision of a theory until about age 12. Thus it appears that the criterion of precision may be late to develop.

Formalism   The literature on children's theories of the natural world suggests that the criterion of formal or mathematical expression is not one shared by children. Children essentially never produce theories in formal or mathematical form.

Fruitfulness   We know of no evidence of children adopting a criterion of fruitfulness in theory evaluation. In general, it seems to us that children are in the business of making sense of their world, not in producing new data, so that it seems unlikely that children would evaluate explanations using this criterion.

Child versus Scientist   Our examination of the criteria that children use to evaluate theories suggests that children apply all of the criteria for quality of explanations that are used in evaluating general explanations, but that they are much less likely to use the special criteria used by scientists to evaluate explanations.

Types of Explanations Used by Children

Causal or Mechanical   The literature on children's theories of the natural world shows that children make wide use of causal explanations and, in fact, may have a strong preference for causal theories (Andersson 1986; Reiner, Chi, and Resnick 1988). For example, Chinn (1997) found that most explanations children gave for chemical processes such as rusting were causal or mechanical. The three astronomy examples given above are typical examples of children's use of causal or mechanical forms of explanation.

Functional   There is clear evidence that children use functional forms of explanation of the natural world. Samarapungavan and Wiers (1997) found a range of functional explanations in their research on children's accounts of biological phenomena. For example:

Rob (age 9) E: "How did polar bears acquire their white fur?" C: "From their parents. All polar bears have white fur. It helps them hide in the snow." E: "Is that why they got white fur—to hide better?" C: "No . . . they always had white fur—that is why they are called 'ice bears' [Dutch word for polar bear]." E: "Penguins have wings but they cannot fly. Why do they have wings?" C: "They use the wings to steer—in swimming."

Intentional There is a large literature showing that children use intentional explanations of human behavior at a relatively young age (Wellman 1990). There is also some evidence (Piaget 1960; Kelemen 1996) that children sometimes employ intentional explanations for domains that adults would not find appropriate (e.g., animism—applying intentional accounts to inanimate objects).

Subsumption We use the term *subsumption* to cover a variety of cases, such as explanation by reference to a lawful regularity or to class inclusion. We find this form of response very confusing. We are not sure that this set forms a natural kind, and we are not sure how explanatory people think these cases are. Samarapungavan and Wiers (1997) report examples such as E: "Why do penguins have wings?" C: "Because they are of the bird family. They all have wings. That is something for all birds." Chinn (1997) reports examples such as E: "Why is steel harder than chalk?" C: "Because chalk is a . . . soft rock."

We also have difficulty deciding if scientists find subsumption to be explanatory. We feel sure that most scientists would not consider "Gold can be flattened because it is malleable" to be very explanatory. However, we are not clear about examples such as "This liquid boiled at 100°C because it is water and all water boils at that temperature." We think that many scientists might consider "The stick looks bent in water because of the laws of refraction" to be explanatory. Clearly, this is a topic in need of conceptual clarification and empirical investigation.

Macro to Micro Children often apply macro properties to micro entities. Although this is not an explanatory framework at the same level of breadth as the others we have discussed, it has interesting characteristics.

In the areas of chemistry and properties of matter, children show a strong tendency to apply macro properties to micro entities (cf. Chinn 1997). Ben-Zvi, Eylon, and Silberstein (1986), in an article with the delightful title "Is an Atom of Copper Malleable?" report that high school students are quite likely to attribute a wide range of macro properties to atoms. This explanatory pattern was also used in the early stages of the development of science. For example, the theory of "preformism" in biology (cf. Gould 1977) postulated that human germ cells contained very small, completely formed humans, although over time this pattern of explanation lost favor among scientists. Thus this explanatory framework is used spontaneously by children, but has been rejected by scientists.

Formal or Mathematical   As discussed earlier, children rarely, if ever, produce formal or mathematical explanations of natural phenomena.

Child versus Scientist   Overall, it appears to us that children use most of the common forms of explanatory frameworks used by scientists, except for formal or mathematical accounts, and may use some additional forms that scientists do not use.

Consequences of Adopting Explanatory Frameworks
Adopting an explanatory framework has a number of interesting consequences for an individual's view of the natural world.

Theory-Ladenness of Data   An explanation provides a framework that in certain circumstances can influence other psychological processes such as perception and memory (Brewer and Lambert 1993). Gunstone and White (1981) report a study in which undergraduates who held a theory that a metal ball would fall faster than a plastic ball of the same diameter were more likely to report seeing the metal ball fall faster. Gauld (1986) gives examples of high school students who misrecalled the data of an experiment they had carried out on electric current so that the data were consistent with their theory of the flow of electricity.

Intelligibility   Explanations provide the frameworks used to make sense of major parts of the world of experience; in that way they determine the intelligibility of phenomena. For example, Samarapungavan and Wiers (1997) have noted that children with essentialist views of biological species (i.e., that species just are—they have immutable essences) typically do not understand questions about the origin of species-specific features. For example:

Jasper (age 11)   E: "How do you think giraffes come to have their long necks?" C: "It [the neck] did not come into being! It was always there. I don't understand what you mean by that."

Vosniadou and Brewer (1992) found similar responses from children who had flat earth beliefs and were asked questions about people living "on the other side of the earth." For many of these children, because the earth was dirt "all the way down," this question simply made no sense.

Conceptual Boundaries   Given that explanations establish the frameworks for understanding the world, they also establish the limits of what can be explained. Samarapungavan (1995b) has noted in the area of biology that when children with essentialist views of biological species are asked questions about the origin of species they often say that this is an unknowable fact. For example:

Jasper (age 11)   E: "How did people first appear on earth?" C: "It's the same as with the animals. No one can know that! That will always be a puzzle."

11.5   Conclusions

Our analysis of the construct of explanation and our review of some of the relevant developmental studies suggest that, although children's explanations of the natural world may have very different content from scientists' explanations of the same phenomena, the underlying form of children's explanations is similar in many respects to that of scientists.

There is remarkably little literature that directly investigates the fundamental issues relating to the development of explanation. In this chapter, we were often able to find examples to make our points, but we did not have sufficient evidence to determine the relative frequencies with which children use particular types of explanations compared to adult nonscientists and compared to scientists. Clearly, this is an area in need of additional work.

Similarly, we did not have sufficient evidence, for the most part, to allow us to trace the development of explanations over the childhood years. It seems likely that some of the aspects of scientific explanations require classroom instruction and may be acquired late, if ever, in the intellectual development of nonscientists.

A number of writers (e.g., Carey 1985) have argued that children learning about the world go about this task in a way similar to that of scientists. More recently Gopnik (1996) has adopted a very strong form of this hypothesis, that there is essentially complete overlap in the processes used by children and by scientists to acquire knowledge of the world. Clearly, we favor the view of the "child as scientist" but think that there are also differences between scientists and children, particularly for those cognitive strategies derived from the historical development of science as an institution. In general, our review suggests that, qualitatively, children show competence with most aspects of everyday explanations at an early age. However, those aspects of explanation that derive from the social institution of science (cf. Brewer and Samarapungavan 1991) are much later to develop and in some cases may never develop without the explicit training involved in becoming a member of the scientific community.

References

Andersson, B. (1986). The experiential gestalt of causation: A common core to pupils' preconceptions in science. *European Journal of Science Education, 8,* 155–171.

Ben-Zvi, R., Eylon, B-S., and Silberstein, J. (1986). Is an atom of copper malleable? *Journal of Chemical Education, 63,* 64–66.

Brewer, W. F., and Chinn, C. A. (1994). The theory-ladenness of data: An experimental demonstration. In *Proceedings of the Sixteenth Annual Conference of the Cognitive Science Society.* Hillsdale, NJ: Erlbaum.

Brewer, W. F., and Lambert, B. L. (1993). The theory-ladenness of observation: Evidence from cognitive psychology. In *Proceedings of the Fifteenth Annual Conference of the Cognitive Science Society.* Hillsdale, NJ: Erlbaum.

Brewer, W. F., and Samarapungavan, A. (1991). Children's theories vs. scientific theories: Differences in reasoning or differences in knowledge? In R. R. Hoffman and D. S. Palermo, eds., *Cognition and the symbolic processes: Applied and ecological perspectives.* Hillsdale, NJ: Erlbaum.

Campbell, N. R. (1957). *Foundations of science.* New York: Dover.

Carey, S. (1985). *Conceptual change in childhood.* Cambridge, MA: MIT Press.

Chinn, C. A. (1997). A microgenetic study of learning about the molecular theory of matter and chemical reactions, Ph.D. University of Illinois at Urbana-Champaign.

Chinn, C. A., and Brewer, W. F. (1992). Psychological responses to anomalous data. In *Proceedings of the Fourteenth Annual Conference of the Cognitive Science Society.* Hillsdale, NJ: Erlbaum.

Chinn, C. A., and Brewer, W. F. (1998). An empirical test of a taxonomy of responses to anomalous data in science. *Journal of Research in Science Teaching, 35,* 623–654.

diSessa, A. A. (1988). Knowledge in pieces. In G. Forman and P. B. Pufall, eds., *Constructivism in the computer age.* Hillsdale, NJ: Erlbaum.

Driver, R., Guesne, E., and Tiberghien, A., eds. (1985). *Children's ideas in science.* Milton Keynes, U.K.: Open University Press.

Friedman, M. (1974). Explanation and scientific understanding. *Journal of Philosophy, 71,* 5–19.

Futuyma, D. J. (1983). *Science on trial: The case for evolution.* New York: Pantheon.

Gauld, C. (1986). Models, meters and memory. *Research in Science Education, 16,* 49–54.

Giere, R. N. (1985). Philosophy of science naturalized. *Philosophy of Science, 52,* 331–356.

Gopnik, A. (1996). The scientist as child. *Philosophy of Science, 63,* 485–514.

Gould, S. J. (1977). *Ontogeny and phylogeny,* Cambridge, MA: Harvard University Press.

Gunstone, R. F., and White, R. T. (1981). Understanding of gravity. *Science Education, 65,* 291–299.

Hesse, M. (1967). Models and analogy in science. In P. Edwards, ed., *Encyclopedia of philosophy.* Vol. 5. New York: Macmillan.

Kelemen, D. A. (1996). The nature and development of the teleological stance. Ph.D. University of Arizona. Abstract in *Dissertation Abstracts International, 57,* 2897B.

Kitcher, P. (1981). Explanatory unification. *Philosophy of Science, 48,* 507–531.

Kornblith, H., ed. (1994). *Naturalizing epistemology.* 2d ed. Cambridge, MA: MIT Press.

Kuhn, D. (1991). *The skills of argument.* Cambridge: Cambridge University Press.

Kuhn, T. S. (1977). Objectivity, value judgment, and theory choice. In T. S. Kuhn, ed., *The essential tension.* Chicago: University of Chicago Press.

Laudan, L. (1977). *Progress and its problems.* Berkeley: University of California Press.

Levin, I., Siegler, R. S., Druyan, S., and Gardosh, R. (1990). Everyday and curriculum-based physics concepts: When does short-term training bring change where years of schooling have failed to do so? *British Journal of Developmental Psychology, 8,* 269–279.

Miller, A. I. (1984). *Imagery in scientific thought: Creating 20th-century physics.* Boston: Birkhäuser.

Nagel, E. (1961). *The structure of science.* New York: Harcourt, Brace and World.

Piaget, J. (1960). *The child's conception of physical causality.* Totowa, NJ: Littlefield, Adams.

Reif, F., and Larkin, J. H. (1991). Cognition in scientific and everyday domains: Comparison and learning implications. *Journal of Research in Science Teaching, 28,* 733–760.

Reiner, M., Chi, M. T. H., and Resnick, L. (1988). Naive materialistic belief: An underlying epistemological commitment. In *Proceedings of the Tenth Annual Conference of the Cognitive Science Society*. Hillsdale, NJ: Erlbaum.

Salmon, W. C. (1990). *Four decades of scientific explanation*. Minneapolis: University of Minnesota Press.

Samarapungavan, A. (1992). Children's judgments in theory choice tasks: Scientific rationality in childhood. *Cognition, 45,* 1–32.

Samarapungavan, A. (1995a). Do children understand the burden of public proof in science. Paper presented at the annual meeting of the Society for Research in Child Development, Indianapolis, March.

Samarapungavan, A. (1995b). Establishing boundaries for explanatory frameworks: Children's epistemologies in context. In J. Astington, ed., *Theory of mind at school: Children's scientific reasoning.* Symposium conducted at the annual meeting of the American Educational Research Association, San Francisco, April.

Samarapungavan, A., Vosniadou, S., and Brewer, W. F. (1996). Mental models of the earth, sun, and moon: Indian children's cosmologies. *Cognitive Development, 11,* 491–521.

Samarapungavan, A., and Wiers, R. (1994). Do children have epistemic constructs about explanatory frameworks: Examples from naive ideas about the origin of species. In *Proceedings of the Sixteenth Annual Conference of the Cognitive Science Society*. Hillsdale, NJ: Erlbaum.

Samarapungavan, A., and Wiers, R. W. (1997). Children's thoughts on the origin of species: A study of explanatory coherence. *Cognitive Science, 21,* 147–177.

Schank, P., and Ranney, M. (1991). Modeling an experimental study of explanatory coherence. In *Proceedings of the Thirteenth Annual Conference of the Cognitive Science Society*. Hillsdale, NJ: Erlbaum.

Thagard, P. (1992). *Conceptual revolutions*. Princeton: Princeton University Press.

Toulmin, S. (1961). *Foresight and understanding*. New York: Harper and Row.

Vosniadou, S., and Brewer, W. F. (1992). Mental models of the earth: A study of conceptual change in childhood. *Cognitive Psychology, 24,* 535–585.

Vosniadou, S., and Brewer, W. F. (1994). Mental models of the day/night cycle. *Cognitive Science, 18,* 123–183.

Watson, J. B. (1919). *Psychology from the standpoint of a behaviorist*. Philadelphia: Lippincott.

Wellman, H. M. (1990). *The child's theory of mind*. Cambridge, MA: MIT Press.

Woodward, J. (1989). The causal mechanical model of explanation. In P. Kitcher and W. C. Salmon, eds., *Minnesota studies in the philosophy of science.* Vol. 8, *Scientific explanation*. Minneapolis: University of Minnesota Press.

12

Explanation as Orgasm and the Drive for Causal Knowledge: The Function, Evolution, and Phenomenology of the Theory Formation System

Alison Gopnik

There is a lust of the mind, that, by a perserverance of delight in the continual and inde-fatigable generation of knowledge, exceedeth the short vehemence of carnal pleasure.
—Thomas Hobbes

What is explanation? Both our ordinary everyday concept of explanation and refinements of the concept in the philosophy of science seem to have a curiously circular quality. Theories are good because they explain things, but explaining things turns out to be very much like having theories of them. We explain something, we are told, when we characterize it in terms of some set of abstract underlying laws and entities. But this characterization seems to reduce to having a theory itself. Alternatively, we may say that we explain something when the explanation satisfies our explanation-seeking curiosity. But then explanation-seeking curiosity seems only to be definable as that curiosity which explanation satisfies. The ordinary concept of explanation seems to involve both a kind of knowledge, hence the link to theories, and a distinctive phenomenology, hence the link to the feeling of curiosity. This sort of amalgam of cognition and phenomenology is quite characteristic of our ordinary folk psychological concepts, of course.

I do not think there is some set of necessary and sufficient features that will account for all the things we call "explanation," anymore than there is a set of necessary and sufficient features that will account for all the things we call "bird." Instead, I want to suggest the everyday notion of explanation as a jumping off point for a noncircular and interesting cognitive concept of explanation. Moreover, thinking about explanation suggests some interesting, if still untested, hypotheses about how our cognitive system might work. Although my concept of explanation, like the everyday concept, includes both cognitive and phenomenological elements, I propose a particular, and more precise, relation between them. Explanation may be understood as the distinctive phenomenological mark of the operation of a special representational system, which I call the "theory formation system." This system was designed by evolution to construct what I call "causal maps." Causal maps are abstract, coherent, defeasible representations of the causal structure of the world around us. Moreover, the distinctive phenomenology of the theory formation system impels us to action as well as to knowledge; it reflects a sort of theory formation drive. Hence the title of this chapter. My hypothesis is that explanation is to theory formation as orgasm is to reproduction—the phenomenological mark of the fulfillment of an evolutionarily determined drive. From our phenomenological point of view, it may seem to us that we construct and use theories to achieve explanation or that we have sex to achieve orgasm. From an evolutionary point of view, however, the relation is reversed, we experience orgasms and explanations to ensure that we make babies and theories. Moreover, I suggest that the distinctive phenomenology of explanation may be important methodologically. By using phenomenological evidence we may be able to identify when and how the theory formation system is operating.

12.1   The Theory Formation System

Over the past ten years, developmental psychologists have increasingly used the model of scientific theory change to characterize cognitive development (Carey 1985; Keil 1987; Gopnik 1988; Gelman and Wellman 1991; Wellman 1990). I have called this idea the "theory theory" (see Bartsch and Wellman 1995; Gopnik and Wellman 1994; Gopnik and Meltzoff 1997); it has been consistently productive in explaining the child's developing understanding of the mind and the world. One way of interpreting the theory theory is as a claim about a special and distinctive set of human representational capacities. These capacities are most visible in scientists and in children but are part of every human being's basic cognitive equipment. In this view, science is successful not because it invents special new cognitive devices (though, of course, this is part of what science does) but because it capitalizes on a more basic human cognitive capacity. The analogy to science has two aspects. First, children's knowledge is structured in a theory-like way, and second, that knowledge changes in a way that is analogous to theory change in science.

Children learn their environment (including the people and the cultural biases promoted by those people).

This theory formation system may have evolved specifically to allow human children to learn. Human beings' evolutionary advantage stems from our ability to adapt our behavior to a very wide variety of environments. In turn, this depends on our ability to learn swiftly and efficiently about the particular physical and social environment we grow up in. Their long, protected immaturity gives human children an opportunity to infer the particular structure of the world around them. The powerful and flexible theory formation abilities we see in childhood may have evolved to make this learning possible. In this view, science takes advantage of these basic abilities in a more socially organized way and applies them to new types of problems and domains. Science is thus a kind of epiphenomenon of cognitive development. It is not that children are little scientists but that scientists are big children.

The theory theory is still relatively new and controversial and there is not space here for a detailed explication or defense of the idea (for such an explication and defense, see Gopnik and Meltzoff 1997). Instead, I will assume that the general idea is correct, namely, that there are general mechanisms of cognitive development very much like the mechanisms of theory change in science, and will develop some hypotheses about explanation within that general framework. Moreover, thinking about theory formation in the context of explanation may also point to some interesting hypotheses about the details of the theory formation system itself. Much of the work that has been done in the field thus far, including my own work, has primarily been devoted to elaborating on the similarities between scientific theory change and cognitive development. My colleagues and I have constructed lists of features of science, its abstract, coherent structure, its interwoven web of laws and entities, its capacity for dynamic change, and pointed to similar features of children's developing understanding of the world around them. If we assume that the general parallel to science is correct, however, we can go on to the question of developing a more detailed understanding of the theory formation system as a system in its own right. In what follows I point to some possible features of the system that are especially relevant to explanation and have not been sufficiently emphasized before.

Theories as Causal Maps

One way of thinking about the theory formation system is that it is a way of uncovering the underlying causal structure of the world from perceptual input. In this respect, it is analogous to our systems for representing objects in space. The visual system takes retinal input and transforms it into representations of objects moving in space. Although not perfectly veridical, these representations of objects at least approach a greater level of veridicality than the retinal input itself, which, presumably, explains the evolution of perception and spatial cognition. Similarly, we can think of the theory formation system as a system that takes the input of the perceptual system and transforms it into representations of the underlying causal structure of the world. The theory formation system is designed to go beyond perceptual representations, just as perceptual representations go beyond sensory input. The representations that result, representations formulated in terms of abstract theoretical entities and laws, more closely approach the actual causal structure of the world than the representations of perception. Again, this is true at the level of the exercise and use of theories as well as at the level of theory change. To apply a theory to some pattern of evidence is to assign the evidence a particular causal representation. Theories change in the face of evidence in order to give better causal representations.

In our earlier formulations (Gopnik and Wellman 1994; Gopnik and Meltzoff 1997) of the theory theory, the causal character of theory formation was simply seen as one feature among many. I think this is probably partly because scientific theories have been our model. Science may include cases of theories and explanations that we need not think of as causal, though clearly causal claims play an important, indeed a central role in most scientific theories and explanations (see, for example, Cartwright 1989; Salmon 1984). It increasingly seems to me, however, that uncovering causes is the central feature of the theory formation system from an evolutionary point of view, in the same way that uncovering the spatial character of moving objects seems to be central to the visual system.

Of course, theory formation is far from being the only way that the cognitive system can uncover causal structure. Just as there are many ways in which perceptual systems detect the spatial character of objects, and no creature could survive without some abilities to detect the external world, so we might think of even the most primitive conditioning capacities as a kind of causal detection device. On the other hand, just as our spatial cognition is different from the simple detection systems of other creatures, so it seems plausible that our systems for detecting causal structure are also different.

Work on evolutionary cognition suggests an interesting analogy. It is well known that different species of animals, even closely related species, may use quite different strategies and systems to uncover the spatial character of the world around them. Some of an animal's understanding of space may be hard-wired in the perceptual system. For example, we may be hard-wired to translate two-dimensional retinal information into three-dimensional representations.

But animals may also use information to learn about the specific character of their spatial environment. In particular, O'Keefe and Nadel (1978) point out that some species do this by keeping track of the effects of their movements in the world and using that information to guide their future movements. If turning first to the left and then to the right leads to a food reward, animals will repeat that sequence of movements. They use a kind of egocentric spatial navigation system. However, other species use what O'Keefe and Nadel (1978) call "spatial maps." Although these species also learn from their movement through space, they do so by constructing a coherent, nonegocentric, and often quite complex picture of the spatial relations among objects, a kind of map. Significantly, spatial maps are not hard-wired. As animals move through the world, they update the information in their spatial maps, and they may revise and change them as they learn more about their environment. Animals with this kind of representation system have some real advantages. They can, for example, find food in a maze they have previously explored even if they are placed in a different starting point (and thus cannot simply reproduce their earlier movements).

Maze Learning

Tolman

We can make a parallel distinction between a kind of egocentric causal navigation system and a kind of causal map (see Campbell 1994). One interesting possibility, in particular, is that other animals primarily understand causality in terms of the effects their own actions have on the world. In a process like operant conditioning, they record the causal effects of their actions on events in the world and modify their actions accordingly. In contrast, human beings seem to equate the causal powers of their own actions with those of objects independent of them. They construct and update causal maps of their environments.

Causal maps have the same advantages as spatial maps. Once we represent the causal relations between ourselves, our conspecifics, and objects, we can intervene in a much wider variety of ways to get a particular result. For example, we may imitate what we see another animal do because we assume the causal effects of our actions will be like theirs. We may be able to do this even if we ourselves have never performed the action before. Causal maps also let us use tools in an insightful, rather than just trial-and-error, way. If we understand the causal relations between objects, independent of us, we can immediately use one object to cause another to do something, even if we have never used the tool that way before.

In fact, a number of recent empirical studies of nonhuman primate cognition suggest that human beings may be specialized in just this way. While chimpanzees, for example, are extremely intelligent and very good at detecting contingencies between their actions and the effects of those actions, they seem unable to either imitate the solutions of other animals or to use tools insightfully (Povinelli forthcoming; Tomasello and Call 1997). They do not seem to construct causal maps.

We can think of a theory as precisely this sort of causal map. A theory postulates a complex but coherent set of causal entities, the theoretical entities, and specifies causal relations among them, the laws. Just as a spatial map allows for new predictions and interventions in the world, so a causal map allows for a wide range of causal predictions and interventions, including experiments. And just as theories are revisable in the light of new experience, rather than hard-wired, so causal maps, like spatial ones, can be updated and revised.

Recent work in developmental psychology in the context of the theory theory suggests that children are sensitive to the underlying causal structure of the world and seek to form new causal representations at a much earlier age than we had previously supposed. There is evidence for causal understanding even in infancy (Leslie and Keeble 1987; Oakes and Cohen 1994; Gopnik and Meltzoff 1997). By two and a half or three, children show extensive causal reasoning both about living things and about psychological processes (Gelman and Wellman 1991). Moreover, nine-month-old infants, apparently unlike chimpanzees, can learn a new action on an object by imitation (Meltzoff 1988); eighteen-month-old infants, again apparently unlike chimpanzees, can use tools insightfully (Piaget 1952; Gopnik and Meltzoff 1984).

In recent empirical work (Gopnik and Sobel 1997), we have shown that, by three, children will override perceptual information in favor of causal information when they classify objects. In a series of experiments, we showed children a "blicket detector," a machine that lit up and played music when objects were placed on it. Perceptually identical objects were placed on the machine with differential causal effects, some made the machine light up and some did not. Similarly, perceptually different objects might have the same effect on the machine. Children were shown an object that had set off the machine, told it was a "blicket," and then asked to show us the other blicket. Even three-year-olds were willing to override perceptual features in favor of causal powers: they said that the other object that had set off the machine was a blicket, even when it was not perceptually similar to the original object. Moreover, a control condition demonstrated that this was genuinely causal reasoning. The children did not classify objects together when the experimenter held them over the machine and pressed a button that made the machine light up. A mere association between the object and the event was not enough to influence the children's categorization. Like scientists, these young children seemed to organize the world in terms of the underlying causal powers of objects and to seek explanations of new causal relations.

12.2 Causal Maps and Computation: Could Theories Be Bayes Nets?

One question about the theory theory has always been whether there is any perspicuous way that it could be implemented computationally. In earlier work (Gopnik and Meltzoff 1997), we have simply seen that as a question for the future, no computational representation that we knew of seemed particularly likely as a candidate. It is still true that this is very much a question for the future but there is a recent candidate that may be interesting. The computational formalism "Bayes nets" has been used to precisely represent networks of causal relations among events. Moreover, there are formal results that suggest how such structures may be derived from empirical evidence of the sort available to children (such as conditional dependencies and independencies among events). Similarly, formal results show how these representations may be used to predict future events, to interpret current evidence, and to design appropriate experimental interventions (Glymour, chap. 7, this volume). Finally, at least some adult judgments of causal powers seem to be well represented by this formalism (Cheng, chap. 9, this volume). It is conceivable that the causal maps we have described are represented as Bayes nets, and that children use similar algorithms to learn the structure of these nets and to use them for prediction and control.

Domain Specificity and Generality

Another important feature of the theory formation system is that it combines domain-specific and domain-general mechanisms. We have proposed that infants have innate and quite specific theories of a number of particular domains. In our view, however, these initial theories are subject to revision and change, and the inductive mechanisms that lead to that change may be quite generally applicable (Gopnik and Meltzoff 1997). As a result of differences in their initial theories, and in patterns of evidence, the specific content of children's later theories may be also be quite different in different domains. Similarly, in science, the basic entities and laws of physics may be quite different from those of evolutionary biology. On the other hand, as in science, the processes of hypothesis testing, prediction, falsification, and evidence gathering will be quite similar across domains. Moreover, as in science, the assumption that there is some underlying causal structure to be discovered remains constant across domains. Conceptual change that is the result of these mechanisms may and often will take place within a particular domain. However, there may be radical restructurings of the domains with development, again, as in science. One well-known if controversial example is the emergence of a distinctive folk biology in the school-age years (Carey 1985). In our own work (Gopnik and Meltzoff 1997), we have suggested that children initially have a theory of action that includes aspects of both folk physics and folk psychology.

Folk [handwritten margin note]

Change

The dynamic properties of theories are also distinctive. The representations of perceptual systems seem to be relatively fixed, at least in adulthood, and perhaps in childhood as well. For example, many fundamental features of the visual system such as basic object segregation and distance perception appear to be in place at birth. When the systems do change as a result of experience, they seem to do so in a fairly restricted set of ways. Typically, this process is described in terms of processes like triggering or parameter setting, rather than in terms of the inductive inferences that are the result of new experiences in science.

In contrast, it is part of the very nature of theory formation systems that they are perpetually in flux. In general, the perceptual system seems to work by taking in sensory input and trying to assign some coherent representation to that input. When the system cannot find such a representation, it simply stops. The theory formation system also seeks to find a coherent causal representation of perceptual input. However, when the system fails to find such a representation in enough cases and over a long enough period, it restructures both the very procedures it uses to assign causal representations, and the kinds of causal representations it assigns. In other words, the theory changes. The system takes all forms of evidence into consideration and seeks a consistent causal account of objects on that basis. The theory formation system is perpetually faced with counterevidence and perpetually revises theories on that basis.

The representations that the perceptual system will come up with are highly constrained, but the theory formation system is much less constrained. In the most extreme cases, for example, it may come up with the representations of relativistic physics or quantum mechanics. It is a representational system that both computes representations from inputs and, also and in consequence, alters the way it computes new representations from new inputs.

In recent empirical work (Slaughter and Gopnik 1996), we have explored the dynamic character of children's changing conceptions of the world. In particular, in a series of training experiments, Slaughter and I showed that we could induce general conceptual changes in three-year-olds' understanding of the mind by presenting them with relevant counterevidence to their earlier theories. Children who received evidence that was conceptually relevant showed a new understanding of the mind, and extended that understanding to contexts very different from those in which they had been trained.

Exploration, Experimentation, and the Theory Drive

If we think for a minute about the dynamic features of theory change, moreover, we can see that using theories and, to an even greater extent, changing theories generally involves active intervention in the world. Schwitzgebel (1997) has suggested that theories are closely connected to what he calls a "drive to explain."

Let us return to our earlier analogy with spatial maps. Animals that use such maps also display distinctive patterns of spatial exploration. A rat that constructs spatial maps, for example, will systematically explore a new spatial environment, even if that exploration has no immediate payoff. Presumably the expenditure of energy involved in free-ranging exploration has its payoff in the long term predictive advantages of constructing a spatial map.

Similarly, we might expect creatures that depend on constructing causal maps would intervene in the environment in a way that lets them determine its causal structure. The most obvious example of such intervention is the process of experimentation. In experimentation, we systematically act on the world in a way that is designed to obtain evidence relevant to the theoretical problems we are trying to solve. Sometimes we may experiment to see how a particular piece of evidence should be interpreted in terms of an established theory. Sometimes, we may do so in search of a new, more adequate theory. Sometimes, particularly in organized science, this process of experimentation is designed to carefully and systematically elicit particular pieces of evidence. Often, however, the process is more akin to exploration, to what scientists disparagingly call a "fishing expedition". This sort of experimental intervention in the world is notoriously one of the most powerful ways of determining its causal structure.

We see both extensive causal exploration and even some more systematic experimentation in children's spontaneous play. Piaget (1962), for example, charted how object manipulation and play were related to cognitive change in infancy. Indeed, Piaget defined "play" as the process of assimilation, that is, what we would now consider the process by which evidence is interpreted in terms of existing theories. We have suggested (Gopnik and Meltzoff 1997) that infants fondness for "Drop the spoon" games at fifteen months is related to their changing conception of space, that the earlier hide-and-seek games are connected to object concept understanding and that the later "terrible twos" behavior is related to an understanding of differences in desires. In each of these cases, infants actively try to produce new phenomena, phenomena at the leading edge of their theory formation, in an apparently experimental way.

Indeed, the degree to which infants and children actively and spontaneously explore the world is almost a cliché of parenting. We talk about how toddlers "get into everything" or how preschoolers are always asking "Why?" We "childproof" our houses to try to keep this exploratory behavior under control. Although we take this for granted, it is a striking fact about childhood ecology. These exploratory and experimental behaviors require enormous expenditures of energy and have little obvious function; in fact, they may be, superficially at least, quite dysfunctional. Not only do babies expend enormous energy on getting to the lightbulb or the lipstick; we adults expend enormous energy trying to keep them away from it. Interestingly, work from a very different tradition of developmental psychology, namely, attachment theory, supports this picture of a fundamental exploratory drive. Indeed, in its original formulation, attachment between infants and mothers was supposed to function precisely to mediate between infants need for protection and security and their equally strong need to explore and manipulate objects (Bowlby 1969).

If active intervention in the world is necessary to infer its causal structure, then there needs to be some sort of motivational system to bring about such intervention. In formal organized science, of course, we have an elaborate set of incentives and rewards to ensure that such intervention takes place. Children, however, and to a lesser extent ordinary adults, seem to continue to explore and experiment with the world quite independently of such external incentives. Children, in particular, spontaneously attempt to interpret patterns of evidence in terms of the underlying causal representations of their theories, they spontaneously reorganize their theories when this sort of interpretation fails, and they spontaneously expend energy on the sort of active exploration and experimentation that this entails.

There is a payoff for this activity in the long run, of course. Getting a veridical causal map of the world allows for a wide range of accurate and nonobvious predictions, and these accurate predictions, in turn, allow one to accomplish other types of goals that are more directly related to survival. The relation between assigning the causal interpretations and making the useful predictions may be quite long-term and indirect, however (as scientists are always assuring congressmen). Again, the analogy to sexual drives should be obvious. Nature ensures that we do something that will be good for us (or at least our genes) in the long run, by making it fun (or at least compelling) in the short run.

12.3   Theory Formation and the Experience of Explanation

The Phenomenology of Explanation

What I have proposed above, then, is that there is a special representational system that has a number of distinctive qualities. How is explanation related to the operation of this theory formation system? We could simply identify explanation with the successful operation of the system. In particular, we could define explanation as a relation between theories and evidence. In the terms I have been using, we might say, very roughly, that a theory "explains evidence" when it assigns the evidence a particular causal representation. There is a long tradition in the philosophy of science, dating back to Hempel (1965) that follows this line.

Intuitively, however, this way of treating explanation seems to leave something out. Explanation is a goal-directed human activity. It depends on what is relevant or important to the explainer, it satisfies a special kind of explanation-seeking curiosity, it answers "why" questions. Again there is a tradition of pragmatic accounts of explanation in the philosophical literature that emphasize this aspect of explanation (e.g., Bromberger 1965; Van Fraassen 1980). As is often true in the philosophy of science, there seems to be little relation between the two traditions, logical and pragmatic.

Although pragmatic accounts are rarely phrased in this way, I think what they point to has as much to do with phenomenology as it does with pragmatics per se—what the purely logical view leaves out is that there is something it is like to have or seek an explanation. I suggest that there is a distinctive phenomenology of explanation. Such phenomenological claims are, of course, difficult to justify initially, except by appeal to intuitions. Moreover, in the case of sophisticated adults, almost any particular experience will reflect a complex mixture of different types of phenomenology. Visual experience may reflect extensive implicit inferences as well as reflecting the operation of the visual system itself. The experience of an emotion like anger may run the gamut from cold withdrawal to helpless depression to irresistible rage. Nevertheless, it seems right to say that there is a "phenomenology of anger" consistently related to a particular set of psychological functions, and that there is a "phenomenology of vision" related to the operation of the visual system. In the case of anger, some have suggested there is even evidence of a "basic emotion," an evolutionarily determined complex of facial expression, psychophysiology, and phenomenology (Ekman 1992).

In the same way, I suggest that there is a distinctive phenomenology associated with explanation, involving both the search for explanation and the recognition that an explanation has been reached. We might call these experiences the "hmm" and the "aha." In English, they seem to be expressed by "Why?" and "Because." These experiences are obviously close to what we more broadly call "curiosity" or "interest," but they are not identical with them. We may engage in purely exploratory behaviors (the desire to open a locked cupboard, say, or climb a mountain, or see around a bend) that have no "aha" at the end of them. Often they are connected to goal-directed or problem-solving behavior, but they do not simply reflect the satisfaction that comes from achieving a goal. We may blunder our way to the exit, or use trial and error to find the right key to delete the file, and be happy we have done so, but without any "aha." Conversely, we may experience a splendid moment of illumination when we realize just exactly why it is thoroughly impossible to get what we want.

This explanatory phenomenology also appears to be strikingly domain general. We seek and are satisfied by explanations of physical objects, animate beings, psychological agents, and even social groups. We seek and are satisfied by explanations in terms of physical laws, biological processes, reasons, or rules. The "aha" of understanding why the wiring does not work seems quite like the "aha" of understanding why the electrician will not tell you why the wiring does not work. Even in children "Why?" and "Because" seem to cut across domains in this way (Schult and Wellman 1997; Wellman, Hickling, and Schult 1997).

Moreover, explanation, unlike many other experiences, seems to combine some of the properties of both cognitive and motivational phenomenology. Like vision, but unlike, say, anxiety or depression, or even hunger or lust, explanation seems intrinsically referential, an explanation must be of or about something in particular (we cannot usually experience free-floating explanation, or even free-floating explanatory curiosity, anymore than we can experience free-floating vision). Indeed, explanation, even more than vision, seems to require some sort of propositional representational capacity.

But explanation, also unlike vision, has some of the phenomenological character of a motivational or drive system. We not only know an explanation when we have one, we want explanations, and we are satisfied when we get them. Even in adults, the "hmm" is, to varying degrees, an unsettling, disturbing, and arousing experience, one that seems to compel us to some sort of resolution and action (the two great resources by which popular fiction holds our attention are titillation and mystery— there is nothing like unsatisfied fundamental drives to keep the pages turning). Conversely, finding an explanation for something is accompanied by a satisfaction that goes beyond the merely cognitive.

In children, the drive for explanation may even override other more obvious and straightforward motivations. We have suggested that in "the terrible twos" children are conducting experiments to understand the nature of differences in desires, even though the immediate consequence of those tests is maternal rage. This may even be true in adults, as when, in *Swann's Way*, Swann compulsively tests Odette in search of her secret life, in spite of the emotional and practical pain this will cause him, a rather advanced case of "the terrible twos."

It even seems possible that some aspects of explanatory phenomenology might qualify as a kind of "basic emotion." Surprise and interest, phenomena very closely related to the "hmm" are, in fact, often taken to be basic emotions. There is some evidence for distinctive and universal facial expressions associated with these states, which are distinct from the mere reflex of a startle response or from other emotions like anger or fear. The "aha," in contrast, is often accompanied by an expression of joy. This expression is less clearly distinct from the expression of other positive emotions, but this is characteristic of positive expressions in general (see Ekman 1992). In our own work with children, even with infants, we see a distinctive set of affective responses and facial expressions that accompany exploration and problem solving. In our experiments, children who are in the intermediate stages of theory formation often exhibit a great deal of puzzlement and even distress, furrowed brows, pursed mouths. This contrasts with the behavior of these same children on easier tasks, and with the behavior of children who are firmly in the grip of an earlier or later theory. Children who are presented with problems that are relevant to a newly formed theory, in contrast, often display intense satisfaction and joy.

This sort of "cognitive emotion" has been surprisingly neglected in the psychological literature, perhaps because of the old oppositions between emotion and cognition, or perhaps because it is more commonly and dramatically expressed in children than in adults. Nevertheless, evidence of this sort of phenomenon appears in variety of quite disparate contexts, even in the psychology of adults. A "theory drive," for example, seems to be involved in the Zeigarnik effect, or in the social psychologist's notion of a "need for closure" (see, for example, Kruglanski 1989). I suggest that this sort of experience is at least an important part of what we talk about when we talk about explanation.

The Contingency of Explanation

Thus far, I have claimed that there is a special representational system, the theory formation system, and that it is accompanied by a kind of theory drive. I have also suggested that there is a distinctive set of experiences that are at least part of what we mean by explanation. Now I want to talk about the relation between the cognitive system and the phenomenology. It should be clear by now that I think the explanatory phenomenology—the "hmm" and the "aha"—is closely related to the operation of the theory formation system. The "hmm" is the way we feel when we are presented with evidence to which the theory has not yet assigned a causal representation. The "aha" is the way we feel when such a representation is assigned, either by applying the theory or by revising it.

But is this returning to the circularity I began with? I want to suggest that is not. In our folk psychology, and indeed in conceptual analysis in philosophy, the connection between phenomenology, psychological structure, and function often appears to be transparent and necessary. Before we knew in detail about the visual system, it might have seemed obvious that visual experience and object perception were one and the same thing. Similarly, accounts of explanation often seem to move back and forth between the description of the phenomenology of explanation and its cognitive function, thus, for example, the tension between logical and pragmatic accounts in philosophy. But in fact, the relation between the phenomenology of explanation and its cognitive function is quite complex and contingent.

To see this, let us return to the example of vision. A hundred years of perceptual research have shown us that visual cognition and visual experience, though closely related, are conceptually and empirically separable. It is possible to have a system that functions cognitively like the visual system, but that lacks visual phenomenology, as in the case of computer vision or "blindsight." Alternately, visual phenomenology may be produced by systems outside the visual system itself, as in the case of images, hallucinations, and certain kinds of illusions, such as the top-down illusion of experts that they "see" things they actually infer. The same point may be made even more obviously about the case of sexual phenomenology. Even though the canonical example of sexual phenomenology is connected with sexual activities that lead to reproduction, it is notoriously true that sexual phenomenology is in another sense only contingently related to those activities. Sex need not be attended by desire, and desire may be associated with everything from shoes to conversation to deep-sea diving equipment.

In other rather different cases, both the phenomenology and the appropriate activity might occur, but the system might not successfully fulfill its evolutionary function. Although the function of the visual system is to obtain a veridical picture of the outside world, in practice, the system will often end up with nonveridical representations. The fact that there are visual illusions is not an indicator that perception, in general, is unveridical, or an argument against the idea that the perceptual system evolved because it is veridical in general and over the long run. Again, the case is even clearer for sexual phenomenology. While the very existence of sexual phenomenology and activity depends on its reproductive function over the long evolutionary run, there may be no connection at all for individual humans in the grip of desire, and most experiences of desire will not result in reproduction. There is an interesting additional and seldom considered aspect of this point that may be particularly relevant here. A system may evolve, in particular, to serve a function at one developmental phase of an organism's life and yet continue to operate at some other phase. Women continue to have orgasms after menopause, and have breasts and wombs even when they are not pregnant.

Thinking about explanation in this way may help to resolve what seem like puzzles and paradoxes. What I am suggesting is that the phenomenology of explanation is, in the canonical case, connected with the operation of a distinctive cognitive system, the theory formation system. Moreover, that theory formation system evolved because in general and over the long run, and especially in childhood, it gives us a more veridical picture of the causal structure of the world around us. In a particular case, however, explanatory phenomenology may be divorced from the operation of this cognitive system. Perhaps the most dramatic cases of this, the equivalent of visual hallucinations or sexual fetishes, are certain types of mystical experiences. Some cases of mystical experience seem simply to involve being washed over by a sort of generalized positive affect. But, in at least some such cases, the experience is more pointedly cognitive, the mystic suddenly experiences all the positive affective phenomenology of explanation with no apparent cognitive content. Suddenly, it all becomes clear; all at once, everything makes sense. Something like this also seems to happen in certain kinds of paranoia. Less dramatic but still striking instances of this are the "middle of the night" solutions, which dissolve as we decipher our scribbled bedside notes.

Conversely, it may be possible to engage in something like theory use and theory formation without explanatory phenomenology. It might be argued that automated theorem provers, of the sort whose results are published in physics journals, do just that. Sadly, the same may be true for the scientist who has been thoroughly corrupted by the system of social incentives, so that the greed for the Nobel prize utterly outweighs the joy of discovery. Indeed, given the complex social organization of science, it may be that a whole group of scientists scattered over many places comes upon the correct theoretical answer to a question without any single scientist experiencing any phenomenology at all. (It is striking, and comforting, however, to see the phenomenology of explanation persist even in relatively sophisticated and socially organized scientists. The scientists in the recent Mars probes almost without exception described their joy and excitement by saying it felt "like being a little kid again." None of them said it felt "like getting a raise.")

It is also possible that the theory formation system may genuinely operate, and the related explanatory phenomenology may occur, without achieving a more veridical causal map. The function of theory formation may be to obtain veridical causal maps, in general and over the long run, and particularly in childhood, but this is perfectly compatible with the idea that the products of theory formation are often not veridical. The function of sex is still to reproduce even if reproduction does not occur in the vast majority of cases. These cases would be more like visual illusions than hallucinations, more like having sex on the pill than like fetishism.

Some of the notorious cognitive illusions offered by Kahneman and Tversky and others may be instances of this sort of case (Kahneman, Slovic, and Tversky 1982). Magical, mythical, and religious explanation, and certain types of social explanation, may also be examples. This may help resolve the otherwise puzzling question of whether having a bad explanation or a pseudo-explanation is the same as having no explanation at all. From the normative cognitive view of philosophy of science, this may indeed be true. From the psychological point of view I am developing here, however, genuine explanation, and indeed genuine theory formation, can take place whose outcome is normatively deficient, even, very deficient much of the time. This is perfectly consistent with the view that the system evolved because, in general, over the long run, and especially in childhood, it gives us veridical information about the causal structure of the world.

It appears that one of the differences, perhaps the most important cognitive difference, between organized science and spontaneous theory formation is precisely that science contains additional normative devices

designed to supplement the basic cognitive devices of the theory formation system, and to protect them from error. We might think of science
as a kind of cognitive optometry, a system that takes the devices we usually
use to obtain a veridical picture of the world and corrects the flaws and
distortions of those devices. The fact that most people over forty wear
glasses is not, however, usually taken as an indictment of the visual system.
In fact, the analogy might even be taken further, perhaps science compensates for our deteriorating adult theory formation abilities the way
optometry compensates for our deteriorating adult vision. By twenty, most
of us have done all the theory formation evolution requires; by forty, most
of us have done just about everything that evolution requires.

In this view, then, the relation between explanation and theory formation, though close and principled, is not circular. We can have theory
formation without explanation and vice versa. Nevertheless, most of
the time and overall, explanatory phenomenology will be attended by
theory-like cognition, and there is a principled psychological reason for
this.

12.4   Methodological Issues

This view of explanation as the phenomenological mark of a cognitive
process also has methodological implications. Like other cognitive scientists of my generation, I grew up a functionalist. The basic tenet of func-
tionalism was that cognitive science would proceed by characterizing the
input and output to the human mind and providing a computational
account of the relations between them. The difficulties, both practical and
philosophical, of implementing that project have, however, become increasingly clear. Mere functional information seems to deeply underdetermine
the possible computational accounts of the mind. Many have turned to
neuroscience for salvation in this dilemma. But while neurological
accounts may indeed help us to untangle competing accounts of mental
structure in low-level cognition like vision and motor control, they appear
to be much less applicable to higher-order thinking, reasoning and
problem solving.

There may be another source of evidence in cognitive science. The
evidence comes from phenomenology, from the internal structure of our
conscious experience. Recently there has been a great deal of speculation
in cognitive science about Capital-C "Consciousness," the "Big Problem"

of how phenomenology is possible at all, and how it relates in general, to the functional structure of the mind. We do not seem close to a solution. For the entire history of cognitive science, however, specific relations between conscious experience and function have been the source of some of the most productive work in the field, even though the cognitive scientists who use this evidence have kept fairly quiet about it.

The most striking example is vision science, arguably the most productive branch of psychology in this century. Psychophysicists have never adhered to a strictly functionalist program, though often they pretended to, and continue to pretend to. (A famous and spectacularly hard-nosed psychophysicist I know regularly shows slides of various psychophysical functions he is investigating. The slides have initials in the corners, identifying the subjects, and establishing that this is an objective scientific enterprise. But somehow, the initials always correspond to those of the psychophysicist and his coinvestigators.) Psychologists in psychophysics and perception have always begun from the structure of conscious percepts and then produced accounts of the relation between those percepts and underlying functional, computational, and (most recently) neurological structure. Indeed, the phenomenology in some sense even defined the field of inquiry. We do not need an elaborate set of inferences to work out whether a particular phenomenon is due to the visual system, as opposed, say, to the auditory or kinesthetic system. The evidence of phenomenology itself gives us at least a very good first guess at an answer. More generally, without this phenomenological evidence, our understanding of vision would be severely impoverished.

Psychophysicists used phenomenological evidence but they never assumed that that evidence constituted mental structure itself. Rather they outlined quite complex and contingent relations between the phenomenology of visual experience and the functional relations between the mind and the world. Indeed, it is arguable that the first great cognitive revolution in psychology, sixty years before Chomsky and Bruner, and evident in psychologists as diverse as Freud, Piaget, and the Gestaltists, came when psychologists began to treat phenomenology as evidence for psychological structure, with complex relations to underlying theoretical structures that were themselves unconscious. This contrasts with the practice of earlier philosophers of mind, from Descartes to Hume to Brentano, who still assumed that the theoretical entities of psychology would themselves be conscious experiences.

I would argue that, despite the contingent relation between explanatory phenomenology and theory-like representations, we can use the phenomenology as a guide to the underlying psychological structures. In particular, a purely functionalist account may make it difficult to discriminate the theory formation system from other types of representational systems. For example, as Irvin Rock (Rock 1983) elegantly demonstrated, the formal structure of perceptual representations may involve "inferences" about underlying theoretical entities from the "data" of sensation. When the moon looks larger at the horizon than at the zenith, it is because the perceptual system draws a set of "inferences" about the relation between size and distance. Similarly and more generally, "modular" representational systems may mimic the functional architecture of theories. Indeed, modularity theorists will sometimes talk about "theories" in just this way (e.g., "theory of mind module"; Leslie 1987 is not an oxymoron). Chomsky famously characterized the highly automatic, unconscious, and indefeasible processes of syntactic processing as a kind of knowledge, if not quite a theory.

Elsewhere (Gopnik and Meltzoff 1997) I have suggested that developmental evidence may be crucial in discriminating between modules and theories. Another important type of evidence may come from examinations of the phenomenology of theories, and from explanation, in particular. However modules mimic the architecture of theories, they are strikingly lacking in explanatory phenomenology. There is no internal "aha" when we look at the large moon on the horizon, just a big moon. Similarly, we do not seem to be driven to parse in the way that we are driven to explain. We simply hear (or fail to hear) a meaningful sentence. Again, I do not want to suggest that explanatory phenomenology is a necessary indicator of theory-like processes, only that it is a reliable indicator. In particular, it may be that very well-practiced and well-established theories often lose their explanatory character. Nevertheless, in general it seems to me that theory-like knowledge in adults will at least potentially support explanatory phenomenology. Even in the case of a well-practiced theory such as folk psychology, it should be possible to formulate "why" questions and "because" answers, and to experience the "hmm" and the "aha."

These ideas may have particularly interesting implications for developmental psychology. In the past, developmental psychologists have been rather shy about attributing phenomenology to infants and children, perhaps because we have enough trouble getting our colleagues to agree that children have minds at all. The conventional phrase, for example, is to say that children have "implicit" rather than "explicit" theories. This shyness, however, seems more political than rational. There is every reason to believe that infants and children have rich phenomenal experiences, even if those experiences differ in many ways from our own. But do children experience explanatory phenomenology?

Recent work by Wellman and his colleagues suggests that at least one index of explanatory phenomenology, explicit linguistic explanations and requests for explanation, is in place much earlier than we previously supposed. In adults, we think of explicit "why" questions and "because" answers as the quintessential index of explanation, just as we take color reports to be an index of visual phenomenology. In an analysis of children's spontaneous speech recorded from the CHILDES database (Wellman, Hickling, and Schult 1997), Wellman and colleagues found explanations and requests for explanation in children as young as two, indeed, almost as soon as the children could speak at all. These explanations also changed, and changed in interesting ways, as the children grew older. The changes seemed to reflect those independently attributed to theory formation. For example, two-year-olds who were more likely to explain behavior in terms of desires and perceptions, whereas three- and four-year-olds began to explain behavior in terms of beliefs. A similar shift occurred in children's predictions about behavior at about the same time (Bartsch and Wellman 1995).

Are there other indicators of explanatory phenomenology in young children? The fact that explanatory phenomenology in adults is accompanied by distinctive affective and motivational states may provide a clue. We suggested above that we see very similar patterns of affect, action, and expression in young children, and even in infants, who show characteristic patterns of surprise, interest, and joy, and characteristic attempts at exploration and experimentation in some circumstances.

These patterns may be an interesting tool in sorting out whether infants form theories and which of their other behaviors are indicative of theory formation. In particular, there are currently interesting discrepancies in the literature between the inferences we can draw from infants' active behavior and those we can draw from their visual attention. The best-known case is the discrepancy between the object knowledge children demonstrate in their search behavior and the knowledge they demonstrate in "looking time" paradigms [In these paradigms, children look longer at unexpected events than at familiar events.] (see Baillargeon 1993; Spelke et al. 1992). The children's behavior in the looking time paradigms is often described in terms of explanatory phenomenology: the children are said to be "surprised" or "puzzled" by the unexpected event, or to have "predicted" that the event would not take place and to be "registering the violation of their prediction." Similarly, the children's later search behavior has also been described in these terms: children "predict" that the object is in a location, search for it there, and are "surprised" and "puzzled" when it is not there. However, neither the children's actions by themselves nor their visual attention by itself necessarily supports this interpretation. The children's looking time may reflect some automatic modular perceptual preferences that are detached from theory-like knowledge. Alternately, the children's actions may be the result of some automatic habit rather than the result of an inference about the object's location.

In either case, searching for signs of explanatory phenomenology might be helpful. Are children genuinely surprised by impossible events? Do they furrow their brows or show distress? Do they show signs of exploratory behavior that might be relevant to the conceptual problems such events pose? Do they smile if a more coherent explanation of the event is made available to them? If these behaviors do accompany search or visual attention, we are more justified in concluding that they reflect something like the operation of a theory formation system.

More generally, being able to identify the operation of the theory formation system in this way, with reasonable reliability if not perfect accuracy, could be helpful as a first step in working out the functional and, eventually, computational structure of the system. Imagine if we tried to do vision science by calculating every possible relation between visually accessible information and behavior. By using phenomenology as a mediating form of evidence, we can narrow the psychological problems to something more tractable, though still very hard. The same might be true for the psychological problem of characterizing theory formation. For example, the drivelike phenomenology of explanation may lead us to think of theory formation as a more active exploratory process than we might have done otherwise; exploring the temporal unfolding of the transition from "Hmm" to "Aha" may give us clues about how the theory formation system works on-line; and so on.

Finally, understanding the nature of the psychological process of theory formation and explanation may contribute to the more traditional normative questions of philosophy of science. We may learn not only how evolution constructed the best causal inference device we know about but also how the limitations of that device can be corrected and supplemented. In this way, explanation might actually explain things.

Note

This research was supported by National Science Foundation grant DBS9213959. I am very grateful to Henry Wellman, John Flavell, Clark Glymour, John Campbell, Dacher Kelther, Daniel Povinelli, Lucia Jacobs, and Eric Schwitzgebel, as well as to the editors and reviewers, for helpful discussions.

References

Baillargeon, R. (1993). The object concept revisited: New directions in the investigation of infants' physical knowledge. In C. Granrud, ed., *Visual perception and cognition in infancy*. Carnegie Mellon Symposia on Cognition. Hillsdale, NJ: Erlbaum.

Bartsch, K., and Wellman, H. M. (1995). *Children talk about the mind*. New York: Oxford University Press.

Bowlby, J. (1969). *Attachment and loss*. New York: Basic Books.

Bromberger, S. (1965). An approach to explanation. In R. J. Butler, ed., *Analytic philosophy*. Oxford: Blackwell.

Campbell, J. (1994). *Past, space and self*. Cambridge, MA: MIT Press.

Carey, S. (1985). *Conceptual change in childhood*. Cambridge, MA: MIT Press.

Cartwright, N. (1989). *Nature's capacities and their measurement*. Oxford: Clarendon Press; New York: Oxford University Press.

Ekman, P. (1992). An argument for basic emotions. *Cognition and Emotion, 6*, 169–200.

Gelman, S. A., and Wellman, H. M. (1991). Insides and essence: Early understandings of the non-obvious. *Cognition, 38*, 213–244.

Gopnik, A. (1988). Conceptual and semantic development as theory change. *Mind and Language, 3*, 163–179.

Gopnik, A., and Meltzoff, A. N. (1984). Semantic and cognitive development in 15- to 21-month-old children. *Journal of Child Language, 11*, 495–513.

Gopnik, A., and Meltzoff, A. N. (1997). *Words, thoughts and theories*. Cambridge, MA: MIT Press.

Gopnik, A., and Sobel, D. (1997) Reexamining the role of causality in children's early categorization of objects. Poper presented at Society for Research in Child Development.

Gopnik, A., and Wellman, H. M. (1994). The theory theory. In L. Hirschfield and S. Gelman, eds., *Mapping the mind: Domain specificity in cognition and culture.* New York: Cambridge University Press.

Hempel, C. G. (1965). *Aspects of scientific explanation, and other essays in the philosophy of science.* New York: Free Press.

Kahneman, D., Slovic, P., and Tuersky, A, eds., (1982). *Judgment under uncertainty: Heuristics and biases.* Cambridge: Cambridge University Press.

Keil, F. C. (1987). Conceptual development and category structure. In U. Neisser, ed., *Concepts and conceptual development: Ecological and intellectual factors in categorization.* Emory Symposia in Cognition. Vol. 1. New York: Cambridge University Press.

Kruglanski, A. (1989). *Lay epistemics and human knowledge: Cognitive and motivational biases.* New York: Plenum Press.

Leslie, A. M. (1987). Pretense and representation: The origins of theory of mind. *Psychological Review, 94*, 412–426.

Leslie, A. M., and Keeble, S. (1987). Do six-month-old infants perceive causality? *Cognition, 25*, 265–288.

Meltzoff, A. N. (1988). Infant imitation and memory: Nine-month-olds in immediate and deferred tests. *Child Development, 59*, 217–225.

Oakes, L. M., and Cohen, L. B. (1994). Infant causal perception. In C. Rovee-Collier and L. P. Lipsitt, eds., *Advances in infancy research.* Vol. 9. Norwood, NJ: Ablex.

O'Keefe, J., and Nadel, L. (1978). *The hippocampus as a cognitive map.* New York: Oxford University Press.

Piaget, J. (1952). *The origins of intelligence in children.* New York: International Universities Press.

Piaget, J. (1962). *Play, dreams, and imitation in childhood.* New York: Norton.

Povinelli, D. (Forthcoming). Folk physics for apes? New York: Oxford University Press.

Rock, I. (1983). *The logic of perception.* Cambridge, MA: MIT Press.

Salmon, W. (1984). *Scientific explanation and the causal structure of the world.* Princeton: Princeton University Press.

Schult, C., and Wellman, H. (1997). Explaining human movements and actions: Children's understanding of the limits of psychological explanation. *Cognition, 62*, 291–324.

Schwitzgebel, E. (Forthcoming). Children's theories and the drive to explain. *Science and Education.*

Slaughter, V., and Gopnik, A. (1996). Conceptual coherence in the child's theory of mind. *Child Development, 67*, 2967–2989.

Spelke, E. S., Breinlinger, K., Macomber, J., and Jacobson, K. (1992). Origins of knowledge. *Psychological Review, 99*, 605–632.

Tomasello, M., and Call, J. (1997). *Primate cognition.* New York: Oxford University Press.

Van Fraassen, B. (1980). *The scientific image*. Oxford: Oxford University Press.

Wellman, H. (1990). *The child's theory of mind*. Cambridge, MA: MIT Press.

Wellman, H., Hickling, A., and Schult, C. (1997). Young children's explanations: Psychological, physical and biological reasoning. In H. Wellman and K. Inagaki, eds., *Children's theories*. San Francisco: Jossey-Bass.

V

Explanatory Influences on Concept Acquisition and Use

.

13

Explanatory Understanding and Conceptual Combination

Christine Johnson and Frank Keil

Cognitive psychology has come to embrace a view of concepts long held in the philosophy of science, namely, that coherent sets of beliefs, or "theories," are essential to a full specification of concept structure (e.g., Murphy and Medin 1985; Neisser 1987; Keil 1989). In this view, concepts can no longer be modeled merely as probabilistic distributions of features or as first-order reflections of feature frequencies and correlations in the world. The seductive power and reliability of probabilistic models for predicting judgments of typicality, similarity, and category membership (e.g., Smith, Shoben, and Rips 1974; Rosch and Mervis 1975; Tversky 1977) have limited our progress in discovering more about the underlying theoretical relationships. When concepts are characterized as lists of features, the relations between those features can be obscured, and the influence such relations have on concept structure becomes difficult to bring to light (see Cohen and Murphy 1984; Medin, Wattenmaker, and Hampson 1987; Medin and Shoben 1988).

How concepts combine has been an area of active interest (e.g., Jones 1982; Zadeh 1982; Cohen and Murphy 1984; Smith and Osherson 1984; Hampton 1987, 1988; Medin and Shoben 1988; Kampt and Partee 1995) ever since Osherson and Smith (1981) showed the limitations of certain fuzzy set operations for predicting the typicality of modified categories. A common assumption in this work is that interpreting a combination of concepts reveals something of the internal structure of the concepts themselves. This revelation is particularly effective when the combinations are novel and the interpreter must "reason out" their meaning. By examining such novel combinations, we may gain some insights into the underlying theoretical structure in which such concepts are embedded. We will examine how combinations of concepts reveal the explanatory relations intrinsic to the structure of many of those concepts.

Such "depth" of processing, however, is not always necessary for interpreting conceptual combinations. That is, in many cases, the typicality structure of the constituents alone does a strikingly good job of predicting the typicality of the resulting combinations. Hampton (1987, 1988) demonstrated in a series of studies that the structure of conjunctions like "sports that are games" could often be predicted from the typicality structure of their constituents, subject to certain rules of attribute union. Hampton suggested that such a reliance on typicality may predominate in everyday discourse where rapid processing and comprehension are essential (but see Rips 1989). Moreover, Smith and Osherson (1984; see also Smith et al. 1986) have also developed successful models, relying almost exclusively on typicality structure, to predict outcomes of adjective-noun combinations involving simple modifiers. (See also Hampton 1996 for further discussion of the limits and powers of probabilistic models in understanding conceptual combinations.)

There are other cases, however, where typicality alone cannot work (Medin and Shoben 1988; Murphy 1987; Murphy, chap. 14, this volume; Rips 1989). Medin and Shoben (1988), for example, show that the adjective "straight" when applied to boomerangs and bananas (both typically curved) has very different effects on the resulting combinations' membership in their superordinate categories (see also Keil et al. 1998). That is, "straight boomerangs" are judged much worse members of the "boomerang" category than "straight bananas" are of the "banana" category. Similarly, the factors that affect similarity only partially overlap with those affecting categorization. For example, participants rated a 3.5-inch disk as more similar to a quarter ($0.25) than to a pizza, but less likely to be member of the category "quarter" than of the category "pizza" (Rips 1989). Even Hampton (1987), in his research on conjunctions, found that participants' judgments of the "importance" of constituent features was better than typicality as a predictor of inclusion in the conjunction, although a combination of the two functions was better still.

Thus there is a dilemma of sorts. Typicality structure is an important aspect of concept structure, which can sometimes help us to understand conceptual combinations. At the same time, however, it is increasingly clear that something else is also having an impact on such combinations (for further discussion, see Cohen and Murphy 1984; Barsalou and Medin 1986; Wisniewski 1996). Rather than simply documenting that something beyond typicality is at work, in this chapter we explore what that something might be. In effect, we are working toward generating an operational definition of theory and explanatory insight. Rather than seeking to predict how concepts "compose" (Fodor 1997), we wish to determine whether there are patterns in conceptual combinations that reveal deeper aspects of how explanatory insight is involved in concept structure.

13.1 Experimental Explorations of Explanation and Conceptual Combination

We describe here studies that focus exclusively on noun-noun combinations. However, unlike most prior work, our noun-noun combinations will form modifier-head noun pairs (such as "arctic rodents"), rather than conjunctions (such as "tools that are also weapons"). The modifiers used in these pairings are more complex than those (such as "red" or "striped") used in Smith and Osherson's work (Smith and Osherson 1984) and, as a consequence, we expect their role in the combinations to be more complex as well. Our primary focus, however, will be on the head noun (i.e., the second noun in each pair), partly in response to the common assumption that in processing such combinations, the main action is of the modifier on the head noun, with the latter acting as a passive recipient of a feature-weighting process. But perhaps theory relations in the head noun itself can have an impact on which features are seen as salient in the combinations. We think it useful to see how some of the broad issues concerning theory, explanation, and concept structure can be linked to detailed patterns of experimental data. It is one thing to claim that explanatory relations implicit in concept structure influence conceptual combinations. It is quite another to develop methods that uncover the actual explanatory structures at work and show the nature of their effects. We describe here an early attempt to uncover such structures as a way of seeing how they might relate to other senses of explanation discussed in this volume.

Study 1

Our first study asked whether the most typical features of constituents can nonetheless be only minor participants in specifying the important features in the resultant combinations. Establishing a set of combinations in which this is the case is the first step toward learning more about the "deeper" structures that might influence interpretation.

In this study, one group of 36 college undergraduate participants was asked to generate features for individual nouns and a second group of 16 undergraduates was asked to generate features for noun–noun combinations constructed out of those constituents.[1] The amount and kind of overlap between these sets of features was examined. The modifier nouns were environments that would present a complex set of conditions in light of which the head nouns would be assessed. These environments were either natural ones, such as DESERT, or artificial ones, such as HOSPITAL. The head nouns were also chosen from the two general categories of artifacts and natural kinds. The artifact versus natural kind contrast enabled us to explore possible differences in theory structure between members of these two categories (for further discussion, see also Ahn 1999).

The stimuli used in all three studies were chosen on the basis of pilot work that attempted to rule out the processing strategies shown to operate in some modifier–noun interpretations. We chose combinations that were novel (although at least moderately plausible, such as HOSPITAL RODENT or ARCTIC BICYCLE) so that participants would not refer to stored exemplars. Similarly, we did not reverse the pairs (e.g., RODENT HOSPITAL or BICYCLE MOUNTAIN) because, in such cases, pilot participants tended to state simply that the environment was the setting where the modifier noun could be found. We wanted the participants to have to do some conceptual work in interpreting the combinations, testing the assumption that such work taps into underlying explanatory knowledge. Thus the goal of this research was not to identify which sorts of processes operate in which combinations but instead to determine what the modification of nouns can reveal about the explanatory structure underlying those concepts. In our first study, we specifically wanted to determine the extent to which explicit feature listings in constituent noun phrases contributed to explicit features in the resulting contribution. Given difficulties in predicting the nature of conceptual combinations from constituents, we did not expect great success. The key issue in this study was to establish the extent of the disparity and to explore possible patterns in what sorts of features "emerge" in combinations and how they might be related to constituent concepts even though they do normally appear in standard feature lists of those constituents.

Method The phrases used in all three studies were constructed from twelve common nouns selected from two general categories: natural kinds and artifacts. The six nouns used as modifiers were the natural environments MOUNTAIN, ARCTIC, and DESERT and the artificial environments HOSPITAL, LABORATORY, and KINDERGARTEN. The six head nouns were the natural kinds RODENT, BIRD, and SEED and the artifacts BICYCLE, KNIFE, and DANCE. Combinations of these nouns were formed such that both kinds of modifiers were used with both kinds of nouns. For a full list of the combinations and features, see table 13.1.

Each participant was instructed to list features "common to or characteristic of" six nouns or six combinations. Participants in part A were requested to list thirty-six such features for each individual noun. (This number was determined in pilot work as the typical maximum number of features participants would generate when asked to produce as many as they could in 5 minutes.) Participants in part B were requested to list "at least 5 features" for each combination. It was assumed that finding features to list for the combinations might be considerably more difficult, hence fewer were requested as a minimum. Setting such a low number puts a conservative bias on any findings of emergent features because a higher threshold would almost surely have caused far more novel features to be produced.

In part A, the responses for all participants on a given item were compiled and a master list constructed, ranking each feature according to its frequency of mention. A typical noun features (TNF) list was then derived that included only those features that were mentioned by over half the participants on that item. The responses for all participants on a given item in part B were also compiled. A typical combinations feature (TCF) list included the combination features mentioned by at least half of the participants. Then both the TCF and master combination lists were compared to the TNF and master lists for the relevant nouns.

In part A, most participants listed 36 features for each item and took from 20 to 60 minutes to complete this task. Ten lists generated for each noun contributed to the final master list for that noun. The derived TNF lists (included in table 13.3) varied in length from 9 to 18 features, with an average length of 11.2 features.

In part B, all participants listed at least five features for each combination, taking from 5 to 20 minutes to complete this task. Eight lists generated for each combination contributed to the master list for that combination. The derived TCF lists included a total of 28 features (127

Table 13.1
Typical Combination Features (TCF) Listed by at Least Half the Subjects in Part
B of Study 1

Combination	Typical features	Source[a]
HOSPITAL BICYCLE	meters and dials[b]	Atypical (head noun)
	stationary	Unique
	adjustable difficulty	Unique
HOSPITAL RODENT	sneaky and quick[b]	Atypical (head noun)
	nocturnal	Unique
LABORATORY DANCE	lab coats	Typical (modifier)
	wild and crazy[b]	Unique
LABORATORY SEED	plentiful	Unique
	hybrid[b]	Unique
KINDERGARTEN KNIFE	small	Atypical (modifier)
	plastic	Atypical (head noun)
	dull[b]	Atypical (head noun)
KINDERGARTEN BIRD	sings	Typical (head noun)
	caged[b]	Atypical (head noun)
ARCTIC BICYCLE	two wheels	Typical (head noun)
	spiked tires[b]	Unique
ARCTIC RODENT	white[b]	Typical (modifier)
	thick coat	Unique
DESERT DANCE	primitive ritual[b]	Unique
DESERT SEED	cactus	Typical (modifier)
	Hot	Typical (modifier)
	long dormant[b]	Unique
MOUNTAIN KNIFE	large[b]	Typical (modifier)
	sharp[b]	Typical (head noun)
MOUNTAIN RODENT	fur	Typical (head noun)
	burrows	Typical (head noun)
	eats plants	Atypical (head noun)
	thick coat[b]	Unique

[a] "Typical" appeared on typical noun features (TNF) list. "Atypical" appeared on master noun list, but was not typical. "Unique" did not appear on noun list.
[b] Feature used in studies 2 and 3.

responses) and are presented in table 13.1. Table 13.2 summarizes the results of comparing the combination features with the corresponding noun features: 68% of the combination features (both from the typical and the master lists) failed to appear on the TNF lists; compared with the

Table 13.2
Proportion of Combination Features That Do Not Appear on Noun Feature Lists

Source	Typical combination feature lists	Master combination feature lists
Typical noun feature lists	68%	68%
Master noun feature lists	38%	30%

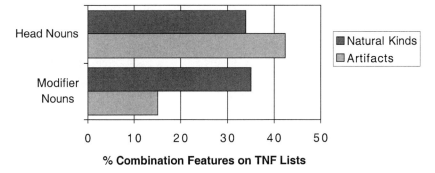

Figure 13.1
Proportion of combination features (mean = 34%) that also appear on the typical noun feature (TNF) lists for the four noun types in study 1.

master noun lists, 30% of all combination features and 38% of the typical combination features also failed to appear.

Considering just those combination features that did overlap with the noun lists, there are significant differences in the contributions made by the various nouns. Overall, the head nouns contributed nearly twice as many features as did the modifier nouns (head nouns: 57 features; modifiers: 32 features). In addition, although natural kinds and artifact head nouns contributed about equally, among the modifier nouns the natural environments contributed about twice as many features as did the artificial environments (see figure 13.1).

Discussion of Study 1   As seen in table 13.2, over two-thirds of the features of these novel noun-noun combinations do not appear to be directly "inherited" from their constituent prototypes. The weighted concatenation of typical constituent features seen, for instance, in many of Hampton's conjunctions (Hampton 1987), cannot account for most of the combination features generated here. More of these features do appear on the

master constituent lists—that is, they do occasionally surface when participants are given ten or more minutes to generate features. But this finding
offers no hint as to how those features are accessed for the constituents,
evaluated for inclusion on the combination lists, or even whether such a
"feature selection" process is involved.

The more telling finding was that nearly 40% of the combination
features on which subjects agreed strongly were never mentioned by any
subject for the individual nouns. Indeed, participants reached consensus on
these "unique" features in 9 out of 12 of the combinations (see table 13.1).
Thus any model that relies strictly on constituent feature lists is inadequate to explain this frequent result. Although the unique features seem
to appear out of nowhere, they may well have been explicitly stored for
these concepts before the participants encountered our task. Certainly
these unique features are not unreasonable or even unusual. Few of us
would find it difficult to accept, for example, that rodents can be nocturnal, or seeds hybrid, or bicycles stationary, or dances ritualized. Nevertheless, even when given up to an hour for a traditional feature-listing task,
the participants in part A did not seem to access such information, while
the majority of participants in part B did. Apparently, in interpreting familiar nouns in novel combinations, something beyond constituent feature
lists is brought into play.

The higher incidence of features inherited from the head nouns than
from the modifiers probably follows from the nature of adjective-noun
relationships. That is, an ARCTIC RODENT is a type of RODENT (and
not a type of ARCTIC) and thus would be more likely to include features of the general RODENT category. But why include some typical
RODENT features (such as "has fur") and not others (such as "used in
experiments")? Smith and Osherson (1984) have suggested that it is the
function of modifiers in such combinations to weight certain dimensions
in the head nouns and thus increase their diagnosticity for the combination. Although we consider this proposition more closely in study 2, an
examination of the modifier features generated in study 1 offers insight
into some of the complications that can arise in noun modification (see
table 13.3).

The typical features listed for the artificial environments tend to be
the entities, objects, and events commonly associated with those environments. For LABORATORY, for example, typical features included "scientists," "apparatus," and "experiments."[2] About half of the typical features

Table 13.3
Typical Noun Features (TNFs) Listed by Over Half the Subjects in Part A of
Study 1, for Modifiers and Head Nouns

Natural modifiers	Typical features	Artificial modifiers	Typical features
MOUNTAIN	snow	LABORATORY	apparatus
	made of rock		experiments
	tall, high		scientists
	thin air		chemicals
	plants		microscopes
	animals		lab coats
	trees		tables
	massive		test tubes
	steep		shelves
	skiing		
ARCTIC	cold	KINDERGARTEN	crayons
	ice		play
	snow		friends
	polar bears		kids
	white		learn
	seals		teachers
	Eskimo		ABCs
	iceberg		bus
	polar		small furniture
	freezing		
	water		
DESERT	dry	HOSPITAL	waiting room
	cactus		patient
	sand		nurses
	dunes		doctors
	snakes		beds
	hot		medicine
	lizards		operating room
	vast		white
	oasis		maternity ward
	mirage		emergency room
	bones		needles
	flat		surgical
	barren		instruments
	death		visitors
	horizon		large building
	sandstorm		
	Arabs		
	camels		

Table 13.3
(Continued)

RODENT	sharp teeth	DANCE	music
	used in experiments		rhythm
	fur		groups of people
	tail		fun
	claws		dressing up
	small		exciting
	burrows		partner
	pest		social event
	not liked		romance
			movement
BIRD	eggs	BICYCLE	two wheels
	wings		seat
	nest		chain
	fly		spokes
	beak		reflector
	feathers		transportation
	migrate		pedals
	chirp or sing		pump
	eyes		metal
	worms		frame
SEED	plant	KNIFE	sharp
	growth		slice
	soil		tool
	water		blade
	sunlight		cut
	small		serrated
	sunflower		metal
	hard		stab
	life		shiny
	garden		harm
	pit		handle
			weapon
			carve

for the natural environments also fall into these categories. The other half, however, might be considered general physical conditions, such as "cold" and "white" for ARCTIC, "hot" and "vast" for DESERT, and "massive" and "made of rock" for MOUNTAIN. These conditions account for about 75% of the features inherited from these modifiers. The near absence of such physical condition terms in the artificial environments may account for the much lower incidence of inheritance from those modifiers.

The inheritance of such features is not always a straightforward business, however. Although MOUNTAIN KNIVES are "large," for instance, they are not "made of rock." Such a difference might be accounted for by a "consistency" judgment (Hampton 1987) in which the typicality structures of the two constituents are compared. Because KNIVES are typically "made of metal," this may preclude the inheritance of "made of rock." However, a closer look reveals that the comparison process involved can sometimes be more complex.

The feature "white," for example, was listed almost as frequently for HOSPITAL as it was for ARCTIC, but only one subject listed "white" for HOSPITAL RODENT, while all but one listed it for ARCTIC RODENT. If participants were, in both cases, merely making a consistency judgment between RODENT and whiteness, such a result would be surprising. That is, if HOSPITALS are nearly as typically white as the ARCTIC, it is not clear why HOSPITAL RODENTS are not also listed as "white" more often. Instead, a different sort of judgment, based on causal or explanatory relationships, seems to be involved in this case, rather than a simple reliance on the strength of associative relations between features and categories. Participants may recognize that the color of a hospital would be unlikely to influence the biological processes responsible for a rodent being white, while the color of the arctic might well play a vital role in those processes. In the absence of strong exemplar or typicality effects (LABORATORY RODENT, for example, probably would be described as "white"), the dimension of color would not be diagnostic for RODENT in most artificial environments because it is not causally important.

In more general terms, one basis for evaluating the appropriateness of combination features may depend on causal explanatory links between selective conditions and useful, adaptive traits. Such causal links might concern the evolution of a natural kind in a particular habitat or, for an artifact, its purposeful design. However, participants seldom included purposes or goals on their lists of features. For instance, participants never listed such terms as "diagnose," "heal," or "recuperate" for HOSPITAL. Nonetheless, they were surely aware of these goals and of their interactions with the features they did list, such as "doctor," "medicine," and "beds." These may have been more implicit in these tasks. The importance of goals in organizing both concept structure and use converges with work by Barsalou (1985).

If we look again at the typical modifier features with causal explanatory relationships in mind, we see that the entities, objects, and activities listed might be interpretable as agents and means that serve implicit goals. For example, a LABORATORY's "scientists" and "apparatus" imply the goal of discovery; a KINDERGARTEN's "teachers" and "ABCs" imply the goal of literacy. In addition, the condition terms (such as "cold," "dry," and "made of rock") listed for the natural environments might act as constraints on the types of causal relationships possible in those environments. Thus, although these relations are not explicit in participants' feature lists, this omission does not mean that such knowledge is absent from these concepts or unimportant in their combination.

Whether explanatory relations are "hidden units" driving conceptual combinations can only remain speculation if we persist with the feature list approach to the study of concepts. As study 1 demonstrates, this approach seems to preclude direct access to the relevant knowledge base. A different technique is needed to prompt participants to reveal their knowledge of causal relations. Study 2 was an attempt to elicit such tacit knowledge. More generally, this second study explores the extent to which we should not think of theory and explanation effects on concepts as invariably operating at a fully explicit level.

Study 2

Piloting and speaking-out-loud protocols suggested that participants often engage in a form of problem-solving while interpreting novel combinations. That is, the combination features that they ultimately produce often have the flavor of "conclusions." Therefore, in our second study we decided to ask participants to be explicit about the premises that led to these conclusions. This was done by presenting them with sentences such as the following:

Since the ARCTIC _____
and since RODENTS _____
then arctic rodents have white fur.

Study 2 thus asks whether this sort of explanation-based frame might elicit constituent features different from those listed by participants in study 1. The conclusions stated for the combinations were all features drawn from the typical combination feature (TCF) list generated in study 1 (see table 13.1), which helped ensure that the participants would find the conclusions reasonable and thus have little difficulty in generating the appropriate premises. Furthermore, the TCF chosen for a given combination was one that required a causal explanation.

For example, "cactus" was not chosen for DESERT SEED because, if one were to ask why a DESERT SEED has the characteristic "cactus," the response would probably simply refer to what might be called "categorical knowledge." That is, because seeds come from plants, and a cactus is a typical desert plant, a DESERT SEED is probably from a cactus. This associative process, or something very like it, was most probably in effect when the participants originally produced the combination feature "cactus." (For discussion of such processes, see Medin and Smith 1984.) Because, however, our goal was to use conceptual combinations to learn more about causal or explanatory knowledge, the TCF "long dormant" was chosen for DESERT SEED. An answer to why DESERT SEEDS are long dormant would probably require a more causal explanation involving, for instance, climatic seasonality and the requirements for germination. By using, as conclusions, combination features that seemed to require knowledge not just of category structure but also of real-world constraints and tendencies that govern the interactions between these entities and their environments, this study attempted to explore the structure of the participants' underlying explanatory understandings. Twelve fill-in-the-blank frames (as shown above) were created, one for each of the combinations used in study 1. The conclusion presented for each combination was selected from the TCF list derived in part B of study 1. The full set is indicated by the starred items in table 13.1.

Method   All eighteen participants received six frames, each on a separate sheet of paper. The order and selection of items varied across participants. Participants were given virtually unlimited time to complete this task. Each frame required participants to complete clauses for a given head noun and modifier in order to generate a set of premises that the subject felt would lead to the presented conclusion. In particular, the participants were asked to provide "the critical attribute for each individual category that would lead you to the conclusion stated for the compound category."

The critical features generated in this task were analyzed as follows. First, the critical features for a noun used in one combination were compared to the critical features for that same noun used in a different combination. Second, all critical features for a given noun were compared with the typical features for the corresponding noun (TNFs) in study 1. Finally, the number of matching responses for a noun in a given combination was assessed by three independent judges, who were asked to write a summary version of the most frequent responses for each combination. These summary versions were used to compose a summary critical feature set for each noun in each combination. These summary critical features were then compared, as above, across combinations and against the TNFs of study 1.

On average, only 19% of the critical features listed for a given noun appeared in both contexts for that noun. Among the head nouns, the average overlap was 14%. Among modifier nouns, it was 31%, although over one-third of these responses could be accounted for by ARCTIC, for which there was nearly complete overlap (i.e., of the feature "ice and snow"). Among the 24 summary critical features, only those derived for ARCTIC overlapped (see table 13.4). Only 34% of the critical features (74/216 responses) generated in this study were judged synonymous with the TNFs derived in study 1.

The summary critical features showed a similar pattern: 33% (8/24 responses) were synonymous with the TNFs. Only 26% of the head noun critical features matched TNFs, while 43% of the modifier critical features did. Among the head nouns, artifacts and natural kinds each had 14 responses that matched the TNF lists. Among the modifiers, natural environment shared twice as many critical features (31 responses) with their respective TNF lists as did the artificial environments (15 responses; see figure 13.2).

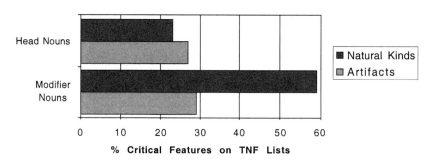

Figure 13.2
Proportion of critical features (mean = 32%) that also appear on the typical noun feature (TNF) lists for the four noun types in study 2.

Table 13.4
Summary Critical Features Derived from Most Frequent Responses in Study 2

Combination	Conclusion	Summary critical feature
HOSPITAL BICYCLE	meters and dials	needs to monitor patients' health requires physical exertion
HOSPITAL RODENT	sneaky and quick	needs to be kept sanitary tries to avoid extermination
LABORATORY DANCE	wild and crazy	has serious scientists allows people to relieve stress
LABORATORY SEED	hybrid	does experimental manipulations contains genetic material
KINDERGARTEN KNIFE	dull	needs to protect small children can be dangerous if mishandled
KINDERGARTEN BIRD	caged	has boisterous, inquisitive kids tries to fly when frightened
ARCTIC BICYCLE	spiked tires	is covered with ice and snow requires traction to move
ARCTIC RODENT	white fur	is covered with ice and snow must blend in for protection
DESERT DANCE	primitive ritual	is a difficult, demanding habitat is a means of communing with god
DESERT SEED	long dormant	has long, dry periods requires moisture to sprout
MOUNTAIN KNIFE	large and sharp	is wild, dangerous place can be used for protection
MOUNTAIN RODENT	thick coat	can be cold at high altitude needs to keep warm

The critical features generated in this study were, on average, nearly four times longer than the noun features produced in study 1. Although some were concatenations (e.g., "dangerous, hot, and not well populated" for DESERT), others were statements of relation (e.g., "if misused or mishandled can cause serious bodily harm" for KNIVES). In fact, many critical features showed such goal-oriented or means/end phrasing (for more examples, see table 13.5). That is, phrases like "need to," "in order to," "enables," "allows," and so on, which appeared in only 2% of the noun features on the master lists of study 1, occurred in over 40% of the critical features for the same nouns. In fact, for every combination in this

Table 13.5
Examples of "Goal Phrasing" in Subjects' Critical Feature Responses

Combination	Noun	Critical feature response
ARCTIC BICYCLE	BICYCLE	"need traction to run effectively"
LABORATORY DANCE	DANCE	"enable us to let our hair down"
KINDERGARTEN KNIFE	KNIFE	"if misused, mishandled, or thrown can cause serious bodily harm"
DESERT SEED	SEED	"require moisture to sprout"
KINDERGARTEN BIRD	BIRD	"try to fly away when frightened"
ARCTIC RODENT	RODENT	"need camouflage to protect them from predators"
HOSPITAL RODENT	HOSPITAL	"are kept sanitary to prevent the spread of infection"
LABORATORY DANCE	LABORATORY	"require workers to be serious and composed"
KINDERGARTEN KNIFE	KINDERGARTEN	"need to protect children in their care"
DESERT DANCE	DESERT	"have primitive peoples who want to control the weather"

study, at least three responses showed such phrasings. The number of natural head nouns, artificial head nouns, and artificial modifiers that displayed this goal-oriented phrasing was about equal; such phrasing was only rarely seen among the natural modifiers.

Discussion of Study 2   Several issues are raised by this exploratory study. Consider, first, the finding that only minimal overlap in critical features occurs across contexts for a given noun. For head nouns, this finding is consistent with other research on context effects (Bransford and McCarrell 1975; Anderson and Ortony 1975; Barsalou 1982; Roth and Shoben 1983) in that certain aspects or dimensions of head nouns tend to be differentially weighted in different contexts (see also Murphy 1987 and Murphy and Andrew 1993 for such effects in conceptual combinations). A similar finding for the modifier noun is more provocative, however.

Omitting the exceptional ARCTIC case, over 80% (95/117) of the participants' responses for modifiers paired with one head noun differed from their responses for that same modifier paired with a different head noun. For example, when the modifier HOSPITAL was paired with RODENT, its most common critical feature was "must be kept sanitary." However, when paired with the head noun BICYCLE, its most common critical feature was "needs to monitor patients' health." Even with the apparently ambiguous ARCTIC (where the summary critical feature in both contexts was "ice and snow"), it is not unreasonable to suppose that in the case of ARCTIC RODENT ("has white fur"), it was the color of ice and snow that mattered (as indeed one subject spelled out). Similarly, for ARCTIC BICYCLE ("has spiked tires") it was probably the type of surface that ice and snow present (i.e., "slippery ice" and "soft snow," as two participants wrote) that was important.

Although this finding does not rule out the function of the modifier as weighting relevant aspects of the head noun, it does suggest that this process may be more reciprocal than has generally been assumed in the Smith and Osherson model. That is, when the modifier is complex, the head noun may itself play a role in determining what aspect of the modifier is relevant to the combination. With a simple modifier like RED or PEELED, the dimension to be weighted is usually obvious (although, even these cases can show changes; Murphy and Andrew 1993). But with a complex environment like HOSPITAL, the relevant dimension is not at all clear at the outset. As discussed above, even the relatively "simple" environment ARCTIC, with its few dominant features, shows evidence of being influenced by the head noun with which it is paired.

Medin and Shoben (1988) found similar results in a study where they had participants rate the similarity of triplets of modified nouns. For example, they paired BRASS, GOLD, and SILVER with the head nouns RAILING and COIN. Participants rated GOLD and BRASS more similar when they modified RAILING, and GOLD and SILVER more similar when they modified COIN. Apparently, combining with RAILING made the color of these metals salient while combining with COIN weighted their monetary value. Although just how such reciprocal influence may operate is still a mystery, it is clear that the head nouns in such combinations cannot be viewed as simply the passive recipients of a dimension in the weighting process.

In study 2, only about one-third of the critical features were synonymous with the typical features for the same nouns. This key result again points to the inadequacy of traditional feature lists for predicting combination features. This is especially true for the head nouns: only 25% of their critical features also appeared on the true/false (T/F) lists for those nouns. Thus the question again arises as to the source of these critical features.

Far from being obscure or unusual, the critical features can be considered common knowledge about the nouns in question (see table 13.4). Consider BICYCLE, for example. Surely both "requires traction" and "requires physical exertion" are a part of most people's concept of bicycles, yet these features never appear on the noun lists generated in study 1. Apparently, there is something about the sort of knowledge that is revealed in the current study—and, presumably, that enters into the interpretation of novel combinations—that is not readily captured in the standard feature list or prototype model.

The distinctive character of this knowledge may be revealed by a closer examination of those critical features judged as synonymous with the TNF. In study 1, for example, nearly all the participants listed "water" as a feature of SEED. In study 2, in listing the critical features for SEED in DESERT SEED ("is long dormant"), most participants also mentioned "water." However, in every case in study 2, the word "water" (or "moisture," "rain," etc.) was embedded in a phrase such as "requires water" (or "needs adequate moisture to sprout"). Although these phrases are, in one sense, synonymous with the typical feature "water," the difference between the responses in the two studies may be important.

When participants list "water" for SEED alone, the contingency "required for sprouting" may well be implied. But when such contingencies are implicit rather than explicit, that difference can influence how models of concept structure are constructed. Although the participants' abbreviated responses on the feature listing task may be rich in implication for them, this richness remains unavailable as data. When such feature lists are further taken to be "summary representations" of concepts (see Medin and Smith 1984), not only is much important conceptual structure inaccessible to experimental manipulation, but it is also at risk of being left out of our models altogether.

The causal or goal phrasing observed in many of the critical features in this study may offer a unique and revealing glimpse into the structure of theory. By phrasing the feature as a conditional relationship, rather than merely a perceptual or functional attribute, subjects appeared to reveal a new facet of their underlying conceptual organization. These relationships may not only determine the organization of features and dimensions within a concept but also dictate how that concept can interact with others.

To use a concrete example, the purpose or goal of a hospital influences many aspects of its physical structure and associated events. This goal also influences our conceptual organization of those features. Similarly, the artificial head nouns used in this study represent artifacts that were created with a purpose that influences both their design and the way we think about their features. The natural head nouns, representing living entities, also have a kind of causal or intentional structure. This is based not on human purposes but on evolutionary, adaptive goals such as survival and reproduction. The presence of such relations in at least three responses for every combination in study 2—and their virtual absence from the constituent lists in study 1—suggests that such knowledge may be particularly relevant in interpreting novel combinations.

This suggestion receives further support from the finding that natural environments shared twice as many critical features with their respective TNF lists as did artificial environments. It is no coincidence that this pattern duplicates the inheritance of features from these environments in the combinations (compare figures 13.1 and 13.2). The majority of natural environment features that turned up on the critical feature lists were the general physical conditions discussed above. Although these features do not, in themselves, imply a particular goal (note the lack of goal phrasing in this category of modifier), they do present prevailing conditions that constrain the sorts of goal relations that can apply. For example, the cold of the high-altitude mountains dictates that a rodent has a "thick coat of fur" to meet its need to keep warm. Similarly, a parched heat so dominates the desert that dances there must be "primitive rituals" with the goal of producing rain. In addition, the head nouns paired with these modifiers showed a stronger tendency toward goal phrasing than those paired with the purpose-rich artificial environments.

Despite the intuitive power of these interpretations, study 2 does not explicitly address whether these relational critical features are qualitatively different from the typical features of study 1. It still remains to be demonstrated that the goal phrasing of many of these features is an indication of their theoretical or "deep" conceptual status, in contrast with the "surface" features that appear on the prototype lists. Many researchers have proposed dichotomies between "core," "defining," or "central" features, on the one hand, and "identifying," "characteristic," or "prototype" features, on the other (e.g., Armstrong, Gleitman, and Gleitman 1983; Miller and Johnson-Laird 1976; Smith and Medin 1981). A common assumption in these models is that the centrality of a feature is reflected in the degree to which a change in that feature influences the integrity of the concept: the greater the impact, the more "central" the feature (see Gentner 1983; and Sloman, Love, and Ahn 1998). Study 3 examined the centrality of the goal-oriented features generated in study 2 versus that of the high-frequency prototype features generated in study 1.

Study 3

To test for the centrality of what we are calling "explanatory" or "theory relations" over that of typical features, participants were presented with made-up "facts" that discounted one or the other type of knowledge. The participants were asked to accept these "facts" as true. They were then asked, in light of these facts, to rate the feasibility of the typical combination features used in study 2. If the explanatory relations were indeed more central, altering them would be more likely to affect the interpretation of the combinations than would altering the typical features. In addition to rating the combinations' features before and after the presentation of the pseudo-facts, participants were also asked to rate how "likely to be true" both the theory relations and the typical features were of the combinations. These ratings were intended to confirm the relevance of these attributes and to justify contrasting the effects of their alteration in the final phase of this study.

Only the possible centrality of the head nouns' attributes (rather than those of the modifier nouns) was examined in this study. This was, in part, because every head noun in study 2 produced responses that showed the goal-phrasing thought to be indicative of theory relations; not all the modifiers produced such responses. Because the structure of this experiment is somewhat complex, consider the following example. (For a schematic of this paradigm, see table 13.6.) In part A, a given subject might rate the likelihood that the sentence "Arctic rodents tend to be white" is true. Like all the target sentences in part A, this sentence is composed of one of the noun-noun combinations used throughout these

Table 13.6
Structure of Study 3 (Example: ARCTIC RODENT)

Study phase	Instructions	Theory condition	Feature condition
A	Rate likelihood: "Arctic rodent . . ."	Typical combination feature: ". . . is white."	Typical combination feature: ". . . is white."
B	Rate likelihood: "Arctic rodent . . ."	Theory relation for head noun: ". . . must blend in."	Typical feature for head noun: ". . . has fur."
C	Accept as fact: "Arctic rodent . . ."	Discounting of theory relation: ". . . smell repels predators."	Discounting of typical features: ". . . has naked hide.
D	Rerate likelihood: "Arctic rodent . . ."	Typical combination feature: ". . . is white."	Typical combination feature: ". . . is white."

studies and the TCF (typical combination feature) used as a conclusion in study 2.

In part B, half of the participants rating the above sentence would now rate "Arctic rodents have fur." The predicate of this sentence is a typical feature of the head noun of the combination (feature condition). The other half of these participants rated "Arctic rodents must blend in with their surroundings to avoid detection by predators." The predicate of this sentence is a theory relation based on the summary critical feature for this head noun (theory condition).

In part C, the participants in the feature condition were presented with a "fact" that discounted the typical features used in part B. This discounting was achieved by denial or by the substitution of an incompatible feature. The participants were instructed to accept the "fact" as true and then to rerate the original target sentence. For example:

Given the FACT:
Arctic rodents have no fur, but a heavy layer of blubber.
Now rate:
Arctic rodents tend to be white.

1———2———3———4———5———6———7———8———9
very   very
likely   unlikely

The participants in the theory condition were presented with a fact that discounted the theory relation used in part B. This discounting would be achieved again by substitution or by eliminating the need for the relation. For example:

Given the FACT:
Arctic rodents give off a strong, repulsive odor
that discourages predators from approaching them.
Now rate:
Arctic rodents tend to be white.

1————2————3————4————5————6————7————8————9

very   very
likely   unlikely

A comparison of the ratings of part C with those for the same sentences in part A yields a measure of the centrality of the manipulated attribute.

Materials   Nine different versions of the materials used in this study were prepared, each with a different subset and order of stimuli. The same instructions accompanied all versions. Across these versions, all 12 of the combinations appeared 42 times, half the time in the "theory condition" and half in the "feature condition" (see table 13.5).

Part A of this study consisted of 14 sentences, each with its own 1–9 rating scale where 1 = very likely, and 9 = very unlikely. For a given version, these 14 sentences included 8 target sentences. The subjects of these target sentences were the combinations used in the previous studies; the predicates were the frequently mentioned combination features used as conclusions in study 2. The remaining 6 sentences were fillers, constructed to be rated as unlikely (e.g. "Library windows look out on vast deserts," or "Library grass tends to be red."). These fillers were added to help balance the likelihood ratings.

Part B of this study consisted of 14 sentences each again accompanied by a 1–9 likelihood rating scale. These 14 sentences were composed of the same subjects used in Part A, but with different predicates. Six of these were fillers. In the remaining eight target sentences, four used head noun typical features (feature condition) in their predicates. The TNFs selected for these sentences were judged by the experimenters to be the most relevant to the predicates used in part A. (For example, a

RODENT having "fur" is more relevant to an ARCTIC RODENT being "white" than the equally common RODENT features "teeth" and "tail" would be.) The other four target sentences used the theory relations (theory condition) suggested by the summary critical features in study 2.

Part C of this study 3 used the same eight target sentences that were used in part A for a given version. In part C, however, each sentence was preceded by a "fact" in light of which that target would be rerated, as shown in the example above. In the feature condition, this fact discounted the typical feature rated in part B. In the theory condition, the fact discounted the theory relation rated in part B. The length and complexity of these facts was equated across conditions. No filler sentences were used.

Procedure and Analysis   Each of 63 participants was given a pamphlet that included the above-described materials and two pages of instructions. The first page of instructions asked participants to rate a set of sentences on a 1–9 scale as to their likelihood of being true. The 14 sentences of part A and the 14 sentences of part B followed on pages 2 through 5, with no special distinction made between them. A second set of instructions appeared on page 6 of the pamphlet in which the participants were told that they were again to rate a set of sentences (on pages 7 and 8) as to their likelihood of being true. These instructions went on to say: "However, this time each such sentence is preceded by a 'FACT'. This 'FACT' may be more or less believable (some are quite farfetched) but you are to accept all such 'FACTS' as TRUE. Then, in light of this 'TRUE FACT', you are again to rate one of the sentences you rated in the first part of this study."

The data from this study were analyzed in two ways. First, the ratings for the target sentences in part B were compared across participants for a given combination to determine whether there was a significant difference in feasibility between the typical feature and the theory relation. Second, the changes in ratings within participants for the target sentences from part A to part C were compared across the two conditions for a given combination to determine whether the impact on the combination's interpretation was significantly different when the relevant typical feature versus the relevant theory relation was discounted.

In comparing rating changes (part A ratings minus part C ratings for a given target sentence), we found a significant difference between the theory and the feature condition (F [1,124] = 53.09, p < .001; see figure 13.3). That is, when the theory relation was discounted in part C, participants tended to alter their ratings 2 to 2.5 points more than they did when the typical feature was discounted. We also found a significant artifact/natural kind (head noun) effect, with combinations involving the latter shifting more under both conditions (F [1,124] = 25.46, p < .001).

In comparing the ratings in the theory condition versus the feature condition in part B of this study, we found no significant differences (figure 13.4). Consider first the implications of the participants' ratings in part B of this experiment (see figure 13.4). The two types of head noun attrib-

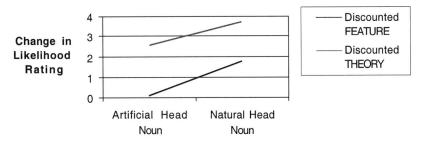

Figure 13.3
Change in the likelihood of combination features in response to discounting a typical feature (feature condition) versus discounting a theory relation (theory condition).

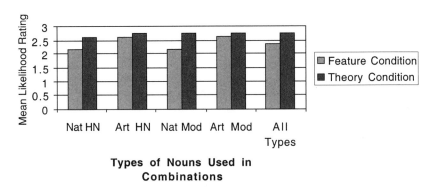

(HN=headnouns; Mod=modifier nouns; Nat=natural kinds; Art=artifacts.)

Figure 13.4
Mean likelihood ratings of head noun typical features (feature condition) versus head noun theory relations (theory coditions) across different types of combinations. None of the differences was significant.

utes were rated as equally likely to be true of the combinations. This result was not unexpected because both the typical features and the theory relations were selected for use in this study based on their presumed relevance to the combinations. But this finding does more than confirm that supposition. Consider its implication in conjunction with the primary finding of this study.

In comparing the pre- and postmanipulation ratings, changes in the theory relations were found to have a significantly greater impact than changes in the typical features had on the interpretation of the combinations. This greater centrality to theory relations might also be thought of as greater psychological stability. The ratings in part B show that the attributes in question were equally true of the combinations. But when threatened by facts that challenged this truth, the typical features were more easily dismissed. Thus, even though ARCTIC RODENTS may be just as likely to have fur (average rating: 1.50) as to require camouflage (average rating: 1.67), eliminating fur was less disruptive to the integrity of the combination than was eliminating the need to blend in (at least as far as being "white" is concerned).

This effect also shows important differences across noun types. In both conditions, the ratings for the combinations with natural head nouns shifted more than those with artificial head nouns (see figure 13.3). In fact, in the feature-discounting case, altering the artifact's typical feature had almost no effect on the combination's feature rating, whereas altering typical features of the natural kinds produced, on average, a two-point rating shift. This difference may be attributable to the nature of the causal links in natural kinds, which are more richly homeostatic and interconnected (see Ahn 1998; Boyd 1999; Keil 1989). Artifacts, on the other hand, may be more amenable to the substitution or modification of features. That is, the impact of altering an artifact's typical features may vary more, depending on how closely tied it is to the artifact's function or purpose.

A KNIFE, for example, may typically be made of metal, but plastic would do if it were hard and sharp enough to enable the knife to be used as it was intended. A BICYCLE may typically have two wheels, but giving it six wheels may not critically affect how or why it is used. Changing a RODENT's fur to feathers, on the other hand, or giving a BIRD six wings instead of two, would be more likely to prompt us to rearrange our understanding of these creatures to fit them into an acceptable framework of evolutionary adaptations. That is, the surface features of natural kinds are more inextricably bound up in our theories of their adaptive functions (for discussion, see Carey 1985; Keil 1989).

Similarly, the typical features of most natural kinds are felt to be caused by something intrinsic to the kind (e.g., genetic code, chemical interactions, etc.). The typical features of most artifacts, on the other hand, are usually caused by extrinsic factors. Thus changing the features of natural kinds may be seen as having more of an impact on the intrinsic nature of those entities. This is compatible with suggestion that even preschoolers may see richer, underlying causal structure for natural kinds as opposed to artifacts (Gelman and Hirschfeld 1999).

13.2   Explanatory Relations and Conceptual Structure

In these three studies, we have demonstrated the inadequacy of the feature list model of concepts for predicting the features of novel combinations of those concepts. The causal explanatory knowledge contained in such concepts, which is only rarely included in participants' lists of typical features, can nonetheless be elicited if participants are asked for the premises that would lead them to the conclusion of those combination features. The premises are often phrased as conditional relationships and appear to reflect the participants' underlying understandings about why the properties associated with concepts cohere as they do. These conditional relationships are more central to the concepts than even highly typical features: changes in the relationships have a greater impact on how the nouns are interpreted in the combinations.

A closer look at what we have not demonstrated is also in order. The "critical features" generated in study 2 are necessarily post hoc. Because the combination features are provided as a (foregone) conclusion, subjects are actually constructing these critical features after the fact. Thus the role such features play in the original generation of the combination features is not directly assessed. Even the significant impact of altering the explanatory relations on the subsequent reinterpretation of the combinations does not prove that these relations originally participated in that interpretation. This limitation is less troubling, however, given that our primary goal was not to investigate the processes by which novel combinations are interpreted but to use such combinations to examine the more explanatory facets of concept structure.

As the accumulating literature on conceptual combinations indicates, there seem to be several strategies used to generate interpretations. Each of these strategies reflects a different aspect or level of conceptual organization. For example, the inheritance of typical features seen in many of Hampton's conjunctions (1987, 1988) confirms the hiqh accessibility of such features and reveals that information on their relative importance is also available. Smith and Osherson's work (1984) on nouns modified by simple adjectives shows that feature values depend, in part, on the diagnosticity of their dimensions, which are weighted by the contexts in which the nouns appear. Although this weighting process becomes more complicated as the modifiers increase in complexity, Smith and Osherson's model captures the probabilistic nature of conceptual structure. Smith and Osherson have shown how this structure, described by the first researchers to break from the classic tradition of necessary and sufficient features (e.g., Smith, Shoben and Rips 1974; Rosch 1975; Rosch and Mervis 1975; Hampton 1979), influences—and in fact permits—conceptual combination. Medin and his colleagues (1982; Cohen and Murphy 1984; Malt and Smith 1984; Medin and Shobin 1988) have shown that information on feature correlation is also available and relevant in the interpretation of conceptual combinations. Such correlations often reflect underlying causal relationships. Detecting these correlations may provide a rapid means of assessing the validity of combination features without having to explicitly engage in causal reasoning.

Finally, a variety of work, including our own pilot studies, suggests that stored exemplars are consulted whenever possible in these interpretations (e.g., Hampton 1987, in press; Medin and Schaffer 1978; see Medin and Smith 1984). If the combination is sufficiently novel that no exemplar has previously been stored for it, the interpreter can search for a related exemplar, as by considering other members of the noun's superordinate category. For example, for ARCTIC RODENT, one might search the category ARCTIC ANIMALS, find the highly typical polar bear, and then transplant POLAR BEAR features—such as "white"—into ARCTIC RODENT. But this "shifting up" strategy cannot be applied blindly because it would seem to usually involve considerable interpretation of the combination to know when choices of the superordinate exemplars and properties are appropriate.

The above set of strategies is not exhaustive, however, and there is at least one aspect of conceptual structure that is not revealed by them. We have already examined the inadequacy of the constituents' typical features for predicting novel combination features and the complications engendered by using complex modifiers. A further look at some of our combinations shows that exemplars and feature correlation are also insufficient to produce the consensus of response obtained in these studies.

Although the use of related exemplars may at times be helpful, there seem to be noncategorical factors that constrain their applicability. For example, even though ARCTIC ANIMAL may seem an obvious default category in the ARCTIC RODENT case, shifting up to HOSPITAL ANIMAL gains one very little for interpreting HOSPITAL RODENT. Clearly, something about the specific combination influences the usefulness of such a strategy. There may be, for instance, theoretical biases that affect which exemplars or categories of exemplars, if any, are relevant. Consider HOSPITAL BICYCLE. The common combination feature of "meters and dials" may indeed be true of the general category of HIGH-TECH EQUIPMENT found in a hospital. But when not constrained by this context, subjects would be highly unlikely to characterize a bicycle as a member of the category HIGH-TECH EQUIPMENT. Moreover, none of the typical HOSPITAL features (objects) actually generated by our subjects could readily be characterized as HIGH-TECH EQUIPMENT. Nonetheless, when the two terms are combined, the hospital's goal of "monitoring health" and the bicycle's requirement of "physical exertion" seem to work together to bring out this perspective.

A similar process was probably also at work in participants' listing of "hybrid" for LABORATORY SEED. If LABORATORY dictates, as study 2 suggests, that the relevant feature be something that can be "experimentally manipulated," why was that something not size or color or how many can fit in a quart jar? We suspect that an active interaction of theoretical information in both constituents—for example, the goals of scientific research and the causal reasons for why seeds are what they are rather than the fact they have the superficial features they do—is involved in the comprehension of such combinations (as also argued in Murphy 1987). Thus information that explains the constituents also plays a role in how they can interact.

Missing, therefore, from most models of concept structure are what might be called "explanatory relations." Where prototypical features are descriptive, and exemplars embody particular perceptual traits (such as can be represented in a mental image), explanatory relations organize a concept's structure and direct its interactions. Such explanatory relations are the stuff of theories. Feature correlations reflect this organization, but they are not synonymous with it.

Consider again the difference between "water" as a typical feature of SEED and "requires water in order to sprout" as its critical feature. The "requires . . ." version is an explanation for the observed correlation between water, seeds, and sprouting. This explanation, captured by the relation "requires . . . in order to," helps to organize the fundamental structure of the concept SEED. The "requires," "enables," "in order to" phrasing that emerged in study 2 captures an essential characteristic of explanatory relations. These are relations of contingency, where one element is a necessary condition or means to the other, which may account for the difficulty in teasing typicality and feature correlation apart from explanatory structure: such features and correlations are often essential elements in these contingencies.

This partial extractability of explanatory relations from their elements illuminates the results in study 3. For example, the need for camouflage explains why an arctic rodent has white fur. However, if "fur" is removed, another element can and will be substituted (e.g., "white hide") in order to continue to meet that need. The elements that are appropriate for such a substitution are, of course, limited. The explanatory aspect of concept structure can be thought of as a set of constraints that determines just which sorts of elements can be used in such relations.

Finally, such explanatory relations do not just account for observed correlations—as with seeds, water, and sprouting—but can also help to establish such correlations in the first place. Our perception of our world, how we choose to organize what we see, will be influenced by the intuitive theories—or sets of explanatory relations—that we already possess for a given domain. For instance, we often produce "illusory correlations" (Chapman and Chapman 1967, 1969; see Murphy and Medin 1985; Wisniewski 1997), where our prior theories cause us to create or enhance correlations central to these theories and to ignore or discount equally strong, but more peripheral correlations. Although biased by our preconceived ideas about what sorts of contingencies should or should not exist, without such sets of relations, we would be unable to make sense of our world. Our theories organize what we have learned, direct our search for new information, and sometimes change to accommodate violations or novelties inconsistent with previously held beliefs.

These three studies suggest a particular perspective on explanation and its influences on concept structure and use. Explanatory relations are the contingencies that organize a concept, explaining and selecting feature correlations. These deep relations remain constant (within limits) as surface features change and dictate which surface features can be incorporated. As conditional explanatory relations, they reflect the causal or intentional design of the entities they represent. This design constrains the concept's interaction with others by requiring that goal-serving conditions be met and that established contingencies be maintained. Although superficial concept structures such as feature typicality and correlation and representative exemplars may often be relied on for diagnostic help, explanatory relations may underlie structures and direct their productive use.

One complex issue remains. As seen in other chapters in this book, explanation itself is almost never exhaustive in a domain and indeed is often surprisingly shallow and fragmentary. It might therefore seem that such a partial and fragmentary structure would not be a very reliable way of constraining and guiding concept use, particularly in such cases as conceptual combinations. It might seem that, with so much uncertainty about the details of explanatory structure, people's intuitions about the interpretations of the same conceptual combinations would vary wildly as they filled in different details. Certainly, there are examples of such variability, but even more striking is the extent to which we routinely and successfully communicate meanings through conceptual combinations. It would seem that the skeletal nature of explanatory understanding might nonetheless be highly structured and systematic and that a key challenge is to find better ways to describe that structure and its cognitive consequences.

Notes

This research was supported by National Institutes of Health grant R01-HD23922 to Frank Keil.

1. Hereafter we adopt the convention of using all capital letters (e.g., RODENT) to indicate concepts or categories, and quotation marks (e.g., "has fur") to indicate features.

2. This sort of judgment may be reflected in Hampton's "importance" rating (1987).

References

Ahn, W. (1998). Why are different features central for natural kinds and artifacts. *Cognition*, *69*, 135–178.

Anderson, R. C., and Ortony, A. (1975). On putting apples into bottles: A problem of polysemy. *Cognitive Psychology*, *7*, 167–180.

Armstrong, S. L., Gleitman, L. R., and Gleitman, H. (1983). What some concepts might not be. *Cognition*, *13*, 263–308.

Barsalou, L. W. (1982). Context-independent and context-dependent information in concepts. *Memory and Cognition*, *10*, 82–93.

Barsalou, L. W. (1985). Ideals, central tendency, and frequency of instantiation as determinants of graded structure in categories. *Journal of Experimental Psychology: Learning, Memory and Cognition*, *11*, 629–654.

Barsalou, L. W., and Medin, D. L. (1986). Concepts: Static definitions or context-dependent representations? *Cahiers de Psychologie Cognitive*, *6*, 187–202.

Boyd, R. (1999). Homeostasis, species, and higher taxce. In R. A. Wilson, ed., *Species—New Interdisciplinary Essays*. Cambridge: MIT Press.

Bransford, J. D., and McCarrell, N. S. (1975). A sketch of a cognitive approach to comprehension. In W. Weimer and D. Palermo, eds., *Cognition and the symbolic processes*. Baltimore: Erlbaum.

Carey, S. (1985). *Conceptual change in childhood*. Cambridge, MA: MIT Press.

Chapman, L. J., and Chapman, J. P. (1967). Genesis of popular but erroneous diagnostic observations. *Journal of Abnormal Psychology*, *72*, 193–204.

Chapman, L. J., and Chapman, J. P. (1969). Illusory correlation as an obstacle to the use of valid psychological signs. *Journal of Abnormal Psychology*, *74*, 272–280.

Cohen, B., and Murphy, G. L. (1984). Models of concepts. *Cognitive Science*, *8*, 27–58.

Fodor, J. (1998). Concepts: where Cognitive Science went wrong. Oxford: Oxford University Press.

Gelman, S., and Hirschfeld, L. (1999). How Biological is Essentialism? In D. L. Medin and S. Atran, eds., *Folkbiology*. Cambridge: MIT Press.

Gentner, D. (1983). Structure-mapping: A theoretical framework for analogy. *Cognitive Science*, *7*, 155–170.

Hampton, J. A. (1979). Polymorphous concepts in semantic memory. *Journal of Verbal Learning and Verbal Behavior*, *18*, 441–461.

Hampton, J. A. (1987). Inheritance of attributes in natural concept conjunctions. *Memory and Cognition*, *15*, 55–71.

Hampton, J. A. (1988). Overextension of conjunctive concepts: Evidence for a unitary model of concept typicality and class induction. *Journal of Experimental Psychology: Learning. Memory and Behavior*, *13*, 1–21.

Hampton, J. A. (1996). Conceptual combination. In K. Lamberts and D. Shanks, eds., *Knowledge, concepts and categories.* London: UCL Press.

Hampton, J. A. (••). Concepts and prototypes. *Mind and language.*

Jones, G. V. (1982). Stacks, not fuzzy sets: An ordinal basis for prototype theory of concepts. *Cognition, 12,* 281–290.

Kamp, H., and Pantee, B. (1995). Prototypes and Compositionality. *Cognition, 57,* 129–191.

Keil, F. C. (1989). *Concepts, kinds and cognitive development.* Cambridge, MA: MIT Press.

Keil, F. C., Smith, C. S., Simons, D., and Levin, D. (1998). Two dogmas of conceptual empiricism. *Cognition, 65,* 103–135.

Malt, B. C., and Smith, E. E. (1984). Correlated properties in natural categories. *Journal of Verbal Learning and Verbal Behavior, 23,* 250–269.

Medin, D. L. (1986). Comment on "Memory storage and retrieval processes in category learning." *Journal of Experimental Psychology: General, 115,* 373–381.

Medin, D. L., Altom, M. W., Edelson, S. M., and Freko, D. (1982). Correlated symptoms and simulated medical classification. *Journal of Experimental Psychology: Learning, Memory and Cognition, 8,* 37–50.

Medin, D. L., and Schaffer, M. M. (1978). Context theory of classification learning. *Psychological Review, 85,* 207–238.

Medin, D. L., and Shoben, E. J. (1988). Context structure in conceptual combinations. *Cognitive Psychology, 20,* 158–190.

Medin, D. L., and Smith, E. E. (1984). Concepts and concept formation. *Annual Review of Psychology, 35,* 113–138.

Medin, D. L., Wattenmaker, W. D., and Hampson, S. E. (1987). Family resemblance, concept cohesiveness, and category construction. *Cognitive Psychology, 19,* 242–279.

Miller, G. A., and Johnson-Laird, P. N. (1976). *Language and perception.* Cambridge, MA: Harvard University Press.

Murphy, G. L. (1987). Comprehending complex concepts. *Cognitive Science, 11,* 1–21.

Murphy, G. L. (1990). Noun-phrase interpretation and conceptual combination. *Journal of Memory and Language, 29,* 259–288.

Murphy, G. L., and Medin, D. L. (1985). The role of theories in conceptual coherence. *Psychological Review, 92,* 289–316.

Murphy, G. L., and Andrew, J. M. (1993). The Conceptual Basis of Antonymy and Synonymy in Adjectives. *Journal of Memory and Language, 32,* 301–319.

Neisser, U. (1987). *Concepts and conceptual development.* Cambridge: Cambridge University Press.

Osherson, D. N., and Smith, E. E. (1981). On the adequacy of prototype theory as a theory of concepts. *Cognition, 9,* 35–58.

Rips, L. J. (1989). Similarity, typicality and categorization. In S. Vosniadu and A. Ortony, eds., *Similarity and analogical reasoning*. Cambridge: Cambridge University Press.

Rosch, E. (1975). Cognitive representations of semantic categories. *Journal of Experimental Psychology: General, 104*, 192–223.

Rosch, E., and Mervis, C. B. (1975). Family resemblances: Studies in the internal structure of categories. *Cognitive Psychology, 7*, 573–605.

Roth, E. M., and Shoben, E. J. (1983). The effect of context on the structure of categories. *Cognitive Psychology, 15*, 346–378.

Sloman, S., Love, B., and Ahn, W. (1998). Mutability of features. *Cognitive Science, 22*, 189–228.

Smith, E. E., and Medin, D. L. (1981). *Categories and concepts*. Cambridge, MA: Harvard University Press.

Smith, E. E., and Osherson, D. N. (1984). Conceptual combination with prototype concepts. *Cognitive Science, 8*, 337–361.

Smith, E. E., Osherson, D. N., Rips, L. J., Albert, K., and Keane, M. (1988). Combining prototypes: A modification model. *Cognitive Science, 12*, 485–527.

Smith, E. E., Shoben, E. J., and Rips, L. J. (1974). Structure and process in semantic memory: A featural model for semantic decisions. *Psychological Review, 81*, 214–241.

Tversky, A. (1977). Features of similarity. *Psychological Review, 84*, 327–352.

Wisniewski, E. J. (1996). Construal and similarity in conceptual combination. In T. B. Ward, S. M. Smith, and J. Viad, eds., *Creative thought: An investigation of conceptual structures and processes*. Washington DC: American Psychological Association Press.

Wisniewski, E. (1997). When Concepts Combine. *Psychonomic Bulletin and Review, 4*, 167–183.

Zadeh, L. A. (1982). A note on prototype theory and fuzzy sets. *Cognition, 12*, 291–297.

14

Explanatory Concepts

Gregory L. Murphy

Over the past 15 or so years, researchers have come to agree that concepts are not learned and represented solely as associative structures based on the intrinsic similarity of category members but are instead part of a broader knowledge representation scheme and thus constrained by the content of that knowledge. This realization has been incorporated into a view of concepts sometimes called the "theory view" or, in a more cutesy vein, the "theory theory" of concepts, on the assumption that people have a theory or theories of a domain that is partially incorporated into concepts in that domain. In some sense (to be discussed shortly), these theories provide explanations of the concepts. However, as I will argue in this chapter, even when people have successful explanations for concepts, they do not rely solely on their explanations but continue to learn and use other information about the concepts. Nonetheless, the influences of knowledge can be profound, as shown by recent research my colleagues and I have carried out. In this chapter, I review this work and address its consequences for a theory of concepts. This work documents both the importance and limitations of such knowledge and shows how the knowledge influences the learning of properties apparently unrelated to it.

Because the term *theory* is somewhat charged, I will usually refer to *knowledge* that people have. Some writers (e.g., Carey 1985; Gelman 1990), restrict the word "theory" to refer to knowledge structures meeting stringent criteria, such as coherently defining a domain and providing the basic principles or laws of a domain. Although people may well have theories of this sort, the effects of knowledge are not restricted to domains that can be characterized by such theories (such as numbers, music, or psychology—see Gelman 1990). In a related vein, Wilson and Keil (chap. 4, this volume) propose that a theory should have a range and depth of coverage that goes beyond a simple explanation. However, I do not think that conceptual effects are limited to such broad and powerful explanatory systems either. Knowledge can be fairly mundane and simplistic, and even such knowledge can influence what people learn about a concept. Indeed, past demonstrations of knowledge effects have used very specific and mundane knowledge such as the fact that adults can blow up balloons more easily than children can (Pazzani 1991) or that a flat tool is not appropriate for stabbing bugs (Murphy and Wisniewski 1989). The kind of knowledge I will discuss includes broad-ranging theories, but also narrower and more mundane explanations. For all these reasons, I will generally use the word "knowledge" instead of the word "theory."

14.1   Knowledge and Explanations

One way some people describe the use of knowledge in concepts is to say something like "People have a theory of dogs, which is their concept of them." However, this gives the impression that people have knowledge that is sufficient to predict the *existence* of dogs, with most of their properties. Although, in some sciences, such as subatomic physics, the existence of unknown entities is predicted by theories in advance of their empirical discovery, I doubt very much that people's knowledge is that powerful in most cases. If you had mundane knowledge about marine biology, you would not be able to predict the existence of, say, sea slugs or dolphins, if you didn't know that they existed. Instead, the kinds of explanations people can generate are post hoc ways of understanding why a category is the way it is. I will illustrate this with two simple examples.

Consider the category of birds. Most people think of birds as being feathered, two-legged creatures with wings, which fly, lay eggs in nests, and live in trees. Why do birds have these properties? In asking this, I am not asking a question of evolution but of justifying this particular configuration of properties. With fairly simple, mundane knowledge, one can explain many of these features. Consider the feature flying. In order to fly, birds need to support their weight on wings. Feathers are important for a lightweight body covering that also help create an aerodynamic form. By virtue of flying, birds can live in nests in trees, because it can easily fly into and out of the trees. This is a useful thing to do, because many predators are unable to reach nests in trees. Birds need nests for brooding, and for the babies to live in until they are able to fly.

This line of reasoning, which virtually any adult in our culture could perform, does not rely much on book-learning or courses but on everyday mundane knowledge. This knowledge may be incomplete or even wrong in detail (e.g., most people's ideas about how wings support a bird are probably wrong), but it is close enough to account for a number of generalizations about the world. For example, most things that fly have wings; almost everything with wings flies. The exceptions can be explained by the mundane knowledge as well. For example, ostriches have wings and do not fly, but this is easily explained by the tiny size of the wings relative to the size of the ostrich. The surface area of the wings is manifestly unable to lift the ostrich's weight. So, even if people do not really understand the aerodynamic principles by which wings support a body, what they do understand (or believe) about them does a fairly good job in explaining why some things can fly and some cannot.

Consider another, even simpler example, table knives (i.e., knives used for everyday eating). Most table knives are simple, two-part affairs made out of metal: one part is the handle, which is longer and thicker, and the other part is the blade, which is shorter and sharp. They are used to cut food while eating. These properties can be explained, largely through the function of cutting combined with constraints on our motor control. Knives must be sharp in order to cut tough food, and so metal is the best material, especially for the blade. However, the handle must not be sharp, to avoid cutting our hands, and it must be fairly long so that it will sit in the hand comfortably and so that sufficient pressure can be put on it. But the knife cannot be so long as to be unwieldy and heavy. Similarly, the handle is usually thicker than the blade and often has rounded edges, so that it is comfortable to grasp.

Again, this kind of reasoning could probably be verbalized by a schoolchild, though it seems unlikely that many parents sit down and explain why knives have the properties they do, any more than they explain why chairs have seats or why cars have windshields. The experience of seeing different kinds of silverware and tools and of encountering different materials eventually results in implicit knowledge of why such artifacts are the way they are. Thus, people can use their background knowledge to provide explanations for a category's properties.

In what sense are these explanations? I should emphasize that I am not claiming a very strong or interesting form of explanation here. I am not claiming that people could deduce the properties of table knives in the absence of experiencing them. (No doubt some people could, such as physical anthropologists, but this would be a bit much to expect of the average person, and especially the average child.) What I am claiming is that people can infer reasons for many of the properties of common categories being the way they are, *given the other properties these categories have*. That is, the properties fit together in a way that allows one to construct relations between them.

In some sense, then, these explanations are a bit circular. One cannot just explain why birds have wings. One must explain why they have wings, given that they fly, live in nests, and so on. Furthermore, one can explain why they live in nests, given that they have wings, fly, lay eggs, and so on. And the explanation for flying is based on having wings, living in nests, and so on. Rather than a logical chain of one property or fact explaining another, which in turn explains another, the properties of many concepts are closely intertwined. Richard Boyd (1999; Keil 1989) has proposed that such properties are in a mutually reinforcing or homeostatic relationship. Rather than independently contributing to the concept, the properties conspire to causally support one another. The reason I am emphasizing this is that there is a temptation to view explanations and background knowledge as providing deductive evidence for a concept as a whole. However, in most cases, it seems more likely that it is the properties within a concept that can be explained by virtue of how well they fit together, and perhaps by virtue of how well they fit into a particular role—functional, evolutionary, social, or whatever. But because the identification of such roles depends on the properties of the category as well, this does not escape the circularity either.

Circularity is not the only shortcoming of such explanations; Wilson and Keil (chap. 4, this volume) point out their shallowness as well. For example, although even a child understands that metal is good for cutting, even an adult may not be able to say much about why that is. Why do metals have the properties of strength and the ability to hold an edge, when other substances do not? Explanations may work well at their own level without providing an explanation at a lower level. One might wonder, then, whether such relatively weak explanations actually provide any benefit in acquiring real concepts. If learners could not predict in advance that a knife should be made out of metal, perhaps there is no advantage in learning concepts that have these properties, even if they make sense after the fact. Is it useful simply to be able to think of reasons for things being the way they are? The results reviewed in section 14.2 suggest that it is. Also, post hoc explanations may be useful for purposes other than initial learning. Wilson and Keil have suggested that developing such explanations may help people make better decisions about objects and events and understand them more deeply, even if the explanations do not aid learning in a predictive sense. This is certainly consistent with the view proposed here, although the experiments I discuss will not explore such uses of knowledge.

14.2 Basic Experimental Evidence on Knowledge and Concept Learning

For the past few years, my students and I have been examining how concept learning is influenced by certain kinds of knowledge relations. In particular, we have been interested in how people use inferential relations of the kind discussed above in learning new concepts. Since the explanation one gets from such concepts is rather post hoc, it is possible that they will not be very helpful during the initial acquisition of a concept. For example, if it is only after knowing that knives are metal and that they have sharp blades that one thinks how well these two features fit together, then perhaps the features have to be learned prior to the explanation. If so, then the explanation will probably not be very helpful in initially learning about knives. In contrast, it may be that the explanation is inferred very quickly: after the features are encountered, but before they are well learned. If so, then having such an explanation available could speed up the learning of which features go with which category (which is typically the biggest problem in learning categories—of the sort studied in experiments, at least). Furthermore, if this explanation is formed post hoc for two or three features, it may increase in power to become more actively predictive for later features. For example, once one has figured out how flying, having wings and living in trees go together, one might develop a more complete explanation of what birds are like, which could in turn allow one to predict other features, such as living in nests or eating flying insects.

Many of our experiments have followed a paradigm that is extremely common in the concept-learning literature, in which subjects view exemplars of two concepts and are asked to guess which of two categories each exemplar is in (the categories are usually given nonsense names, like "Dax" and "Kez"). After their response, subjects are told which category the exemplar is in, and they have a few seconds to study it. At the beginning, subjects must simply guess which category each item is in, but eventually they learn the differences between the categories and form representations of what each one is like. The main dependent measure, then, is how long it takes people to learn different kinds of categories. In order to understand more precisely what people have learned, we have recently also performed posttests in which subjects are asked various questions about the two concepts.

We have also used a somewhat different paradigm, which is less prevalent in the literature (see Ahn and Medin 1992; Medin, Wattenmaker, and Hampson 1987), called "concept formation." In this paradigm, subjects do not learn concepts specified by the experimenter but instead form their own concepts of a set of items. Most typically, they are given cards with exemplars on them to study. Then they are told that the items represent two different categories, and they are asked to divide them up into the categories that seem "best or most natural" to them. No other information or restrictions on the categories are given. In our version of these experiments, we often present the items on a computer a number of times first, so that subjects become familiar with them before sorting the cards. (We discovered early on that when simply given cards, some people would start to form "concepts" after looking at only one or two items; Spalding and Murphy 1996.)

For the concept formation paradigm, the dependent measure is whether subjects discover the category structure that underlies the items. For example, it is usually the case that two categories were constructed so that different features are typical of each one. Perhaps surprisingly, subjects generally do not discover these categories. The most common response is a unidimensional sorting of the cards, in which a single feature or dimension is used to divide up the items. For example, if the items were pictures of animals, subjects might divide them into items with long versus short tails, regardless of all their other attributes (Medin, Wattenmaker, and Hampson 1987).

In order to study the effects of knowledge, we vary the categories that people learn. In some cases, the features of the items are not obviously related. This is of course the typical situation as studied in hundreds of concept-learning experiments over the past thirty years. In most past research, people have been taught concepts that have unrelated properties, such as geometric figures that are green, triangular, and large. Our stimuli are usually presented as lists of short phrases, which together are intended to describe a single object. In some conditions, these phrases can be linked through an explanatory schema or theme of the sort discussed earlier. In control conditions, they cannot be so linked. The question, then, is whether the presence of knowledge linking features materially affects the learning of the concept or the formation of a new concept. The reason we use linguistic descriptions of this sort is that many of the properties that might be related to background knowledge are difficult to depict pictorially. It would be difficult to indicate the usual diet, habitat, and reproductive habits of an animal in a single picture. The function or manufacturing history of an artifact could be difficult to depict as well. Furthermore, subjects often derive different features from pictures than the ones experimenters intended to present, which destroys the intended category structure. The use of phrases allows us to indicate fairly abstract or nonperceptual properties without ambiguity (although it should be noted that knowledge effects have also been found in picture categorization as well; Lin and Murphy 1997).

Let me present a concrete example. First, imagine that you are a subject in the control condition (of course, subjects do not know this). You might get a sequence of examples like the ones shown in table 14.1,

Table 14.1
Examples of Two Categories Not Related by Knowledge

Dax	*Kez*
Fish are kept there as pets	Wood exterior
Scandinavian furniture	Scandinavian furniture
Has a patio	Has wall-to-wall carpeting
Large front yard	Non-central heating
12-month lease	Large back yard
Dax	*Kez*
6-month lease	Has rugs
Has a patio	Large back yard
Brick exterior	12-month lease
Central Heating	Wood exterior
Has rugs	Has a porch

Note: In the actual experiments, the features were presented—randomly ordered—without the category name present. Subjects guessed the category and then received feedback.

which presents categories of building types. (As described above, in the actual experiment you would first read the description, guess the category name, and then get feedback. That being impossible here, I just list the category name before each item.) Read over each item for 10 seconds, say, and then go on to the next one. When you are done, think about what you have learned about the Dax and Kez categories. If you are like our actual subjects, you may not have learned very much about them based on this minimal exposure to category members. Fortunately for you, you do not have to view these examples (and a dozen others like them) over and over until you classify them all correctly—the usual criterion for learning the concept.

Now read over the cases in table 14.2 (also building types), which I will call the "knowledge" condition.[1] (Actually read them! Don't skip.) Here you may find the categories to be somewhat easier to learn. A number of these features within each category are linked by relation to a theme. Kez could be characterized by the theme "underwater building," and Dax by "building that floats in the air." Again, in the actual learning experiment, subjects are not asked about themes but simply go through the items one by one until they are able to correctly identify which category each item is in. An important point in all of our experiments is that the knowledge and control conditions are structurally identical. That is, across conditions, the items are made up of the same numbers of features; each feature occurs the same number of times within a category; the cat-

Table 14.2
Examples of Two Categories, Each Related by Knowledge

Kez	Dax
Fish kept there as pets	Astronauts live there
12-month lease	Floats in air
Has rugs	6-month lease
Divers live there	Thin light walls
Get there by submarine	Has wall-to-wall carpeting
Kez	Dax
Modern furniture	Has rugs
Under the water	Get there by plane
Thick heavy walls	Victorian furniture
Get there by submarine	Astronauts live there
6-month lease	Birds are kept there as pets

egories overlap to the same degree; and so on. So, if you were to take each feature and replace it with a letter (e.g., "Fish are kept there as pets" = A; "Scandinavian furniture" = B; etc.), you would see that the items in each condition are identical in terms of the A's, B's, and other features. So, the concepts are structurally, the same; the only difference between them is that it is possible to relate the features through this explanatory schema in one condition but not the other.[2]

In describing these experiments and their results, I will generally not mention the exact way the categories were constructed and other details of procedure or testing that sometimes differed across experiments. Although these details can be important to the size of the results, they are not germane to the current discussion. Also, although I will use the air building/underwater building example throughout the chapter, all the experiments used multiple category pairs, so that nothing hinges on this example in particular.

The basic finding in the learning experiment is that categories whose features are related by knowledge (like the one in table 14.2) are learned much faster than those whose features are unrelated (like the one in table 14.1). For example, Murphy and Allopenna (1994) found that subjects were 4 blocks faster in one experiment and 2 blocks faster in a second when the categories were related through knowledge (a block is a complete run through the stimuli). If one looks instead at the total amount of time subjects spent in learning, those in the knowledge condition took less than half the time of those in the control conditions.

One might worry that the knowledge condition does not actually require learning. Perhaps subjects think that the underwater building is just a submarine and the building that floats in air just a space station. That is, perhaps the categories seem to be familiar to subjects, and so this condition has an unfair advantage. However, this is not the case. We designed the categories so that they would be unfamiliar objects, even though they can easily be made sense of. Furthermore, when we asked if the items appear to be familiar objects, subjects in the knowledge condition denied this, whereas those in the control condition actually tended to affirm it (Murphy and Allopenna 1994; Spalding and Murphy 1999).[3] Thus the knowledge condition items are not simply categories that are already known, but categories that make sense because their features can be easily related.

The category formation paradigm shows similar results. If subjects receive cards with examples like those shown on table 14.1 and are asked to make the best categories they can out of them, they do not divide the cards up into well-structured family resemblance categories. Instead, they are very likely to divide them up according to the presence or absence of a single feature (like a large front yard). When the items come from the knowledge condition, however, subjects divide them up into the correct categories. For example, Spalding and Murphy (1996, Experiment 1) found that, 44% of the knowledge condition subjects formed the correct categories, whereas only 6% (one) of the control subjects did. In another experiment (the preview condition, Experiment 3), 78% of the knowledge condition subjects formed the categories, whereas none of the control subjects did. The exact number of subjects forming the correct categories depends on various procedural variables, but in a number of studies, we have found that knowledge is a potent force in encouraging subjects to notice the correct categories (see also Kaplan and Murphy 1999).

Why does knowledge have this effect? One possibility is that there is some unique property of background knowledge that allows people to perform better. Informally, people explain the difficulty of the control conditions by saying, "They're meaningless—they don't make sense. Of course they're harder to learn." But what is it about the absence of knowledge that makes these categories harder? It is important to avoid a kind of mystical approach to knowledge effects, in which knowledge confers some unstated goodness on cognitive processing. I have suggested that the benefit of knowledge is in tying together the properties of a concept. Learning that a category of buildings has divers as inhabitants helps one to learn that one takes a submarine to get there. (In real life, there are no doubt other benefits of knowledge, such as those discussed in Murphy 1993; Murphy and Medin 1985; or Wisniewski and Medin 1994. For example, knowledge may be very helpful in deciding what counts as a feature of an object. However, many of these effects do not apply to the present situation in which simple items with unambiguous features are presented.) The knowledge serves to integrate the features of a category, which leads to faster learning. In category construction, knowledge leads people to notice and use many features in constructing categories, rather than using a single dimension.

Lassaline and Murphy (1996) indirectly tested this claim by looking at other ways of integrating features in a category construction task. Their idea was that if people could be encouraged to integrate the features, even without knowledge, there would be an increase in the construction of "correct" categories. In their experiments, subjects first viewed items and then were asked to divide them up into two categories. During the viewing portion, they performed one of two tasks. The *induction* group had to answer questions about the relation of pairs of features. For example, for buildings, they might be asked, "If a building has a brick exterior, what kind of heating does it have?" These questions encouraged subjects to notice that items with brick exteriors tended to have central heating (though not all did), and that items with central heating tended to have large front yards; and so on. *Control* subjects were asked quantitative questions about single dimensions, such as "How many items have brick exteriors?" Because these subjects actually went through the items more often than the induction subjects did, their exposure to the exemplars was greater.

For stimuli like the one presented in table 14.1, Lassaline and Murphy (1996) found that answering induction questions led subjects to discover the correct categories 54% of the time, compared to only 17% of the time when they answered the frequency questions. Furthermore, an experiment using pictorial stimuli found virtually identical results. Thus, encouraging subjects to relate the features to one another increased their sensitivity to the category structure, although the effects were not as strong as the effects of knowledge reported by Spalding and Murphy (1996). Although it is difficult to compare effects across experiments, I think these findings reflect a real difference between induction questions and knowledge effects. The reason is that induction questions require subjects to notice and remember the specific feature-to-feature connections. Subjects would have to remember that the brick exterior went with noncentral heating, and the patio with having fish as pets. Such a set of arbitrary feature relations may be difficult to remember and then use as the basis for forming a category. In contrast, the underwater buildings and air buildings can be learned as a general theme, and then individual features compared to that theme. Subjects did not have to memorize all the features, because they could be derived from the theme. This made it easier for subjects to use multiple features when constructing new categories.

14.3   More Complex Experimental Evidence

The story I am telling so far is a fairly simple one. When people study category members, they seek explanations for why the items are the way they are. This is not something that we need to tell them to do—they notice and use such explanations spontaneously. Furthermore, the resulting improvement in learning and category construction can be in large part explained by the relation of the features to the explanation. If the explanation says why underwater buildings should have thick walls, it is no surprise that subjects learn this feature for the category. The more features subjects learn, the better their performance in the task (because not every item has every feature, and so they cannot just learn one or two features). If the explanation said nothing about these features, then they would presumably be harder to learn. Thus, on this view, it is the direct relation of features to explanations that accounts for the knowledge effect.

This story is consistent with other accounts of knowledge effects in category learning. For example, Pazzani (1991) proposed that knowledge might help by focusing subjects' attention on the critical features of a category involved in explaining it. Those features would then be incorporated into the category representation. Similarly, Wisniewski (1995) argued that knowledge led subjects to weight knowledge-relevant features more than others (see also Heit 1998).

One way to examine the effect of knowledge is to look at what people have learned about categories that have these kinds of explanatory bases. One possibility is that they have simply learned the theme or general knowledge structure that could be used to separate the categories. For example, they might simply learn that Daxes are underwater buildings and that Kezes are air buildings. Of course, it is a bit unlikely that they learn only this. When they first view the exemplars, people must be learning individual features, because they haven't figured out the theme yet. But perhaps it is the theme itself that becomes the focus of the concept, with other information being largely ignored, or even suppressed, once the theme is identified.

An alternative view is that the knowledge actually aids in the learning of the category's details. If the role of the explanation is to make a category's features comprehensible, it may be that noticing the theme improves learning of the features. That is, once one thinks about why underwater buildings should have thick walls, one may have formed a representation of Daxes that includes the feature "thick walls." Although one might have been able to *derive* this feature from the theme (i.e., without learning it), it is also possible that the specific feature was encoded during the learning phase. As a general rule, people may need to remember specific features, rather than rely on more general knowledge, in order to categorize items quickly and efficiently. For example, if you want to find a knife, it would be more efficient to know what a knife looks like than to have to decide for each object in the kitchen whether it could serve the function of cutting your steak. Knowledge may aid the process of learning specific features.

Murphy and Allopenna (1994) made the first proposal mentioned above, that subjects may have been learning the themes without much information about the particular features. That is, the knowledge condition subjects would be expected to learn less about the features than the control subjects would. This is a bit tricky to test, because one cannot simply ask subjects which features go with which category, since the knowledge condition subjects could derive the answer without having really learned it. Therefore, Murphy and Allopenna varied the frequency of individual features to see whether the different groups were sensitive to this. They predicted that the control group would find the infrequent features harder to learn and would rate them as less typical of the category (based on much work showing a relation between frequency and learning). However, the knowledge group may simply have learned the theme, thereby preempting learning the detailed structure of the features. If so, then these subjects would probably not have noticed that some features were fairly infrequent, especially since they were consistent with the theme.

The results were consistent with this prediction. That is, the control subjects were less accurate with the infrequent features, and they rated them as atypical. The knowledge condition subjects showed neither effect, which suggests that background knowledge substitutes learning of a theme for learning the details of the category. That is, once you have the explanation, you do not need to know much more, because the features can be derived from the explanation. Or so we thought.

Later research has cast doubt on this story, suggesting that the effect of knowledge is different and in some ways more interesting. Thomas Spalding and I became concerned over the somewhat indirect measure of what subjects had learned in the Murphy and Allopenna study. Because knowledge condition subjects had learned essentially all of the features, the lack of a frequency effect in their classification accuracy was not very diagnostic. The other main measure was the typicality of the features, which might not be telling us exactly what subjects learned about the features. For example, suppose that the infrequent feature for the air building category was "has screen windows." When the knowledge condition subjects saw this, they may have realized that it was infrequent. But when asked how typical it was of the Kez category, they may nonetheless have rated it quite high, under the reasoning that screen windows could be useful in an air building but impossible for an underwater building–that is, ignoring the frequency. In contrast, the infrequent feature for the control group would not be thematically related to either category, and so the only basis for rating typicality would be frequency or salience. In short, perhaps the knowledge group did learn the frequency differences but simply did not use them to rate typicality.

In Spalding and Murphy (1999), therefore, we directly asked subjects to judge the frequency of the features. They engaged in a learning task for three blocks. We then gave them a list of features and asked them to judge how many times per block these features had occurred. For half of the subjects, the categories could be explained by a theme, and for half, they could not. (Through careful selection of features, we were able to use the same high- and low-frequency features in the two conditions. Thus the frequency effects across conditions were not confounded with item differences.) Somewhat to our surprise, we found that subjects were actually more accurate in estimating frequency in the knowledge condition (nonsignificantly in Experiment 1; significantly in Experiment 2). To be sure that there was no unexplained difference in subjects or procedure that could explain the result, we replicated Murphy and Allopenna's finding in Experiment 3: When asked to judge typicality, only the control subjects showed an effect of frequency. The difference between these two measures is shown in figure 14.1.

The main point of interest here is that the proposal that background knowledge inhibits learning about the category details is clearly wrong. If there is any effect of knowledge, it is the opposite—it actually improves the accuracy of frequency judgments. How, then, can we explain the apparently opposite effect in typicality ratings? The answer is that knowledge seems to preempt other kinds of information when category judgments are made. That is, screen windows can be easily related to the other

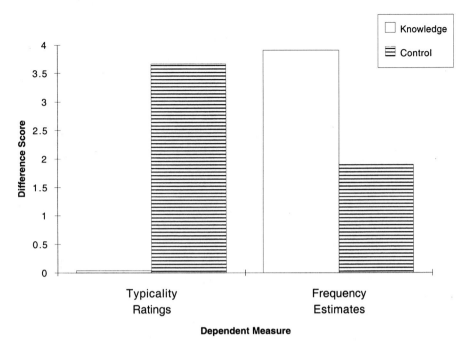

Figure 14.1
Results from Spalding and Murphy (1999). The bars show the difference between frequent and infrequent features on typicality ratings (left pair) and frequency estimates (right pair). Knowledge groups showed virtually no effect of frequency in typicality ratings, but a larger effect of frequency (close to the correct difference of 4) in frequency estimates.

features of Kezes and so are judged a typical feature, even though subjects clearly know that very few exemplars have screen windows.

This finding is analogous to a result of Wisniewski 1995. He taught subjects categories in which some of the features were related and others were not. Wisniewski found that subjects were more swayed by the features involved in the relations than by other features that were actually statistically better predictors of the category. That is, when the two were placed into conflict, the knowledge relation seemed to trump the more structural variable. Of course, in most cases, both kinds of variables are important, and they are probably correlated as well. It is intriguing nonetheless that, when making typicality judgments, people use knowledge to the exclusion of more statistical information with these categories (and see Barsalou 1985 for studies of natural concepts).

Minimal Knowledge

In more recent experiments, Audrey Kaplan and I have been looking at a somewhat different kind of category. In the experiments described thus far, the use of knowledge has been extreme. In the knowledge conditions, all of the features of a category were related to the theme; in the control conditions, there was no theme, so none of the features was effectively related to the theme.[4] In real life, categories generally do not have this all-or-none quality. Consider the example for birds that I gave at the beginning of the chapter. I listed some features of birds that I then conveniently forgot to discuss when talking about explaining the features. For example, why do birds have two legs? Although this is certainly helpful for walking, it doesn't seem closely related to the rest of their properties. And why do birds lay eggs instead of giving birth to live babies? Nothing in the rest of the features seems to predict this. (For example, although one might try to relate laying eggs to nesting in trees, birds that don't nest in trees still lay eggs.) If I were to work at this hard enough, I could probably come up with some kind of evolutionary explanation for these features. For example, birds presumably have two legs in part because their other two limbs are used for wings. It is a property of higher vertebrates to have four limbs (though that is also unexplained—to me, anyway), and so this makes some sense. But it is not closely related to the rest of the features I know about birds. Furthermore, I am very doubtful whether children first learning the category of birds (e.g., around two years of age) could generate the same kind of explanation. (Given how difficult I found it to explain, it would be something of a blow to my ego if two-year-olds could do it.) Finally, one can go to categories that are more specific and find even more examples. Why do robins have red breasts? Why do cardinals have a crest? Why are magpies black and white? Again, one can derive very general explanations for some of these features (e.g., the male robin's display indicates its health and suitability for mating), but these are even vaguer than the explanations for the properties of birds (i.e., there is no particular reason in the explanation that the robin's breast should be red rather than blue or green).

In short, real categories are a mixture of what Kaplan and I (in press) have called "rote" and "knowledge-related" features. Although explanations can connect some of the features in a category (the knowledge-related ones), they cannot account for others (the rote ones). Of course, it is possible that a separate explanation could be devised for some of these, and some features may later be incorporated into the explanation as knowledge grows. Nonetheless, especially for natural kinds, which were not designed with a specific purpose in mind, we suspect that people cannot account for all of a category's features through such explanations.

Where does this leave our findings, then? Clearly, the literature shows that knowledge can be extremely helpful in category construction and learning. But the practical consequences of this are somewhat clouded by the observations just made. Past demonstrations have almost always been cases in which all (or almost all) of the features of a category could be related by knowledge. That is true of the studies in my laboratory (e.g., Murphy and Allopenna 1994; Spalding and Murphy 1996), as well as a number of influential studies that have compared conditions similar to the knowledge and control conditions described here (e.g., Pazzani 1991; Wattenmaker et al. 1986). Suppose that it is necessary for almost all of a category's features to be related to a common knowledge structure in order to obtain a knowledge benefit. This would greatly reduce the interest of the knowledge variable. Although it might be theoretically significant, it would simply not be something that could influence many of the every-day concepts we encounter. Thus, this question of how much knowledge is necessary to derive a benefit is a central question about whether knowledge is efficacious in most concept learning.

Kaplan and I devised a rather different category structure in order to address this question. We decided to make categories containing quite a small amount of relevant knowledge to see if they show a knowledge benefit. If they do, then we would feel confident that real-world categories would also show such a benefit. To do this, we constructed two sorts of features within a given domain (e.g., buildings). One set of features consisted of unrelated properties that were not easily integrated into a given theme. For buildings, properties such as "has venetian blinds," "has central heating," and "has rugs" were of this type. These are rote features, because they are not related to a common theme, and so presumably have to be learned by rote. Another set of features consisted of thematically related features of the sort used in the knowledge condition earlier, for example, the knowledge-related features "get there by plane," "astronauts live there," and "it floats in the air." To make up each individual exemplar, we put together five rote features, plus one knowledge-related feature. (Following a common design in this field, we made each exemplar have four rote features from the correct category and one from the incorrect category. Thus, subjects had to view a number of exemplars in order to figure out which features usually occurred in each category.) As a result, the knowledge-related features were a small minority of the total description of each object. Furthermore, each of these features occurred only once, in a single exemplar. Thus, subjects could not learn just one or two of them and get a benefit in learning. To get a better feel for what these exemplars were like, see the examples in table 14.3, for the air/underwater building categories. It is clear that no single exemplar is very evocative of air buildings in particular.

The control condition for this experiment was one in which the knowledge-related features were assigned to categories inconsistently. For example, half the Daxes would have air building features and half would have underwater building features. In this "mixed theme" condition, knowledge would not be helpful (and might be harmful). In the other,

Table 14.3
Examples of Categories with Minimal Knowledge

Kez	*Dax*
Has wall-to-wall carpeting	Has window shades
Has Venetian blinds	Has a small kitchen
Has thick, heavy walls	Has non-central heating
Has central heating	Has colonial style furniture
Has colonial style furniture	Birds are kept there as pets
Has a small kitchen	Has rugs
Kez	*Dax*
Get there by submarine	Has Victorian style furniture
Has colonial style furniture	Has central heating
Has Venetian blinds	Has rugs
Has central heating	Has window shades
Has a large kitchen	Has a small kitchen
Has wall-to-wall carpeting	Astronauts live there
Kez	*Dax*
Has Venetian blinds	Has Victorian style furniture
Has Victorian style furniture	Has non-central heating
Has central heating	Atmospheric research is carried out there
Has wall-to-wall carpeting	Has window shades
Divers live there	Has a small kitchen
Has a large kitchen	Has wall-to-wall carpeting

"intact theme" condition (as in table 14.3), all of Kez's knowledge-related features would be for air buildings and all of Dax's would be for underwater buildings. (Again, keep in mind that this is only one feature per item; the majority of each item's features were rote in both conditions.)

Despite the slight amount of knowledge in these items, Kaplan and Murphy (in press, Exp. 1) found that subjects learned the intact theme categories in less than half the time they took to learn the mixed theme categories. That is, when the knowledge was consistent with category membership, subjects found learning much easier. In another study, we performed a category construction task with these stimuli. Subjects were given the items on cards and asked to divide them into the most natural categories they could find. Even with only one knowledge-related feature per item, subjects discovered the category structure some of the time (33%), but never did so in the intact theme condition (Kaplan and Murphy 1999). Clearly, massive amounts of knowledge are not necessary to confer a benefit, which argues that real-life concepts like birds or knives could benefit from knowledge even if they have a mixture of rote and knowledge-related features.

These results again raise the question of exactly what subjects are learning when going through these items. If the knowledge-related features improve learning, then perhaps people primarily learn the themes, rather than the rest of the features. Because these experiments used both rote and knowledge-related features in the same category, we can now make a comparison of the two to see which ones were learned.

In Kaplan and Murphy (in press) we gave subjects single-feature tests after they had learned the categories. In these tests, a single feature was presented, and subjects had to indicate as quickly as possible which category it was in, by pressing a button. They then gave a confidence rating to indicate how sure they were of their answer (which I will ignore in this discussion). The results showed that the intact theme subjects were faster and more accurate for the knowledge-related features than for the rote features. This is perhaps surprising, given that the knowledge-related features occurred only in one item each, and so they afforded fewer opportunities for learning. In contrast, the mixed theme subjects had very similar performance for the two types of features. It seems likely that the intact theme subjects actually learned the knowledge-related features, rather than simply deriving them from the theme, because this was the fastest condition of those we tested. If subjects had not learned the features but tried to make an inference at the time of test, they presumably would have been much slower.

Thus far, then, the results suggest that the conceptual representation of these intact theme categories is strongly based on the knowledge relating the features: The knowledge-related features are apparently learned better. In a later experiment, we found that this advantage is appears after only one block of learning—that is, after each knowledge-related feature had been seen only once. Thus, people are very fast to notice the theme and to use it to understand the category involved. This is not a process that requires significant learning before being initiated.

Despite the potency of this knowledge, there is much other learning going on. For example, although the intact theme subjects performed better than the mixed theme subjects on the knowledge-related features, they performed no worse on the rote features.[5] For example, in one experiment, intact theme subjects correctly categorized 94% of the knowledge-related features and 78% of the rote features. Since chance on the test was 50%, it is clear that these subjects were learning both types of features.

In the category formation task, this effect is even stronger. Kaplan and Murphy (1999) modified the usual category formation task by not asking subject to form categories (a fairly major change, actually). Instead, subjects studied the items as before but then were asked questions about specific features, in order to discover what they had learned about them during the study period. The categories were much like the ones just described for the learning experiments in Kaplan and Murphy (in press). But because the study task did not provide information about categories (and did not mention Daxes and Kezes), subjects could not be tested by asking them to categorize features. Instead, we asked whether subjects had learned the correlations among different properties that make up the categories. Specifically, if subjects noticed that the items formed two categories, having such-and-such properties, then they should be able to say which properties went together. For example, subjects might have noticed that one kind of item tended to have venetian blinds, central heating, and wall-to-wall carpeting, whereas another kind tended to have window shades, noncentral heating, and rugs. If so, then they should be able to report the relations between these features.

To discover whether they did notice such categories, we asked subjects questions like the following: "If an item had central heating, would it be more likely to have wall-to-wall carpeting or rugs?" In one experiment, we asked only about the rote features, to see whether subjects had noticed these correlations. To our surprise, the intact theme subjects performed above chance on this task, but the mixed theme subjects did not. Even though the theme manipulation by definition involves the knowledge-related features, it had an effect on features unrelated to knowledge. What we think happened is this. The intact theme subjects noticed the thematic features and proposed to themselves that there were two kinds of items, say, underwater and air buildings. However, since most of the features were not immediately related to the themes, subjects had to attend to these other features as well. Indeed they may have tried to relate them to the themes. For example, perhaps they tried to think of a reason why an air building should have central heating but an underwater building noncentral heating. Often one can make up such a reason, even if one could make up a reason for the opposite pairing as well (this is an example of the ad hoc aspect of explanation discussed above). By trying to do this with a number of features, one is essentially relating the rote features together (perhaps analogous to the Lassaline and Murphy 1996 induction task described earlier). That is, once one has tried to figure out why an air building has central heating and why it has wall-to-wall carpeting, one is thereby noticing a connection between these two features.

To get further evidence for this hypothesis, we asked intact theme subjects in a later experiment to answer questions relating the rote and knowledge-related features. For example, they might be asked, "If a building had astronauts living there [knowledge-related], was it more likely to have central or noncentral heating [rote]?" We found that subjects had in fact learned some of the relations between explanatory and rote features. We discovered that this was not just a matter of paired-associate learning (e.g., that "astronauts live there" occurred in the same item as "noncentral heating"), but that subjects had formed generalizations between the theme and rote features (e.g., "the air buildings seem to have noncentral heating"). Thus it seems that making connections between the explanatory features and rote features could be an important part of learning about a category. We are not yet sure whether subjects must be successful in making these explanations, or if it is sufficient to *attempt* to draw such connections. That is, suppose a subject tried hard to relate central heating to air buildings but could not come up with a sensible relation. Is this enough to get that feature incorporated into the category ("The buildings floating in air seem to have noncentral heating, though I can't figure out why"), or is a successful inference necessary? This is a topic for future research.

However, we do have evidence that people are trying to draw such connections in the learning task. In a final experiment, we (Kaplan and Murphy in press) had subjects learn intact theme categories through the usual procedure and then participate in another, unrelated experiment. Later, the subjects were asked to rate the materials of the first experiment, which was presented as a new task. In particular, subjects were asked how thematic and rote features go together *in the real world*. That is, would a real air building be more likely to have rugs or wall-to-wall carpeting? If subjects had been trying to draw explanatory links between the features in the learning phase, then they might now believe that there was a reason for such correlations. If they had tried to think of a reason why air buildings would have rugs (perhaps they would be lighter than carpeting), then this would seem a more natural choice. Of course, the actual pairing of rote features to themes was counterbalanced over subjects (e.g., half of the subjects who learned about air buildings saw exemplars with rugs, and half saw exemplars with carpeting). Perhaps surprisingly, we found that subjects did indeed show such a bias: They believed that the feature they had seen in a thematic category was more typical of the theme in real life. This provides evidence that they had been trying to connect the themes to the features (with some apparent success) during learning. And it also provides evidence for the post hoc nature of explanation, since different subjects selected opposite feature pairings, depending on what they had learned. That is, some subjects thought that real air buildings would be more likely to have rugs, whereas others thought they would be more likely to have carpets, depending in part on which pairing they learned. Apparently, subjects could think of a good reason for either pairing, but they were more likely to have thought of a reason for the one they actually encountered.

14.4   Conclusion: Explanations and Category Learning

People's ability to explain the features of a category has dramatic effects on their learning. When the features fit together nicely, the category can be learned much faster than when the features are arbitrarily related. Furthermore, people are much more likely to form family-resemblance categories in the category formation task when the features can be linked by knowledge. The latter effect is particularly strong, given that in many experiments no subjects at all form the correct categories when there is no knowledge linking the features (Kaplan and Murphy 1999; Medin, Wattenmaker, and Hampson 1987; Regehr and Brooks 1993; Spalding and Murphy 1996). From the perspective of ecological validity, it is also important to know that the benefit of knowledge is not confined to the rather artificial situation in which all of a category's features are related to the knowledge. If some of the features are connected, then this may be sufficient to confer a fairly large benefit as well.

In part because of the finding just mentioned, explaining the explanation effect is not quite cut and dried. It would be easy to account for the effect of background knowledge if there were a direct connection between that knowledge and what is learned. For example, if only features related to that knowledge were learned, or if only the knowledge structure itself were acquired, then the speed of learning—as well as the result of the learning process—could be easily explained. It is clearly a lot easier to learn something like "Kezes are air buildings" than to learn the specific features associated with Kezes. But people do not simply learn the general themes, as I have reported. Alternatively, if people simply learned the features connected to the themes, then this might explain the learning advantage. For example, the knowledge would make it easier for knowledge condition subjects to encode the fact that Kezes have astronauts living there, whereas the control subjects would have no equivalent aid to help them learn that Daxes have large front yards. In fact, we did find evidence of this kind of knowledge effect (in the single-feature tests of Kaplan and Murphy, in press). However, what is not explained by this is why subjects with knowledge also learn the other, rote features of the category. For example, they are well above chance in categorizing such features after category learning (Kaplan and Murphy, in press), they learn these features' frequencies very well (Spalding and Murphy 1999), and they learn some of the relations among rote features in the category construction task (Kaplan and Murphy 1999), whereas subjects without the knowledge do not. Thus, knowledge does not have the kind of limiting effect one might expect of it. People learn properties that are not easily connected to their knowledge, and in fact, they may learn them better than people who do not have knowledge.

One could say that these unexpected effects reflect a far-reaching motivation for explanation that characterizes much of our higher-level cognition (see Gopnik, chap. 12, this volume). We do not require or even encourage subjects to use knowledge in our tasks—they do so spontaneously, and they rely on the knowledge even when they have learned details of the category structure (Spalding and Murphy 1999). We have proposed that the benefits of knowledge may derive in part from the attempt to explain things that are not yet and perhaps never are explained. In trying to figure out why the underwater buildings have noncentral heating, subjects are learning this property of that category of buildings. Thus, the benefits of explanation can extend beyond the properties that are easily explained.

Of course, such effects will not always be found. In many psychology experiments, subjects simply wish to get the task over with as quickly as possible. If they arrive at a single feature that can explain the categorization, they may not feel the urge to explore that category further or to think about why and how its properties are related. This is one reason, I think, why subjects are very likely to divide up exemplars unidimensionally in the category formation task (see also Lassaline and Murphy 1996 for discussion). It is also a common finding that in early stages of a learning task, subjects attempt to use single-dimension strategies (e.g., "Maybe the Daxes all have central heating") to learn the categories (Nosofsky, Palmeri, and McKinley 1994). Especially when such simple strategies are successful, knowledge effects may not be found in experimental contexts.

Furthermore, this use of explanation can be risky. If people are overly flexible in their explanations, and if they attempt to explain things that do not really submit to explanation, they can arrive at bogus explanations that seem valid. For example, it was a common joke when I was a child to tell younger children that brown cows give chocolate milk. One could then lead on the unsuspecting sibling or friend to draw interesting implications about the milk of different colored cows or about how one gets strawberry-flavored milk, and so on. The farther down the garden path the victim went in explaining the cow–milk flavor connection, the more hilarious the joke was (to the seven-year-old mind).[6] Although we are usually not so cruelly deceived by our friends and family, we can also develop similar explanations for things that do not really exist. For example, Hirschfeld (1996) has argued that people are primed to accept racial explanations for human behaviors and physical properties in part because they are so ready to accept underlying causal explanations for natural phenomena. Thus, such explanations can seem plausible even for properties that are manifestly unrelated to "biological" race (which is how most people think of race), like driving skill. This tendency is problematic for learners in general because incorrect properties can be explained post hoc too easily, leading learners to incorrectly incorporate them into the category representation. However, all of this testifies to the power of explanation. Although the possibility of bogus explanations limits the value of conceptual explanations in general, it is nonetheless impressive that people are so driven to explain natural phenomena that they will accept even bad explanations.

In the experiments I have described, explanations have had a generally positive effect. Surprisingly, we have found that categories with clashing or inconsistent features (like the mixed theme cases discussed in Kaplan and Murphy 1999, in press) are no harder than categories with simply unrelated features. Although subjects identify the themes almost immediately and try to use them to help learning, when the themes are actually inconsistent with the category structure, subjects quickly discover that the knowledge they activated is simply not helpful, and they are able to ignore it. This is reassuring, but it also points to the importance of rote features and the feature structure per se. One cannot rely too much on these explanations in learning concepts. Categories contain other features that are learned, and these are important to performance as well (especially in the category construction task). Furthermore, as most of the concept literature shows, it is possible for people to learn arbitrarily constructed categories that have a strong category structure. Even without a strong structure, people eventually do learn artificial concepts with enough practice. Thus, being able to explain a concept is by no means a prerequisite to learning, even if it is a very powerful aid. But it seems likely that people would not be able to acquire new concepts as rapidly as they normally do without the knowledge that allows them to explain the concepts' features.

In much of the literature in concept learning, there is a tension between approaches that investigate and emphasize the importance of background knowledge and approaches that view concept learning as a kind of associative learning, related to classical conditioning, for example. Although I obviously am more interested in the former, the results suggest that there is an important interaction between the two aspects of learning. People do not simply derive a knowledge structure, nor do they simply learn exemplars or features of the category. Instead, these two aspects of concepts seem to be closely integrated. The category themes greatly improved learning of features related to the themes. However, even other features not intended to be related to the theme were learned, perhaps because subjects attempted to connect them to the knowledge structure as well. Clearly, as some other recent writers have also suggested (most notably Wisniewski 1995; Wisniewski and Medin 1994), the present tendency of the field to carry out these two approaches independently is not the right way to understand concept learning. The difficulty is in developing models combining these two approaches that will make specific quantitative predictions about what is learned. Although that prospect is unfortunately still in the future, the work described in this chapter argues strongly that such an integrated approach is required.

Developing Accounts of Knowledge

The research I have reviewed here is one particular slice through the set of possible ways that knowledge and concepts could interact. Future work will need to take different slices (much like an MRI scan) in order to complete the picture. I think that one of the main areas for future investigation is the issue of how different kinds of knowledge may have different effects. Although I can only speculate on possible differences here, let me mention some of the possibilities that come to mind.

The first issue returns to a point raised in the introduction to this chapter, namely, the difference between the rather catholic approach to knowledge I have taken and the approach that focuses on domain-specifying theories, a much more abstract and fundamental kind of knowledge structure that specifies the basic ontology and principles of a whole domain. For example, Carey (1985, 5) discusses the change between Aristotelian and a more modern notion of mechanics: "One cannot understand the process by which [these changes] occurred without considering the changes in the whole theory—in the domain of phenomena to be explained and in the kinds of explanations considered acceptable. All three kinds of change—in domain, concepts, and explanatory structure—came together." Similarly, Wellman (1990) discussed the importance of *framework theories*, which set the stage for the representation of more specific facts and generalizations. In this sense, ". . . subscribers to a theory share a basic conception of the phenomena encompassed by the theory, a sense of how propositions about these phenomena are interdependent, and consequently what counts as a relevant and informative explanation of changes and relationships among the various phenomena" (p. 7; see also ch. 5). He contrasts framework theories with specific theories of particular phenomena, which take place within the more general framework, presupposing the ontology and principles that the framework specifies. In short, the domain theory is a highly abstract one that does not describe specific facts so much as delineate separate domains, by describing the kinds of entities and processes that take place within those domains.

The kinds of knowledge examined in most studies of concept learning are usually more specific than these broader, framework theories. For example, in my work, we have used themes such as air buildings/underwater buildings, predators/prey, and arctic/jungle vehicles. The fact that arctic vehicles would be more likely to have treads than wheels is not an implication of one's general knowledge of vehicles or artifacts, but a specific fact about how vehicles work in different environments. Of course, this, like any other specific fact, is also related to more general constraints on a domain (e.g., the fact that vehicles must have some way of exerting force so as to move). However, the particular facts included as parts of concepts in most experiments (e.g., Pazzani 1991; Wattenmaker et al. 1986; Wisniewski 1995; in addition to the experiments discussed above) are much more specific than the general principles and properties that define an entire domain. In that respect, the framework theory is probably not providing much help in these experiments. That is, the fact that vehicles need some means of propulsion does not tell you whether an arctic vehicle should have treads or wheels—which is what subjects must learn in order to master the categories.

What is not clear is how framework theories might influence learning in real life. To answer this, we would have to do the kinds of experiments reviewed here, but varying framework knowledge instead. One might expect that such knowledge would be even stronger and have more powerful effects than the more specialized facts about vehicles or buildings investigated here. Indeed, Keil (1989) found that young children thought that it might be possible to change a raccoon into a skunk (with the appropriate medical procedure) but not to change a porcupine into a cactus. Children seemed to respect the major ontological boundaries between animals and plants from very early ages, even before they had a complete understanding of the identity of natural kinds. Thus, it is possible that domain theories of the sort proposed by some authors would have effects similar to—or even stronger than—those shown here. However, this is not necessarily the case. In some experiments, Murphy and Allopenna

(1994) used a control condition in which features of different domains were jumbled together. For example, a single category would have features of a vehicle, building, and animal—clearly violating ontological boundaries. Such categories were harder to learn than categories that followed a theme (like underwater building), but they were not reliably harder than categories without themes that did not violate ontological boundaries. It is possible that these results were due to the artificial experimental setting, where subjects did not necessarily expect the stimuli to be reasonable. Perhaps a more realistic setting would show differences between framework and more specific theories, but such comparisons have not yet been made.

A second issue has to do with the specific relations that connect the features. Again, in our research, we have been very open-minded (or, some might say, careless) about selecting the features and their relations. Given five or six features typical of an experimental category, one cannot always choose properties that have a specific kind of relation to every other feature. For example, a building that is underwater might have thick walls for important reasons having to do with resisting the pressure of the water. Thus, thick walls causally enable the building to be underwater. In contrast, having fish as pets is a general thematic similarity in that fish are aquatic; and so, being under water, one might expect to have pets that could be found under water as well. But there is clearly no direct causal relation. I know plenty of people who have fish as pets, and their houses are only under water when the storm sewers back up. Furthermore, there is little direct connection between having fish as pets and thick walls per se—there is only an indirect connection via the underwater building schema. Thus there was no single relation between features—or between the features and the theme—in these categories.

I think that this diversity of relations is fairly realistic. There are all kinds of reasons for categories to have the properties they do, and this results in all kinds of relations among the properties themselves. One issue, though, is whether some kinds of relations are more critical than others. It has often been suggested that causal relations in particular are critical (Boyd 1999; Keil 1989; Murphy 1993; among many others). This would not be surprising, because causal relations are by definition important to explaining how particular patterns of features come about. However, even the word "causal" is a simplification, because there are different possible causal connections (see Waldmann and Holyoak 1992, for example). A could cause B; A might not directly cause B to occur, but it might permit or enable B; A and B might together cause C; A and B might both be caused by C; or A and B might both be on the same lengthy causal chain. All of these relations between A and B might help people to learn that they are features of the same category.

I will not expand on the importance of causal relations or on the diversity of relations further, because I have no data about these issues. There is some reason to believe that causes are considered to be more important than effects in determining category membership (Ahn 1998), and this might be consistent with the view that people believe that there are underlying essences to categories that help to explain their superficial characteristics (Hirschfeld 1996; Medin and Ortony 1989). However, there is also anecdotal evidence for children paying great attention to clearly noncausal information in learning concepts—for example, insisting that it's not a birthday party without a clown, for instance. More generally, it seems very likely that some expectations about features will be easier to over-rule than others. For example, it would not surprise me much if a bird with normal-looking wings turned out not to fly. No doubt there is some reason in its evolutionary history that made flying not worth the effort. On the other hand, it certainly would surprise me if an animal without wings did fly. Understanding the different relations between properties and how people reason about them in learning concepts is an interesting topic for future work.

Closely related to this is the question of how specifically relations predict features. For example, I used the example of the robin's red breast as a kind of rote feature. I know of no reason why the robin's breast should be red in particular, nor why it should be the breast that is distinctive instead of the beak or crest, and so on. On the other hand, having a distinctive feature that is typical of males is a general feature of birds. This is an example of what Goodman (1965) called an "overhypothesis": It is not a regularity of a specific feature, but a hypothesis about what general kinds of regularities are found in certain domains. In birds, males often have a colorful distinctive feature, and so the male robin's red breast is related to this very general domain knowledge. I am not in fact certain that such knowledge is all that helpful. That is, violating such knowledge might cause problems in learning, but the fact that male birds often have distinctive plumage would not help that much in learning that robins, in particular, have red breasts in particular, because it doesn't help in noticing or remembering the specific features involved. Or so my intuition goes. Again, this is an area in which careful empirical comparisons have not yet been made.

In some sense, then, I am suggesting that we need a better taxonomy of the kinds of background knowledge people have, and then a more complete investigation of how each kind of knowledge is involved in learning concepts. Given that such knowledge is a critical component in explanation, such an investigation would serve to further spell out the relation between explanation and concept acquisition.

Notes

Many thanks are owed to my collaborators in the research described here, especially Audrey Kaplan and Thomas Spalding, and to the editors for very helpful comments on drafts of the chapter. The research was supported by National Institute of Mental Health grant MH41704, and the writing of this chapter was also supported by National Science Foundation grant SBR 97-20304.

1. I use this terminology throughout for consistency, though the full reports of the experiments cited sometimes use different, more specific names.

2. One might argue that relating features in this way changes exactly what a feature is, and so changes the structure as well. If this is true, it is not then explaining the differences between conditions by a pure structural difference. Instead, it is making the structure dependent on the explanatory links. My point here is that simple formal models of category learning that do not make any reference to knowledge and rely on feature overlap will not predict any differences here.

3. The reason for this is that the control categories usually could be interpreted as a familiar objects like a suburban house or a car, even though the features did not pick out a house or car in particular. For example, there is no known category of house that specifically has a brick exterior and fish as pets, but such features are certainly consistent with houses in general. Thus, when asked what they think the category is, subjects simply reply "house." This would not be sufficient to learn the two categories, though, because *both* categories could be interpreted as houses. See Murphy and Allopenna 1994 for discussion.

4. In fact, some of the features were the same in the two conditions. But if only one or two thematic features were present, subjects did not identify them as being related. For example, having thick walls and fish as pets was not enough for subjects to identify a category as an underwater building, when none of the other features were related to this theme. Thus, these features remained functionally unrelated in the control conditions.

5. The intact theme subjects were often—but not always—a little less accurate on the rote features, but this was a small effect that was never statistically reliable. In contrast, the intact theme subjects' advantage with the knowledge-related features was always reliable.

6. I am not condoning this behavior.

References

Ahn, W. (1998). Why are different features central for natural kinds and artifacts? The role of causal status in determining feature centrality. *Cognition, 69*, 135–178.

Ahn, W., and Medin, D. L. (1992). A two-stage model of category construction. *Cognitive Science, 16*, 81–121.

Barsalou, L. W. (1985). Ideals, central tendency, and frequency of instantiation as determinants of graded structure in categories. *Journal of Experimental Psychology: Learning, Memory, and Cognition, 11*, 629–654.

Boyd, R. (1999). Homeostasis, species, and higher taxa. In R. A. Wilson, ed., *Species: New interdisciplinary essays*. Cambridge, MA: MIT Press.

Carey, S. (1985). *Conceptual change in childhood*. Cambridge, MA: MIT Press.

Gelman, R. (1990). First principles organize attention to and learning about relevant data: Number and the animate-inanimate distinction as examples. *Cognitive Science, 14*, 79–106.

Goodman, N. (1965). *Fact, fiction, and forecast*. 2d ed. Indianapolis: Bobbs-Merrill.

Heit, E. (1998). Influences of prior knowledge on selective weighting of category members. *Journal of Experimental Psychology: Learning, Memory, and Cognition, 24*, 712–731.

Hirschfeld, L. A. (1996). *Race in the making: Cognition, culture, and the child's construction of human kinds*. Cambridge, MA: MIT Press.

Kaplan, A. S., and Murphy, G. L. (1999). Interactions of structure and knowledge in family resemblance category learning. *Memory & Cognition, 27*, 699–712.

Kaplan, A. S., and Murphy, G. L. (in press). Category learning with minimal prior knowledge. *Journal of Experimental Psychology: Learning, Memory, and Cognition*.

Keil, F. C. (1989). *Concepts, kinds, and cognitive development*. Cambridge, MA: MIT Press.

Lassaline, M. E., and Murphy, G. L. (1996). Induction and category coherence. *Psychonomic Bulletin & Review, 3*, 95–99.

Lin, E. L., and Murphy, G. L. (1997). The effects of background knowledge on object categorization and part detection. *Journal of Experimental Psychology: Human Perception and Performance, 23*, 1153–1169.

Medin, D. L., and Ortony, A. (1989). Psychological essentialism. In S. Vosniadou and A. Ortony, eds., *Similarity and analogical reasoning*. Cambridge: Cambridge University Press.

Medin, D. L., Wattenmaker, W. D., and Hampson, S. E. (1987). Family resemblance, conceptual cohesiveness, and category construction. *Cognitive Psychology, 19*, 242–279.

Murphy, G. L. (1993). Theories and concept formation. In I. Van Mechelen, J. Hampton, R. Michalski, and P. Theuns, eds., *Categories and concepts: Theoretical views and inductive data analysis*. New York: Academic Press.

Murphy, G. L., and Allopenna, P. D. (1994). The locus of knowledge effects in concept learning. *Journal of Experimental Psychology: Learning, Memory, and Cognition, 20*, 904–919.

Murphy, G. L., and Medin, D. L. (1985). The role of theories in conceptual coherence. *Psychological Review*, *92*, 289–316.

Murphy, G. L., and Wisniewski, E. J. (1989). Feature correlations in conceptual representations. In G. Tiberghien, ed., *Advances in cognitive science*. Vol. 2, *Theory and applications*. Chichester: Ellis Horwood.

Nosofsky, R. M., Palmeri, T. J., and McKinley, S. C. (1994). Rule-plus-exception model of classification learning. *Psychological Review*, *101*, 53–79.

Pazzani, M. J. (1991). Influence of prior knowledge on concept acquisition: Experimental and computational results. *Journal of Experimental Psychology: Learning, Memory, and Cognition*, *17*, 416–432.

Regehr, G., and Brooks, L. R. (1993). Perceptual manifestations of an analytic structure: The priority of holistic individuation. *Journal of Experimental Psychology: General*, *122*, 92–114.

Spalding, T. L., and Murphy, G. L. (1996). Effects of background knowledge on category construction. *Journal of Experimental Psychology: Learning, Memory, and Cognition*, *22*, 525–538.

Spalding, T. L., and Murphy, G. L. (1999). What is learned in knowledge-related categories? Evidence from typicality and feature frequency judgments. *Memory & Cognition*, *27*, 856–867.

Waldmann, M. R., and Holyoak, K. J. (1992). Predictive and diagnostic learning within causal models: Asymmetries in cue competition. *Journal of Experimental Psychology: General*, *121*, 222–236.

Wattenmaker, W. D., Dewey, G. I., Murphy, T. D., and Medin, D. L. (1986). Linear separability and concept learning: Context, relational properties, and concept naturalness. *Cognitive Psychology*, *18*, 158–194.

Wellman, H. M. (1990). *The child's theory of mind*. Cambridge, MA: MIT Press.

Wisniewski, E. J. (1995). Prior knowledge and functionally relevant features in concept learning. *Journal of Experimental Psychology: Learning, Memory, and Cognition*, *21*, 449–468.

Wisniewski, E. J., and Medin, D. L. (1994). On the interaction of theory and data in concept learning. *Cognitive Science*, *18*, 221–281.

Index

Index